Number One Lowchen
Club Show BIS Winner
Group 2 Midland Counties

... Never looking back!

CARMEN

TRANSCEND TIDAL BABE Brogansian Amadeus with Transcend x Taradona Pearly Queen

Owner
Andrea Wylie

Multiple Best Puppy In Breed Winner
rBCC at Darlington CH Show
where her sire won the DCC and BOB.

A Huge
Thank You to
Lyanne Murray
for handling
Carmen so
beautifully &
the judges
who have
thought
so highly
of Carmen

Top Winning
Chihuahuas
Maltese &
Mini Bulls

BROGANSIAN AMADEUS
WITH TRANSCEND
2CCs, 3rCCs

andrea.w@chesters.co.uk

Liza

A balanced vital picture
of symmetry, proportion
and harmony.

AM GCH Irvonhill Leave It To Me

Multiple Group Winner
Regional Specialty Winner
National Specialty Winner

Best of Breed WKC 2015
Best of Breed Montgomery 2015

Handlers R C Carusi
& John Averis

Owners Tony & Jean Barker, Irvonhill
and John Averis

annual 2016
Contents

The 2014 Pup of the Year final was the last to be sponsored by Pro Plan after many years' association with the prestigious competition. The final at Crewe Hall was judged by Jeff Horswell who chose Tim Jones and Steve Jepson's Beagle Eardley Stew Pendous, who has since gained his title plus group places.

The year has seen two POTY finals; the 2015 event, now sponsored by Eukanuba with Dog World, was held in October in conjunction with the Eukanuba champion stakes final at the Chesford Grange Hotel. Jean Lanning chose as winner Sharon Lambert's Labrador Mattand Exodus who had enjoyed an exciting puppy career.

Our mouth-watering NEW wet dog food.

"IT'S NOT BRAGGING
IF YOU CAN BACK IT UP"

Group	2	Crufts		2015
Group	1	Crufts		2014
Group	1	WDS	Milan	2015
Group	1	WDS	Helsinki	2014
BIS	SWKA	Championship	Show	2015
BIS	European	Winners	Show	2015
BIS	European	Winners	Show	2014
BIS3	World	Dog	Show	2014
BIS	Eurodogshow	Kortrijk		2014
BIS	Mechelen	International	Show	2014
BIS2	Green Dog Show,	Libramont		2014
BIS	Hatboro	Dog	Club 1	2014
RBIS	Hatboro	Dog	Club 2	2014
BISS	National Terrier	Champ	Show	2015
BISS	Interra	Terrier	Show	2015
BISS	Interra	Terrier	Show	2014
BISS	Terrier Club Of Norway EDS Oslo			2015
BISS	World Terrier	Specialty	Show	2014
BISS	European Top	Terrier	Show	2014
BISS	European Royal Fox Terrier Show			2014
BISS	Terrier	Club of	Michigan	2014
BISS	WFTA	Championship	Show	2015
BISS	WFTA	Championship	Show	2014
BISS	WFTA	Centenary	CH Show	2013
BISS	FTC of Scotland	CH	Show	2013
BISS	FTC of Wales Championship Show			2013
BISS	The Fox Terrier Club CH Show			2015
BISS	The Fox Terrier Club Open Show			2013

Owner Victor Malzoni Jr.

With breeder co-owners
Rony de Munter &
Dieny Uiterwijk

Toys chase Top Dog title

Alan V Walker

At the time of going to press, the identity of the winner of the Dog World/Arden Grange Top Dog 2015 competition is not yet known, but it seems likely that it will be one of two toy dog males.

Currently topping the table is the Papillon Ch Gleniren Shootin Starmaker Sunshoo, bred and owned by Glenn Robb and his mother Irene. He has headed the toy group seven times during the year and was best in show at East of England, where they are pictured with judge Rodney Oldham, chairman John Orbell and new secretary Julie Robb. Among his other wins were RBIS at UK Toydog, Leeds and Driffield.

Currently runner-up in the Top Dogs league, having been third in 2014 when he took his first best in show at South Wales, is Lesley Adams' Longcoat Chihuahua Ch Hollyel Topaz Chancer. He is pictured winning best in show at Midland Counties under Andrew Brace. He too won seven groups during the year, including BIS at UK Toy, and was reserve BIS at Manchester, Paignton and Darlington.

Production

Annual editor: Simon Parsons

Project leader: James Morrissey

Production: Colin Swaffer, Dave Mugridge, Caroline Robinson

Editorial: Simon Parsons, Adrian Marett, Damian Durio and Chrissy Smith

Advertising: Adrian Marett, Gary Doran, Beckie Sutton, Dael Carter, Pam Blay, Alan Walker

Published and distributed by:
The DOG WORLD Ltd
Williamson House, Wotton Road
Ashford, Kent TN23 6LW

Telephone 01233 621877
Fax 01233 645669

Email annual@dogworld.co.uk

Website www.dogworld.co.uk

Subscriptions www.dogworld.co.uk/subscribe-now

Also publishers of DOG WORLD, Britain's top selling weekly canine newspaper

Copyright The Dog World Ltd

Printed by:
Advent Print Group
19 East Portway Industrial Estate,
Andover, Hampshire, SP10 3LU

ISBN: 978-0-9567535-3-3

Front cover:
Featured on the front cover is the Lowchen Ch Jameneli Cream Craicer, owned and bred by Joanne Graham, photographed by Lisa Croft-Elliott.

See also the inside front cover and page 1.

FSC MIX
Paper from responsible sources
FSC® C008152

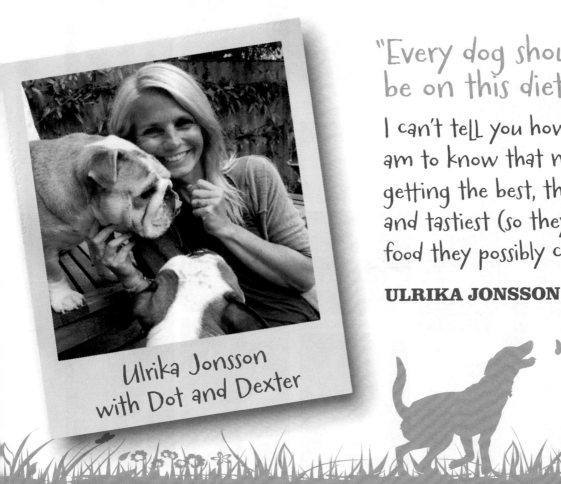

The Dog World in **2015**

The power of the proxies

AT FIRST glance the agenda for the Kennel Club's annual meeting of members did not look as contentious as in some years, but as in 2014 the increase in 'power to the people' resulting from proxy voting soon became evident.

This resulted from the club's new constitution as a company limited by guarantee and would seem to make it more likely that motions not necessarily supported by the club's leadership can be approved nevertheless.

One proposal was made by former Committee member Jean Lanning who had a few minutes earlier been elected an honorary life member.

She asked that the KC set up a small working party 'to review the whole current registration policy; comparing and contrasting the approaches to purebreds and crossbreeds'.

It is obvious that a significant proportion of the membership felt that the club has in recent years been over-emphasising its commitment to 'all dogs', perhaps at the expense of its traditional support for pedigree dogs in particular.

Miss Lanning spoke at length on her proposal, saying: "I believe that purebred dogs and the KC are synonymous, and must always be paramount over crossbreeds and mongrels'.

The Committee did not support her motion, and in reply vice-chairman Mike Townsend pointed out there had been a review of registration policy just two years before. He said that pedigree dogs were the core of the KC's work, but that they have to recognise that 'designer dogs' do exist and will continue to do so. There was no intention of putting them onto the breed register.

The vote among members present was so close that a paper ballot was needed, but when the proxy votes were added in the result was a victory for the proposal.

Dr John Symonds was responsible for two further proposals for new working parties. One was to look at the club's governance, considering aspects such as a reduction in size of the General Committee, time limits for directors, ensuring a balance in representation of the various disciplines, and clarifying the relationship between the board and its sub-committees, especially the Finance and General Purposes.

The chairman, Steve Dean, accepted there needed to be some kind of review but wondered whether now was the right time.

Again the vote seemed evenly split and again the proxies carried the day for the proposer.

The power of the proxies was revealed even more clearly with Dr Symonds' other proposal, for a working party to review the KC's communications strategy, looking into aspects such as whether a more proactive strategy could be adopted. Only seven members present – many did not return after the lunch break – supported him but the weight of the proxy vote ensured that the motion was carried by 210 to 150.

So we have three new working groups; the new KC chairman Simon Luxmoore chairs the Governance Working Group; other members are new KC vice-chairman Steve Croxford, Tony Allcock, Dr Symonds, Paul Eardley and an adviser from solicitors Farrer & Co, Anne-Marie Piper.

Mark Cocozza is chairing the communications group, with Frank Kane, Mr Allcock, KC secretary Caroline Kisko and staff members Helen Fox, Heidi Ancell-day and James Skinner. Chairman of the registrations working party is Gerald King, with Mike

Townsend, Jan Wood and Mrs Kisko.

More may join the groups as time progresses, and anyone who has expressed an interest in contributing will have been invited to speak at meetings. ■

Unlike most recent years, the best in show rings have not been dominated by just one or two dogs during 2015, and it was not until Welsh Kennel Club that we saw any dog take more than one BIS award. As we go to press, only four have done so. The first was not even a British resident, but the Standard Poodle from Sweden and bred in the US, Charlotte Sandell's Sw/Norw/Fin Ch Da Maya Huffish Copyright Woman, who won at Bournemouth and then two weeks later at Welsh Kennel Club. Her first CC had come at Crufts and her second at the breed club's golden anniversary show. At Bournemouth they are pictured with secretary Kirsten Rotchell, new chairman John Appleby and judge Ron James.

A second-generation BIS winner for breeders Lee Cox and Tom Isherwood is the Toy Poodle Ch Vanitonia As You Wish, a daughter of eight-times winner Ch Vanitonia You'll See and co-owned by Vanitonia with Ann Evans. Handled by Lee, she took top spot at both Birmingham National and the August Scottish Kennel Club. At the former the judge was Robin Newhouse and on the left is new chairman Tony Foulston. She had won two RBIS awards in 2014, and took another at Three Counties '15.

The Dog World in 2015

Kennel Club chairman voted out

FOR WHAT is thought to be the first time ever, a Kennel Club chairman has been voted out of office.

In June, at its first meeting following the annual general meeting, the General Committee voted Simon Luxmoore to the chair, replacing Steve Dean who had been in office for four years.

Steve Croxford was elected vice-chairman, replacing Mike Townsend.

Both Professor Dean and Mr Townsend remain as trustees and therefore as committee members; the latter will be retiring in 2016. Mr Luxmoore is also a trustee and a member of the Finance and General Purposes Sub-Committee and had been chairman of the Judges Sub-Committee.

He has been involved with Siberian Huskies since 1971 under the Zima and more recently Hushwing affixes, campaigning a one-time CC record holder. His dogs were also successful in the racing world and he wrote breed notes for DOG WORLD for many years.

Professionally, he is chief executive of the Royal Aeronautical Society.

Mr Croxford has been a regular competitor in agility for over 25 years and is a professional agility trainer. He managed the KC's international agility team for ten years, during which time it won medals almost every year.

Events began to unfold shortly just after the annual meeting in May when KC member Geoffrey Davies publicly called for the General Committee to appoint a new chairman. He said he had support from more than 50 other members and was 'increasingly concerned' about the way the club was being led.

"Is it unreasonable to expect the chairman of any organisation to listen and accept the views and opinions of others that are at variance with his own views?" Mr Davies asked. He had been chairman of the *Kennel Gazette* working group before his resignation in December.

One of his concerns was that the chairman was the only member allowed to give his views in the online KC *Journal*, and that Prof Dean had expressed his opinions in advance on motions to be raised at the annual meeting which he was to chair.

Presumably Mr Davies' concerns were shared by a proportion of the General Committee for it has usually been a formality for the chairman to be re-elected if they stand again.

Mr Luxmoore had been one of the candidates at the time Prof Dean was

Alan V Walker

Best in show at Blackpool under Mike Gadsby was Fiona Lambert's Bouvier des Flandres Liskport Lord Of The Rings, who had been runner-up in the Pup of the Year final. He quickly completed his title and won another BIS at Richmond. Michael Craig was the handler and on the left is secretary Steve Hall. Fiona has been an owner and/or breeder of all four UK Bouvier BIS winners.

elected in 2011, following the resignation of Ronnie Irving.

It is hard to be specific about any one factor which brought about this situation. DOG WORLD had high hopes of Prof Dean's chairmanship when he was elected, having known him well as he was the paper's veterinary correspondent for two decades, continuing to contribute through his chairmanship until early in 2015.

Combining a background in breeding, exhibiting and judging Border Terriers, with practical and administrative experience in various aspects of the veterinary world, and a fluent and often amusing speaker, he seemed the ideal choice.

But within less than a year of his taking office came the introduction of the veterinary checks for the high profile breeds at Crufts 2012. They way in which this was implemented alienated many within the world of show dogs, and somehow Prof Dean's chairmanship never seemed to recover from this, with the impression given, however falsely, that the KC was not on 'our side'.

It did not help that even some positive moves were implemented badly, such as the changes to the Assured Breeder

Scheme or, this year, the suspension of the unbeaten dog rule.

Increasingly, even the KC's own members seemed prepared to rebel, over the arbitrary decision to kill the *Kennel Gazette* and then in 2015 with the support for, in particular, Jean Lanning's proposal at the annual meeting, which was personally opposed by the chairman.

Prof Dean's substantial legacy, and that of his predecessor Ronnie Irving, will surely be the KC's spanking new offices in Clarges Street, made possible by the handsome property deal which came to a successful conclusion during his term in office.

Regarding his successor, he is featured on pages 74-77. No doubt in next year's edition we will be able to analyse the KC's actions during his initial year in the chair. There was plenty of goodwill behind him, so time will tell!

In his speech at the Welsh Kennel Club dinner, Mr Luxmoore stressed that 'the days of being able to organise and manage any governing body, let alone ours, along autocratic lines are gone'. He ended by saying: "I believe good people make good things happen and I believe the ne'er-do-wells have had their day. If we all pull together we can make real progress". ∎

The Dog World in 2015

A great Crufts despite 'tailgate' and a poison scare that wasn't...

Crufts 2015 was its usual immaculately organised self, and no one could have predicted the two incidents which cast a shadow over what was for the vast majority of exhibitors and visitors a highly successful event.

The show drew an entry of 21,427 dogs, slightly down on the previous year's figure of 21,614 but enough to retain its status as the world's largest dog show. Labradors with 539 dogs just edged out Golden Retrievers by seven dogs.

As usual the number of overseas participants increased, the 2,995 dogs from 45 countries accounting for 14 per cent of the total entry. For some reason, several national newspapers decided that this caused resentment among UK exhibitors, and the KC responded by saying it was proud to welcome the overseas visitors.

Nearly 160,000 people visited the show, very slightly up on 2014. Television viewers of the Channel 4 and More4 coverage increased more significantly, with a cumulative peak of 6.4 million and a cumulative average of 5.1 million.

Following a degree of confusion after the 2014 show, prize money was sent to those eligible after the show, within 30 days.

Ramps were available for Basset Hounds, Bulldogs and Chows, if exhibitors wished to use them, following the trial with Bulldogs in 2014.

The show had three new sponsors, and more are sought for both Crufts and Discover Dogs.

Gundogs were on the first day and two days later came the news that an Irish Setter who had been exhibited at the show, Thendara

Ronnie Irving's choice as best in show at Crufts was the Scottish Terrier Am/Rus/Blr/Ukr/Cro/Lit/Lat/East/Slo/Pol Ch McVan's To Russia With Love, bred by Dr Vandra Huber and Michael Krolewski in the US, owned by Marina Khenkina from Russia and handled by Rebecca Cross. Martin Phillips (left) had judged the group. 'Knopa' was winning her second CC; she had also been BOB at Crufts two years before, her sister doing so the year before that. She returned to England with her owner for Windsor where she gained her UK title. She is a BIS winner in both Russia and the US where she was twice top Scottie, and has been BOB at Westminster and twice at the national specialty.

Satisfaction, had collapsed and died on his return to Belgium where he lived with Willem and Alexsandra Lauwers, who co-owned him with British breeders Dee Milligan-Bott and Jeremy Bott.

A post-mortem examination suggested poison had been put in cubes of meat, it was claimed.

Immediately social networks went into overdrive and the story was quickly taken up by the national press with headlines such as 'Murder at Crufts', even though the illness occurred more than a day after 'Jagger' left the show.

The Kennel Club said they were supporting the owners, but that there was no evidence that the poisoning had taken place at the show.

Rumours of other dogs becoming ill or worse began to emerge, but none was substantiated except that two big winning Shetland Sheepdogs were distinctly off colour on the day.

In the days after the show the KC took a more definite line in its statements, saying the a toxicology report showed that Jagger was not poisoned at the show; it appears he had consumed two pesticides, aldicarb and carbofuran, which would have taken effect within half an hour to three hours.

The club felt it was 'almost certain' that he had consumed the poison after he returned to Belgium. It therefore 'reassured all dog lovers who came to Crufts' that it was 'not possible' he was poisoned at the show. The club sent its sympathy to the dog's owners who were nevertheless 'disappointed' at the way the KC had handled the tragedy.

The KC also said that 'absolutely no dog has been shown to have been sick at or after Crufts due to poison ingested at the show'.

The incident led to the KC carrying out research into and offering advice on poisonings and the substances which can cause accidental deaths. At the 2016 show exhibitors who enter a single dog will receive

PHOTO RBT

At Crufts Per Iversen from Norway awarded the first CCs in Bracchi Italiani. BOB was Lauren, Michaela and Dorne Carr's Ir Ch Laumidorn Rachel Carson, and BD went to James Galea's Dingligem Spider, from Malta.

PHOTO RBT

...betan Mastiffs gained CC status at Crufts where Terry Munro was the judge. BOB was the bitch, Pat and Mark Leak's ...eronsview Runi Bea for Madire, and DCC, Caroline Hughes' Darchen Jampo at Jamalaca.

PHOTO RBT

...wedish judge Dan Ericsson awarded the first CCs in Havanese at Crufts. His BOB was the bitch, Tracy and Paul Clayton's ...arwinsca Lady Guinivere, and DCC went to Jennifer Harper-Dediu and Mick and Sylvia Bambrook's Immeleon Hellz-A-...oppin. This pair won the CCs at the next two shows, thus becoming the UK's first champions in the breed.

Beaucerons had breed classes at Crufts for the first time. Meg Purnell-Carpenter's BOB was Barbara Bucinel's Grimmuss du Pays des Songes, bred in Slovenia.

an extra pass for a helper.

Another rumour alleged harsh handling of an obedience competitor in the car park; again the KC said there was no evidence this had occurred.

The best in show line-up for Ronnie Irving was an exciting one, and more cosmopolitan than ever. The only one of the seven dogs to be both owned and bred in the UK had an American-bred sire living in Europe. It was a particular exciting show for Sweden.

Ronnie's choice was the Scottish Terrier, the first Russian-owned dog and amazingly the first one bred in the US to take the top spot, and the first of the breed to do so since her tail-male ancestor Ch Heather Necessity in 1929.

All well and good – though the BIS judging was briefly interrupted by a protestor with a notice 'Mutts against Crufts' – but then another social media storm began as Rebecca Cross, Knopa's American handler, had lifted her down from the table with one hand under her neck and the other holding the tail.

Although this is a traditional way of handling terriers, particularly overseas, and it is very unlikely that with the breed's thick short tail any harm would have been done, there is no doubt that this does not look good. Delve into the depths of the show schedule and you find that lifting a dog this way is forbidden, and the KC said it had made 'repeated requests' to Ms Cross not to use this method. She apologised and said: "I didn't do it on purpose, it was just habit".

Later, following this and another alleged incident at a small show, the KC updated its specimen schedules emphasising that picking up dogs by tails and leads is not acceptable – there is no suggestion, however, that the Crufts winner was picked up by the lead.

The question of whether Ms Cross should be punished or even whether Knopa should lose the win was extensively debated on social media; in the event the KC decided simply to warn the handler. ∎

THE CRUFTS GROUP WINNERS
PICTURED OVERLEAF:
The Crufts best in show winner, the American-bred Scottish Terrier Am/Rus/Blr/Ukr/Cro/Lit/Lat/East/Slo/Pol Ch McVan's To Russia With Love, owned by Marina Khenkina from Russia and handled by Rebecca Cross, surrounded by the other group winners, Sue Ellis' Alaskan Malamute Ch Chayo My Prerogative; Justine Waldron's French-bred Bearded Collie Ch Victory Wind's Ghost Whisperer for Snowmead; RBIS, Anette Dyrén's Flat-coated Retriever Sh Ch/Int/Norw/Sw Ch Castlerock Simply Magic, from Sweden but UK-bred; Age Gjetnes and Elsa Storesun's Miniaure Poodle from Norway, Am Ch Montserrat Caballe; Niclas and Ingunn Ericsson's Saluki, Sw/Norw/Fin Ch Qirmizi Ovation, from Sweden; and Stefano Paolantoni and Franco Prosperi's Maltese It/ Gre/Rom/Fin/Sp/Port Ch Cinecitta' Sacha Baron Colen, from Italy, handled by Javier Gonzalez Mendikote.

PHOTOS ALAN WALKER

The Dog World in **2015**

Crufts 2015
Group winners on the move

Nora

CH Bayard Forgetmeknot JW

dob 03/01/2014

23 CCs 16 BOB including 4 CLUB BESTS IN SHOW

Presented by Sarah Gibbons

jill@bayardbeagles.co.uk   www.bayardbeagles.co.uk

Top Breeders feed and recommend Eukanuba

EUKANUBA

THE
PAWSCARS
Recognising success at every level

For the second time, on the night before Crufts the Pawscar awards ceremony was held in the Metropole Hotel just next door to the National Exhibition Centre.

Once again the night was a sell-out with 450 people coming together to celebrate success in the world of dogs.

The Pawscars recognise success at every level of the sport from the training clubs and open shows to stewards, breed note writers, championship show judges and those who have given their lives to the pedigree dog and the show scene.

Hosted by Lee Cox and Suzy Roffey and sponsored by some of the leading businesses in the dog world, the Pawscars was once again a huge success with plans already well in hand for the event to take place again in 2016.

Money raised from the event goes to the Peek A Boo Trust, a charity formed after the success of Jilly's Jolly Jaunt in 2013. The Trust is committed to aiding children's charities and canine welfare organisations.

Plans announced on the night by Pawscars co-founder Gavin Robertson for a UK-wide sponsored walk, involving every Kennel Club recognised breed, had to be put on hold for 2015 but will go ahead in 2016 with money raised earmarked for six charities all working with children and dogs.

STUART BAILLIE

Trade Stand of the Year was Hub International. Pictured are Dave and Hilary Barrett, Gordon and Cathy Urquhart and Barry Canty.

Championship Show of the Year was the Welsh Kennel Club, represented by Ann and Graham Hill. Also pictured are Stuart Baillie and Melanie Spavin.

The Steward of the Year was Colin Woodward, pictured with Jenny Fairhall and Simon Luxmoore.

Open Show of the Year went to Luton. Pictured are John Howie of sponsor Lintbells, Jenny Alexander, Ben Reynolds-Frost, Paula Reynolds-Frost, Trevor Rabson and Anne Defaye representing last year's winner, Coventry LKS.

Breeder of the Year was the Gunalt kennel of Patsy and Stephen Hollings, pictured with last year's winner Zena Thorn-Andrews.

Breed Note Writer of the Year went to West Highland White Terrier writer Marjorie Dickinson, pictured with Dawn Coates from sponsor Herbal Solutions.

Journalist of the Year award went to Dog World's Simon Parsons, pictured with Peter Nicholas from sponsor Nutriment.

Junior Handler of the Year was Teigan Harp-Jones, pictured with Kay Baillie representing Dog World, and Will Croxford.

Exhibitor of the Year was Judith Carruthers, pictured with Jo Boughton-White from sponsor Dorwest and Mark Cocozza.

Group Judge of the Year was John Thirlwell, pictured with Liz Cartledge and Antony Bongiovanni of sponsor Royal Canin.

Training Class of the Year went to Middleby and Waterbeck. Pictured are Andy Reed of sponsor Royal Canin, Charley Donaldson, James Winkley-Balmer and Rosemary Balmer, with Chris Blance.

Achievement Awards

The Outstanding Achievement Award went to Mike Gadsby and Jason Lynn's Afterglow kennel, pictured here with Sara Robertson.

All Breed Judge of the Year, Frank Kane, pictured with Michael Coad and Anthony Smallman from sponsor Natural Instinct.

Photographer of the Year was Alan Walker, pictured with Sharon Pinkerton and Angela Phillips, representing sponsor Challenge Dog Food/Mariners Choice, and Richard Stafford.

Lifetime Achievement Award went to Marion Spavin, pictured with Geoff Corish, Ken Sinclair and Andy Griffiths, representing sponsor Happy Dog.

The Dog World in 2015

Ups and downs in the British show season

Paul and Hayley Seal's Bulldog Ch Sealaville He's Tyler enjoyed a great run at the autumn shows, having earlier topped the Contest of Champions. Within three weekends he was RBIS at Richmond and then went one better at both Darlington and Belfast, handled at both by David Salkeld as his owners were on holiday. Secretary David Guy, Alicia Salkeld and judge Albert Wight complete the line-up at Darlington.

CHAMPIONSHIP show entries in the early part of the year showed an encouraging trend, most being up on 2014, Windsor and Manchester rising by over 600 dogs. This tailed off later in the season, with slight declines in most cases.

From LKA 2014, 13 general shows had bigger entries that the previous year, and 13 fewer. Of the group and Scottish Breeds shows since BUBA '14, seven were up and five down.

After ten years at Kelso, the Hound Association of Scotland moved to the Lowland Hall at Ingliston. Although many enjoyed the April outdoor shows, they were often rather cold, and fears about the weather were exacerbated by the end to benching.

Belfast show moved out of town to the new Balmoral Park at Maze Long Kesh, site of the former prison. In fact the main building was exactly the same, having been moved bodily from the old Balmoral venue.

The show was granted permission to be unbenched, just like all the championship shows run under Irish Kennel Club rules throughout Ireland – it seemed an unnecessary expense to have the benches transported over the Irish Sea for just this one event. Entry fees were reduced and the dinner dance revived.

Blackpool also saw a change of venue. Its former site suffered when the weather was windy or rainy, and twice in recent years the show had to be abandoned before it could be completed. The new ground bought by the society is at Redwood Fields near Inskip, and although more work needs to be done, it coped with what were again at times rather challenging weather conditions.

The 'docked and denied' campaign celebrated a victory when Leeds championship show dropped its admission fee so legally docked dogs (mainly imports or working gundogs) could be shown at the event in Harewood park. A car parking fee was charged instead.

The only shows which now charge admittance are Crufts and LKA at the National Exhibition Centre, and East of England. LKA has negotiated a much lower car parking fee than in recent years, and is to accept spectator dogs.

One of the first decisions to come out of the deliberations of the Kennel Club's working party looking at ways to encourage show entries was a two-year suspension of the 'unbeaten dog' regulation, so that dogs could still compete in groups and best in show even if beaten in variety classes.

It came into effect at the start of 2015 but there was some confusion about exactly when – did it depend on the show date or the closing date for entries? The change was applied at the first big show of the year, Boston, but Manchester a week later decided, on KC advice, that the old rule was still in place as entries closed during 2014.

After protests on the first day, a u-turn was effected and an announcement was made in the afternoon that beaten dogs could after all compete further.

In general the change has been welcomed and seems to have run smoothly at shows run on the group system, with more dogs actually competing in the stakes than was previously the case.

However, the situation was much more complicated at open shows not run on a group basis and there is still often confusion about who is eligible for BIS, some ludicrous situations emerging.

Another change has been allowing two sets of CCs to be offered in a breed on the same day at the same venue. The first all-breed show to do this was Windsor, with a Bichon breed club show taking place after the Windsor breed judging. Other societies, including the Houndshow, are building on this idea in future years.

Breeds which have CC status may now qualify for Crufts through class placings at shows where they do not have CCs on offer. Previously only the BOB and best puppy did so; this has been extended to first, second and third in puppy, junior, post graduate and open. There must be more than three breed classes on offer, more than five in Stud Book band E breeds.

Another idea of the working party was to allow more of what it describes as 'all-breed' championship shows, with CCs on offer for all eligible breeds, in addition to Crufts, the National and the Scottish and Welsh Kennel Clubs. A number of shows applied for this status and six have been shortlisted as possible contenders. An announcement is expected in 2016. ∎

Why do breeders work with Petplan?

Petplan®

Each month in 2015, over
1,000
puppies have been bought Covered For Life® insurance, thanks to Petplan breeders

90 % of claims are for illness

Over **£4.4 million**
paid out in claims per week

Over **£8 million** paid by the Petplan Charitable Trust since launch

£2,815,512
paid to charities in 2014

£139,405 Argos
£127,795 M&S

worth of vouchers issued by the Breeder Bonus Scheme to breeders in 2015

97%

of claims paid

20,500
Breeder e-newsletters sent every month

88% of our claims team have a veterinary qualification

Source: Petplan.

Every pet deserves Petplan

The Dog World in 2015

Radical ideas suggested at revived November KC members' meeting

PHOTO ALAN WALKER

The runaway Top Dog of 2014, the Wire Fox Terrier Ch Travella Striking Steel, completed an amazing year when he won his 13th best in show of the year at LKA, making 21 in all, thus confirming his record as Britain's top BIS winner of all time. He was handled by Richard Allen for Victor Malzoni of Brazil, who also co-owns his main rival Ch Kingarthur van Foliny Home. After Crufts 2015 he began a successful show career in South America. Judge at LKA was Michael Quinney, seen with secretary Jane Valentine and vice-chairman Anne Bliss, who has now taken over the chair after the retirement of Ferelith Somerfield.

ONE OF the first actions by new Kennel Club chairman Simon Luxmoore was to write to all KC members to inform them of the intention to revive the second general meeting of the year.

Members had voted to stop holding a bi-annual meeting in 2008, but it wasn't long before many began to regret the move, especially as the latter part of that year saw so much going on about which they might have liked to be kept informed face to face.

The revival of the meeting did not require a rule change as it is within the General Committee's power to call a special meeting at any time.

The meeting duly took place in November and was a busy and productive one, well attended by members, many of whom were keen also to get their first view of the new clubhouse.

The Committee had previously held, for the first time for many years, a long meeting to discuss its strategic objectives. These are to be revealed at next year's annual meeting.

Much of the November meeting was devoted to progress reports from the KC's five working parties, three having been set up as a result of the motions carried at the May AGM.

Mr Luxmoore spoke for the membership group, saying that the survey which had gone out to both members and others on the subject had been entirely inconclusive, revealing greater concern about the way in which the club does things than about how to become a member, though there was a general view that membership should recognise achievements and commitment to the world of dogs.

The UK membership ceiling was doubled to 1,500 back in 2002, and various routes not requiring a proposer had been put in place. But none of these had been fully subscribed, ordinary membership even now still only at 1,250.

The group is considering two modifications which might encourage greater take-up of membership, a 'town and country' two-tier system whereby those who never or rarely use the club premises pay a lower fee but retain voting rights; and joint membership for two people in the same household.

One of the new working parties concerns itself with corporate governance. John Symonds, who proposed its formation, revealed that it is thinking on radical lines, modernising the way the club is structured now that is an incorporated company limited by guarantee.

Ideas include getting rid of the Finance and General Purposes Sub-Committee, to prevent any domination by a small group, and instead setting up three new committees for finance, audit and risk, and performance and remuneration.

The role of the trustee might also go; members would not be able to delegate their proxy votes to someone else for Board elections; the Board should co-opt members if there is thought to be a 'skills shortage', and the term 'General Committee' finally be replaced by 'Board', or 'directors'.

Another new group is looking at the club's communication strategy, and Mark Cocozza said it was carrying out a much broader and more far reaching review than had originally been intended by Dr Symonds when he put forward the idea.

The third new group was suggested by Jean Lanning who felt the club should do more to promote purebred dogs and wished the approaches to purebred and crossbred dogs to be compared.

The initial thoughts of the resulting working party, chaired by Gerald King, are that the KC should continue to concern itself with ALL dogs, while still strongly promoting pedigree dogs.

With its UKAS accreditation, the Assured Breeder Scheme could not exclude crossbreeds. although this 'sits poorly with the specialist pedigree world',

The group is considering a unique crossbreed register – separate from the KC – which would offer, among other things, health testing and published results.

"We recognise that it is vital to support the pedigree breeders and not upset the KC's core constituents while offering something to all breeders, exhibitors and the wider pet dog-owning public," said Mr King.

The final group to report was the show promotion working party, chaired by Keith Young. We have already looked at most of those recommendations which are already in practice; another is for 'have-a-go' shows aimed at encouraging newcomers. Two pilot events were held in 2015, which proved popular, and it is hoped they will be rolled out further.

Currently, the working party is analysing the breed club shows that will have an impact on the proposed 'all-breed' shows; reviewing the CC allocations for 2019, '20 and '21, so that licences and allocations can be granted for three years at a time, making the show organisers' task simpler; and addressing the number of CCs for numerically small breeds.

Next it will look at open shows and breed club shows, aiming, following consultation, to reduce the number of dates in the show calendar, perhaps through amalgamation. Future topics include champion classes, benching and judges and judging. ∎

The Dog World in **2015**

The Kennel Club's hot properties

WHEN THE Kennel Club came into its £12 million windfall from its property deal, one of the areas members voted to spend some of the money on was dog activity sites around the country. Progress in this area was slow and it was disappointing that the first attempt to buy somewhere, the Hand Equestrian Centre in Clevedon, Somerset, was unsuccessful.

At the annual meeting the then chairman Steve Dean admitting that spending the money was proving a 'less than straightforward task'. The Committee was looking at a ten-year strategy for developing regional centres of excellence around the UK. which could be a 'go-to location' for anyone wishing to find out about dogs and canine activities.

Also established after the property windfall was a £3 million legacy fund; applications could be made to help finance worthwhile projects. By the time of the special meeting in November only £8,500 had been spent, through there were four applications in process, including a proposal for a canine gene bank project, for a total of £936,000.

It was clear that the plan for activity centres would cost a lot more than the £4.5 million originally allocated, so it was proposed at the November meeting that this be increased to £9m, using in addition money from the legacy fund, cash reserves and investment monies.

Members overwhelmingly supported the idea; just as well, for the next proposal was to complete the purchase of the Emblehope Estate in Northumberland, as a venue for field, working and Bloodhound trials. An agreement had been reached to do this, at a price of £4.5m, plus £250,000 for equipment and stock, provided that a management agreement can be concluded with Natural England. If a contract is in place by March 2016, there will be a saving of £900,000 in capital gains tax.

The case for purchase was put by Board member Alun Rountree. Around 100 days a year would be available for field trials and training days. The economic case had clearly convinced the committee, including an income of over £300,000 a year from various government schemes.

A lively debate ensued, some members commenting on the area's remoteness (others feeling this was in fact an asset), the fact that it had not previously been able to find a buyer, and various technical considerations.

But there was heavyweight support and the plan was approved by 75 per cent.

The meeting also heard about other property ventures. Some were already complete or under way – the very handsome new headquarters, a little further down Clarges Street than the now demolished 1-5, opened for business in October, while a site and design have been agreed for the new office building in Aylesbury, the land to be sold freehold to the club by the local council. It is hoped that it will be open by the end of 2017.

For the future, Graham Hill told the meeting of well advanced plans for an activity centre at Chepstow Racecouse, where a building, similar to that at Stoneleigh, could be erected on the site of a derelict grandstand. Use would be shared with the racecourse, with dog people being able to occupy it on 32 weekends a year. A 125-year last would cost the club £2 to 2.5 million.

The KC would fund construction costs; the racecourse owners would provide the land and be responsible for maintenance and administration. Other parts of the racecourse could be used for various canine activities.

Mark Cocozza revealed plans for partnership agreements with the owners of the Stafford Showground and the Royal Highland Showground at Ingliston, to create activity centres based on the Stoneleigh model.

The two sites between them already host five all-breed and several group championship shows, so securing their continued use for the future clearly makes good sense. ■

Internationally, one of the most successful dogs of recent times has been the Wire Fox Terrier Ch/Bel/Am/Cz/Fin Ch Kingarthur van Foliny Home, bred in Belgium by Rony de Munter and Dieny Uiterwijk and co-owned with Victor Malzoni from Brazil. King has won a group and G2 at Crufts, twice BIS at the European Show, in Brno and Oslo, twice a group winner and once BIS3 at the World Show and much more. In the UK in 2015 he was BIS at National Terrier and finally took his first British all-breeds BIS on his handler Warren Bradley's home ground at South Wales under Stuart Plane. Also pictured are secretary Bridget Croucher and president Isobell Dyke.

PHOTO FARLAP

A scene from the Emblehope Estate.

PHOTO KENNEL CLUB

Dogmatic does the triple and wins 'product I can't live without' award for third time!

Dogmatic are extremely proud to announce that they are winners of the 'Product I can't live without' category of the Your Dog Magazine and Pet Industry Association Product Awards 2015/16.

This is a wonderful achievement, winning this for the third time, in a category that spans the pet product market.

Thank you so much to all of you for taking the time to vote for us and for this wonderful win! It really does mean a great deal to us.

We are delighted to hear how much the Dogmatic Headcollar has helped owners and their dogs and it is their 'must have' product.

What a great start to 2016!!

The award-winning Dogmatic Headcollar stops dogs pulling on the lead

DO YOU WANT A HEADCOLLAR THAT'S COMFORTABLE TO WEAR AND DOESN'T RIDE UP OR GO NEAR THE EYES?

We offer the widest range of dog headcollars in leather and padded cushioned webbing, all with matching collars and specialised leads/training leads. They fit all sizes from small dogs to giant breeds in a choice of colours, and are recommended and endorsed worldwide by behaviourists, trainers, vets, rescue centres and breeders.

WHY IS THE DOGMATIC HEADCOLLAR DIFFERENT/UNIQUE?

It is very comfortable to wear and offers complete but gentle control.

The unique strapping under and at the sides of the chin ensures the Dogmatic stays in place and the nose band does not ride up under or into the eyes which causes distress and discomfort to your dog.

The loop under the chin to which the lead is attached works independently of the other straps and can be moved forward, downwards, back, upwards or sideways as required without causing any other straps to lose their position. This means the handler can move and alter their dog's head position leading to total control.

An extra bonus is that, in an emergency, the Dogmatic can be used to close your dog's mouth and turn its head to enable

Quote from a client of the Animal Behaviour Clinic, Chorley:
"Just wanted to say that the Dogmatic is fantastic! After struggling desperately for eight months with Rocky (St Bernard), walking him now is an absolutely pleasure. After only five minutes of protesting, he now walks right by my side with no pulling at all – it's amazing! He also had a tendency to walk from one side to the other constantly and this has also been eliminated on the very first use of the Dogmatic. Even my 70 year old parents are able to walk him now and he's 12 stone of sheer power! I can't thank you and Dr David Sands enough for recommending it … it's such a refreshing change to buy a product which does exactly as it promises. I shall certainly be recommending the Dogmatic to all my friends and family."

Quote from Dr David Sands:
"I have no hesitation in recommending dogmatic to all dog owners who wish to have complete but gentle control of their dogs in public.

Who could imagine a horse without a halter?

I cannot now imagine a dog being walked without a dogmatic headcollar."

you to keep it safe but the loop immediately releases again, allowing your dog to once again pant, drink, carry a toy, eat a treat etc.

We have combined safety with comfort and use top quality materials, fittings and workmanship because your dog deserves the best!

Don't just take our word for it, TV dog behaviourist **Dr David Sands** endorses the Dogmatic …

"This superb product was first brought to my attention by a client. Not only did this client praise the product but she also made kind comments about the helpful advice given by Zoe".

Zoe says, *"Since that unsolicited endorsement over two years ago, I have received numerous endorsements from my clients including the special one from Dr David Sands (left)".*

Visit www.dogmatic.org.uk for customer testimonials.

Phone: 01952 245330.

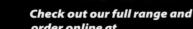

The Dog World in 2015

Chipping compulsory next April

COMPULSORY microchipping becomes law in April 2016. But how actively will it be enforced?

The dog sub-group of the Associate Parliamentary Group for Animal Welfare (APGAW) said at the end of 2014 that Westminster had already stated it did not expect enforcement to be 'proactive' and that it would be 'light touch in nature'. The latter phrase was used by DEFRA minister Lord de Mauley during a 2012 debate.

By this it meant compliance would be encouraged rather than offenders prosecuted, APGAW said.

"Enforcement is expected to largely fall to local authorities, which, with increasingly restricted budgets, may find it difficult to have the resources to tackle non-compliance," the report reads.

"The sub-group is concerned about the lack of resources available to tackle this and the other dog-related issues in an effective and meaningful way.

"While we hope that education will assist with ensuring compliance in the majority of cases, it is important that there are resources available to deal with the minority who do not comply."

A DEFRA spokesman said: "We expect that local authorities will enforce the regulations as they are already responsible for caring for stray dogs.

"It is estimated that microchipping will save local authorities £4.6 million a year because they will be able to reunite dogs more quickly with their owners."

With less than a year to go, the British Veterinary Association estimated that a quarter of the UK's dogs had still not been microchipped.

It had been planned that Wales would have a year's head start on England. But deputy minister for farming Rebecca Evans asked for the draft regulations to be withdrawn to ensure they were fit for purpose, and now the regulation will come into force at the same time as in England and Scotland.

Those whose dogs are already chipped have been advised to check that the microchip still works; it will be an offence is a chip has migrated from the point of implantation and the owner does not report it.

Dogs will have to be chipped by the age of eight weeks, with their details registered on a database. It will be up to new owners to ensure that the details have been changed on the database. DEPRA advises breeders to keep records of the sale and transfer of ownership, to confirm the animal is no longer in their possession.

At the Kennel Club annual meeting, the then chairman Steve Dean reassured members that the club's microchipping registration service Petlog would be 'at the forefront when the new law comes into place'.

Sam and Sharron (right) Dyer's Pointer Sh Ch Sharnphilly Juici Cuture was Sigurd Wilberg's choice as best in show at Southern Counties, having been reserve at the National and at the Scottish Kennel Club in 2014. Secretary Angela Cavill, James Barker, chairman David Cavill and chief steward Bill Bunce complete the line-up. Later in the year Juici was BIS at Gundog Society of Wales, and reserve BIS at the Scottish gundog show where she beat the breed CC record.

"One of our primary intentions is to aid the pedigree dog breeder by streamlining the processes of puppy registration and microchip registration," he said.

Later it was announced that from April, breeders of pedigree dogs who register their puppies will receive Petlog Premium free. ∎

Advisory Council bids farewell

THE FINAL meeting of the Advisory Council on the Welfare Issues of Dog Breeding took place at the end of 2014, attended by representatives of most of the stakeholder groups including Bill Lambert, the Kennel Club's health and breeder services manager.

Chairman Sheila Crispin said she hoped that the Canine and Feline Sector Group would take its recommendations forward.

This group, chaired by then KC chairman Steve Dean, comprises representatives of the industry, welfare and rescue organisations and will advise the Animal Health and Welfare Board for England and DEFRA ministers on the key issues affecting dogs and cats.

The council, which was formed three and a half years earlier in the wake of the furore caused by *Pedigree Dogs Exposed*, announced in August 2014 that it was to wind down at the end of that year. One of its main aims, which proved a sticking point, was the creation of a new breeding standard.

The KC and the council suffered an uneasy relationship and at one time were unable to agree on 200 points in the standard. The KC feels such a standard is unnecessary because of its Assured Breeder Scheme (ABS).

Prof Crispin said: "The council's standard and that of the ABS are now quite close," she said. "By modifying both standards, the position had been achieved whereby the ABS standard and guidance when taken together deliver equivalent welfare standards to the council's standard.

"Perhaps more importantly, as far as the majority of dogs are concerned, the council's standard aligns closely with the Chartered Institute of Environmental Health."

She expressed disappointment at the lack of response from DEFRA ministers to the council's recommendations.

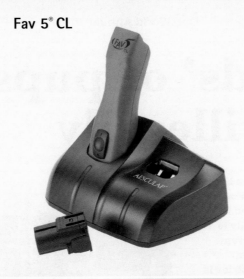
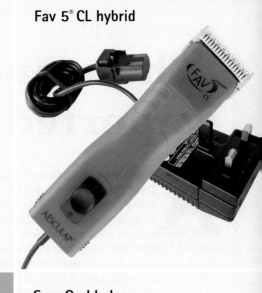

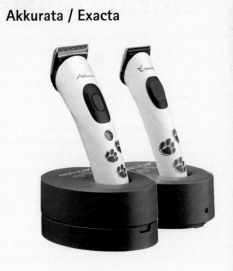
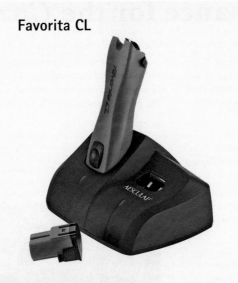

The Dog World in 2015

'Thousands' of pups imported illegally

AN UNDERCOVER investigation by Dogs Trust in 2014 revealed what many suspected, that thousands of puppies are being sent illegally to Britain each year by dealers from Eastern Europe. The enormous increase in legally declared imports from these countries is believed to be just the tip of the iceberg,

Vets in countries such as Hungary and Lithuania were prepared, apparently, to falsify pet passports to show that the puppies had received rabies inoculations when they had not. Some breeders made weekly shipments of under-age puppies to the UK.

Canine groups have continued to lobby the Government about the dangers of the illegal puppy trade, the RSPCA pointing out once again the risk of rabies arriving in the UK. Dogs Trust and MP Neil Parish hosted a briefing on the topic at the House of Commons.

Meanwhile Battersea Dogs' and Cats' Home warned about the dangers of buying from undercover breeders in the UK; it would like to see a minimum age of sale of eight weeks and any household licensed which produces two or more litters a year. ∎

Border Union's best in show winner under Patsy Hollings was the Pyrenean Mountain Dog Ch Charibere Simply Speical at Chezanna, owned by Christine Kenyon (second right) and Arthur Ward and handled by Louise Bermingham. Also pictured are secretary Brian Stevenson and show chairma Douglas McKay. He had won BIS at a group show in 2014, and in '15 was RBIS at East of England.

Stormy renaissance for the *Gazette*

THE *KENNEL Gazette* finally reappeared at the end of June. It had been killed off in December 2013, without any consultation with Kennel Club members, but at the annual meeting the following year members supported Simon Parsons' proposal that it should reappear on a monthly basis.

Its rebirth was by no means trouble-free as in November 2014 several members of the editorial group resigned, including its chairman Geoffrey Davies who said he and other members of the panel felt 'demotivated, hurt and insulted' by the KC's response to their plans. He cited a lack of encouragement and 'continual delaying tactics'. Mr Parsons also resigned, but for personal reasons.

The remaining members of the working party, appointed from members who had supported the original proposal, continued their work. They were Ron Stewart, Pat Brigden, Gay Robertson and Philippa Gilbert.

Subsequently an editor was appointed, Pembroke Corgi enthusiast Carrie Thomas. Some expressed surprise that the company chosen to publish the magazine was Pet Subjects, whose managing director Beverley Cuddy has often been an outspoken critic of dog showing, but the company merely produces the magazine and has no influence on content.

The first issue consisted of 44 pages, including traditional features like *Judges' Choice* and *Viewpoint*. Each month a different General Committee member makes a contribution, and there have been reports on events and profiles of prominent personalities.

After some comment on the first issue, the quality of the covers was improved.

A few readers regret that the lists of shows, judges etc which appeared in the old *Gazette* are now published only in the online *Journal* (of which a printed version is available on request) but most accept that this would have driven up the cost of producing the *Gazette* to an impossible level. ∎

On her first appearance at a UK show the Greyhound Int/Norw/Sw/Dan Ch Jet's Moonlight Serenade owned by Åge Gjetnes and Espen Engh from Norway, and subsequently in partnership with Pauline Oliver, took best in show under Jane Lilley (left). With them are patron the Earl of Buchan, group judg Jan Pain and secretary Irene Terry. She quickly won her UK title, taking BIS at the breed show and RBIS at the August Scottish Kennel Club.

ROYAL CANIN®

Breeder Club

Tailored nutrition for every cat and dog

 **Preferential prices**

FREE kitten and puppy recommendation packs
benefits for you and your kitten or puppy's new owner!

FREE 48 HOUR delivery
on orders over 20kg

Earn FREE food and branded items
through our Loyalty Points Scheme

Great benefits
for our members

 Breeder Management Software
(Making daily kennel and cattery life easier!)

Unique PRO bag sizes
up to 20kg in all PRO ranges

SAVE **Exclusive promotions**

 Dedicated breeder team and technical helpline

Enrolment requirements - To be involved in the scheme you will need to have:
- 2 or more breeding bitches/queens
- 4 or more dogs or 10 or more cats in total
- Registered Prefix
- Kennel Club Affix/IKC assured breeder certificate for dog breeders
- Boarding License for kennels or catteries

For more information on the ROYAL CANIN® BREEDER CLUB please call 0845 300 5965 or visit

royalcanin.co.uk

The Dog World in 2015

Breeders' licences: 'gaping holes' in the system

LATE IN 2014, the All-Party Parliamentary Group for Animal Welfare (APGAW) Sub-Group for Dogs launched a report which it hoped would be used by governments as part of their policy-making process.

It was compiled in partnership with a group of key stakeholders including the Kennel Club, British Veterinary Association, Battersea Dogs' and Cats' Home, Blue Cross, Dogs Trust, PDSA and RSPCA, with input from cross-party politicians.

The recommendations covered almost every issue related to dogs. With regard to breeding, dealing and trading the group called the laws outdated and in need of review and updating.

There needs to be a robust system of checking breeders, including spot checks, and a decision made on how breaches are to be dealt with, the report said.

It felt that the existing models, from the Assured Breeder Scheme and the Advisory Council, should be considered further to explore opportunities for developing some form of self-regulation similar to that used in farming.

Parliamentary Under Secretary of State George Eustice pointed out that the Breeding and Sale of Dogs Act states that anyone carrying on the business of breeding and selling puppies must have a licence irrespective of the number of litters their bitches produce.

"However, owing to complex wording within the Act, local authorities have misinterpreted this and only license those with five litters and above," the recommendation reads. "It seems that there is a lot that can be done by simply clarifying the existing legislation to local authority inspectors and ensuring consistency across the councils."

That vets should offer advice about inherited disorders and promote screening programmes, is another recommendation.

The sub-group believes dangerous dogs legislation should be consolidated; in particular it should move away from the breed-specific approach, protect the welfare of the dogs concerned and focus on early intervention and prevention supported by an effective education programme.

All serious and fatal dog bite incidents should be investigated fully including using an independent behaviourist. On this issue, a meeting of experts was

Boston's best in show winner under Robin Searle was Nick and Angela May's Bearded Collie Sengalas Court Jester who became a champion on the day. His litter sister Ch Sengalas Breaking Dawn for Clovabrae won BIS at Scottish Breeds in 2014. Their sire Ch Sengalas Indiana Jones also produced the group show BIS winner Ch Potterdale Platinum Plus. On the left is secretary Pat Dufty.

later held at the KC, where a strategy of reducing such incidents was set out, emphasising the need for education of the public, especially children, and for a 'robust' central database which will give information on the causes of dog bites. The KC runs its Safe and Sound programme to this end and Battersea Dogs' And Cats' Home has a film to help children interact with dogs.

Latest it was revealed that the number of people taken to hospital with dog-inflicted injuries had risen by 76 per cent in ten years.

The threshold for breeders requiring a licence remains a bone of contention. At long last new breeding regulations were introduced in Wales in 2015, and any breeder with three or more breeding bitches must be licensed there. There is a minimum staff ratio of one person to 20 adult dogs and breeders must adopt socialisation plans for puppies and 'enhancement and enrichment programmes' for all dogs.

DEFRA has written to local authorities in England saying that the wording of the 1999 Act had been interpreted incorrectly by some as a 'five-litter' test, and that there

had been concerns that many breeders who produced fewer than five litters a year but who are operating as businesses were not being licensed.

Durham County Council appears to be the first to take a more muscular approach to licensing and will be assessing breeders in its area to determine whether they were considered to be operating as 'traders'.

A report by Battersea suggests that 88 per cent of puppies in the UK are bred by unlicensed breeders, and that there are 'gaping holes' in enforcement of the system. Over a third of councils have no licensed breeders and 77 per cent license no new breeders in 2014. The few large establishments are responsible for 'a disproportionate amount of breeding', and there are huge variations in the cost of a licence.

There are just 895 licensed breeders in the UK who keep a total of 13,425 breeding bitches. Battersea estimates they would produce around 67,000 puppies a year, which is less than a third of the number registered by the KC.

The charity would like to see anyone breeding two or more litters a year be licensed. ■

Hill's

In
safe
hands

Your love, our protection.
Specially for small dogs.

Hill's™ Science Plan™ Small & Miniature is precisely balanced nutrition to support immune system health and long life expectancy in small breed dogs.

- Precisely formulated with clinically proven antioxidants
- Chicken & turkey as No.1 ingredient
- Small easy-to-chew kibble tailored for small dogs' tender mouths

Learn more at **www.hillspet.co.uk/smalldogs** or **www.hillspet.ie/smalldogs**

Hill's
SCIENCE PLAN.
VETERINARY FORMULATED

Adult 1-6   Small & Miniature
Chicken & Turkey

The Dog World in 2015

Progress with testing for health

A PIECE of significant progress on the health-testing front is that the Kennel Club is to record the results of BAER (brainstem auditory evoked response) hearing tests for Dalmatians. The KC worked with breed clubs to develop the programme, with the aim that the various testing centres around the country will eventually send their results to the KC so that they can be recorded on the dog's registrations, It is hoped that this can be extended to other breeds in which deafness can be a problem.

A DNA test for primary open angle glaucoma in the Petit Basset Griffon Vendéen, and indeed Basset Hounds in which the problem has now also been found, is now available at the Animal Health Trust, as is one for sensory neuropathy in Border Collies.

The Kennel Club has also approved DNA testing schemes for polyneuropathy in the Alaskan Malamute; for multi-drug resistance and Imerslund-Grasbeck syndrome (IGS) in the Border Collie; for hereditary footpad hyperkeratosis in the Irish Terrier; for factor VII deficiency and IGS in Beagles; for Collie eye anomaly in the Lancashire Heeler; and for exercise-induced collapse in the Clumber Spaniel. Labradors can now be screened for macular corneal dystrophy.

The KC will no longer register Cardigan Corgis whose parents are not clear (either hereditarily or by DNA test) of progressive retinal atrophy–rcd 3.

The KC and BVA will now record eye test results in breeds which are not on schedule A of the scheme.

Controversy continues about health testing in Cavaliers with some activists demanding that all breeding stock should be tested for syringomyelia, the chiari malformation and mitral valve disease. One study suggested that heart problems in the breed were even more prevalent than had been suspected, whereas the recorded incidence of the other two was far lower.

The KC refused to an accept an 8,000-signature petition on this topic at Crufts, but the KC Charitable Trust and the British Veterinary Association pledged up to £30,000 to support breeds affected by SM and CM.

The estimated breeding value scheme, launched at Crufts 2014, has now been extended to 13 more breeds giving a total of 28. ■

Best in show at Manchester under Tom Mather was Jenny Killilea and Arlene Clure's Akita Ch Redwitch Will I Am, handle by Jenny's husband Dave and seen with secretary Paul Harding and chairman Bob Gregory. Will had taken five best puppy in show awards at championship shows and is the second BIS winner for his dam EchoStar's Portrait at Redwitch

Frenchie numbers double in two years

KENNEL CLUB registrations for 2014 totalled 222,638, a small drop of just over 1,000 on the 2013 figure. As ever Labradors were top breed with 34,715 puppies, followed by Cocker Spaniels (22,366) and English Springers (10,616).

French Bulldogs continued their seemingly unstoppable rise to reach fourth place with 9,670 registrations, which had doubled in just two years.

Next in line are another fast growing breed, Pugs (9,245), German Shepherds (7,926) and Golden Retrievers (6,977). Border Terriers, Bulldogs and Miniature Schnauzers completed the top ten, the latter overtaking Staffordshire Bull Terriers.

Pembroke Corgis and Irish Wolfhounds fell below 300 registrations to join the 'vulnerable' British and Irish native breeds list.

In 2015, registrations for the first three quarters of the year, 165,732, were more than 2,500 down on the same period in 2014.

Andy and Heather Morris' Shar-Pei Ch Ashowai Ready To Rock was best in show at WELKS under Ken Sinclair. On the left is Sheila Jakeman whose last show in the secretary's role this was after 21 years. Ready To Rock later achieved the breed CC record previously held by his sire Ch/Am Ch Asias Red Marsh Whip It Good who was also a BIS winner.

The Dog World in 2015

Welcome to the Jack Russell

THE JACK RUSSELL Terrier is to be recognised by the Kennel Club. An interim Standard will be published and breed classes will be available from April 1, 2016.

Although the breed has been developed as a show dog in Australia, rather than in its country of origin, it will not have to go onto the imported register.

It appears that registration will be available to dogs registered with overseas kennel clubs; to those with a three-generation pedigree from the pre-existing UK clubs from the breed (at least one of which is strongly against having anything to do with the KC); or to those whose owners provide photographs for the dogs to be determined as typical.

The breed is recognised Down Under, by the Fédération Cynologique Internationale, and in the US where it is known as the Russell Terrier, and is frequently successful at group level worldwide.

The Griffon Fauve de Bretagne has competed in imported register classes since December 2014, the Hungarian Pumi and Azawakh since June 2015 and the Picardy Sheepdog since September '15, while the Cirneco dell'Etna came off the imported register in October 2015. The Greater Swiss Mountain Dog will do so in April 2016.

Dogues de Bordeaux gain challenge certificates in 2016 and Cesky Terriers and Spanish Water Dogs in 2017. ■

At the May Scottish Kennel Club, best in show was John Averis and Tony and Jean Barker's Irish Terrier Ch Lakeridge Cahal, following in the footsteps of his sire Ch/Am Ch Kells Touch Of Fleet St and his grandsire Ch/Am Ch Fleet St Fenway Fan. In the line-up are secretary Beth Harrison, judge Keith Nathan, Alison Morton representing Royal Canin and convener Irene McManus.

KC and FCI agree on approval of judges

AT LONG last an agreement was reached between the Kennel Club and Fédération Cynologique Internationale on the mutual acceptance of judges. Briefly, British judges may award CACIBs in breeds in which they have been passed for CCs. Formerly, a certain number of UK judges were allowed to award CACIBs in all breeds which have CCs in the UK; we understand that this will still apply.

UK judges who have previously done groups at FCI international shows can continue to do so, otherwise they will have to have awarded CCs in half the breeds which have CC status in that group. Those who have done BIS at FCI shows can continue to do so, otherwise they will have to have done no fewer than five FCI groups.

As for FCI judges officiating in the UK, the previous sticking point was that they had to fill in questionnaires for their first UK appointment even if they had been judging the breed for years. Now they will no longer have to do so if they have been judging the breed at international shows in countries other than their own for five years. Group and BIS judges will have to fulfil the same criteria as our own.

Responsibility for checking that overseas judges are suitably qualified is down to the inviting society, who will be responsible for the judge's performance. An evaluator must be appointed by the society. Overseas judges must not form more than 20 per cent of the total number of judges appointed.

Some felt that the agreement was rather one-sided in that British judges gained nothing over what they previously had, indeed may conceivably have lost out, whereas some FCI judges, unlike our own, no longer have to complete questionnaires. In theory they could be passed having judged a breed just once in each of two countries five years ago.

Clearly a lot depends on the common sense of the show societies in only inviting overseas judges with genuine knowledge and experience of the breeds concerned.

One breed which clearly wasn't too convinced about this was the Border Terrier, and the breed clubs later wrote to general championship show secretaries asking them to ensure that foreign judges awarding CCs have the same experience as those in the UK. ■

PHOTO ALAN WALKER

An American-bred junior Deerhound was best in show at Bath, Foxcliffe Classic Liberty Freedom at Beardswood, owned by Sarah Helps and her breeders Cecilia and Scott Dove. She is a daughter of Westminster BIS winner Am Gr Ch Foxcliffe Hickory Wind. Also pictured are secretary Ben Ford, president Chris Laurence, judge David Cavill and Councillor Dine Romero.

The Dog World in 2015

Red tape call from Europe

THE EUROPEAN Union Dog and Cat Alliance is asking for strict new measures governing the breeding, sale and transportation of dogs.

The Alliance, which is made up of 45 groups from 14 European states – including Dogs Trust, Battersea Dogs' and Cats' Home, Blue Cross, Wood Green and British Veterinary Association in England – at its first meeting in Brussels called for:

- More robust EU-wide legislation including compulsory identification and registration of dogs and cats on a database which is linked to an EU database.
- EU legislation requiring the compulsory licensing of dog and cat breeders by member states.
- Harmonised EU standards for dog and cat breeders which clarify a definition of 'commercial breeder'. Standards should include requirements to prevent 'selective breeding practices leading to reduced genetic diversity, inherited diseases and the expression of exaggerated conformations'.
- A ban on the sale of dogs and cats in pet shops, at markets, shows or exhibitions as well as in the street. Only registered breeders should be allowed to import dogs and cats from another state's registered breeders and sell them in their premises.
- Controls on the internet trade of dogs and cats.
- A 'full ban' on all surgical mutilations which are still allowed, other than for medical reasons.

The report has been shared with all 751 Members of the European Parliament, all 28 national governments and the European Commission.

Ann Arch's choice as best in show at Three Counties was Di Jenkins' Norfolk Terrier Ch Kinsridge Top Tip, seen with dog show chairman David Coode.

Meanwhile the Eurogroup for Animals has put forward a proposal that all breeders and puppy sellers would have to be registered from 2020. ∎

Find judges on the internet

THE KENNEL Club extended its online 'Find a Judge' service beyond merely listing approved CC judges and their contact details.

You can now see details of their previous and future appointments, along with how many dogs were entered and how this compared with the breed average for the year. An unexpected bonus was that the system revealed Crufts judges for several years ahead!

The minimum time period between judging appointments with CCs is to be 18 months from 2018, rather than 12. The KC has said that breed clubs, particularly those from numerically small breeds, must make sure there are enough names on their judging

The Petit Basset Griffon Vendéen Boom Chicago v Tum-Tums Vriendjes, owned by Anouk and Gwen Huikeshoven from the Netherlands, spent a successful weekend in the UK, taking group 4 at the Houndshow and then travelling to Paignton where he was Frank Kane's choice for best in show. Secretary Aileen Hodsoll and chairman David Creech complete the line-up.

PHOTO ALAN WALKER

Britain's top hound of 2014, Jeannette and Alan Glaister's Saluki Ch Classicus Cassander, won BIS at Leeds under Stuart Mallard. Secretary Liz Stannard made the presentation.

lists. It hopes the change will allow a greater rotation of judges and give them more opportunities. Many societies already insist on an 18-month gap in their contracts, but it hasn't always been easy to insist on this in some breeds.

Judges who award CCs in one breed will now have to pass at least one breed-specific seminar for the second and third breeds before being able to award CCs in them. ∎

Police had 'no right' to kill 22 dogs

A HIGH Court judge ruled that Merseyside police force had no right to destroy 22 dogs of what it claimed were banned breeds.

The crackdown took place in March 2014 when police said that the dogs' owners had failed to abide by court conditions when the were granted permission to keep dogs of the banned breeds, but Mr Justice King said a court should have had the final say and the police had no legal power to put down the dogs.

Another development is that police now have the option to grant 'bail' to dogs suspected of being banned breeds, allowing the return home subject to certain conditions.

Later in the year, police chiefs said that kennelling costs for seized dogs are putting a serious strain on police force budgets. It has cost £5million to kennel 7,000 dogs over the past five years. ∎

All vet checks passed but three

THE VETERINARY checks for the category three breeds' BOB winners and new champions have almost invariably resulted in passes; the first failure of the year did not occur until Blackpool where a big winning Neapolitan Mastiff did not pass. A Bloodhound failed at Leeds. A Pekingese failed at Midland Counties but the problem had cleared up two days later when it was tested again and passed.

One of the breeds still on the list is the German Shepherd and at a meeting between the Kennel Club and breed council, the criteria for the breed to come off the list were explained.

A project is being undertaken at Surrey Veterinary School in which 15 GSD will be used to research the relationship between conformation and health and welfare. The KC Charitable Trust will foot the bill.

A separate study of the GSD, funded by Dogs Trust, aims to determine whether certain factors in a dog's lifestyle or genetics are related to its temperament and health.

Meanwhile some vocal campaigners would like to see the KC split the 'Alsatian' from the 'German Shepherd'.

Longcoat Shepherds and fawn pied Frenchies accepted

THE GERMAN Shepherd Dog Standard has been clarified to include the longcoat variety, though soft fluffy coats are still incorrect. The new wording reads: "In long coats, outer coat longer, not always straight and frequently not lying close and flat to the body. Thick undercoat. Coat distinctly longer inside and behind the ears, forming moderate tufts.

"Longer hair on the back of the forelegs through to the loins and dense feathering on the hind legs. Tail bushy with light feathering underneath."

The two coat types will be shown together, unlike what happens at European shows and at events like the British Sieger.

Fawn pied is now an acceptable colour pattern in the French Bulldog. Changes to the Standard also make clear which colours are not acceptable. Cardigan Corgis also have a more detailed colour clause.

John and Mary Whitton's Ch Zaydah You Win Again at Vaucluse is only the second Hungarian Puli and first bitch to take a UK general championship show best in show. She won at City of Birmingham under Jill Peak. Chairman Bill King made the presentation.

PHOTO ALAN WALKER

After no fewer than 11 group wins, Sue Ellis' Alaskan Malamute Ch Chayo My Prerogative won his first all-breeds best in show at Driffield under Jack Bispham. He was also the only UK-bred and owned dog to take a group at Crufts 2015. Sue owns and bred all three Malamutes to have won a BIS at this level. President Lord Kirkham and secretary Martin Freeman presented the awards.

The Dog World in 2015

Shocking statistics for abandoned dogs

A 'SHOCKING' number of healthy but unwanted dogs are being put to sleep daily as councils and charities buckle under the strain of trying to cope with them.

New statistics have revealed that in the last 12 months more than 47,500 were abandoned in council pounds, unclaimed by their owners.

In total 102,363 stray and abandoned dogs were handled by UK local authorities and 5,142 were put to sleep – equating to 14 a day.

Dogs Trust's research has shown that 280 strays are found each day – and the charity received nearly 44,000 calls in the last year from people wanting to give up their dogs, the equivalent of 120 a day.

Dogs Trust, whose policy is to never put down a healthy dog, questioned the UK's local authorities as part of its annual stray dog survey. ■

The 2014 British Utility Breeds Association was topped by Elaine Emmett and Craig Simons' Dalmatian Ch Dalliviro Reba Mac at Ellemstra. Tom Mather was the judge and president Doug Kitchener presented the rosette.

PHOTO ALAN WALKER

Scottish Breeds' BIS winner, having been runner-up in 2014, was the Gordon Setter Sh Ch Lourdace Fulcrum, owned by David Alcorn, David Crowther, Jose Baddeley and Fiona Swan. Also pictured are breed judge Sandra Tye, trophy steward Moira McErlean, Alison Morton of Royal Canin and judge Peter Bailey. Later Fulcrum topped the Gundog Breeds Association of Scotland.

Bulldog row leads to Kennel Club bans

KENNEL CLUB disciplinary hearings continue to be rare, most of its activities concerning those already banned by the courts. However, a field trial competitor was banned for three years for kicking his English Springer Spaniel at a gundog event, and a Good Citizen Dog Scheme examiner has been warned and banned from some KC activities for a year for falsifying details on test certificates.

A 'juicier' case involved a Facebook posting by a Bulldog exhibitor who accused a judge of being 'bent'. The affair spilled over to Crufts the following day where three exhibitors, two of them championship show judges, were involved in a row with obscenities yelled, fingers pointed, chairs chucked and cages kicked.

The two main participants, including the one who had originally brought the complaint, were fined and banned from KC activities, one for two years, the other for one year. They both appealed, unsuccessfully in one case but the original complainant's ban was commuted by half to six months.

Another exhibitor was also fined and was banned from judging for six months. ■

PHOTO ROBIN BRYDEN

Ch Soletrader Annie Mac became the third generation Petit Basset Griffon Vendéen bitch to win BIS at the Hound Association of Scotland following her famous dam 'Jilly' and granddam 'Dizzy'. She is owned by Sara Robertson with Wendy Doherty of Canada and Ron and Debbie Scott of the US. They are pictured with her namesake, chairman Anne Macdonald, and judge Ken Sinclair.

Breeder Andrea Kirkwood handled Lisa Mair Jones' Samoyed Ch Vandreem Imperial Kai to win BIS at Working and Pastoral Breeds Association of Wales under Jean Lanning. Antony Bongiovanni represented Royal Canin.

SUMMIT

At the peak of Grooming Excellence

The only choice for Dog Grooming Training and Qualifications.

Summit Groomer Training Group Ltd works with groomer training schools to provide a link with City & Guilds and ensure the smooth running of the qualification process. From the registration of candidates, Summit provides the support, advice and communication needed to help and guide through to the final exams and certification.

The qualifications supported by Summit are the City & Guilds Level 2 Certificate for Dog Grooming Assistants and the Level 3 Certificate in Introductory Dog Grooming. Summit also arranges exam days for the Level 3 Diploma which are open to anyone who has successfully completed the Introductory level, whether registered with Summit or any other City & Guilds Approved Centre.

Our satellite training centres

Dashin Hounds – Belfast - dashinhounds.com **Doggrooming.ie** – Dublin – doggrooming.ie **Dazzles Dog Grooming** – Wrexham - Dazzles.vpweb.co.uk

Dee For Dogs – Essex - Deefordogs.com **Handsome Hounds** – Dorset - Handsomehounds.co.uk

Look North Grooming & Training Centre Ltd – Keighley - Looknorth.net **Pretty Paws Grooming** – Huddersfield – Prettypawsgrooming.co.uk

Scotgroom – South Lanarkshire - Scotgroom.co.uk **The Hair Of The Dog** –Hertfordshire - Thehairofhtedog.org

The Muddy Paw – Northamptonshire - Themuddypaw.co.uk **Top Trimz** – County Durham - Toptrimz-doggrooming.co.uk

For more information contact the centre of your choice or alternatively Summit Groomer Training on 01535 661776
www.summitgroomertraininggroup.co.uk   Email: enquiries@looknorth.net

The Dog World in 2015

Brachycephalic breeds under scrutiny

THE SUBJECT of brachycephalic breeds has been exercising the minds of the veterinary profession in both the UK and Sweden.

In the latter country vets are asking the government and kennel club (SKK) to take radical steps to improve the health of these breeds. They want dogs with breathing problems to be excluded from shows, and only healthy dogs to be used for breeding.

They say it is 'high time' a comprehensive approach is taken towards the breeding and importing of dogs who suffer from respiratory difficulties.

A thousand vets signed a petition asking for collaboration between them, the Swedish Kennel Club (SKK) and the Swedish Board of Agriculture to tackle the problems faced by the breeds.

Back home the topic was the subject of research by the Royal Veterinary College, funded by Dogs Trust and the Universities Federation for Animal Welfare, finding that a high proportion of dogs studied in Pugs, French Bulldogs, Bulldogs and Boston Terriers were affected by brachycephalic obstructive airway syndrome.

The researchers say buyers should be aware of the risks and that exaggeration of this conformation should be discouraged. ■

PHOTO TOM CASENTIERI

The Norwegian Buhund Ch/Ir Ch Arnscroft Di To Be A Sailor topped the National Working and Pastoral Breeds show. He is owned by Shirley and Alf Dobson, Sue Cale and Nancy Evans and handled by breeder Di Stirling. With them are judge Jeff Luscott and secretary Ann Arch.

PHOTO ALAN WALKER

Colin Hall and Lucy Ellis' Border Terrier Ch Brackenfell Bok To Bach was one of the year's more consistent winners with RBIS awards at National Terrier, Bath and Border Union. He is pictured at the former with new secretary Stuart Plane and judge Lesley Crawley. He was bred by Colin and Lucy in their first litter.

Jean Blandford gave best in show at the Houndshow to Yvonne Hull and Mike Howgate's Whippet Ch Palmik Live To Tell, pictured with chairman Hector Heathcote, breed dog judge Roz Holland and Kyle Cadmore representing Dorwest Herbs.

PHOTO ALAN WALKER

National Gundog was topped by Karen Whitehead's Weimaraner Sh Ch Gunalt De Ice at Stridview, who had also taken top spot at Belfast in 2014. Handler is Jacqui Ward. With them are president Rosemary Davies, Kyle Cadmore of Dorwest Herbs, judge Rob McMaster and breed judge Richard Stafford. De Ice was later RBIS at City of Birmingham.

Best in show at Working and Pastoral Breeds Association of Scotland was Janet and Mike Lewis' Bearded Collie Ch Potterdale Platinum Plus, who was also RBIS at South Wales. Secretary Sheena Harkins and judge Albert Wight are seen at the Scottish show.

Some like it wet, some like it dry and some like to mix it up a bit.

At Lovejoys® we understand that every owner wants their dog to enjoy a tasty, well balanced diet and we also know that when it comes to din dins, some dogs have very different needs. Not that they're fussy, of course, we would never say that.

To accommodate these needs, our Pure & Simple grain free, complete foods are available as both wet and dry foods. They come in a choice of delicious flavours and are made here in the UK using carefully sourced fresh meat and fish, blended with sweet potatoes, fruit, vegetables, herbs and oils to provide all the nutrition your dog needs for a happy, healthy life.

So whatever your four-legged friend prefers, wet, dry or a little bit of both, if you feed them Lovejoys® Pure & Simple, you can rest assured you will always be giving them the best.

The Dog World in **2015**

Tibetan breeds reject 'China' label

THE FEDERATION Cynologique Internationale, the umbrella organisation for many kennel clubs worldwide, has been much in the news during the year.

First came a stand-off with the American Kennel Club about judges who officiated at shows run by rival kennel organisations in China, Hong Kong and South Korea.

In China in particular, the AKC supported a different national body from the one which is an FCI member. This led to the FCI's Asia Pacific section blacklisting judges who worked at shows run by the 'wrong' organization.

The AKC retaliated by ruling that no judge from the section could judge at its shows; even an acknowledged expert, Hiroshi Kamisato, was prevented from judging the Japanese Chin national specialty. The AKC threatened to extend this to all FCI judges.

Eventually a compromise appears to have been reached at a meeting between the AKC and FCI in May.

Next it came to light in June that at its meeting in March the FCI General Committee changed the official country of origin of the Tibetan Mastiff, Tibetan Terrier, Tibetan Spaniel, Lhasa Apso and Shih Tzu from 'Tibet' to 'China', following a request from the China Kennel Union.

Needless to say, many of those who love the Tibetan breeds are also keen on Tibetan culture in general and have very strong views about how the country has been treated by its giant neighbour. Word such as 'a total betrayal of Tibet' were used.

The cynical wondered why the decision had not been made known earlier, suggesting that perhaps it was to avoid protests at the FCI's World Show at Milan in June.

It was also suggested that the 'country of patronage/development' for the Tibetan Spaniel and Terrier, Lhasa Apso, Chow and Shih Tzu might be changed from the UK to China, even though the latter played absolutely no part in establishing the Standards.

Individuals and clubs involved with the breeds were quick to protest, and within a few weeks the FCI president Rafael de Santiago announced that 'the Kennel Club (England) was to remain the country of patronage of those breeds, though patronage of the Tibetan Mastiff belongs to China'. That was a considerable relief as this means that the traditional British breed Standards will still be followed.

Regarding the country of origin, the KC wrote to the FCI suggesting a compromise: 'Tibet, now part of the People's Republic of China'.

Clearly all the protests worked for a few weeks later the FCI did a u-turn and, claiming it was 'sensitive and attentive' to people's views, changed the country of origin of the Tibetan breeds to Tibet (China). Most considered this to be a fair and reasonable solution. ■

As well as topping the group at Crufts, Justine Waldron's French-bred Bearded Collie Ch/Fr Ch Victory Winds Ghost Whisperer for Snowmead has twice been reserve BIS, at Windsor and Midland Counties where they are pictured with judge Andrew Brace.

PHOTO ALAN WALKER

Sharon O'Brian's Rosanley Aphrodite is the first Tibetan Spaniel to win a RBIS award at a UK general championship show, which she achieved at Blackpool under Mike Gadsby.

Roberta Hall's Afghan Hound Ch Garamond Juniperberry Saxonmill won RBIS awards with her second and third CCs at Hound Association of Scotland and WELKS where they are pictured with group judge Editha Newton and new secretary Helen Wayman. Her litter brother is also a group winner.

MAREMMA SHEEPDOG CLUB OF GREAT BRITAIN

MILWYR ONCE AGAIN UK TOP KENNEL
From right to left
MILWYR WON'T GET FOOLED AGAIN, MILWYR HEIMARMENE, HEMMYLON DELL'ANTICO TRATTURO DEL MILWYR
From right to left
Dad, Daughter, Mum
"Looking to the future"
Advice given, enquires welcome, puppies sometimes available

SALOPLASS MAREMMA SHEEPDOGS
Amy Scales
07492058484
saloplassmaremmasheepdogs
@gmail.com
MILWYR HEDYLOGOS OF SALOPLASS, CIARAMMELLA DELL'ANTICO TRATTURO DEL SALOPLASS, KESALKO IVERLEVEN OF SALOPLASS
"The best is yet to come"
Loved, owned and handled by
Amy

AMICITIA SHOW DOGS
Barbara and Patrick Gold
024767 1137

MILWYR JUPITER LECETIUS DEL AMICITIA

Loved and owned by
Barbara and Patrick

The Secretary, Jacqui Downes on 0774308644 or email jacquinikx@aol.com

The Dog World in 2015

China World Show is catalyst for FCI revolt

FOLLOWING the 'Tibetan breeds' affair, the next problem regarding China and the Fédération Cynologique Internationale was not so easily resolved. At the FCI assembly held after the Milan World Show, member countries voted on the location of the 2019 and 2020 shows. The winners were China and Spain respectively.

Whereupon all hell was let loose…

Unfortunately for the Chinese case, around the same time emerged graphic pictures of the disgusting 'dog meat festival' at Yulin. Even those who can just about accept that eating dog meat is a part of some countries' culture were appalled at what the poor dogs had to go through beforehand.

The Norwegian Kennel Club (NKK) took the initiative in calling for a boycott of the 2019 show in response to a 'serious and general lack of respect and welfare for dogs in China', and strongly advising its judges and exhibitors not to go.

Full details of subsequent events can be found in Norway's pages; briefly, a war of words between Norway and the FCI and especially its Asia Pacific section ensued. The latter's president Dinky Santos said that a boycott of the China show would play into the hands of those who want to see the demise of dog showing. The section supported the China Kennel Union (CKU) in its effort to educate the public and put an end to the eating of dogs.

Things began to get nasty, with the FCI threatening to suspend the NKK for up to two years unless it withdrew its encouragement to other kennel clubs not to attend the show. It set up a meeting with the NKK and CKU but the Norwegians refused to attend.

Our Kennel Club announced that it would not be sending a representative to the show in Shanghai. The reason given was that it did not want to encourage entries from long-haul countries, for the sake of dog welfare, which seemed somewhat strange given that it is happy to boast about how many dogs from far afield come to Crufts.

It subsequently emerged that the KC wasn't intending to go anyway, for logistical reasons.

In fact the KC does not seem to be against the idea of China hosting the show which it hopes 'will help people to see dogs as creatures that can provide their owners with unconditional love and companionship'.

There was condemnation of the Yulin Festival from all sides including the FCI and

For the first time the UK hosted the Bullmastiff World Cup. The two national clubs held their championship shows back to back, with the Bullmastiff Association's designated the World Cup. Cheryl Wright from Australia gave best in show to Grant Slater's Chalfs Naughty Secrets and RBIS to Francesca Pavesi's Indecent Proposal, from Italy, both bitches.

the CKU. The CKU called on the Chinese government to introduce laws on animal protection as soon as possible to regulate and eliminate such events.

The spokesman said that in recent years, under the 'supportive guidance of the FCI' and through the efforts of the CKU itself, the dog industry in China has become more regulated. The aim of the bid for the show is to 'promote and practise dog culture in China', he said. They hope to correct the attitude of Chinese people toward dogs and believe that the attention of the government or society could be aroused by the holding of the WDS.

They were suspicious of the motives of those who had written on the internet and 'angry at this attempt to defame the efforts of CKU and FCI'.

The union asked other FCI members to support its calls for the government to take action, and outline what it and its members have already done for canine welfare.

The Dutch KC did not support a boycott of the show but did hope that the festival would have been closed down by then. The Swedish KC pointed out that China had been a full member of the FCI for just two years, becoming a contractual partner in 2006, an associate member in 2011 and a full

member in 2013.

The fact remained, though, that China had won the vote; it cannot have helped matters that the anti-China vote would have been split three ways, between Spain, Germany and Croatia. China, it emerged, received 33 votes, and the others 14, 13 and eight respectively.

Germany accepted the result as it had been arrived at democratically.

A further complication was that FCI delegates at the meeting had been given – after the vote, it was stressed – 'gold cards' by the CKU, to be used for hotels and other expenses at the show, The NKK subsequently decided it was 'unacceptable' to accept the card and suggested the money, a total of about £70,000, would be better donated to welfare groups.

By the beginning of August the FCI issued an ultimatum to the NKK: that it abides by the FCI rules; leaves the federation; or does neither in which case sanctions would result. A deadline of October 1 was given which, conveniently, was after the FCI European Show which, as luck would have it, was hosted for the first time by the NKK!

Support from Norway came from two of its neighbours. The Swedish KC felt that respect for the World Show would be 'severely damaged' by it being held in a country 'with dreadful dog traditions', and felt it unacceptable that Norway had been threatened with sanctions.

Its statement highlighted the fact that 'democracy' could be considered to have a down side in that all FCI member countries had one vote, regardless of the size of their dog scene or how long breeding and showing has been part of their traditions.

The club is considering changing its membership or even perhaps resigning altogether.

Next the Finnish KC weighed in, saying it was 'deplorable' that the NKK had been threatened and that it felt the FCI's reputation had taken a serious blow.

It pointed out that the operation of the FCI is largely financed by a handful of member countries – referring in particular to Scandinavia, and said: "If these members consider actions disadvantageous to the FCI, the entire economic situation of the FCI may worsen dramatically.".

Even the Danish KC came up with some criticism of the FCI's decision-making process, suggesting that votes are weighted to reflect the number of registrations and dog activities in each country. However the DKK was not reconsidering whether it should be a FCI member, for if it resigned there could no longer be any international canine events in the country, Danish judges would not be permitted to judge abroad and its pedigrees would no longer be recognised internationally.

Quite why all those problems could arise was not clear to British observers; after all the UK, US etc are not FCI members and their judges and pedigrees are still recognised by the FCI, so why should it be any different for countries which resigned?

The case for China took a further blow when a district government there told owners to get rid of their dogs who would otherwise be killed.

The first Pug of the Year competition, judged by Annette Oliver, Bjørn Erling Løken from Norway and Patrick Davis, was won by Holly Attwood's Ch Tsuselena Jimmy Dean.

Obviously, observers of the whole affair were intrigued to see what would happen at the European Show, hosted by the NKK. A press conference led by chief executive Trine Hage made clear the club's overriding commitment to welfare, and showed no signs of backing down on its uncompromising stance.

The show was followed by the general assembly of the federation's European section, attended by FCI president Rafael de Santiago. Could some sort of compromise be reached before the divisions got any worse? Thankfully this appeared to be the case, so perhaps an explosion can be postponed or even avoided.

The section asked the FCI's General Committee to set up a working group to ensure that the statutes, standing orders and byelaws reflect concerns about cruelty against dogs and dog welfare; work out a proposal for changes in the voting and influence structure; and work out proposals for modernising the rules and make the duties and obligations transparent.

It should also consider if the 'five freedoms' can be established as a minimum level of dog welfare – freedom from hunger, thirst and malnutrition; abnormal heat and cold; fear and stress; and injury and illness; and to exercise normal behaviours.

Mr de Santiago confirmed that the General Committee would set up this group as soon as possible.

Latest development is that six kennel clubs have joined forces to demand changes from the FCI.

The Finnish, French, German, Italian, Norwegian and Swedish clubs have come up with a list of propositions they hope will bring about reform quickly.

Together, they account for half the FCI's revenue, it is claimed.

Among the changes they want to are: a weighted voted system based on fees paid; new members to register 3,000 dogs yearly for the three years before being approved as a full member; minutes of any meeting made public within a month; World and section shows to be rotated; the European section to be divided into between two to four sections; alterations to the statutes so that welfare activities of the member kennel club should be improved in every country; the General Committee to comprise a representative of each section, elected by that section; the Committee to appoint a working group to discuss the proposals and to report by the end of March; and an additional general assembly to be held before November '16. ∎

The Standard Poodle Club celebrated its fiftieth anniversary during 2015. At the championship show best in show was Charlotte Sandell's Sw/Norw/Fin Ch Da Maya Huffish Copyright Woman, from Sweden, and RBIS another bitch, Julia Wells' Smart Connection Pay And Play. Judges were Marita Rodgers and Eileen Doyle.

PHOTO SAMANTHA WEBSTER

Ch Dandyhow Dr Walter, Ch Am Ch Chatelet Aradet Rugby (Imp) ShCM, Ch Longsdale's Jen You Win, Sh Ch NED Ch Kavacanne Toff At The Top JW ShCM, Ch Hearthside Man of Mystery at Dialynne JW, Ch Benatone Designer Label, Ch Ir Ch Blackdale Julie, Multi Ch King Arthur Van Foliny Home, Ch Tetsimi Moves Like Jagger, Ch Shalfleet Simply A Lord, Ch Gleniren Shootin Starmaker Sunshoo, Ch Fin Ch Allmark Fifth Avenue JW WW14, Ch Charibere Simply Special at Chezanna, Ch Ir Ch Kebulak Trigger Happy, Sh Ch Sharnphilly Juici Cuture JW, Ch Vandreem Imperial Kai, Ch Arnscroft Di Na Mo Farrah of Koromandel JW ShCM, Ch Am Can Ch Klassic's Girl with a Curl (Imp USA), Sh Ch Bareve Bontebokskraal, Ch Drakesleat Scent Sybil, Ch Salina The Special One, Ch Nikara Iced Diamond JW, Ch Old Manila's Whisky Mac for Optimus, CH Kissangani Caught In The Act For Milukris ShCM, Ch Chelmbull Moon Pilot, Ch Brackenfell Bok to Bach JW, Multi Ch Smiling Snowball Russian Emperor at Samoravich, Ch Austr Ch Costog Mompessons Home Bru, Ch Davricard Harrison, Ch Yakee It Must Be Him, Ch Vandreem Imperial Cruz,

EUKANUBA

Eukanuba Salutes the 2015 Eukanuba Champion Stakes Finalists And Overall Winner

Eukanuba Champion Stakes Final
31st October 2015
Chesford Grange Hotel, Kenilworth

Bred By Experts
Fed By Experts

The 2015 Eukanuba Champion Stakes Overall Winner
Ch Benatone Designer Label

www.Breeders.Eukanuba.co.uk

PHOTO LISA CROFT-ELLIOTT

Winner of the Eukanuba champion stakes final, and therefore the UK's representative at the World Challenge held in December with the Amsterdam Winner Show, was Sarah Jackson and Andrea Wylie's Maltese Ch Benatone Designer Label, seen with judges Mark Cocozza and Jeff Horswell and Annaliese Reekie from the sponsor. The Maltese has three RBIS awards including Belfast in 2015.

PHOTO RBT

Annette Oliver judged the Junior Warrant winner of the year final at Crufts and chose Manuel Fernandez and Chris Purnell's Airedale Terrier Ch Muliebrity Rilletta. Susan Sprung, wife of the American Kennel Club president, presented the trophy.

Colin N Waddell

Before embarking on his exciting run of top wins, Paul (handling) and Hayley (right) Seal's Bulldog Ch Sealaville He's Tyler scooped another major success, winning the Canine Supporters Charity's Contest of Champions. Pictured are sponsors Sharon Evison of Award Board Rosettes and Antony Bongiovanni of Royal Canin, plus judges Tomasz Borkowski (Poland), Jean Pierre Achtergael (Belgium) and Liz Cartledge (UK).

The Kennel Club breeders competition saw its last final take place at Crufts, to the regret of many, though the concept had never really taken hold in the UK as it does in Scandinavia. The winners were the Shalfleet Whippets bred by Jane Wilton-Clark.

News in Brief

A COMPETITION for the 'vulnerable' British and Irish native breeds has been run by the Kennel Club through 2015, replacing the breeders' competition whose last final took place at Crufts '15.

It is sponsored by Eukanuba and run in conjunction with Our Dogs; Points can be accrued at championship and open shows and a final will take place at Crufts '16.

DOG TRAINER Roy Dyer, founder of the Essex Dog Training Centre, a founding director of the county's dog display team and creator of the All About Dogs event at Brentwood, was awarded an MBE in the New Year's Honours. His work with children who were frightened of dogs was particularly noteworthy. Knighted at the same time was David Amess, the Conservative MP who regularly campaigned on behalf of dogs.

when you need them to be at their best...

...why compromise?

 NATURAL

 HYPOALLERGENIC

 VITAMINS AND OMEGA 3 & 6

Introducing DWD, the UK's No 1 Premium Working Dog Food. Our food is healthy, nutritious, hypoallergenic, and free from wheat and wheat gluten.

available now in 8 great flavours
with prices starting at £27.50 for a 15kg bag.

why go grain free?

Some grains have been linked with allergies in dogs, causing symptoms such as upset stomachs or irritated coats.

DWD Working Dog Grain Free contains 50% meat content (with 26% fresh meat content in every variation) with the remaining 50% including fruits and vegetables. Th ecomposition is also high in Vitamins & Minerals which provides lots of energy and nutrition whilst improving the skin and coat making it the ultimate food for your working dog.

available now in 4 great flavours
with prices starting at £38.00 for a 15kg bag.

visit www.dwdfoods.co.uk to find out more

 dwd made in britain

The Dog World in 2015

PHOTO DAVID HUDSON

Winner of the Hunt Point Retrieve Breeds Championship was Howard Kirby's German Longhaired Pointer Wamilanghaar Tash.

Ian Openshaw's Mallowdale Xfactor won the Kennel Club Cocker Spaniel Championship.

PHOTO ANDY BIGGAR/KENNEL CLUB

Winner of the tracking dog stake at the Kennel Club Working Trial Championships was Tony Lockyer with German Shepherd WT Ch Lawinick Come N Get It at Hartshill.

PHOTO DAVID HUDSON

Jon Bailey's Rheastmoor Fizzy won the Kennel Club English Springer Spaniel Championship.

PHOTO GRAHAM COX

The International Gundog League Retriever Championship was won by Richard King's Labrador FT Ch Saxaphone Brown Ale of Lincswolds.

Alan Bexon's Working Sheepdog WT Ch Fly By Night Lad won the patrol dog stake at the Kennel Club Working Trial Championships.

Midland Counties CS celebrated its fortieth year by presenting Dogs for the Disabled with a £16,550 cheque. Pictured are Robert Greaves, Jack Randall and Margaret Everton from the society, the charity's chief executive Peter Gorbing and Laura Viles and Julie Worthington with two of the charity's dogs, Tally and Nala.

PHOTO SAM DAWSON

BIS at the Beagle Club's 125th anniversary championship show was Sarah Jackson's Ch Bayard Forgetmeknot, seen with patron Marion Spavin, judges Sue Bownds (dogs), Christine Lewis (BIS) and Lesley Hiltz (bitches) and president David Webster.

The Kennel Club's Pointer and Setter Championship was won by David O'Neill's Irish Setter Glynlark Aramis.

A group of Golden Retriever enthusiasts has raised more than £24,000 for the Animal Health Trust. Jayne May, pictured to the left of her Golden Zoe who survived cancer, had orginally aimed to raise £5,000 but that figure swelled beyond all expectation.

Tastes change, quality doesn't

We've been making our mark on the pet food industry for over 100 years, but our passion for delivering the best never fades. Made here in the UK, Davies helps achieve the maximum health and performance from dogs through a nutritional range – including a new grain-free variety – that is free from many common allergens. Our heritage and reputation for quality provides peace of mind to our many satisfied customers – and their owners.

Davies Pet Food is part of the Pets Choice family. To find out how to become a stockist, please call **01254 54545** or email **info@daviespetfood.co.uk**

The Dog World in 2015

At Crufts the large dog Agility Championship was won by Charlotte Harding's Ag Ch Rujaff Red Hot Scandal, seen with judge Alan Bray and American Kennel Club agility director Carrie DeYoung.

At Crufts the Obedience Championship for Dogs was won by Jessica Lewis and Ob Ch Pepsanner Atlantic, the first Golden Retriever to win since 1973. With them are judge Sandra Gordon, Crufts chairman Gerald King and chief steward Roy Page who retired after this show.

Dot Watts won a Crufts Obedience Championship for the fifth time when she topped the bitches with Ob Ch Zygdann Rockin Frenzi.

The Northern region won the Inter-Regional Obedience competition at Crufts, managed by Pat Wilson. Members are Ashleigh Foster with Angelo's Wings, Henri Carew with Hens Millie Minstrel, Jackie Muir with Morgansr Made For Me, Brenda Holden with Alfie of Hodge House, Gillian Strickleton with Redistedi High Reality, Fiona Holdsworth with Actadog All For One, Jeny Miller with Foxfold Unexpected Edition CDex, UDex, WDex, TDex and reserve, Louise Frelford with Actadog Aim To Achieve. Steve Barnes was the judge.

Medium Agility Championship winners at Crufts were Sian Illingworth with Ag Ch Arnpriors Made Of Honour.

The team from England won the Crufts Obedience World Cup, judged by Kathy Russell. Members are: team manager Herbie Watson, Philomena Barnes with Ob Ch Bheinn Bewitched, Pat Watson with Ob Ch Forevermagic Itsflicka, Mary Ray and Ob Ch Colliewood Blue Jeans, who won the individual award, and Marie Cartwright with Ob Ch Dodgin Firecracker. The World Cup will cease after Crufts 2016 and will be replaced by an inter-regional rally competition.

Mary Ray's Ob Ch Colliewood Blue Jeans won 13 obedience certificates during 2014, one more than the previous record.

Claire Burrell and Ag Ch Daimonic Expelliarmus won the small dog Agility Championship at Crufts.

News in Brief

CAMPAIGNERS were bitterly disappointed when the Government overturned on appeal a decision to disallow the construction of a new facility to breed Beagles for experiments near Hull. Among those calling for a change of heart are the Kennel Club and the Fund for the Replacement of Animals in Medical Experiments, while Cruelty Free International has lodged a judicial review.

THE COUNTRY Landowners' Association Game Fair is no longer. The 2016 event at Ragley Hall has been cancelled. The event has been part of the calendar since 1958 but for the last three years insufficient visitors have been attracted to make it an economic proposition.

THE ANIMAL Health Trust has repaid the interest-free loan of £1.5million, provided by the Kennel Club in 2011 to build its cancer centre near Newmarket. By February 2015, 130 dogs of 20 breeds suffering from 15 types of cancer had been seen.

DOGS KILLED on main roads must now be scanned for a microchip, and if one is found the owner must be informed of the dog's fate. Campaigners made the case for 'Harvey's Law', named after a dog whose owner spent 13 weeks looking for him. She had not been informed that his body had been found, even though he was chipped.

Why just one food for all dogs?

Although there are several theories nearly everyone is in agreement that all our dogs (Canis Lupus Familiaris) in all their variety are descended from wolves (Canis Lupus), as different breeds. That they belong to the same family (Canis / Canidae) and, in spite of differences in appearance, are still very similar to each other, is apparent from the fact that the basic behaviour of our dogs is still the same as the behaviour of a wolf.

Thousands of years ago, in the course of history, a simbiosis (living together to the advantage of both) arose between man and wolf. Wolves are opportunistic and learned that it was beneficial to stay in the area of people travelling around (nomads). The wolves ate the remains of food from the people during times of scarcity and the people learned that it was advantageous to use the characteristics of the wolf, for example, in hunting and keeping watch.

Just like the basic behaviour of the wolf, the whole digestive system, and all it entails, has remained the same. Amongst wild dogs it was and is a fact that the whole pack, from young to old and from small to big, eat the same food sources in accordance with their requirements, of the prey that is available at the moment. Pups eat relatively more and older dogs somewhat less.

In this respect dogs are comparable with people (also a long living "mammal"), because people also eat the same mix, from baby to senior. The baby eats relatively more of this (blended) food than its parents, and the grandparents in contrast eat relatively much less.

Because dogs, just like their ancestors, eat as much as is necessary to supply their energy needs, with food of the correct composition they also take in all the nutritional substances in the right relative quantities to the energy taken up.

Young dogs, lactating bitches, and working dogs that have to perform, eat more than the average fully grown dog, and in this way their total requirement for the various nutritional substances is satisfied.

The same applies to older dogs that are not expected to perform; these eat less than the average fully grown dog.

Because dogs have a very short intestine (in relative terms seven times as short as that of humans), food for dogs has to contain a lot of energy per kilogram of dry material, so that digestion is not adversely influenced by too much bulk.

Therefore all dogs can eat Farm Food HE (High Energy) throughout their lives. And the "All Life Stages" philosophy of Farm Food has been based on this fact since 1982: one type of food that is suitable for all dogs, from "mini" to "maxi"; from puppy to senior; from working to resting.

The recent years have more than proved that Farm Food HE is extremely suitable for puppies and seniors, very large and very small breeds, hard-working and resting dogs, and that special puppy food, senior food, or hypo-allergenic food is unnecessary, just like in nature.

For small dogs (puppy or a small breed) there is Farm Food HE Mini, precisely the same composition but then in a smaller sized pellet (6 mm) and in a smaller bag.

www.farmfood.co.uk
info@farmfood.co.uk

Since 1982

FARM FOOD®
Natural Dog Food

The Dog World in 2015

Lucy Creek and Harriot Skiffle King won both the Freestyle and Heelwork to Music finals at Crufts.

The International Freestyle winner at Crufts was Slovakia's Monika Olsovka with Arsinoe z Rose Wa.

PHOTO ALAN WALKER

PHOTO ALAN WALKER

Among the winners at the Siberian Husky Club of Great Britain's Royal Canin Aviemore races was Colin Stewart with his eight-dog team.

PHOTO SIBERPRINT

Overall winners of the gamekeepers' classes at Crufts was Paul Drewery's English Springer Spaniel Master Bojangles, handled by Helen Fox. Judge was Helena Sully and Alan Jarrett of the British Association for Shooting and Conservation presented the Northesk Memorial Trophy.

PHOTO ALAN WALKER

Marnee, an 11-year-old Golden Retriever, was named Pets As Therapy Dog of the Year. She has been a PAT Dog since she was nine months old with her owner Noel Austin. Dog trainer Victoria Stilwell and Tony Parkinson of HiLife Petfood made the presentation.

News in Brief

DAVID Guy replaces Steve Croxford (who is now Kennel Club vice-chairman) as chairman and Mark Cocozza takes over from Mr Guy as vice-chairman of the KC's Disciplinary Sub-Committee.

On assuming the chair of the club, Simon Luxmoore stepped down as chairman of the Judges Sub-Committee and has been replaced by Anne Macdonald, and Ron James takes on the role of vice-chairman from her.

Irene McManus has taken over as vice-chairman of the Show Executive Sub-Committee from Rod Price.

Babs Sharp took on the Malinois Jazzed U when she was a stray dog who had run the streets of London and was within a week of being put down. After less than two years' training they won the Kennel Club Good Citizen Dog Scheme pre-beginnner obedience competition at Crufts. With them are Heather Hardaway, scheme working party chairman Maurice Cooke and judge Michael McCartney.

Agility Team GB won the gold medal in the large team competition at the World Championships in Bologna. Here are Matt Goodliffe with Turboed Widewater Wizard Jess Clarehugh with Ag Ch Lynwood Cara Fuzzy Logic, Charlotte Harding with Ag Ch Rujaff Red Hot Scandal and Greg Derrett with Devongem Rehab Sproglett.

The Dog World in 2015

Four pioneering scientists have been honoured with International Canine Health Awards: David Argyle for his work on stems cells and cancer, James Swann for his research into haemolytic anaemia, eye specialist Sheila Crispin and geneticist Cathryn Mellersh, pictured with sponsor Vernon Hill (centre).

Gladys Ogilvy-Shepherd of the Gbos Rottweilers received an MBE in the June Queen's Honours List for her service to animal welfare and veterinary education. In particular she has supported the Royal (Dick) Veterinary School's hospital for small animals.

Di Johnson was the winner of Dog World's award of excellence, presented at the 2014 Pup of the Year final. Andrew Brace, Stuart Baillie and Simon Parsons made the presentation.

PHOTO ALAN WALKER

Kari Wilberg has announced her retirement from judging.

Helen Wayman has succeeded Sheila Jakeman as secretary of the West of England Ladies' Kennel Society.

Jean Faulks, a leading figure in the working trials world, particularly with Dobermanns, celebrated her hundredth birthday.

Vivien Phillips of the Debucher Bassets Griffons Vendéens has been awarded a Medal d'Honneur by the French breed club for her part in helping to develop a DNA test for primary open angle glaucoma in the Petit variety.

Annette Oliver has retired from the Kennel Club General Committee. She is pictured as KC representative at a Buckingham Palace garden party, along with her son David. Tony Allcock MBE has joined the Committee. As well as being a successful toy dog exhibitor, he has immense experience as competitor and administrator in the bowls world.

Clarissa Baldwin, for many years chief executive of Dogs Trust, was awarded a CBE in the Queen's birthday honours list in recognition of her contribution to animal welfare over 40 years.

Ferelith Somerfield has retired as chairman of the Ladies' Kennel Association after more than 40 years' involvement. She is seen (right) with her successor Anne Bliss.

Two of Britain's best known multi-breed judges, Stuart Mallard and Rodney Oldham, married at a ceremony in Bakewell.

Dr Claire Guest, co-founder and director of Medical Detection Dogs, was presented with a British Citizen Award by Baroness Cox (left).

Paul Doyle with the painting of Crufts 2014 best in show winner Ch/Am Ch Afterglow Maverick Sabre which he undertook for the Kennel Club Arts Foundation.

The Dog World in 2015

PHOTO ALAN WALKER

At eight years old, Lauren Bridges must surely be the youngest handler to win a championship show group. She did so at Richmond handling Jane Fulierova's Samoyed Ch/Svk Gr Ch Smiliesam Strike Home. Judge was Mark James and Darren Clarke represented the committee.

PHOTO ALAN WALKER
©V.Woods/C.Wi

An encouraging aspect of Crufts was the number of young handlers who won bests of breed or other top awards. Star of them was Ryan Ross, 12, who handled the English Toy Terrier, new champion Witchstone China Girl for Poshpins, to group 3.

First Russian Black Terrier to win a group at a UK championship show is Mike Smith's Rohantia Nikolai at Fernwood who scored at East of England under Sue Garner, handled by Sarah Gibbons. Show manager Alan Hards made the presentation.

PHOTO ALAN WALKER

Irene Collier's Belatarr Mahalia Jackson is the first Hungarian Wirehaired Vizsla to win a championship show group in the UK. She did so at Boston under Aidine Howes. Phil Rundle represented sponsor CSJ.

PHOTO ROBIN BRYDEN

New Portuguese Water Dog CC record holder is Rachael Reddin's Ch Rarjo For Your Eyes Only, succeeding his sister Ch Rarjo She's The One. He was also the first of the breed to win a championship show group in the UK.

Robert and Tracey Hargreaves' Large Munsterlander Sh Ch/Int/Dutch/Ger Ch Ghyllbeck Holcus has taken the breed CC record formerly held by his great-great-grandsire from the same kennel, Ch Ghyllbeck Holcus.

Racquel Walker' Ch/Norw Ch Condalf Baldur is the new Leonberger CC record holder.

PHOTO ALAN WALKER

Britain's first Tibetan Mastiff champion is Richard Gardiner's young American import Sierras LL Cool Jay at Heronsview, seen with Ron James who gave him his third CC.

Britain's first Bracco Italiano show champion is Lynne Bowley's Gunsyn Aafia.

News in Brief

A CANINE act won the popular *Britain's Got Talent* TV show, but there was controversy afterwards when it was revealed that Jules O'Dwyer used a second dog, in place of the winning Matisse, to perform a tightrope walk which was part of the act. Ofcom agreed that viewers had been misled and ITV offered to refund or donate to charity what viewers had spent in voting for the winning act.

A STUDY by researchers at the University of Liverpool suggested that one in four dogs competing at Crufts was overweight. Dog people didn't take much notice as the claims were made just from looking at photographs, some as far back as 2001, and the Kennel Club expressed its displeasure.

IN A pilot scheme Richmond invited hound breed clubs and councils to nominate breed judges for 2016 and '17. Blackpool had already asked for nominations for a number of breeds for 2017 and this has been extended to '18.

The Dog World in 2015

PHOTO ABBOTT

©Maxine Abbott Photos

The first mantle Great Dane to win a CC since the colour pattern was included in the Standard in 2006 is Ravendane Flash Gordon at Roiucandane, seen with owner Sheena Booth, breeder Joanne Walton and judge Adam Chappell.

PHOTO LLOVALL DESIGN

Top Stud Dog 2014 in the Dog World/ Royal Canin competition was the American-bred Keeshond Ch/Am/Can Ch Kemont's Skyline's Game Boy, owned during his British stay by Joan Miles with Kristen and Susan Cullen.

PHOTO LISA CROFT-ELLIOTT

For the second year running, Dog World/Yumega Show Dog Top Brood Bitch 2014 was Neil and Angie Allen and Robert Harlow's Australian Shepherd Ch Allmark Careless Whisper, dam of eight CC winners of the year and five new champions.

PHOTO HEIL

The second International Dog Health Workshop took place in Dortmund, Germany, organised by the German Kennel Club. It saw the launch of the DogWellNet website which contains a wealth of information on canine health issues. Pictured are Brenda Bonnett and Pekka Olson, chief executive and chairman of the International Partnership for Dogs, Steve Dean the then chairman of the Kennel Club, its secretary Caroline Kisko and health information manager Aimee Llewellyn and German KC chairman Peter Friedrich.

PHOTO ALAN WALKER

Alan O'Wells

The Cirneco dell'Etna came off the imported breeds register in October and the first championship show breed classes were at Midland Counties where Tom Mather gave BOB to Michele Farleigh's Hadranensis Violetta via Kinabula.

PHOTO ALAN WALKER

Joanne and John Blackbuirn-Bennett's Sandanca Silver Lady at Stargang is the first dapple Miniature Smooth Dachshund champion for over 50 years, and the first silver dapple champion ever.

PHOTO PAUL KEEVIL

To celebrate the 200th anniversary of the publication of Sir Walter Scott's *Guy Mannering*, after a character in which the breed is named, Dandie Dinmont Terrier people from around the world organised a celebration, visiting Scott's home at Abbotsford and several other sites in the Scottish borders connected to the early days of the breed. Here they are pictured at Bowhill, home of the tenth Duke of Buccleuch (centre front); Old Pepper, the founding father of the breed, was a poacher's dog who was found caught in a trap on the estate then owned by the fifth Duke.

News in Brief

THE KENNEL Club Assured Breeder Scheme produced a film which can be seen on the KC website to dispel any fears breeders may have about what is involved in an inspection under the scheme.

The scheme had 6,690 members at the beginning of 2015, 1,694 fewer than a year earlier, perhaps the result of the changes introduced during that year.

'GROUND-breaking' research which it hopes will help breeders improve genetic health and protect the future of dog breeds has been launched by the Kennel Club. The review covers 35 years of data and is said to be is the most comprehensive research project of its kind, covering the years from 1980 to 2014 for all 215 recognised breeds.

Where numbers allow, it has allowed the calculation of the rate of loss of genetic diversity within each, which is quoted as the estimated effective population size (EPS), which indicates the sustainability of a population.

The KC says the research shows that since 2000 the rate of inbreeding has declined in the majority of breeds to sustainable levels. It believes this suggests the future for many breeds is brighter, including some of the vulnerable native breeds whose lack of popularity and low numbers have been a cause for concern.

After her Japanese Shiba Inu, Sylvia, went missing on a Anglesey beach and was later found drowned, Janice Bannister launched a fund in her memory which raise £7,000 for the island's coastguard service. A total of 75 Shibas and their owners gathered for the presentation

Juniors

Winning juniors in the picture

PHOTO ALAN WALKER

Daria Moiseeva, representing Belarus, won the International Junior Handler of the Year competition at Crufts.

At Crufts Hollie Kavanagh became the Young Kennel Club Handler of the Year.

Jack Bispham chose the Australian Shepherd Ch Allmark Spirit Of St Louis, handled by Sarah Gibbons, to win the Young Kennel Club stakes final at Crufts. Valerie Foss made the presentation.

For the second year running Connie Critcher was declared Young Kennel Club Groomer of the Year at Crufts.

PHOTO O'BRIEN

PHOTO ALAN WALKER

PHOTO ALAN WALKER

PHOTO ALAN WALKER

Scottish Handler of the Year is Bethany Green, who had previously been runner-up and fourth in the finals. She is pictured with her mentor, previous double winner Ashley Place.

Young Kennel Club Agility Dog of the Year, judged at Crufts by Dave Deaville, was Holly Ryan's Abbicher Dreaming. Crufts chairman Gerald King (left) made the presentation.

Rebecca Williams (right) chose Catherine Webb as Welsh Junior Handler of the Year. With them are organiser Dr Phillippa Pearson and Jackie Stubbs of sponsor Happy Do

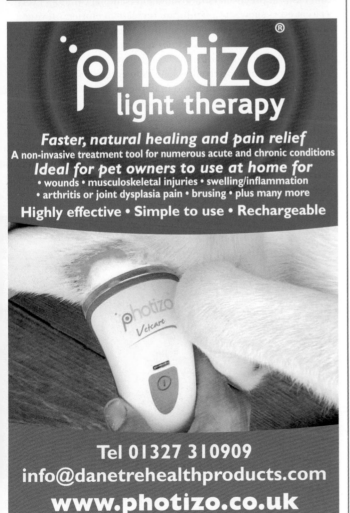

Juniors

A new format for the Junior Handling Association

Report by
Marina Scot

Big changes for the Junior Handling Association were seen in 2015. It was the first year when the semi-finals were moved from Richmond championship show and spread across the six national group championship shows.

The year also saw the organisation hold its own junior handling training day for members and it was also the first time in many years when the JHA final was moved to a new venue and date.

In August 2014, it was revealed in DOG WORLD that the JHA was to move its semi-final competition from Richmond. This came as quite a surprise to many juniors and their parents but once they understood the reasons behind the move, many embraced the decision and looked forward to the start of the new chapter.

Richmond is one of a handful of shows that does not rotate its groups so hound and toy exhibitors remain on the Friday. As the semi-final competition mirrors these groups, it meant that junior handlers showing hound or toy breeds were at a disadvantage because schools go back the week before Richmond.

Getting time off for dog shows is becoming more and more difficult as the education system now takes quite a strict view on taking time off school in term time – they can even go as far as to fine parents for doing this. So with this in mind, it was decided, sadly, to move the semi-finals away from Richmond, where they have enjoyed wonderful hospitality since the 1970s.

Each national group show welcomed the opportunity to stage two classes of the semi-finals and in December 2014, British Utility Breeds Association hosted the first two classes, attracting bumper entries, almost a 20 per cent increase on the utility classes at Richmond.

And the rise in entries continued right across all the group shows in 2015 from UK Toy, National Terrier, National Working

and Pastoral Breeds to Houndshow and National Gundog. Every class at every show saw a significant increase in entries, proving that allowing juniors the opportunity to compete on a Saturday or Sunday and at more central venues such as Stafford and Malvern le[ ] to an increase in popularity.

Another change was to allow juniors to enter each and every semi-final with a different breed until they won a class and qualified for the JHA final. There were many juniors who took up this opportunity and handled breeds that they were more unfamiliar with to class placings and even wins – namely Paige Spencer who won through with a Lowchen compared to her usual Bernese Mountain Dog and Antonia Leech who won a place in what must b[ ] a record fifth final, this time handling a Dobermann rather than a Bearded Collie.

Winner of the Junior Handling Association final, sponsored by Dog World and held at Discover Dogs, was Harvey Small with a French Bulldog. The final six all also handled a Nova Scotia Duck Tolling Retriever.

PHOTO ALAN WALKER

The 14 finalists in the JHA competition were for the first time selected at the national group championship shows. They were: front, Lauren Bridges, Lauren Goddard and Oliver Stone; middle, Ella Findlay, Tamsin Blyton, Paige Spencer and Alice Potter; back, Connor Bartlett, Harvey Small, Ffion Thomas, Antonia Leech, Jazmine Bellenie, Molly Cousins and Min Witheyman. Antonia was runner-up, followed by Lauren B, Lauren G, Jazmine and Min.

The Junior Handling Association, Dog World and Kennel Club team who help run the event: front: Jo Gordon, Irene Terry, Liz Cartledge, judge Suzy Roffey and Marina Scott; back, Gerald King, commentator Jonathan Daltrey, Ben Hanney and Adrian Marett.

Juniors

PHOTO ALAN WALKER

Scenes from the Junior Handling Association training day.

PHOTOS MARION B YE

Dog World and Royal Canin have supported the JHA all year with prizes and goodies and I and Adrian Marett from DW have regularly met with JHA organisers Liz Cartledge and Irene Terry to help in various ways.

Another new branch to the JHA was the launch of its first handling training day. There was an amazing response and 25 juniors spent a day at the Dobermann Club's venue in Digswell, Hertfordshire with trainers myself, former UK Junior Handler of the Year Hollie Kavanagh and top Scottish ex-junior handler Lisa Moir.

We put the attendees through their paces, making sure the handlers were handling their dogs in the manner that they would in the breed classes and then tweaking any extra handling points to get the best out of the handler and dog.

Former Young Kennel Club Show Handler of the Year winner Lucy Carter, who now works with Royal Canin, attended along with breeder manager Gary Gray who engaged the juniors in a wonderful, aptly named talk 'how to get the best out of your show dog experience'.

He went through all the other activities juniors could get into, such as stewarding, judging, committee and other official work.

The training day itself was a huge success and more are to be organised so watch this space!

So the last big change of 2015 for the JHA was the final itself. This has been traditionally held within the main ring of Discover Dogs in November but the old venue, Earls Court in London, closed in December 2014 to make way for a new residential site.

So, its new home became London's ExCel Arena and for 2015 the event was moved to October 17 and 18. It felt just like Discover Dogs that we knew and loved, except in a slightly different shaped building!

The JHA final was moved to Sunday morning at 10am instead of its usual spot on Saturday morning opening the main ring programme.

Suzy Roffey was this year's judge, a former winner of the event herself (1989) and currently a successful exhibitor in gundog and utility breeds.

She awarded UK Junior Handler of the Year 2015 to 17-year-old Harvey Small from Devon handling a French Bulldog. He became only the second male handler to win the title in the past 16 years, almost as long as he's been alive! It's the first time a junior handler has won with a Frenchie and five years since a utility breed made the top spot.

In fact, the last utility winner was Charlotte Page with a Dalmatian in 2010, who put Harvey through from the semi-final at BUBA!

He goes forward to represent the UK at the International Junior Handling final at Crufts in 2016.

A wonderful and successful year for the JHA – let's hope 2016 continues this exciting momentum. ■

Juniors

Report by: **Haley Jones and Sarah Gibbon**

Starting at the beginning...

Jodie Forbes competing in heelwork to music with Bramble and Hazel.

Caitlin Forbes practising her grooming on Solo.

Everyone has got to start somewhere, no matter your activity, whether you want to compete or just have some fun.

Starting a new activity, you will always make mistakes; many people remember something that went wrong but no person or dog is perfect and part of improving is making the mistakes to learn from.

Jodie Forbes, a competitor in heelwork to music, says: "Now I realise that actually, some of the best moves come about purely by accident, so mistakes aren't all that bad! Just stay positive and have fun!"

A brilliant way to improve is to find a local club for guidance, Rebecca Foster did just this when she began flyball training: "I train at my local club, Bassett Allsorts near Swindon, which has been running for 20-plus years."

We asked her what advice she would give to someone who wanted to start taking part in flyball: "Be consistent in your training and never give up on your dog. Speed is just one element and enjoyment is above all most important."

Unfortunately, depending on where you live, there is not always a training club near you. Someone who experienced this was grooming competitor Caitlin Forbes. One of the best ways to learn for her was to "Speak to other groomers in your chosen breed, ask as many questions as you can and be willing to learn. Take photos of the dogs that you think are presented well – but ask permission from the owner. If you can, attend grooming seminars and possibly breed seminars so you know how the breed should look.

"Practice makes perfect. From speaking to other groomers, I learnt that every show and every experience will teach you something new, whether it is a new way to hold your scissors or a new way to trim the head. The phrase 'you learn something new every day' definitely applies in grooming."

You can learn a lot by watching others and reading books or articles on the internet. Jodie Forbes, a heelwork to music competitor, advises anyone who wants to begin in her discipline: "I would definitely recommend joining a local heelwork to music group, or joining an online group, to anyone who is interested in dog dancing. I'd also recommend watching videos on YouTube and, if possible, going to watch the HTM competitions, or Mary Ray, at Crufts for inspiration."

For many, having a role model like Mary Ray is essential as it gives you something to aim for. You can watch your role model and see what they are doing and if you watch carefully you will pick up tips that you can then go home and use in training.

Some people use this method to teach themselves the basics and then later find a training club to help them to progress up to a higher level. This was how Ella Armstrong, an obedience competitor, began. She said: "I was very proud to have originally been self-taught and have been successful with a breed (Whippet) that you don't tend to see in an obedience ring. However, I do now go to a brilliant club which specialises in competitive obedience and believe I would not be at the level I am now if it wasn't for their help."

When starting a new activity it's not just you who is learning but it's also your dog. Your dog doesn't understand the new activity straight away and doesn't have someone explaining what is expected of them, except for the information that the handler is giving them.

This is why communication is so important. If you teach a dog a movement with a command the dog will remember this and in the right frame of mind the dog will perform this command in many environments. Your dog can only learn a command if he's consistently given the same commands while you are practising.

This isn't just learning verbal commands; our dogs watch our body language constantly no matter what we are doing with

Cameron Bunce with Jay going over the A frame.

Rebecca Foster's Brandy jumping a flyball jump

them so when training you must keep any hand signals and body movements consistent to help your training and give your dog the best chance of understanding.

There's no reason why you must train only one activity; many handlers teach their dogs a number of activities as they all help build a special bond with your dog and all require your dog to be responsive to commands.

Agility requires your dog to listen as carefully as obedience and even in a show ring you are still ask your dog to listen to certain commands like wait, stand and turn.

When you are starting out often you will be unsure of what activity you want to take part in. A few of the main ones such as obedience, agility, flyball, heelwork to music, grooming and Canicross are all brilliant to try before you decide on what to train regularly.

Many young handlers join the Young Kennel Club (YKC) which offers a number of events, training days and camp throughout the year where you can try training and even competition for beginners as well as for those who are advanced.

Someone who began a new activity at YKC camp was Bobbi Shepherd who started Canicross at YKC camp in 2009: "I would say the only thing that inspired me was YKC camp as I had never heard about it before but it was really fun to learn."

We asked her what advice she could offer to someone who was thinking of starting Canicross. She said: "I would suggest trying to find someone who competes in and trains Canicross so you can learn about the correct equipment you need to use."

This type of event, put on by the YKC, aims to encourage young people to begin and continue in new activities. They are usually led by people who have completed or trained in the activity and usually these people have also been taught at one of these training days.

Many young handlers enjoy competing in exciting and active sports and this is why agility is such a hit. Not only is it exciting but it is hugely popular around the country as well as having a large number of different categories so everyone can complete in a fair manner.

One young handler who enjoy competing in agility is Cameron Bunce who offered a bit of advice to someone who wanted to start taking part in agility: "Have a good relationship with your dog and work hard!" Agility involves a large amount of trust and concentration from the handler and dog.

Whether you are first starting out with training your dog or have been competing for years in one activity and want to try

Ella Armstrong's Wilf practising obedience.

Bobbi Shepherd and Twinkle competing in Canicross.

another, it's clear that many competitors say the same thing: watch, learn, and listen to those who are already competing.

Find out how they began and what they think is important to the individual sport and first and foremost make it an enjoyable experience for your dog.

If you are both happy and having fun you will achieve your full potential together. So what canine sport will you trial in 2016? ■

Moving forward in CLARGES STREET

Simon Parsons talks to new Kennel Club chairman **SIMON LUXMOORE**

SP: Simon, What sort of feedback have you had from both Kennel Club members and ordinary dog people since you became chairman?

SL: Having attended many different events, shows, working trials, field trials and so on – the feedback I'm getting is that people seem to be very positive and upbeat at the moment.

The General Committee are in the process of addressing many topics – people tell me that they believe there is a new approach towards openness and transparency and a real desire to resolve issues and move forward together, all of which is good to hear.

SP: What can you tell us about the work of the Governance working party, which was set up after the 2015 AGM?

SL: At the special general meeting (see page 26) you will be made aware of the issues that the Governance Group has been discussing. The agenda items have in the main come from General Committee members who were asked to submit their ideas and concerns which they wanted the working group to consider. The conclusions and recommendations of the working party will be submitted to the GC for their consideration. Then, and only then, will the GC make recommendations to the membership by way of proposals for change which will be aimed at supporting a 'modern' and effective KC organisation. Hopefully this will be achieved in time for the May 2016 AGM.

SP: There are some areas of the Kennel Club's work which seem to have taken a long time to address – coat testing, for example?

SL: I would agree with that sentiment and I am keen to address some of those long outstanding issues. Whether, as some would suggest, there has been a deliberate tactic of 'delay' in addressing difficult issues I couldn't comment, but I believe that a governing body has a responsibility to move as quickly as is reasonably possible to resolve matters that arise.

Of course we hope to get our decisions 'right first time' but on occasion we will make a mistake and in those circumstances we will have to make amends. However I believe making no decision at all is far worse than making the occasional error!

SP: You were closely involved in the incorporation process, by which the KC became a company limited by guarantee. Certainly it has made a difference at the AGMs, particularly the proxy voting, for example on the formation of the working parties which wouldn't have been passed without the proxy votes. Was this meant to happen?

SL: The matter of proxy voting is something else the Governance Working Group has been asked to look at, however I believe it is a facility that 'absent' members should always be able to use when necessary. Having two meetings a year should help the membership to be far better informed on day to day issues, that combined with regular

New Kennel Club chairman Simon Luxmoore.

correspondence which I believe the membership also appreciate.

SP: Can you tell us more about the strategy meeting which the General Committee held in September?

SL: The strategic discussion we had in September was the first time the KC strategy has been reviewed formally and collectively by the General Committee for over ten years. A business should look at is strategy each year and tweak it, or not. The fact that this hasn't happened meant that the General Committee of today has no ownership of the former strategy, because it wasn't involved in its creation.

This is not to say the old strategy was wrong, it's just that the current board of directors didn't understand where it came from or who put it together.

Having had this discussion in September, next year the General Committee will sit for a couple of hours and say we did this last year, we all understand it, we recognise it – do we need to do a little bit here, have we done that. Having spent years working in the arena of business strategy its use and purpose is all very clear to me, and if I said to you, where do you expect the KC to be in ten years' time, you'd have a view. The board is working on putting together a ten-year vision for the KC. I had hoped to be able to share the first part of our discussions at the SGM but the GC wanted a further meeting to 'tidy' our first deliberations and we will do this in mid-November.

We started with a clean sheet of paper, and we asked one question: "What do you believe the KC will be doing and who will it be associated with in ten years' time?" This started a lot of brainstorming about what it could be doing and for whom!

SP: We had this survey on the membership issue which wasn't quite ready for the AGM. Since then we have heard nothing.

SL: The objective was to get a view about membership, from both members and non-members. We discovered that before people wanted to alk about membership, they had things to say about the KC itself.

In the pilot study beforehand, Helen Watts rang people to ask bout membership. But they said, before we talk about that, have I got omething to tell you… So we had a two-part survey, so people could get ther matters off their chest, and then talk about the membership.

From part one we ended up with a huge data bank of comment about he KC, which in in my opinion is useful feedback primarily for the staff. Iowever the key message from that data collection and feedback was not o much a concern about actually what the KC did but on occasion there vere concerns about 'how it actually did it'!

Then we came to the membership, and of all the membership models vhich were suggested – regional, activity-based etc – no one was interested. Ve had in mind the British Horse Society, the Royal Aeronautical Society, ll sorts of different models, but people were not interested.

The general feeling was that actual KC membership isn't the issue. There doesn't seem to be a significant number of people out there vanting to be members in any way, shape or form.

The key comments were that membership should recognise some sort f achievement in or contribution to the world of dogs. It was quite clear hat people didn't realise that in the existing model, there exists capacity o take on more members. We have got to market that better.

One issue that came up is that perhaps there should be another grade f membership which isn't as expensive. The member wouldn't have ccess to KC facilities, but would have a vote, like a 'country membership'. t would answer the question: "I never come to London so why would I vant to be a member?"

Caroline Kisko and her team and the membership group plan to come ip with a proposal to put to the next AGM about whether or not the nembers want to consider an alternative membership model.

The Kennel Club's new home at 10 Clarges Street, opened in October.

SP: Do you think the KC has more influence externally than it did a few years ago

SL: Yes, I think there has been change. We met with senior members of he veterinary profession not so long back. There is undoubtedly a much greater willingness by the vets to be supportive of what we are doing. The British Veterinary Association, Royal College and British Small Animal Veterinary Association are all very much on side. Within the political rena we are in a good position to be able to influence that we didn't have n the past. The RSPCA are always a challenge so let's just leave it at that.

SP: So what are the big challenges now? Are hey, for example, from groups in Europe which say all breeders should be licensed?

SL: No, the main challenges are still within the UK. The KC is doing more for dog health and welfare than any other kennel club in the world, bar none.

If you are a board member, you are aware of a lot of things the KC is doing on the health front but you are not quite sure how it all fits together. One of the first things I did was get together a presentation which was given at a General Committee meeting to try to paint an overall picture of what we are doing and where we are going to go.

Everyone has different views on a particular topic. Health is one. We have vets on the General Committee, we have big breeders, 'hobby breeders' like us and so on, they don't necessarily share the same view. I think pulling people together on subjects like that is important.

It's the same with the Dog Show Promotion Working Party – everybody has a view. On the General Committee you have people who are thinking about how we can increase numbers at shows and their popularity and go back to the good old days, but they all think of it from a slightly different perspective.

SP: Are we expecting more ideas from the working party?

SL: Absolutely. A few months ago we appeared to have almost ground to a halt. The working party has been going now for a couple of years

and we weren't getting very far. This is an example of where we have now managed to re-energise the activity and come up with some ideas and solutions.

The dog press recently wrote about the six shows shortlisted for possible 'all-breed' status before we had reached any final decision on this matter. People talked and got the wrong end of the stick which caused a great deal of confusion.

SP: What about the crossbreed working party?

SL: There's a lot of work going on there. Our mission statement will almost certainly continue to reference 'all dogs' but we will have a first-line emphasis on pedigree dogs. We will, however, provide services for those that are not pedigree dogs. These services are likely to be branded somewhat differently but will of course be coming under the larger KC brand banner. I can understand why people have been confused – we haven't been clear about what we are doing. Crossbreeds will not be part of the KC breed register.

Gerald King is chairing this group and they have undertaken a great deal of consultation.

SP: And what of the progress of the communications working party?

SL: As with all these working parties I'm really pleased. Under the chairmanship of Mark Cocozza, Caroline Kisko and her team are doing a good job with supporting the communications working group, explaining what her team currently does.

We are all working together and she and I have a good understanding about issues that crop up. I would say that communication does revolve a bit around style, because I'm different on that – a couple of issues have cropped up and because my training on communications has been more involved with aircraft incidents there clearly are some differences in approach.

Our communications work has taken on a life which is much broader ▶

PHOTO DAVID DALTON

PHOTO MARC HENRIE

Dana Stafford won the Kennel Club Good Citizen Dog Scheme's outstanding achievement award, receiving it from KC chairman Simon Luxmoore and Gary Gray of Royal Canin. Other GCDS awards went to John McNeil so set up the scheme's first listed status club, Leven Dog Training Club, The K9 Academy in Tyne and Wear, The Southern Finnish Lapphund Society and Aberdeenshire Council.

than that probably intended by Dr Symonds when he proposed the motion at the AGM. It covers every single aspect of the KC communications, not just the press office.

SP: What more can we all do to get across the right message about where to buy a dog and so on?

SL: You have to keep repeating the message and make sure that it's loud enough. It's the only way we are going to do it, unless someone sensible makes a TV programme, and that's when people will start to take it on board. We are working with someone at the moment about a programme for the BBC whose whole focus is how to go about buying a dog.

SP: What about the Assured Breeder Scheme?

SL: We were aiming in the right direction, but the timing of the changes to the fee structure was very poor, but beyond that I don't think anyone is ever that keen on a price rise! If you are going to do the inspections, there has to be a cost.

When you are challenged, and you haven't really thought it through as much as you might have done, you are vulnerable. We are looking at the financial model of the ABS at the moment and we have been for six months. We've got one more chance to get it right.

If you go all the way back to the start of the ABS – great idea, something we had to be involved with, but it's very complex and a far bigger and more far-ranging issue than we ever thought. And one that needed to be developed. We are looking to make the business model at least cost-neutral. And of course you have to understand the huge cost to us of ABS membership and everything that goes with it. It's not easy. If you are just a hobby or occasional breeder, that presents an entirely different proposition to someone who is having a dozen litters a year, and it's that sensitivity which is difficult to grasp.

SP: Might the American model be a possibility, with one scheme aimed at 'show' people, and another more towards commercial breeders?

SL: We would be very loath to make the ABS just about commercial breeders. Eighty per cent of the puppies from people who register the dogs are bred by small breeders, so that's whom people are buying from.

SP: What about the KC in the international arena?

SL: First and foremost we need to make sure we've got our own house in order. We want to be recognised as a good governing body in the UK. We will continue to have meetings with all our friends and colleagues both at home and abroad. We have various arrangements with various organisations, and I think our aim should be to be a respected and influential international player on the world scene.

SP: No possibility of being an associate member of the Fédération Cynologique Internationale?

SL: I'm not saying no possibility, but I can say it's very unlikely! I don't know what advantage it would bring. You only have to look at what's happening elsewhere to see why other people are going in the opposite direction. If people want to join with us and like what we are doing, then that's a compliment to us, and that's what I would want people to do. I think it would be wrong for us to cluster with any group of kennel clubs 'just because' – it's so limiting, you lose control over your own kennel club.

SP: Are you happy with the agreement with the FCI over judges?

SL: I'm absolutely happy. At the end of the day we put in place an agreement which could increase the number of judges judging in this country, all predicated on someone wanting to invite them. That individual is responsible for making sure they are qualified. Exhibitors will not see an FCI judge unless someone invites them.

SP: What do British judges get out of it?

SL: They get an opportunity to judge FCI groups, which is now a lot easier under the agreement. Then there is reinstatement of the 'top 16' judges, who were appointed before. We tried to get people on the B lists approved (to award CACIBs in those breeds), but we didn't get that.

Don't forget that our judges had been 'kicked into touch'. It seems the FCI never understood what it was they were giving us when they granted privileges to the top 16 judges, so they decided to take them away. So our judges had nothing, and now they have been reinstated, and now we have a common understanding, and some of our breed judges have the chance to judge groups over there on far more favourable terms than FCI judges.

SP: It is rumoured that there are going to be changes to the training of judges?

SL: There has long been a view that the numbers-based judging approval system is not appropriate going forward. There is the training board chaired by Gerald King, the Judges Sub-Committee now chaired by Anne Macdonald, and in between there is a small group who sit on both committees and they are looking at a new basis for the training of aspiring judges. This is the single topic I find of most interest in the near term.

SP: Returning to communications, you have said several times that there will be a more open approach and we now have both the *Gazette* and *Journal*. In what way is the club going to communicate more than it did before?

SL: The principle of General Committee members getting their personal views out there is a good one – look at Gerald King's piece on continuing development of judges which has been so well received. I believe the membership at large deserves to be given the chance to hear from all the Board members. Of course there are those who will decline the opportunity and that is their choice. If we are giving a collective 'Board' view on a particular topic then it will be considered by the Board first and then appear in the *Gazette*.

From a personal perspective, you are unlikely to hear too much from me as I'm busy doing other things. My style is to build a team to do the job, and the same with the staff. It's not about an individual.

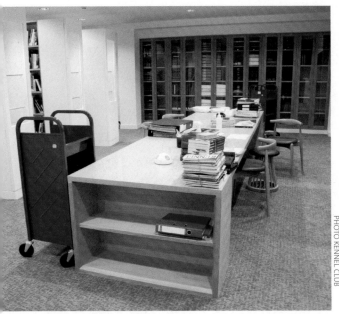

Part of the library in the Kennel Club's new building.

SP: You have talked previously about the challenges of an organisation led by volunteers but with a paid staff.

SL: I think there is a challenge particularly now that we have a significant business with a members club rather than a members club with a business element. I think perhaps that too much is expected of the volunteers, the executive and staff should have more freedom to act and be more empowered to deliver the business performance and be accountable for that, without feeling the need to reference the volunteers. Both groups need each other. We are beginning to work together and build a far better understanding.

If you look at the different styles of the Committees, and the chairmen that went with them, these have changed so much down the years. Sometimes the staff were not involved at all; at others they may have been too involved. So it can be hard for the staff to know exactly where they stand.

SP: When it comes to re-electing board members, at present we have no idea what their performance has been like.

SL: In the past people have largely been elected on their personal popularity and as we move forward this is not going to be sufficient. We now need to consider business skills as well as knowledge of the sporting aspect.

By example we are going to lose Mike Townsend in the near future – we will need someone with his skills and business perspective or he will be leaving a significant gap. I am going to write to the membership with a person and job spec to fill a finance role. That will need to be done, for Mike, who will be standing down, has fulfilled a very important role.

If I was casting a vote at an AGM to elect a committee member, I would want to know what their skill base was and how well they contributed to the work of the General Committee, or if they were a new candidate what they will 'bring to the table'. If I didn't know sufficient to have an opinion I would make it my business to find out by asking one or two people 'What's this person like?" and "How should I cast my vote?" People should vote carefully, even if they don't cast all of their votes. Far better that they cast their votes from a position of knowledge.

I will be writing a letter before the AGM reminding members that they need to remember the important role the Board now plays and that members should have the requisite skills to carry out these roles. A shared interest in dogs is very important but you are electing someone who is going to play a part in managing millions of pounds worth of assets and is responsible for the governance of pedigree dogs.

SP: Is there any prospect of change on the veterinary checks?

SL: It's an ongoing review. My personal desire is that every breed in category three knows what they need to do to go to category two and is working in that direction. We have just carried out a health review, which is a work in progress. We will be working with a number of breeds, not only in category three, helping the breeds to help themselves.

SP: Are there any special plans for Crufts in 2016?

SL: It's 125 years! I think we are inviting the leaders of various kennel clubs around the world to come and join us. We will be supporting Pawscars as usual – we're very keen to be part of that.

SP: What about the property issues?

SL: Volunteers have put in a ridiculous amount of time flying or driving up and down the country making visits.

People have got to look at the business case, they have got to look beyond their own disciplines, and they have got to think whether this is a good use of the Kennel Club's assets. Nothing will come before the membership which hasn't been really well thought through and if it comes with General Committee support, then in my view it deserves support. I would be disappointed if as a result of the special meeting we didn't move forward because the board would be looking at each other and saying: "Whatever do we do now?"

SP: Next year will see compulsory microchipping for all. Do you think it will in be enforced?

SL: I don't think it will be enforced as such, because there has never been the plan for one body to be responsible for doing so. But responsible breeders already do it and most others will follow. My view is that the things that have been said about it being a panacea for all ills are so off beam. We will just have to wait and see.

The KC's wish is that it increases the protection that microchipping gives to the dogs. Our position has always been that it's all about getting your dog back if it gets lost, rather than law enforcement. The KC is well in advance of many other organisations on this issue and some of the conversations we have had reveal that some people just can't see it coming down the line.

SP: Thank you Simon. ∎

Discover Dogs was forced to move from the now defunct Earls Court to the ExCeL exhibition centre on the other side of London. No one knew whether the public would still support it but in the event attendance at the more spacious venue was encouraging, with a gate figure of 27,272, 6,000 down on 2014. It featured all the usual attractions including the Junior Handling Association final and the Junior Warrant competition semi-finals, but its core remains the breed booths. The competition for the best of these was won by the Pugs. Elaine Arnold-Strong is pictured with the judges, Eukanuba's Mike Bloxsome and the Kennel Club's Gerald King.

THE MAJESTY DIGNITY & TYPE

Selmalda ZiZi's Journey JW

Selmalda Angel
Of Harlem JW

Bred, Loved, Owned,
Conditioned & Presented by:
Lesley & Adam Chappell

©advertising &
photography Croft-Elliott

www.selmalda.com

CH Selmalda Koochie Ryder JW

Selmalda
Journey
To Melody
At Samdice

SELMALDA
GREAT Danes

Lesley & Adam Chappell

ELEGANCE MAJESTY DIGNITY

SPLENDOUR IN ST LOUIS

The Dog in Art
Nick Waters

The American Kennel Club Museum of the Dog

Terry Chacon: *Final Cut*, 2013, gift of Terry Chacon.

The American Kennel Club Museum of the Dog is one of the oldest, largest and arguably the most important collection of dog-themed art in the world.

As well as fine paintings and sculpture in their multitudes, there is art in its many guises: a fairground carousel piece, a 19th century bronze doorknob, film posters, etchings, a Palladian dog house by interior designer Juan Pablo Molyneux and much, much more.

It was known originally as the Dog Museum of America, but for the sake of brevity will be referred to here as the museum.

The curators, in common with those at the Swedish Kennel Club museum, have a policy of encouraging and collecting work by contemporary artists, work that at times goes beyond the boundaries of traditional purebred dog portraiture. In fact the Swedish museum has an example of street art in its collection.

Comparatively recent contemporary acquisitions include Terry Chacon's *Final Cut*, of Afghans being judged, and Christine Merrill's portrait of President George H W Bush's English Springer Millie on the lawns of the White House.

Christine Merrill, *Millie on the South Lawn*, 1990, gift of William Secord Gallery Inc.

It all began in the early 1970s when a group of interested individuals devoted to dogs met to discuss the possibility of a national museum of art and books focusing on the dog. In 1973, the Westminster Kennel Club Foundation conducted a survey to explore the level of support for such a project. Encouraged by the results and with a broader level of support needed, in 1979 the American Kennel Club Foundation was formed to help meet this need.

In 1981 William Secord became the first director of the Dog Museum of America and in 1982 the first exhibition, *Best of Friends: The Dog in Art*, opened at the AKC offices in the New York Life Building on Madison Avenue.

With a rapidly expanding collection and a need for larger space, in 1985 the board voted to relocate the museum to its present home, the historic Jarville House in St Louis, Missouri, a

Abraham Hondius: *Study for The Dog Market*, c 1677, gift of Marie A Moore.

Percival Rosseau, English Setter in a field, 1908, gift of the Westminster Kennel Club Foundation.

Greek revival mansion built in 1853.

The museum does not have a buying policy and has always relied totally on donations. The US is unique inasmuch as it is home to so many wealthy patrons of the sport who share a passion for dog art and through their generosity are prepared to share their collections with others. Not all donations, though, have been vast; smaller collections and single items are equally well appreciated.

Frank Sabella, a Poodle legend in his own lifetime, forever holds the distinction of being the first contributor of art with his gift of several paintings with a heavy leaning towards the Poodle.

Other major donors have included horse breeder, Saluki fancier and art collector Cynthia Woods, Glen Twiford, who

Sir Edwin Henry Landseer, The Two Dogs, 1839, gift of Cynthia S Wood estate.

collected Royal Doulton sets of every breed, and Marie Antoinette Moore.

Mrs Moore amassed an unimaginably large collection of Mastiff paintings and sculpture and what was America's gain was England's loss. She had intended the bulk of her collection to go to the National Trust property, Lyme Hall in Cheshire, spiritual home of the Mastiff, indeed part of her collection was already there on loan.

However, on a surprise visit to Lyme she was exceedingly unhappy to discover just how it was housed and displayed, so had it all shipped back to the States. Her gift is sufficiently large to warrant its own museum and includes many of the early pictures in the collection, particularly ones by Abraham Hondius (c1615/30-1695). ▶

Edwin Megargee: the Great Pyrenees (Pyrenean Mountain Dogs) Ch Estat d'Argeles of Basquaerie and Ch Estagel d'Argeles of Basquaerie, 1930, gift of the estate of Mary Crane.

William Henry Hamilton Trood, A Domestic Scene, 1888, gift of Marie A Moore.

Reuben Ward Binks, Our Cocker Friends, c 1935, etching and aquatint, gift of Jay and Mary Remer.

Charles van den Eycken, Willpower, 1891, gift of the estate of Cynthia S Wood.

Charles Olivier de Penne, Tricolour French Hounds, 19th century lithograph, gift of William Secord Gallery Inc.

Enjar Vindfeldt, Dachshund mother and puppies, c 1950, gift of Catherine Burg estate.

Detail from Jean-Baptiste Oudry, White Pointer, 1726, gift of Mr and Mrs Phillip S P Fell.

Louis-Eugène Lambert: Bichon Frisé 1854, gift of Mr and Mrs Alvin E Maurer Jr.

Like Britain, America has had its own gifted sporting and canine artists but unlike the British ones who have found fame in the US, their American counterparts have never been appreciated here.

Naturally, work by American artists is well represented, from the evocative sporting pictures of gundogs in the field by John Martin Tracy and Percival Leonard Rosseau to show dog portraiture in its purest form from the likes of Edwin Megargee.

The museum's holding of Megargees is a virtual catalogue of the artist's work. Among the best-known dogs he painted were the Blakeen Poodles of Hayes Blake Hoyt, whose dogs defined the breed in America at that time, and the Basquaerie Pyrenean Mountain Dogs of Mary Crane who introduced the breed into the States.

Theme exhibitions have always played a role at the museum and a recent one was the Reuben Ward Binks Wall honouring the collaboration between the artist and the Geraldine Rockefeller Dodge, for whom Binks painted virtually every dog in her extensive kennel. Spring 2016 will see *Tiny Toys: the Smallest Group*, a selection from the museum's permanent collection.

When I asked what their signature work is, without hesitation the reply was Sir Edwin Landseer's *The Two Dogs* which he painted in 1838, a gift from the estate of Cynthia Wood. The reason for choosing this picture was Landseer's ability to inject human qualities and emotions into his depictions and how that influenced other artists, his connection to the Victorian age through Queen Victoria, and the fact that he is considered one of the top animal artists of the 19th century.

Other well-known signature works from the 19th century include William Henry Hamilton Trood's *Domestic Scene*, a gift of Marie Moore, and Belgian artist Charles van den Eycken's *Sweet Temptation*, also from Cynthia Wood.

Richard Ansdell, *The Poacher*, 1865, gift of Marie A Moore.

John Sargent Noble, *On The Scent*, c 1880, gift of Mr and Mrs Robert Lindsay.

Arthur Wardle, *Realisation*, 1920, gift of Lakeshore Kennel Club.

John Henry Frederick Bacon: Maud, daughter of Colonel Temple, with her two Schipperkes, 1899, gift of Mrs Paul R Willemsen.

Frederick Thomas Daws, the Miniature Poodles Ch The Laird of Mannerhead and Ch Limelight of Mannerhead, 1931, gift of Frank T Sabella.

William Secord wrote *A Breed Apart, the art collections of the Dog Museum and the American Kennel Club*, a large tome of well over 300 pages and 400 illustrations, so selecting just a handful to show the breadth of the museum's collection was no easy task.

Pictures by Continental artists include French Hounds by Charles Olivier de Penne who specialised in pack hounds; a Dachshund bitch with her puppies by Danish artist Enjar Vindfeldt, a breed synonymous with the artist; a white Pointer by the 18th century French master of the genre, Jean-Baptiste Oudry; and a very decorative picture of an early Bichon type by the Parisian artist, Louis-Eugène Lambert.

Few would deny that it is 19th and 20th century British artists who have made the greatest contribution to the genre, both decorative and historical. The British artists represented reads like a *Who's Who* and included alongside the aforementioned are Richard Ansdell and John Sargent Noble whose work is Victorian sporting dog art at its most monumental, and purebred dog portraiture from Arthur Wardle, Maud Earl, John Emms, F T Daws and others.

A particularly beautiful and well observed decorative picture is John Henry Frederick Bacon's portrait of Maud, daughter of Colonel Temple, with her two Schipperkes painted in 1899.

I haven't even touched on porcelains and bronzes of which there are enough for a separate article.

Every museum has at least one mystery and one the museum has is a recently acquired gift from the great Maud Earl collector, Marjorie Raike. It is a life-size portrait by Miss Earl of a lady with her two dogs – but who is the lady? Every road travelled so far has led to nowhere. As Maud Earl was not known as a human portraitist, why would the lady commission her, or why would Maud want to paint her? Perhaps a close friend or family member?

I visited the museum when it was in New York but have not made the trek to St Louis – I'm sure it is well worth doing. ■

James Ward, Salukis, 1807, gift of Cynthia S Wood estate.

Maud Earl, portrait of a lady with two dogs, 1897, gift of Mrs Marjorie Raike.

Have open shows lost their way?

by Sheila Atte

Over the last few years the 'ordinary dog folk' – the grass roots exhibitors who provide the bulk of the entries at any show, often without much realistic hope of going home with any of the major awards – have felt increasingly side-lined.

Without them there would be no shows, but they often feel that they are an irrelevance, that to some the breed judging is merely an inconvenience that has to be endured before the serious business can start.

In too many breeds there is the impression that one exhibitor assumes that they have the right to represent the breed at the higher level and that the other exhibits are only there to make the achievements of the chosen one look even more impressive.

The UK is perhaps the only place where breed judging still has much importance. Few other countries regularly see the level of entries that we achieve on a weekly basis, and in many the championship shows barely reach the numbers that we have at our open shows. So perhaps it doesn't matter? I think it does.

Dog ownership is increasingly coming under pressure in our modern world, and the more people we can attract to the sport of dog showing, the greater the influence we can have in an increasingly anti-dog environment. To attract, and more importantly to keep, new exhibitors,

Some open shows, including many single group shows, continue to flourish. At the Hound Club of East Anglia's 25th anniversary show, Zola Rawson gave BIS to Carol Allchorne's Basset Brackenacre Intrepid. With them are secretary Celia Mortlock, Terry Cole and Jenny Collett.

we have to offer them something over and above any other hobbies that might take up their spare time.

We do start with an advantage. To those who own dogs any time spent with them is a bonus, and offering a hobby which means they get to be with their canine companion at the same time has to be a bonus.

But we mustn't lose sight of the fact that there are many other canine sports that offer enjoyment as well as the buzz of competition. Many of these also, it has to be admitted, are somewhat more spectator-friendly than watching a judge assess a large breed entry in a draughty, noisy sports hall or equestrian centre.

For the non-doggy members of the family, cheering on their pet in an agility round has to be rather more exciting than watching mum or dad standing in a ring for half an hour and walking once round the ring on their own – even if the final result is a red rosette.

The new Kennel Club chairman has taken up his post at a time when morale seems to be at an all time low. The show scene has weathered the financial crisis that threatened to send many societies to the wall, but there seems little sign of a revival. On the contrary, many shows seem to have been cancelled in the latter part of 2015 due to lack of support.

This isn't necessarily fading interest from exhibitors, but more likely to be the

The Pets As Therapy Show Dog of the Year competition at Crufts was won by the Pyrenean Mountain Dog, Christine Kenyon (third left) and Arthur Ward's Ch Charibere Simply Special at Chezanna, handled by Louise Bermingham. With them are Tony Parkinson of sponsor HiLife Pet Food and PAT Dogs' chief executive Paul Lawrence. In addition to his championship show successes, the Pyrenean also won South Wales KA's Open Show Dog of the Year contest.

ocieties themselves failing to attract ew committee members. There re so many other calls on the time f those who have the skills to act s secretaries and treasurers, as well s those whose main qualification s quite simply enthusiasm – erhaps the most valuable asset or any committee member. If the ommittee are tired and apathetic, s it any wonder if their shows lack parkle and innovation?

So, assuming that we think that the pen shows are worth saving – and hat is perhaps a question that needs o be answered before any major lecisions are made – then what can ve do to make them more enticing?

In my view, grass roots are mportant. Think of Premier League ootball. Hugely talented and highly paid players attract massive support nd spectators pay large sums and ravel long distances in order to upport their teams. But that doesn't top the rather less talented from njoying a game of football, whether as player or supporter, and both live in the hope that one day their efforts will be ewarded with promotion to a higher evel.

Maybe this is a model that could be ooked at with regard to dog showing?

We already have to qualify for Crufts, o is it practical to insist that every dog hould qualify at open show level before being entered at a championship show? Probably not, but that's the sort of question that needs to be tackled.

Are there just too many open shows? What is the furthest distance that exhibitors will travel to an open show? Would having a cluster of shows at the same venue over a weekend entice more exhibitors to enter?

Rescinding the unbeaten dog rule seems o have worked well at championship how level but there seems to be much confusion at open shows as to how it hould work. When people are given conflicting advice, and club officials appear confused, this leads to a lack of confidence in the organisation.

Perhaps the time has come for the KC o rewrite the show rules in simple, easy o understand language, and make them readily available to all exhibitors. Yes, the regulations are downloadable from the nternet, but that doesn't really solve the problem, especially for the new exhibitor.

So, it seems to me that there are two separate problems. The first is the 'them and us' divide, which alienates many exhibitors. They feel that, however good their dog is, unless they know the right people they will never reach the heights.

The second problem is that, being honest, many open shows have lost their way. These should be the training grounds

James Rogerson was overall winner of Coventry Ladies' Kennel Society's adult handling finals.

PHOTO ALAN WALKER

for new judges but all too often it is the same few names that crop up time and again, and all too often they don't have the knowledge to judge across a variety of breeds so that it is, just as at the championship shows, the same few faces who take the major awards, irrespective of the quality of their dogs.

Again, I wonder if there are just too many shows? We are all sad to see the demise of a once respected society, but perhaps we should be more realistic. Is it better to have ten bustling, exciting shows, with a mix of respected, experienced judges and novices just starting out

on their careers, rather than a hundred small, mediocre shows, badly organised, recycling the same incompetent judges week after week?

I know a remarkable number of serious exhibitors who simply won't go to open shows. They regard them as boring and irrelevant. But if new judges don't get the opportunity to go over excellent examples of a breed they are always going to regard mediocrity as the norm – and might not even recognise quality when they do come across it. This is not the way to develop the next generation of judges.

We sometimes forget that there are people with other interests apart from showing who also have an stake in the running of the KC, and it's only right that they too should have their fair share of KC resources.

However, the show scene, showcasing as it does the achievements of breeders, contributes financially very large sums to the KC coffers – and if the enthusiasm for dog showing diminishes, so will the KC's income, so it is important that the new administration really gets to grips with the problem of falling numbers.

This is perhaps the biggest challenge to face Simon Luxmoore and his team as they enter 2016. There are no easy answers, but one thing is certain – just tinkering around the edges will not solve anything. There needs to be radical change, perhaps not popular, but necessary if our shows are to survive, let alone prosper. ∎

Channel Island Dog of the Year was Nikki Brouard's Alaskan Malamute Dreamwolves Cauz For Aplauz, seen with judge Meg Purnell-Carpenter and Kennel Club of Jersey president Dr Margaret Bayes. Runner-up was Fiona Officer and Stuart Mottershaw's Afghan Hound Shumakays A Perfect Match for Elangeni.

The Generation Game

Talent in breeding and showing dogs often runs in families. There are many cases of parents and children all successfully involved in the show scene, but in this feature we present a number of examples where three generations – and in one case four – have owned, bred or been connected with UK champions.

WATTEAU:

Frank Calvert Butler, Mary Blake and Antonia Thornton

Frank Calvert Butler.

It all began in 1906 when my grandfather Frank Calvert Butler started to breed Fox Terriers. He bred a number of Wires and Smooths and I have a photograph of one of the earliest, Redcroft Wrangler, whelped in 1906.

The first champion was Miss Watteau, who was by Camp Watteau ex Oxalis, a bitch bred by Desmond O'Connell by Ch Oxonian ex Odonta. Thus started the Watteau prefix which has continued up to the present day.

My grandfather had a number of successful Fox Terriers of both coats, some homebred, some not, but his interest was also in other terrier breeds, notably Kerry Blues and Irish.

He owned two exceptional Kerrys in Ch Black Prince of the Chevin, bred by Miss Toft, and Ch Muircroft Thora, both of whom were hugely successful in the ring, Black Prince being the first Kerry Blue to win BIS at a general championship show.

He also bred Clydesdale horses, Wensleydale sheep and pedigree Shorthorn cattle.

He was on the Kennel Club's General Committee and the Show Committee, and was a renowned judge. He was also a founder of the Wire Fox Terrier Association.

Most of the kennel was dispersed during the war and sadly my grandfather died in 1942. The early days of the kennel were overseen by Herbert Johnson, the kennel manager, and it was through his encouragement that the kennel continued with my mother, Mary Blake, after my grandfather's death.

With Johnson's enormous experience and assistance the kennel became successful once more, chiefly with the Smooth Fox Terriers of which there were many, but also with Miniature Smooth Dachshunds which were bred and shown too.

Anthony and Mary Blake.

My mother bred one Dachshund champion, Watteau Ballerina, and although she liked the breed very much she found it increasingly difficult to show two breeds of different groups, and the Dachshunds came to an end.

My mother bred some very influential stud dogs, Ch Watteau Midas, (her first champion), Ch Watteau Chorister, Ch Watteau Madrigal, and her favourite dog of whom she said "I shall probably never breed a better one", Ch Watteau Snuff Box.

Snuff Box held the breed record winning 23 CCs with 22 BOBs under 23 different judges, quite an achievement, and was highly influential at stud.

I joined my mother in partnership of the Watteau kennels in 1967 when she bought a bitch for me from Ireland named Lingrove Linnet. She proved an excellent brood bitch producing two champions in her second litter, by Am Ch Watteau Snufsed, Ch Watteau Last Word and Ch Watteau Happy Talk, as well as an American champion Watteau Small Talk.

Happy Talk continued the success in the nursery by producing Ch Watteau Lyrical, the dam of Ch Watteau Ploughman. Ploughman won BIS at the National Terrier in 1980.

Other champions to be bred by our partnership were Chief Barker, Black Magic, Dominic, Ballad and Painted Lady. The last Watteau champion, bred by me, was Ch Watteau Bandmaster.

As a family we have been very involved with The Fox Terrier Club; my grandfather was a member of the committee from 1913 until his death, my mother was a committee member from 1947 until ill health prevented her from continuing in the 1990s. My father was president of the club for 15 years and I have been both president and committee member, the former for five years and the latter for 38 years.

Antonia Thornton.

Frank's Watteau Battleshaft, an important stud dog and founder of the B line of Smooths.

Mary's Ch Watteau Snuff Box.

Antonia and Mary's Ch Watteau Happy Talk.

My grandfather was president of the Wire Fox Terrier Association when he judged the championship show held in Bradford over two days where there were over 400 entries! My mother and I have both been president of the Smooth Fox Terrier Association – I have actually been president twice which I deemed a great honour.

This is the story of our kennel which is now in retirement! My son and his family have a young Smooth Fox Terrier, a grandson of Bandmaster, and he is the last connection to the past.

I think if my grandfather, my mother and I were able to sit round a table at this minute, the one thing we would all agree on is the great friendship and enjoyment we have received through our interest in our breeds over the past 109 years. ■

ANTONIA THORNTON

BRIGHTON:

Henry Hylden, Frederick Hylden and Lily Ickeringill

Comparable with Watteau among Britain's oldest kennel names is Brighton, an affix fundamental to the history of the Bloodhound.

The kennel was founded in the city of that name by Henry Hylden in 1908 and the first two champions were born in 1911.

Ch Dark of Brighton, pictured, was one of the top winning dogs of all breeds in the years after the first world war, with many triumphs in particular at the Kennel Club's own show. No other British Bloodhound has been so consistently successful in all-breed competition.

The kennel was continued by Henry's son Frederick who, a butcher by trade, was one of the very few able to continue breeding on a small scale during the second world war, and subsequently the Brightons emerged as the dominant force in the breed during the post-war recovery. Among his champions was Ch Buccaneer of Brighton.

Frederick's interest was shared by his granddaughter Lily who, along with her husband George Ickeringill, maintained its traditions with many more champions for themselves or others. She is pictured with Ch Brighton's Nimrod.

BARMAUD:

James Ernest Barker, James Barker, Jennifer North-Row and Emma North-Row

T he kennel was established in 1898 by James Ernest Barker in Huddersfield in the north of England. He was the typical late 19th century dog fancier with interests in different breeds, mainly sporting ones.

However, in the early 20th century JE turned his attention to Whippets, which were considered by many to be rather below Greyhounds in many senses of the word.

He won well and bought Ch Willesbrenda from Willie Beara after her third CC and subsequently won another three CCs. He bred on from her and made two others into champions. The last Manorley champion, Manala, was much of his breeding. If you look at the first post-war champions his breeding figures prominently.

He became treasurer of the Whippet Club in the 1920s and stayed with the club until the 1940s.

He also was interested in Greyhounds and made two into champions but Whippets were his first love and after the second world war he made up Ch Seagift Sunglint.

His son, James, also loved dogs. As well as his love for Whippets, gaining a championship with Barmaud Sungauge and winning RCCs and CCs with others, he loved terriers, especially Wire Fox, Lakelands and Welsh, making up champions in all three.

In fact he was the only person, up to then, to win BIS at National Terrier twice with two different breeds, the Lakeland Terrier Ch Ravelsaye Reflector of Barmaud and the Wire Fox Terrier Ch Barmaud Right Smart. Reflector produced several champions before being exported, but Right Smart was exported to France soon after his win. The last Lakeland Terrier to win BIS there carried our BIS-winning dog's blood.

Jennifer, his daughter, decided to follow tradition and handled her father's Greyhound to her first BIS when she was only 16 – the bitch won her championship soon after. She also handled Sungauge to many wins. Her personal breed was American Cockers and she won a CC and several RCCs with one in the early '80s.

Emma, the fourth generation, was allowed her first dog at ten and was given a Wire Fox Terrier, from the last litter bred by her grandfather, who, handled by the late Frank Kellett, won CC and RBIS at the WFT Association.

Her first 'own' dog was a Deerhound Ch/Ir Ch Drissaig Hesta around Barmaud, who, handled by Jennifer due to Emma's schooling, won her championship and won her Irish title – the first since the Ross dogs in the '30s.

Emma was lucky to be able to buy a Whippet who was part of a litter of three champion sisters. Ch Fullerton Agile Star in Barmaud won her title exactly a hundred years after Emma's great-grandfather, JE, started the kennel. She produced an Irish RBIS winner, Ir Ch Barmaud Sweet

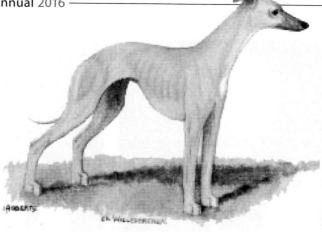

J E Barker's Whippet Ch Willesbrenda.

Shannon, and her sister Barmaud How Sweet It Is won a BIS at a breed club show in Sweden, later producing a Swedish champion for the Fennaur Kennel.

Now based in Ireland, we decided to have Wire Dachshunds. Starting with some of the last of the Silvaes bred by Jill Johnstone, we struck lucky immediately and won a CC with our first Silvae bitch and two RCCs with a dog. We then mated our first Dachshund bitch; three champions ensued including a group winner in our first litter.

In our second litter, when using another Silvae dog, we produced three puppies, one bitch and two dogs, and these three broke records wherever they went. Jessica stayed at home in Ireland and won, at the age of 15 months, the variety's first all-breeds BIS in Ireland since the 1950s. She also won a CC and several RCCs, and finished the year number nine at the Top Dog event.

She went on to produce our first UK champion who also won a BIS at breed championship shows, shown by a novice to Dachshunds, and Am/Can Ch Barmaud Rowan who in a very short show career won BPIS at Lower Mainline Dog Fanciers, Canada's biggest show, under Espen Engh, BIS at specialties and his Junior Earthdog title.

Jessica's brother Am Ch Barmaud Joshua won his title very easily and was then campaigned to win BOS at both Westminster and the national specialty, a feat no Wire Dachshund from this side of the water had ever achieved.

His son Full Circle Roaring Water at Barmaud won majors at specialties before arriving at Barmaud where he won his title in spite of not loving the show ring.

Jessica's other brother Ch Barmaud Jacob won his Irish title as well as a CC and RCC but he is now a beloved pet to Emma's brother and his family although he won a couple of BVIS and BV at Crufts.

He came into his own when used on our other imported bitch Am Ch Full Circle Angel's Song SW; they produced Ch Barmaud Violet, who when shown selectively has won a couple of groups and her title with ease and a CC and several RCCs.

Recently we have been campaigning two Kaninchen Wire Dachshund for the Auchans kennel and have titled both, including a group 2. And a Deerhound has arrived, winning a group at the tender age of ten months. ■

EMMA and JENNIFER NORTH-ROW

James Barker with Greyhounds Barmaud Bubbling Over and Barmaud Celebrity.

Jennifer (centre) and Emma (right) North-Row with Ir Ch Barmaud Jessica after her BIS win.

BOUGHTON:

W G Boggia, A G Boggia, Monica Boggia-Black, Alfreda Boggia and Clare Boggia

The showing dynasty was founded by William George Boggia who came from Truro, Cornwall, in the early 1920s. He had an interest in Rough Collies initially and then showed and bred Smooth Fox Terriers. He was secretary of Truro Canine Society for many years.

The eldest of his three sons was Arthur George Boggia who retained the terrier interest. He too showed Smooth and Wire Fox Terriers, English Setters and Greyhounds. He moved to Kent during the second world war.

At its height the kennels at Boughton House had up to 80 dogs. Perhaps the best known of his SFT was Ch Buckland.

Those who knew him will remember him being very tall, immaculately dressed and wearing a bowler hat!

He judged at championship level including Crufts, and was passed for the terrier group. He also enjoyed judging abroad, including Ceylon as it was then and Hong Kong.

He was a founder member of the Greyhound Club, together with his daughter Monica. Truluswell Princess was his first Greyhound – she had 23 BIS, but not made into a champion due to the war. Some early Boughton Greyhound champions were Boughton Blue Lad and Boughton Damsel; nearly all his Greyhounds where white or white particolours.

A G Boggia had two children, Monica, the well known international judge, and son William George. While his son did not show or breed, his wife Alfreda had a keen interest in the canine world, initially with Whippets and latterly French Bulldogs. She gave CCs in both breeds and was chairman of the French Bulldog club of England before her early death.

Alfreda's grandmother showed landseer Newfoundlands.

Monica Boggia-Black is passed for all groups except gundogs and has judged the hound, utility and terrier groups at Crufts. She has judged extensively abroad.

Monica has made up champions in various breeds including Whippets, Lowchen, Bedlington Terriers and Chihuahuas and is well known for handling her father's Greyhounds and SFT. Her favourite breed is the Greyhound so it was just as well her niece Clare Boggia followed in her grandfather's steps!

Clare Boggia, daughter of Alfreda, now continues with the showing side, primarily with her Greyhounds. She got her first Greyhound from the famous Solstrand kennel of Dagmar Kenis-Pordham. Ch Solstand Fait Accompli was a direct descendant of her grandfather's Ch Parcancady Lancer (sire of the famous Ch Treetops Hawk).

The family has always had an active interest in organising shows. Ashford and Faversham CS was founded in 1941 by Arthur George Boggia. Monica was secretary of this society, together with Whitstable CS and East Kent CS, for many years. She has always taken a keen interest in breed clubs and has had various roles, including secretary of the Southern Border Collie Club, chairman of the Lowchen Club and president of the Smooth Fox Terrier Club and Northern Japanese Spitz Club.

Clare is currently secretary of Ashford and Faversham CS and on the committee of Hound Association.

The affix Boughton was not registered until the 1950s. The name comes from the house that A G Boggia bought when they moved to Kent. Alfreda registered all her dogs as Boughton B…, and this theme is continued by Clare, with the latest champion being Ch Boughton Brigadier – the first champion particolour for Clare, so going back to her grandfather's roots! ∎

CLARE BOGGIA

W G and A G Boggia, 1937.

A G Boggia with a Greyhound, probably Ch Boughton Damsel.

PHOTO FRANCIS PILGRIM.

Alfreda Boggia with a Boughton French Bulldog.

Monica Boggia-Black with a Boughton Smooth Fox Terrier.

Clare Boggia with Epic Generous winning BIS at Skokloster, Sweden.

Walter Edmondson with Crookrise Duncan in the late 1940s.

Julie Wilkinson with her sons Joshua and Joseph.

CROOKRISE:

Kitty and Walter Edmondson, Cicely Robertshaw, Helga Edmondson and Julie Wilkinson

The kennel was started by my parents Walter and Kitty Edmondson in the year of their marriage, 1933. Although my father's name was always on the dogs they were in a joint venture with my mother.

Before the Crookrise affix was taken out, a number of dogs were registered Forest which they thought the Kennel Club had allowed but they were then notified that they could not use this affix. Setters were the first breed before the Pointers.

The first Pointer champion bred in the kennel was Forest Fleet, and he became the breed's first post-war champion. His name was changed to Highflier of Ide when Joe Braddon bought him. In those days one could change the name of dogs.

The litter was repeated and Crookrise Fleet was retained. He became the sire of the first CC winner Crookrise Duncan in the early 1950s. He in turn sired Ch Crookrise Duncanson, the first group winner for the kennel.

There were a few more champions and group winners all coming down from Fleet and Duncan. To this day all our present dogs go back to these foundations, with a few outcrosses along the way.

One day in the early 1960s my father saw a photograph of an Italian dog, the orange and white Dual Ch Barnabes de Valesia. On seeing this picture he was absolutely struck by the beauty of this dog.

My father decided that this was the type of Pointer he would like to strive to achieve. By the kindness of Joe Dub of the Blackfield affix he was fortunate to acquire his daughter who was born in quarantine. She was then bred from to our original dogs, hoping to produce Pointers possessing true breed characteristics capable of top wins in the show ring but also able to give a good account of themselves in the field.

This has always been the main aim of the kennel until this day, by my mother, myself and now their granddaughter Helga.

Much as my father loved showing and judging, he was happiest out on the moor or in the field with his Pointers. This is the same for me.

Both my mother and father were founder members of the newly formed Pointer Club, my mother later becoming secretary and running the first club field trial. Both awarded CCs in many of the gundog breeds, and later my mother judged abroad.

They would offer help and advice to novice owners with a genuine interest in the breed. My father was breed note contributor for DOG WORLD and my mother for *Our Dogs*. I took over the breed notes after the death of my father in 1967 and continued for many years.

I have always been involved in the Pointers right from the beginning, and in the early days always accompanied my father to the shows. From a small child I used to handle the dogs but in those days there were no special classes for child handlers.

When I was a teenager Duncanson was my first titleholder and championship show group winner. When I was 14 years old I judged gundog breeds at a sanction show. Since that time I have judged in many countries, and award CCs in Pointers, English, Irish and Gordon Setters.

For the past 13 years I have run the Kennel Club Good Dog Citizen class each week, something which I feel very fulfilling.

On the death of my father my mother moved to Sedbergh in Cumbria to be nearer my husband and myself. This is where a handful of the Pointers live with me to this day.

The dogs were transferred into partnership with my mother and me and we produced a number of titleholders We almost always chose the same puppy as pick of the litter although I had a soft spot for the dogs and my mother for the bitches but this always worked well .

Most of the success that followed was because we were renowned for selling promising puppies who later became titleholders for their owners and then through owners coming back to us to continue with our planned breeding. Our kennel was never a large concern and we owed a

Kitty Edmondson at Sedbergh, when she was in her eighties.

Ch Crookrise Old Glory.

Helga Edmondson with a puppy from a recent litter.

cely Robertshaw on the fells with a couple of her present-day Pointers, Rosie and Dom.

t to the owners of these dogs.

Since the foundation of the kennels there have been 34 UK hampions, three World Winners, 21 field trial winners and one field ial champion.

Much use was made of the bloodline of Barnabes and we were elighted when Ch Crookrise Flint appeared with a striking resemblance o Barnabes. Flint became famous throughout the world with many ffers being refused for him.

Flint's granddaughter produced our first Field Trial Ch, Crookrise hythm – it was so fulfilling to think that this was the wish of my father to roduce dual-purpose Pointers. He was trained and handled by myself, nd probably this was my greatest thrill in connection with the Pointers.

Again coming down from the same bloodline was Sh Ch Crookrise io, our first best in show winner at an all-breed championship show.

To this day whenever we make an outcross it is always to a field-bred og or bitch.

Now to the next generation, my daughter Julie who owned Crookrise uy and ran him at a field trial. He was the sire of Flint whom she also ter owned. As a teenager she would travel by dog coach on her own to andle the dogs. She has also judged the breed at open show level. Her emory of the pedigrees is excellent, probably by writing out pedigrees r new puppy owners from an early age.

When she married, dog shows took a back seat but there was often a ointer living with her.

Now her family are growing up, once again dogs are coming to the fore, especially as her two young sons are also just as keen.

In 2015 Julie and her two youngest sons entered the agility world with great success. Their dogs are all from rescue sources which makes their wins all the more special. Her sons Joshua, 13 years, and Joseph, 11, have both qualified for Crufts 2016, Joshua in agility over 12 and Young Kennel Club team agility and Joseph in under 12 agility, under 12 jumping and YKC team agility. Maybe one day soon a Pointer will be joining them in their chosen sport.

Now the Pointers are owned in partnership with my niece Helga Edmondson. She is my brother's daughter and there was usually one of the Pointers in their home.

From a very young age Helga would spend her school holidays at Sedbergh, spending time with my mother and always with the dogs. She still has a very good memory of the dogs who were about during those years, often travelling to the shows with her and the occasional field trial. Helga and Julie, a year or two older, would play at showing and judging the dogs.

Helga's first champion of her own, bought as a puppy, was Ch Calderside Love In A Mist at Wherathy. She soon gained her title and surpassed all her expectations, winning best of breed and the group at Crufts 2001. Another thrill for Helga was when she gained her show gundog working certificate, handled and trained by her.

Recently Helga has awarded CCs in the breed and travelled to New Zealand to judge their Pointer specialty

Since then Helga and I have had quite a few titleholders. From my father and mother, down to myself and Helga, we almost always agree on the dogs we choose and breed and both strive to keep the working ability in our dogs.

Another new venture for Helga is the importation of Portuguese Pointers from Tiago Fortuna in Portugal. She first saw the breed in that country in 2009 and was impressed by them, which resulted in her first import Irish Sh Ch Ruy at Perdizcyo who is the current leader in the imported register in the Dog World/Arden Grange Top Dog table. Helga owns these with her good friend Penny Westaway.

As a footnote, in 1978 my mother and I were joint authors of the book *The Pointer* and then in 2000 I wrote and published the book *Pointers Past and Present*. Because I was always involved in the breed from a very young age until this day I felt it my obligation to write this book so the breed history and people who made the breed as it is today were not forgotten. ■

CICELY A ROBERTSHAW

Wattie Irving, Andrew Irving and Ronnie Irving

In our case the story is somewhat disjointed and though our three generations of Irving owners are continuous as far as showing is involved, there is not a continuous line where breeding is concerned. Nor have we ever had a kennel name to help link the dogs together.

When the family came into the Border Terrier breed in the 1920s it ad just been recognised by the Kennel Club and there was still quite n opposition to that recognition. Most of the early Border Terrier ennels in the north therefore didn't have a kennel name and my ther and I continued the tradition when we came to breed and own ogs ourselves.

And of course in 1978 when Kate and I married, I stopped reeding dogs altogether, and it was she who carried on her mother, ertha Sullivan's Dandyhow line.

It was in fact my father Andrew Irving who as a child was given the rst Border Terrier to be shown by the family. At that time they lived t Riccarton Junction, a railway village in the heart of the Border area nd one which had no roads to it at all – only the railway lines. My randfather Wattie Irving was the station master there.

The dog was given to the family by Tommy Lawrence, himself a ation master at the nearby town of Hawick. He himself was the wner/breeder of the first Border Terrier champion, Ch Teri.

Wattie Irving with Ch Rising Light.

Andrew Irving judged the 20th anniversary show of the Swedish Border Terrier Club and is seen congratulating a young Carl Gunnar Stafberg (Bombax) on winning BOB.

Ronnie Irving handled his wife Kate's Ch Dandyhow Dr Walter to BOB at Crufts 2014.

With ease of travel to shows by train, and cheap train travel as well as he was a railway company employee, it was not long before Wattie took over this bitch and she was his first champion, Ch Station Masher.

It took my father about 50 years then to come back into the breed in the 1970s and '80s, by which time I had already started to breed and show the dogs and also to judge. My father always claimed that he started his life in dogs first as kennelman to his father and then later as kennelman to his son! The fact of the matter was that as he too was a railwayman, he originally worked shifts and at weekends, and so he wasn't able to take part in the show world until later in life.

In the pre-war period up to 1939, Wattie owned or bred four champions and was the breeder of three of them. His most successful Border pre-war was the bitch Ch Joyden who took her ninth CC at Crufts at the age of nine in 1939.

But it was through his male line that my grandfather had the greatest effect on the breed with what turned out to be some very influential stud dogs such as Whitrope Don, Knowe Roy and Rab O'Lammermoor. In fact I was interested to read something recently of which I had not been aware about the first of these dogs; namely that from the 86 UK Border Terrier champions made up since 2000, all but two descend in the tail male line from Whitrope Don. Only two descend from the other four influential pre-war stud dogs of the time.

After the war, by which time the family had long since moved away from the Borders to Musselburgh, the major winners were Ch Rising Light (ten CCs), Ch Alexander (four CCs), Ch Rab Roy (three CCs), Ch Brieryhill Gertrude (three CCs) and Ch Bright Light (11 CCs). None of these dogs was bred by Wattie but some were by his stud dogs.

During that period there were other champions owned by the family – Ch Hornpiece Salvia owned by my uncle T M Gaddes and Ch Gay Gordon owned by my cousin Grace Gaddes, later McDougald.

It was in 1966 that I bought in the first champion that I owned in my own name – Ch Bounty Tanner. I paid £20 for him aged 14 months and took him on to win his junior warrant and eventually gain four CCs. He was by a Dandyhow dog, D Samaritan.

From then on the dogs that I bred or owned all had Dandyhow behind them. Up to the time I gave up breeding in 1978 there were six champions, four of them homebred. But the best of them were Ch South Box (six CCs) and his litter sister Ch Din Merry (11 CCs) which I co-bred with my cousin. They were line-bred to the top stud dog Ch Dandyhow Shady Knight who appears as their great-grandfather four times but each time mated to different bitches.

Meantime my father showed and bred a few dogs, none

of which became champions but one of which, Bugs Billy, went to Germany and was successful there for Weibke Steen.

As far as judging was concerned Wattie first awarded CCs to the breed in 1932 and did so consistently until his last appointment in 1965. Then my first CC appointment was in 1967. In fact when I come to judge Crufts in 2016 this will be the twenty-eighth occasion I have awarded CCs to Border Terriers and my second time for the breed at Crufts, the first having been in 1977. (I must have done a bad job then as it took 39 years to be asked back!)

My father Andrew judged the breed at CC level only three times – the first in 1980 and the last in 1982. He died shortly after that.

As far as other activities such as involvement with clubs is concerned, my father who was happy to be the backroom assistant and never held office, but between us my grandfather or I were either chairman or secretary of the Border Terrier Club for a continuous period from 1931 until Kate and I left to live in the US in 1987.

My grandfather was chairman of the Lothian Canine Club and the Caledonian Canine Club over a number of years until the mid 1960s and was also a member of the executive committee of the Scottish Kennel Club and its chief steward for many years also.

I was chairman of the Lothian Canine and then also chief steward of the Border Union championship show from its inception in 1975 until we left for the US. I then, as you know, took up some responsibilities at the Kennel Club.

As far as other breeds are concerned my grandfather was secretary of the Scottish Bull Terrier Club for a number of years and we showed one Bull Terrier mostly locally in Scotland. He never hit the high spots but he did gain a Stud Book entry.

My father dabbled in Miniature Poodles but never had much success with them in the show ring. And the only other breed that I both owned and showed was a solitary Norfolk Terrier bitch by the famous Ch Ickworth Ready out of a Nanfan bitch. I only took her to a few shows and just couldn't get her to show and Kate will tell you how good I am about persevering with dogs that won't show!

As I said at the start of this story, the breeding by our three generations was totally disjointed. My grandfather did line-breed before the war but in the 1950s and '60s was getting older and tended to buy dogs in from people who had used his stud dogs.

My father bred very little and came to it late in life, after me in fact, and I based most of my breeding for the 12 or so years before Kate and I were married, on the Dandyhow line. After that I simply became a handler of the Dandyhow dogs providing the occasional bit of (possibly gratuitous) advice to the breeder! ■

A **DOG WORLD** cartoon of Wattie when he judged at Crufts 1962.

RAGUS:

Grace Marks, Marjorie Bunting and Lesley Crawley

The Ragus affix was registered around 1946 by Marjorie Marks who was then in her mid teens.

Her father Roy Marks was a working terrier man who owned small West Highlands and Sealyahams and eventually heard of a litter of drop-eared Norwich. He brought home, Binkie, who adored my mother, then a teenager.

He tried to put her off breeding for show, but when she seemed determined he took her to shows both local and further away and gave her all the help he could to do well.

Roy's wife and Marjorie's mother Grace encouraged Marjorie in practical ways like whelping litters and rearing pups. Marjorie asked her to be a partner in the affix after her first Norwich began to win but the first champion prick-ear in 1953 was Ragus Regal Sixpence who was owned solely by Marjorie though bred by Grace and Marjorie, who was married by then to Hugh Bunting.

The first bitch champion (half-sister of Regal Sixpence) was Ragus Rock'N'Roll but she was owned by me, Marjorie's daughter, when I was five years old.

Marjorie did not drive at this point so Grace took her to all the shows. Marjorie made all decisions on breeding and handled the dogs, but it was her husband Hugh who did all the grooming and trimming side of things. He had bred and owned a champion St Bernard, Terwin Caliph, but gave up the expensive big breed when they started a family and the terriers really started to win.

Hugh bred Cockers for a time but showed them only locally and was quite happy not to go to all the shows. By the time Grace felt she could no longer drive long distances Marjorie had learnt to drive and after her mother's death I became a partner in Ragus kennels.

Marjorie sat on the Norwich Terrier Club committee for around 40 years and during that time was a committee member, chairman, show manager and newsletter editor at various times, and was also president and patron.

She judged many terrier breeds with CCs and the terrier group and wrote Norwich and Norfolk breed notes and articles for DOG WORLD for many years, the notes for around 30 years.

Marjorie started the original Norwich Club points tables, initially for her own use to find out which were the winning lines to provide her with a basis to breed good dogs. The club then used them. Marjorie used them to help write her breed notes as well. This was probably one

Three generations: Grace Marks, five-year-old Lesley and Marjorie Bunting.

PHOTO JOHN SEYMOUR

Marjorie Bunting in 1957 with Ch/Am Ch Ragus Robin Goodfellow as a puppy, the first champion Ragus Regal Sixpence, Ch Ragus Rock'n'Roll and the drop-ear Ragus Solomon Grundy.

of the first points tables in any breeds.

She was a great statistician and kept all the pedigrees of every champion Norwich from 1932 when the KC recognised them, with their main wins etc on the back of each pedigree.

Her greatest achievement with the dogs was owning Ch Ragus Golden Slippers who won reserve in the group (group 2 these days) at Crufts 1964, the first Norwich to do so at a time when they were considered second-class show dogs.

Marjorie was thrilled when Ch Ragus Gypsy Love won the group and BIS at Windsor 1978, handled by me, and then when Ch Elve The Sorcerer won his first BIS at Windsor owned by her son-in-low Michael Crawley and handled by me. He was the pathfinder for Norwich, winning multiple groups and BIS. His grandson Ch Ragus The Devils Own, and Devil's Own's sire Ch Ragus Lucifers Luck (sired by Sorcerer) were the first Ragus male group winners and luckily Marjorie lived to see this.

I born into the dog showing world and owned my first champion at five years old, went to a show alone on a coach at 13 years old, winning BOB, RBCC and best puppy with three different dogs.

From then on did I most of the handling and took over the grooming from my father.

I first judged at 15 years, awarded CCs at 21 and took over the breeding of dogs, making all the major decisions by my early 20s. I also sat on the club committee and am a past president of the Norwich Terrier Club.

The kennel's hundredth champion was Ch Ragus True Romance and the kennel has now owned or bred 132, the latest being Ch Ragus Hand In Glove. So far this year Ragus has bred three new champions and handled another, Ch Wychcover Moonlighting, in partnership with Jill Stevenson (Brickin).

I have handled 14 different group winners which includes my husband Michael's, five BIS winners and three times BIS at National Terrier with three different dogs. My best dogs are The Devil's Own who won ten groups including National Terrier and an all-breeds BIS; Ch Ragus Truly Unruly, the only Norwich bitch to win two groups including BIS at National Terrier; her son Ch Ragus Rings True, also BIS ▶

Lesley and her husband Michael Crawley after winning BIS at Windsor with Ch Elve The Sorcerer.

at National Terrier, winning 24 CCs, 12 groups, eight in a row, three BIS, one RBIS and 11 other group placements over almost three years, and three BOB at Crufts; and Ch Ragus Merry Gentleman, group winner at Crufts 2012, and twice BOB there, he won 12 CCs, one BIS, two RBIS, five groups and 11 other group placements.

I have handled four top terriers of the year, owning three of them: Michael's The Sorcerer, The Devil's Own, Rings True and Merry Gentleman.

Ragus has held many more records in Norwich and Norfolk Terriers over the years than I can remember, some to this day though won years ago. One Norwich bitch needs special mention as her records are so unusual for her breed. Truly Unruly, born in 2002, was top bitch 2003, top winner 2004, top terrier brood 2005 and top brood in her breed for five years. She is the dam of seven UK champions by four sires. In her first litter of six, four bitches, including True Romance, gained their UK title and a male in Austria became a champion. Her son Rings True holds the breed CC record and was second generation BIS at National Terrier.

Much as I admired my mother and learnt so much from both my parents regarding breeding, showing and trimming, I have always been a very different person from her. She was a brilliant breeder, statistician and writer and a fighter for justice and fairness. She was both admired and feared in equal measure,

PHOTO ALAN WALKER

Ch Ragus Merry Gentleman winning the group at Crufts.

probably mainly for her outspoken tongue and brilliance with a pen.

I am no good at most of these things and while I was younger it was very difficult to live up to other people's expectations of me. They expected me to be exactly like her.

I hope I have proven over the years that I am a different personality but just as successful. My forte is breeding, handling and grooming and there have been times, unfortunately, when I and I alone have kept my breed going, dragged them up from the doldrums both in numbers and improving their health and looks.

I have expanded our gene pool by borrowing many males from other countries and have had to breed in a completely different way from my mother in order to improve health and showmanship.

Health issues did not have to be addressed in my mother's day but today it is just another ball to keep in the air for modern breeders. Being a good and successful breeder is even harder in the 21st century than ever before and people these days do not seem to be as interested in being a good, consistent breeder. They just want to own a winner. Where they think their winners will come from I don't know.

Judy Averis and I were discussing this issue a few years ago and she thought there would be very few truly great breeders in the future in the UK. I agreed and just hope to God we're both wrong. ∎

LESLEY CRAWLE

SAREDON/ BELDON:

Les Atkinson, Judith Averis and John Averis

PHOTO DAVID DALTON

Les and Gladys Atkinson had five children, of whom three were involved in the show scene, Frank, Gloria Marshall and Judy Averis. Judy built up the Saredon kennel, owned by her and her partner Dave Scawthorn (pictured), into one of the most successful terrier kennels of all time. In Airedale, Lakeland and Welsh Saredon is integral to the fabric of the modern breed at home and overseas, and champions came in several more breeds, including some outside the terrier group. They sold potential champions to many other exhibitors and acted as mentors of the great British terrier tradition to countless young enthusiasts at home and abroad. She became the only second generation Crufts BIS winner when she handled the homebred Welsh Ch Saredon Forever Young to the top spot in 1998.

Judy, who died sadly young in 2014, was a respected judge of the terrier breeds, doing BIS at National Terrier.

Have any other families produced three generations, all of whom have won best in show at championship shows, two of them at Crufts?

Les Atkinson was one of the best known professional handlers of the mid twentieth century, specialising in the terrier breeds and known for his sense of humour and for his ability as a raconteur. Later he became a well known judge.

The pinnacle of his many successes has handling the young Lakeland Terrier Rogerholme Recruit, later a champion, to win best in show at Crufts in 1965.

©Johnson

Judy's son John Averis is continuing the family traditions and in recent years has handled many more champions to top honours. His greatest successes have come with Irish Terriers for Saredon and Tony and Jean Barker of the Irvonhill kennel.

Three of their dogs have won BIS at championship shows, the first being the American import Ch/Am Ch Fleet St Fenway Fan. They are pictured at WELKS 2011 with judge Zena Thorn-Andrews, Tony, Maureen Micklethwaite and Sheila Jakeman.

DIALYNNE:

Marion Spavin, Dianna Spavin and Melanie Spavin

The now legendary Dialynne kennel was founded more than 60 years ago by Marion Spavin who had left school at the age of 14 to work in a Sealyham kennel.

Marion says: "I had always loved dogs since childhood. The family didn't have dogs of our own so I would beg, borrow or steal dogs owned by neighbours and friends to walk and play with. My parents weren't keen on my career plans but I was determined and from an early age learnt all aspects of kennel management and husbandry."

Following her marriage Marion started breeding Cocker Spaniels which she showed with modest success; however after the birth of her third child she gave up showing for a while to become a full-time mother.

When Dianna, Marilynne and Derrick were a little older Marion noticed a Barvae Beagle owned by Gladys Clayton at a time when the breed was still relatively new at dog shows and was immediately attracted to the breed – Beagles were similar in many ways to the Cockers but involved no trimming.

The foundation bitch was Derawuda Vanity who won best puppy at her first show and was subsequently mated to the Canadian import Barvae Benroe Wrinkles, which gave Marion her first champion, Dialynne Huntsman. He became the first in a long line of prepotent stud dogs for the kennel, one of his sons being Ch Dialynne Ponder who was really a dog way ahead of his time.

Always a believer in discerning line-breeding, Marion used Ponder on the Huntsman daughter, Ch Dialynne Shadow, and this resulted in the beautiful Ch Dialynne Nettle who was to earn her place in Beagle history as the dam of Ch Dialynne Gamble, who is still considered the father of the breed.

Marion recalls: "In the early days Beagles had become a very competitive breed with many leading figures breeding and showing. I was in competition with the likes of Leonard Pagliero, Thelma Gray, the Appletons, the Suttons and various others who had much

Marion Spavin with Ch Dialynne Augustus.

higher profiles than I did, but I had a vision in my mind of how the breed should look and behave and set about improving heads and temperament in particular."

The stud dog chosen for Nettle was the Appletons' American import, Am Ch Appeline Validay Happy Feller, and this combination produced the legendary Gamble who produced an incredible 26 champions, many of them bred by relative newcomers, which coincidentally tallied with his 26 CCs.

Amazingly, some years later, Ch Soloman of Dialynne, Gamble's son to one of his own great-granddaughters, produced exactly the same number of champions and also won the same number of CCs. Soloman in turn sired Ch Dialynne Tolliver of Tragband who was a very successful BIS and group winner, and also a sire of some note.

For many years the Dialynne kennel was run in tandem with the Manterr Manchester Terriers of Bryan Moorhouse and all the dogs were shown in partnership so Marion was also involved with numerous champions in that breed.

As her children grew up it was obvious that Dianna had inherited her mother's passion for dogs, unlike her brother and sister.

Dianna remembers first becoming involved when she was in her early teens when she would often look after the dogs for her mother to attend dog shows.

"I probably began handling seriously when I was in my late teens and remember actually taking Gamble to the Pup of the Year final. When my mother first started breeding kennel management was a lot tougher; she fed primarily tripe and dog biscuits – and I'm talking of a time when we would often collect bitches for mating at the local railway station and many of them arrived in grubby tea chests… a far cry from the fancy travelling boxes we use today."

Dianna's daughter Melanie was born in 1978 so was literally born into a thriving kennel where Beagles were the priority. When Melanie was five years old the Spavin household teamed up with Stuart Milner and his parents, Stuart being an enthusiastic young Dialynne satellite with his own Copewell kennel name. He remains active within the kennel, albeit as something of a back-room boy.

Over the years there have been countless UK Beagle champions made up, many of them in novice hands, and of course the kennel has exported an infinite number of overseas champions, many of which have helped establish the breed in their adoptive country.

Whilst Beagles have always been the mainstay of the kennel, Dianna developed interests in other breeds and Tibetan Terriers were soon well established at Dialynne, the kennel making up several champions. Marion also returned to her first love of Cockers and bred a couple of show champions.

Dianna Spavin with Ch Araki Masken Kostium.

"I suppose in many ways I felt that the Beagles were very much my mother's," says Dianna, "and wanted to do something more in my own right and this is why I began with the Tibetans, Ken Sinclair being a close family friend and the obvious person to turn to for foundation stock.

"I enjoyed the grooming and Melanie also had a natural talent for grooming and presentation. We also bred Miniature Schnauzers successfully and it was very flattering that several breeders were asking Melanie to handle their Miniatures."

There were several Dialynne champions in both these breeds but then, just as Dianna had felt the urge to establish herself in another breed away from the Beagles, Melanie too began to look at other breeds that she could call her own.

The Australian Shepherd had always appealed to her and back in 2006 she got her first one. Apart from the physical smartness of the breed Melanie liked the temperament and intelligence of the Aussies and, while not a trimmed breed, they had sufficient coat for her to demonstrate her grooming skills.

Melanie points out: "The breed is very cosmopolitan and I have researched it thoroughly which resulted in my importing two Aussies from the US, including Austin who is currently number one pastoral breed in the UK for this year. I have made many good friends overseas in the breed, several of whom have sent me top class Australians to handle in the UK. Also various breeders in other countries have used my stud dogs with great success."

Melanie has established herself as a highly proficient handler in several breeds even though she did not come up through the rather regimented world of junior handling.

"I'm very much self taught as regards both grooming and handling. Obviously in the early days my Mum taught me basic grooming skills and I then studied other successful groomers, looked at many pictures of dogs whose presentation impressed me and tried to emulate the same look. As regards handling, I am always watching the top people both here and overseas as you can always pick up little hints that can prove useful and help hone the finished picture.

"I was always very conscious of the fact that my grandma was something of a legend in the dog world, and that my mum had followed her as an established judge, so this was something of a two-edged sword. I was lucky to have such a great start in dogs and I suppose I might have taken a lot for granted, but at the same time I always felt I had so much to live up to."

These days the running of the kennel is very much down to Dianna,

Melanie Spavin with Ch Hearthside Man Of Mystery at Dialynne.

Melanie and on a practical front Melanie's husband Lee. Marion now takes more of a back seat but is still very much the matriarch of the kennel. Dianna is now the expert when it comes to stud work and whelping while Melanie is perhaps keener on having her hair and nails done! She does however run a grooming business at the kennel.

Over the years the husbandry may have changed somewhat by way of feeding and housing but the same breeding principles apply where Dialynne has always believed in producing the best by using only top quality specimens with sound temperaments in the breeding programmes. Line-breeding still works for Dialynne and gone are the days when in a litter of Beagle puppies there may have been one or two show prospects and the remaining puppies obvious pets. Nowadays the consistency of puppies bred is such that there are no obvious pet quality puppies, which can make puppy selection much more difficult.

Marion demonstrated a passion for dogs at the age of 14 which has thankfully passed through to her daughter and granddaughter. Melanie's seven-year-old son Gabriel was seen recently putting Austin through his paces so who knows… there may well be a fourth generation waiting in the wings. ∎

MARION, DIANNA and MELANIE SPAVIN

MINARETS:

Muriel Harwood, Carol Harwood and Melanie Harwood

We are extremely proud of our three-generation family all of whom are involved in dogs. Over this period we have built up and established ourselves a reputation for consistently producing a strong type, which are sound and healthy.

Muriel was brought up in a house where there was always a dog; it was inevitable that when she had a house of her own a dog would be on the list of things to have. However, as she was out at work all day, it was several years after she married that this became possible.

Our kennel of Poodles started with a black Miniature in 1960 and a white Miniature a year later. The black was a birthday present for Carol and the white was bought for showing. We showed them at local match meetings and then decided to breed a litter, which led us to registering our affix.

After much deliberation this was chosen by Muriel's late husband Fred. He thought Minarets was appropriate because of the roundness of the poms and coat in the traditional lion

Muriel Harwood with Ch Vasahope Court Vogue of Minarets.

im which is used for the Poodle and Minaret is a rounded type of dome. It as registered in 1961 and both Muriel's aughter Carol and Melanie – her granddaughter – have a separate interest although all the dogs are now in Melanie's name.

Melanie was born into our successful Poodle kennel and is very gifted in presentation and handling. She is responsible for showing and trimming our dogs, puts in a lot of work into their conditioning and training and has been rewarded with terrific success in the ring.

Breeding is a joint effort and much discussion goes into it. We were one of the first Miniature Poodle breeders in the UK to OptiGen DNA test for the PRCD form of progressive retinal atrophy, and along with the DNA test we continue to test our stock on the British Veterinary Association/Kennel Club scheme, ensuring that our lines are as healthy as possible while maintaining our 'type, balance and soundness.

With regard to deciding our breeding programme, Muriel is much more of the traditionalist, Carol is the pedigree researcher and Melanie is a bit more radical than her grandma would like at times. However we sit down and discuss fully everything we do and while there might be the odd cross word now and again (let's face it, we all have those!) at the end of the day we are all happy in the choices we make.

Showing was, and still is, very much a family hobby and Muriel, Carol and Fred were all involved with the development of the white line. Over the years five white Miniatures achieved their title. Ch Minarets Dancing Jester was campaigned by Carol and won the group at Bath 1978 under Bill Siggers.

During this time we also bred several litters of black Miniatures and made up several champions in this colour. One of these was Ch Minarets The Maverick; his mother was Carol's first black champion Minarets The Martinette and his father was Muriel's first white champion Minarets Court Jester. Unfortunately we could not use him in our breeding programme because he was too closely related.

Eventually we had to give up the white line partly because our black line had become so dominant, but the main factor was that the gene pool for the white Miniatures at that time was too small and we had nothing to breed our bitches to.

We used Ch Jolda Joshua of Idadoun on one of our black bitches and kept two from this mating; the bitch, Minarets Mercedes, although never titled, is behind all our stock. Then we used Ch Renwin Rappelle several times on different bitches and the progeny from these outcrosses shaped our present stock. We also used the Spanish import Escandalo of Shikarah de Vanitonia which produced Melanie's first champion, Minarets Secret Affair, who in turn produced 'Rodney'.

Several years ago we reluctantly gave in to Ann and Katherine Kennedy (Clarion) in the US who pleaded with us for two long years to let Ch Minarets Reach To The Stars go to live with them. As Rodney was winning CCs by this time we let 'Nicky' go on

Carol Harwood winning a group under Bill Siggers with Ch Minarets Dancing Jester.

Melanie Harwood and Ch Minarets Secret Assignment after their Crufts group win.

the understanding he came home in two years. Nicky however was more than happy living the good life with Ann and Kat so he stayed with them till the end.

We have two of his granddaughters and mated to Rodney they have produced two males for us, the black Ch Minarets No More Secrets and the blue Ch Minarets Out Of The Blue.

We have also incorporated bloodlines from the Czech Republic into our lines, Ch/Cz Ch Cristal de Nigromanta was imported by our good friend Agnes Murphy and her late husband Bobby; due to Bobby's failing health Agnes asked Melanie if she would like the dog in partnership and for 'Kookie' to live with us while Melanie campaigned him. Melanie jumped at the chance and besides gaining his title, Kookie has produced one UK champion for us.

We have produced 36 UK and 29 overseas champions and have won over 260 CCs. From 2003 to 2009 iand 2012 we were the top Miniature Poodle breeder. Rodney (Ch Minarets Secret Assignment), campaigned by Melanie, is by far our most successful show dog. He is the breed record holder with 65 CCs, is the top CC-winning Poodle of all time and is one of the top CC winners of all breeds.

He won seven all-breed championship show BIS and five RBIS, 24 groups including Crufts 2006 under Martin Freeman, 25 other group places and ten breed club BIS.

Rodney was runner-up overall at the champion stakes final in 2005, winner in 2007 and won the last veteran stakes final in 2009 at his first attempt; this makes him the only Poodle to have won both finals. He was top Poodle five times, number three all breeds in 2005, number five in '04 and joint tenth in '06, top utility in '05 and three times runner-up.

Over the years Carol has always had a white male Standard Poodle as her 'pet'. Her current white boy, Reetano Lipizzaner at Minarets, who is by 'Ricky' the Crufts 2014 BIS, has a CC. Muriel also has her 'pet' in the white Toy Poodle Vanitonia Yukiko who has two CCs.

Carol has also had English Springer Spaniels and has had one Sh Ch, Lyndora Choir Boy at Minarets. Our involvement with ESS came from a long-standing friendship with Dorothy and Tom Bury (Lyndora) and Dorothy was Melanie's godmother.

Muriel has always loved American Cockers and this year Melanie was fortunate to be offered one by Jenny Ward and so 'Tiffany' (Mischtikals Manhattan at Minarets owned by Melanie and Jenny) came to live with us and is doing well, including winning the minor puppy bitch stakes at Leeds.

We do believe in giving something back to this hobby that we love and all three of us are long serving members of the North Western Poodle Club and Darwen Canine Society. Carol has been secretary of the NWPC since 1988, and of Darwen since 1990. Melanie and Carol serve on the committee of Blackpool; Carol is chief steward and Melanie is the assistant office manager. Carol has been a member of the Kennel Club since 2003.

Muriel only ever wanted to judge the three sizes of Poodle and has officiated in Australia and many countries in Europe.

Carol, on the other hand, was always interested in other breeds especially within the utility group. She was passed to award CCs in 1981 and is now passed for nine breeds as well as the utility group. She judged the group at Crufts in 2010.

Melanie awards CCs in the three sizes of Poodle in the UK and has judged in Europe, Australia, Japan and at specialties in the US and Sweden. She also judges several other breeds at open shows.

A few years ago she took over the running of the family boarding kennel and cattery. Outside the dog show game Melanie's passion is photography, and she has a degree in wildlife and environmental photography. The interest in photography runs in the family as both Muriel and Carol love taking images. Carol also has a passion for art history particularly from the Italian Renaissance and has a master's degree in art history in which she specialised in the Medici family and their connections to art. ■

MURIEL, CAROL and MELANIE HARWOOD

STARGANG, SHARDAROBA & SHARDAGANG:

Ellen Blackburn, John and Valerie Bennett, Joanne and John Blackburn-Bennett and Heather Blackburn-Bennett

The Stargang prefix was first registered and compounded for life in 1969. My first show dog, bought in 1965, was a red Cocker Spaniel then another in 1966, a black Cocker both from the Lochranza kennel. They were lightly shown and bred from.

At this time I met and travelled with Helen Harriman of the Vienda Dachshunds and fell in love with the breed so in 1967 I bought my first Miniature Smooth.

In March 1969, at Manchester, my Vienda Coffee Liquer was awarded the bitch CC by the famous judge Bill Siggers. I was seven months pregnant at the time and two months later Joanne was born.

The following year my first CC in Miniature Wires was awarded, by top breed specialist Alf Hague (Limberin) to my male Stargang Pink Pill of Cumtru. These two were then mated (we could interbreed the coats back then) to produce the first Stargang champion, the Miniature Wire Ch Stargang Moonshine.

The first Miniature Smooth champion was Ch Stargang Wurlitzer born in 1974. He went on to be top CC-winning Min Smooth dog in 1975 before being sold to Bill Hardie (Sonderbar) in Australia where he quickly made his mark both in the ring and in the offspring he sired.

The wheel turns and over 30 years later I got back from Sonderbar the brother and sister Sonderbar Ben and Sonderbar Billie Jean who had many lines going back to Wurlitzer. Within the first year of being shown both were champions, Ben having a group 3 along the way at Welsh Kennel Club 2010. Billie Jean turned out to be a lifetime dream. She took the bitch CC record, was awarded the prestigious Jackdaw Trophy, was Dachshund of the Year 2013 after being runner-up 2011 and so many BIS and RBIS wins at breed club shows.

Ellen Blackburn with Ch Sonderbar Billie Jean at Stargang.

Joanne was an early starter attending her first championship show, Leeds, at just two weeks of age. She started handling quite young but only at open shows until she was 11 and then was allowed to handle at championship shows.

One of her first ventures into the show ring when about five years old was a children's handling class and when the judge asked the dog's age she replied: "I don't know but she is a champion."

Years later her son Callum made his debut in the ring at a match meeting Christmas final. He handled a bitch who had become a champion after she qualified for the Match Dog of the Year. He came first and said that was it, he was giving up handling while he was at the top.

The first dog Joanne handled to his title was Ch Stargang Black Mink in 1984, when she was 15 years old. She was 16 when she accepted her first judging engagement and just 21 when she first awarded CCs in Longs at Three Counties. She has now judged all six varieties of Dachshund here and has judged abroad on many occasions.

In 1988 she married John Bennett, the son of John and Valerie Bennett who showed Longhaired Dachshunds under the prefix Shardaroba. John and Joanne then took out their own prefix of Shardagang combining the two names.

At this time they also decided to take the name of Blackburn-Bennett

Joanne and John Blackburn-Bennett with Sh Ch Kiswahili Martin at Kanix winning the champion stakes under Jean Lawless and his imported son Sh Ch Coralwood Kanix Mr T winning the puppy stakes at his first show under Graham Hill.

r their name with dogs as there were quite a few Bennetts showing nd judging Dachshunds, namely John and Valerie, Jack and Jenny ennett (Jack later to be secretary of Blackpool) and some others.

In the teens of champions were made up with the Shardagang refix but when Heather also was owning dogs in her own name ut with either the Stargang or Shardagang prefix we decided it was onfusing us, never mind anyone else, remembering which was owned y whom and whether they were Stargang or Shardagang so Joanne nd Heather took out separate interests in the Stargang name.

After about ten years of close breeding interest with Sigurd and Kari Wilberg of the Kanix Min Wires Dachshunds, Sigurd saw a fabulous ointer when he was judging in New Zealand. He persuaded the wners to let him come to the UK on lease. He came to live with and e handled by Joanne.

Aus Ch/NZ Gr Ch/UK Sh Ch Chesterhope Lets Be Serious at Kanix Breeze) stayed for 18 months, won 20 CCs and was the start of a very uccessful Pointer kennel jointly owned and bred by Joanne, John and Heather in partnership with the Wilbergs.

Their most successful dog to date is a son of Breeze, Sh Ch Kiswahili Martin at Kanix who is the record holding male Pointer CC winner nd was BIS at Scottish KC.

Joanne is also showing a Borzoi, Janter Silver Spirit, whom she co-wns with his breeder Terry Crossman, a Min Wire breeder friend of many years. Rocky is the top Borzoi puppy at the end of September. He was unbeaten in puppy classes and won the CC at Manchester, only is second show.

Heather is third generation exhibitor, handler and championship now judge on both the paternal side through her father John and te grandmother Valerie and grandfather John Bennett, well known or their Shardaroba Longhaired Dachshunds, and on the maternal de through Joanne and myself with our Stargang and Shardagang achshunds.

Strangely, Heather's first show was also Leeds, again at two weeks of ge, was this an omen?

Heather is now very much a major force in the Stargang team. She as been handling the Dachshunds from a very early age and now lso handles the Pointers. Her Ch Lokmadi Sea Holly at Stargang is urrently top Miniature Smooth 2015. She was BOB at Crufts and ortlisted in the group. In 2013 her Min Wire Ch Stargang Czarina as BOB at Crufts and group 3.

She works and lives away from home now but is very much involved n what our bitches are mated to and then in the decisions of what we eep from the litters.

Heather is also handler of several of the Pointers that the Kanix eam has made up. She manages to still get to most championship hows although sometimes work has to come first.

Between the three of us we have bred and/or owned 66 UK achshund champions and numerous champions around the world nd with the Kanix team have made up eight show champion Pointers ith others gaining their overseas titles.

Joanne bred and made up the first brindle Min Smooth bred in the K and made up the only silver dapple Min Smooth champion. We lso have had champions in most colours of the Min Wires: brindle, lack and tan, silver dapple and brindle dapple, red and a CC-winning hocolate and tan.

It was pointed out to us that being born and brought up as second nd third generation of a successful kennel of top winning dogs as good as 'living' a constant seminar, learning handling skills, how presentation especially with the Wires and Longs and also ring rotocol, having it drilled into them that win or lose you keep the mile on your face and congratulate those who beat you.

Showing is not life or death, it is a pleasurable pastime where we eet up with our friends and we always take the best dogs home.

ELLEN BLACKBURN

Shardaroba has been the name that Valerie and I have called all the ifferent houses we have lived in since meeting. During the 'dating eriod' it was a regular Roy Orbison record played at the dances we tended each week; the meaning he tells in the lyrics is that 'The

future will be much better than the past'. And so it was! The Kennel Club spelt the original Shahdaroba spelling slightly differently; even so we went ahead and registered the name in the early 1980s.

Heather Blackburn-Bennett with Ch Stargang Czarina.

Our first encounter with showing Dachshunds was in 1967. We already owned a black and tan Long, and Miss Rigley introduced us to Jack and Jenny Bennett at Darwin from whom we bought two red Miniature Longs. Our showing career briefly started, but soon came to a stop, as we had six children (three under three years old including twins) and time to pull everything in was proving to be difficult.

In 1980 we bought a red Long from Fay Skanta. in the early '80s we obtained from Jean Jensen a red Long, our foundation bitch, who became our first champion, Albaney's Iona Celeste at Shardaroba.

These were followed by Ch Shardaroba Sophistication, Ch Shardaroba High Flyer, Ch Shardaroba Sensation (Iona's daughters from repeat matings), Ch Shardaroba Joint Venture, mother and daughter team Ch Shardaroba Stephanie and Ch Shardaroba Noble Risk, Ch Shardaroba Fascination at Tarramist (the first chocolate Long champion, campaigned by Ian and Lesley Negus) and Ch Shardaroba Irresistible at Abbalongdat, campaigned by Ann Booth.

Valerie was the brains, being more interested in the pedigrees and breeding. She also groomed and presented the dogs to perfection, due to her hairdressing ability. I was the brawn, happy to help with the cleaning and maintenance of the kennels, but loved to handle in the ring. We received much advice and support from Mollie Raine, Jeff Crawford and the Gatheral sisters.

Valerie and I carried out many judging appointments at all levels, mostly within the UK but we both judged in South Africa and Australia. We worked in various capacities on several committees, Ashfield Canine Society, the Longhaired Dachshund Club, West Riding Dachshund Club and lately the Dachshund Club, ranging from committee member, secretary and treasurer to chairman.

Most weeks the children would come with us to the shows, although they all took part in the daily kennel duties, walking, grooming, cleaning etc. "Never pass a table without putting a dog on it" was the instruction to everyone.

Weekly visits to dog training classes were a regular occurrence for the family. The three youngest children (Julia, Joanne and John) would be avid participants in the junior handling class, often squabbling over who had the easier dog to handle. The two girls undertook employment in large boarding and breeding kennels.

Everyone was capable of mating and whelping the dogs without supervision, with the grandchildren (and now the great-grandchildren) learning the 'facts of life' at an early age during mating and whelping sessions. They are still capable of assisting in any daily task that is required and will happily pitch in.

Daily life was focused for everyone on canine management, and to have a successful kennels, everyone needs to work, care, and learn all aspects of this.

▶

John and Valerie Bennett with Ch Shardaroba Noble Risk.

In 1985, Julia went over to the Kilspindie kennel, a top Cavalier kennel in Maine, US, and stayed there until she got married. Since then, she has had Dachshunds and Flatcoats, with spells at showing and had judging appointments in the various breeds and working with me. Sadly, family and work commitments have taken priority.

Joanne showed Sadie Lady of Shardaroba until her marriage and subsequently had children. She took employment in top Belgian Shepherd breeding kennels and horse management, horses being a big part of her life. She now has a German Shepherd, previously having run a small rescue centre before rehoming them.

John, before getting married, worked in all aspects of training, grooming, showing whelping etc at home, While attending shows in the 1980s he met Joanne Blackburn and a relationship started.

Joanne decided eventually to move in with us at Teversal in August 1987. She arrived at the same time as we started out in a new venture with an Otterhound from Jean Pretious (Boravin). Eventually John and Joanne got married in 1988 and adopted for clarity their name Blackburn Bennett, due to confusion with there being more than one Bennett. Everyone knows of Joanne's success in the ring.

While a few of the grandchildren have gone on to care for various breeds of dog, and some have attained excellent academic positions, only Heather has fashioned out a successful showing career for herself. I am immensely proud of the work she has put in to her life in general and the achievements she has gained. She works hard in everything she does. The success she has made with Dachshunds and Pointers only go to show her enthusiasm.

In 2000, we semi-retired from the show world, as we had developed a successful business creating a caravan park from a green field. We soc found out this business was very demanding, being often a 24-hour vocation, although several dogs were still present in the house. In ear 2005 all our hard work paid off and the Caravan Club awarded the park Top Caravan Park of the Year.

Due to health problems we sold the park in early 2006, and built a house in the middle of the Peak District, where fences and walls canno be built without planning permission, so the dogs moved in with Julia.

Sadly in 2008 Valerie finally lost her battle with cancer. Following he death I spent time flying all over the world, often at 24 hours' notice! The highlight of these journeys was the trek to see the gorillas in Uganda and Ruanda. Occasionally I would travel to a show, but mainly to meet up with Joanne and John. It was a lonely period in my life.

For the Bennetts, dogs were very much a family activity. As a family, involvement in all aspects of the show world meant anyone and everyone who chose had the opportunity to air their views on whateve subject was being discussed, no one's opinion was discounted withou thought, and as an entire family, mine and Ellen's, we still discuss thes topics when meeting up.

Conformation is always talked about, especially on new puppies, how to further the breed, feeding regimes and all manner of topics. This is the only way a kennel can go forward.

When Daphne Graham (Jadag) and I got together in 2010, she obviously brought her dogs with her, including Breeze, her Silken Windhound. She has been successful in breeding and exhibiting Miniature Longs, the most famous being Ch Jadag Bjorn Veeta. We attended shows together and I began handling her Minis for her.

We flew to Australia October 2010, looking for a Long to import for me, found nothing we really liked enough, but called to see Gopi Krishnan in Kuala Lumpur on the return journey, and fell in love wit Smooth bitch, whom Gopi agreed to allow us to import.

Daphne and I make a good team, and can be found together at most championship shows with her Miniature Longs, my Smooth and Longs. Recently, we have had gained the titles of two Miniature Longs, Ch Hillstar Lexzina at Jadag and Ch Jadag Heir Apparent, and winning two CCs with my Smooth import, though I am now campaigning her daughter. I have two Longs in Ireland owned and shown by Bill Warke and Gerry McFaul. Both are extremely successfu one already gaining his Irish title. ∎

JOHN BENNET

Peter Lockett with a Flatcoat and some of the Smooth Dachshunds.

RALINES:

Freda and Peter Lockett, Ruth Lockett-Walters and Helen Walters

The Ralines kennel was established by my parent Freda and Peter Lockett. Initially mom and dad were besotted by the gundog group and had numerous particolour Cocker Spaniels which they showed just at local shows because of family commitments. However they were both long servin members of Wolverhampton Canine Society, mother at one time being th treasurer and in later years my fathe was chairman and then president.

Apart from the Cockers my mother wa successful with a homebred Flat-coated Retriever who had come down from the very old Halstock kennel.

The first Smooth Dachshund we quired was down to my father who me home one night from the pub with Smooth bitch having caught someone ing to drown her in the canal. She came a member of our family and ally fitted in well and it was then that my other insisted that we bought a quality tch.

She was sound but no world-beater, but oduced a beautiful litter to Ch Silvae rgo. We didn't have the facilities to ep a male at this time so Jill Workman changed all three boys for a quality tch and we were then up and running.

After long-term illness and getting er a family bereavement, mom and d, taking myself along as handler, took e show scene by storm, making up two ampions within the first 12 months us exhibiting at championship level – h Benjamin of Ralines and Ch Ralines ildegarde.

Benjamin was the sire of one of e breed's most dominant sires and ildegarde the aunt of Ch rlshill Troubadour who am sure will always be membered.

I think the most famous our Smooths was the eautiful Ch Ralines Maid Measure who won BOB Crufts three years on e trot and accrued a tal of 31 CCs – it was fate nfortunately that she never oduced us a litter.

However it was a strong ne and in total we oduced 21 Smooth UK ampions with the Ralines fix.

Dad and I were very much volved as committee embers of the Midland achshund Club for many ars. My father was always ore involved with show organisation and other judged at open show level.

After I had a dabble quite successfully owing a Peke and Sussex Spaniels, it was y yearning for a Mini Longhaired which directed the kennel to this variety. My st dog was a quality dog purchased from e Kizzhar kennel and Kavalcade soon ecame my first champion and a prolific ad for the breed.

Our kennel has produced 24 UK iniature Longhaired champions to date d the most famous are the duo Ch alines Royal Acclaim and her son Ch alines Royal Statesman, both of whom on 32 CCs.

My daughter Helen has now joined e partnership and she has so far owned ree champions, the current one being h Ralines One Of Those.

I was taught by my parents the skills of

Freda Lockett with the family's Cocker Spaniels, 1957.

Ruth Lockett-Walters with Ch Ralines Maid To Measure.

Helen Walters with Ch Ralines One Of Those.

line-breeding and this is what I have always done as far as possible, breeding for quality and soundness. I got greatly involved in the research for the development of the DNA test for generalised progressive retinal atrophy cord 1 in the breed, and have given lectures and written hopefully informative pieces on the subject.

I have always done my utmost to make health factors, as well as beauty and soundness, of major importance in a breeding programme.

Our breeding programme has now got to the stage whereby when we do a mating we already know what we are going to do with the offspring down from that line. This is something over which I and Helen take hours of deliberation and with forward thinking to this end we are definitely seeing the required results.

Yes, we do occasionally have bad luck but you have to put your mistakes or disasters behind you and learn from them.

Regarding breeding, I do not feel that anyone should get too involved within their own comfort zone. Outcrosses are essential to widen out your gene pool and give you room to expand venture into the future. I have taken the plunge into foreign lines having used an Australian Import and recently a Dutch import – my kennel type is dominant and so I have been lucky to maintain type and a couple of generations after the outcross got what I fully intended to achieve.

I was lucky to have had my mother and father – it was not always easy; there were times when we would have run on several puppies out of a litter due to differing opinions. I do appreciate that as times have changed it is not possible to do this now but it was from this experience that I learned my breed Standard and the capabilities of a line inside out – upside down and back to front so to speak.

I do hope I have guided Helen in the same way as I was guided – I think this is likely as we have many a heated discussion.

I have to admit that the success of our kennel has been down to team work and having had the opportunity of coming into the dog world during an era where there were many well respected judges who helped and encouraged you. There were many top kennels based in the Midlands area and the quality at small evening sanction shows was immense. One should keep an open mind; it's never too late to learn more. ■

RUTH LOCKETT-WALTERS ▶

ALSTELLA:

Stella Reeves, Chris Reeves-Sargant and Sam Diment

I CANNOT remember my parents' house without a dog in it. Sally the Irish Setter was the first one I recall, in the early 1950s.

They then acquired Miniature and Toy Poodles and decided to register a prefix. Their first choice wasn't accepted so as all the dogs were owned by Mum they decided on Alstella, meaning all owned by Stella.

Italian Greyhounds and Miniature Pinschers were added and I can remember a blue Italian Greyhound bitch was advertised; we travelled to London by train to the Old Bailey and into a top judge's chambers, and bought her home.

Show quality she was advertised but show quality she was not, miles too small, but she stayed with us until she died.

It was with these three breeds that we ventured into the show ring. The only shows entered were exemption and open shows, championship shows were for the other people! Exemption shows were very popular in those days and we showed nearly every weekend; this is where I learnt my trade of showing.

At open shows we were more often successful then not and at one of these my Mum fell in love with the Japanese Chin, a delightful breed which took over the household.

I always loved Borzois and for a birthday present my Dad appeared at my school, took me out of class and we travelled to Mrs Ruggles of the Matalona Borzois – and my dream came true.

The Chins were bought originally from Peggy Searl (Crossgate) and Deborah Gaines (Gaystock). Slowly we became more successful at the shows, and many established breeders bought from my parents, our line helping produce some top winners. Mum and Dad based the kennel on Riu Gu and Yevot lines, and mixed the lines which many didn't at the time, but it proved very successful.

They mated Kosho of Crossgate to Gaystock Rising Sun which produced a dog and two bitches. They kept the dog and Lilian Davis (Gorsedene) bought the bitches, Tekko and

Sam Diment with Ch Alstella Angelino, Ch Alstella Joshua and two puppies.

Yancha. Yancha won Alstella's first two CCs and Tekko produced Pamela Cross Stern's first Chin champion Sternroc Cho Cho of Gorsedene.

Kosho was taken back to Mrs Davis to be mated but this time didn't allow any dog near her. As soon as she got home she escaped into the garden and was mated by her own son – in those days this was allowed. Alstella Teaka was the result; he sired nine champions and won a RCC until a eye injury finished his show career.

We are proud that the Alstella line is behind many of the top kennels of the past and present.

In 1971 we lost my father and at that time Mum had just bred the first litter from Teaka. Dad picked one bitch, Elisa and Mum the other, Samantha. At the Japanese Chin Club show, I showed Samantha to her first CC at ten months; both gaining their titles making them our first two champions. They took CC and reserve under Osamu Honda (Japan) at Birmingham City.

When my Dad died I became a partner in the Alstella affix.

Shinka, Kotogari and Looto Kezzie all won Irish titles, Kotogari going BIS at the first Irish Japanese Chin Club championship show.

Many more champions followed, in Europe, New Zealand and the US. This year we have had a champion made up in the Netherlands.

Mum always had a soft spot for the red and white Chin. We have always had them: pale lemons, clear reds and now the sables. Our most influential sable who was known worldwide is Ch Alstella Joshua. The most outstanding dog of his time, he is behind so many lovely dogs even to this day.

Mum would have been proud of our record for producing top quality reds. Our Ch Jezebelle was BB at the Japanese Chin Club and Going For Gold won the CC at Crufts 2014.

Mum judged at open show level and I believe was the first person to judge the

Stella Reeves with the kennel's first two champions, Samantha and Elisa.

Chris Reeves-Sargant with Alstella Going For Gold, Crufts 2014.

orthern show for the Chin Club. She never reached CC level hich I know disappointed her.

I started showing at the age of nine, the breeds mentioned us Akitas and Shibas. My first show dog was a Miniature Poodle hom I also trained for agility. Exemption shows were the only ace you could learn about handling, so I went to as many as I ould, winning the child handling class at most.

My life revolved around dogs and showing, and nearly every eekend I would disappear with my Dad to a open show. Many ow don't exist. I had many successes with Gypsy my Borzoi nd had just taken her first first at a open show when she died uddenly. Two more Borzois came along, Barthill Alexandrovna nd Springett Marie Celeste. How thrilled was I at the Borzoi lub show when Alex beat two champions in the open class. She as my first Crufts dog in the days of Olympia.

Our Italian Greyhounds had become very successful but we ecided to give them up as their legs were so fragile and we had ur fair share of accidents with them.

As I got older and got married the shows were cut back bit, only showing the Chins. I applied for my own prefix ewisia making up two UK and one French champion. I judged e Midland Counties Chin classes before they had CCs there, the ub championship show and Crufts.

Just before Mum died I added Akitas, and we did have fun nowing them, Luke always protected Mum, somehow knowing he was a older lady. I bred one litter and decided that although vely dogs they were a handful, so back to the Chins.

I imported a sable and white bitch from Italy, mainly American red and carrying a very strong sable line. Quendalina was not show girl but produced champions and top producers. She as worth her weight in gold and is behind most of our line day. Last year we imported two dogs from the Netherlands and weden, while something really new, a Danish-bred Papillon, me in in September.

I have written two books on Japanese Chin Champions of the ritish Isles, the second an updated version of the first.

My daughter Samantha started showing the Chins when she as a little girl, handling them in the garden from the age of four. he was the first to show Joshua in a minor puppy class, winning second. She used to accompany us to the shows handling the ogs, and started straight from the top handling the champions.

As she got older she had her own dogs; her most famous, and e winner of nine CCs, was Ch Angelino, a beautiful little square og who won BIS at the club championship show in 1993. She en showed his son Ch Luigi to his title.

As she got older and married and had children the shows ad to take a a back seat for awhile, but when her grandmother ied she became a partner in the prefix and all the dogs were ansferred into joint ownership. She judged the club show mong many championship shows.

Sam has always loved the Bulldog and so they became a part f her household. Her original bitch was bought from Mrs ruton and she has never been without a Bulldog since, now wning three. She has also owned a rescued Chinese Crested nd a Boston. She lives a busy life combining the raising of two oys and their busy sport schedules and working as a financial anager of a solicitors.

We have been fortunate that as generations go we have always greed with the policies and the breeding programmes of our arents or grandparents. We have had the same understanding of e Standard and what to look for in the breed, and I believe this as helped in that the type of Chin we breed now is as near as we an to the type my parents bred.

Line-breeding has always been our policy with the inclusion f imports to strengthen the line, but always going back into our riginal line.

We both look forward to a few more years yet in the dog world nd showing and breeding beautiful dogs. ∎

CHRIS REEVES-SARGANT

BRONIA:

Dorothy Hanney, Fran Mitchell and Emily Mitchell

Dorothy Hanney's Ch Mr President of Bronia was the kennel's first best in show winner.

I started pestering for a Longhaired Dachshund having met Mrs Coates (Rokerpark) in the local park (Roker Park of course!) walking her five Longs. I was her shadow for about two years before my Mum Dorothy finally gave in and bought two in 1969.

Before buying the pair I started going to local sanction shows with 'Auntie Peggy', as she was now known, and really got the bug!

Once we had the boys Mum started to take me to all the local shows, usually two every weekend. Mostly I was dropped at the door with a dog and left for the day as I had three younger siblings who also needed entertaining.

In 1972 Mum bred the first Bronia litter of Longs which contained Ch Bronia Zodiac campaigned by Mike and Margaret Hall – I wasn't allowed to keep another male. We kept a bitch who wasn't good enough so I persuaded Mum to sell her and buy me something more flashy for the local shows. An American Cocker from Lochranza filled the bill nicely!

I spent a summer at Lochranza in 1973 learning to trim Cockers and Yankees, then most of my holiday time after that was spent with Margaret and Nicky Swann, Margaret teaching me all I know about Dachshunds and Nicky improving my handling skills.

I met some wonderfully interesting people both at Lochranza and Swansford. I spent many an evening just listening to conversation about dogs; visitors included Ferelith Hamilton (now Somerfield) who was at Lochranza to learn more about Poodles one weekend.

Visitors at Swansford included Fred and Julia Curnow, Catherine Sutton and of course regulars were Harold and Peg Roberts. Nicky coached me to the semi-finals of the Dog Centre junior handling run by Joe Cartledge and held at Cheltenham in 1973 where I was runner-up.

When our stock improved we graduated to championship shows and I booked myself a double seat on Bettie Farrand's dog bus. Those were exciting times and I met many great characters of the dog game, many of whom were pretty young back then and we all had a ball!

My mother started taking more interest in dogs and moved house to a more suitable property to accommodate them as it was the bigger dogs that took her eye. She owned Pointers, Golden Retrievers, Labradors and Newfoundlands, all of which she showed.

My mother's first big winner was Ch Mr President of Bronia who won various groups in the 1980s and BIS at Darlington in 1987, at which time I also had my two children, one of whom caught the dog show bug from an early age. ▶

Fran Mitchell with Ch Bronia Conquistador after he won the Pedigree veteran stakes final.

Emily Mitchell with Ch Bronia Lotario.

Emily was always keen to come along to the shows and loved handling. She initially started handling Mini Longs for Margaret Jamieson at club shows, beginning in the junior handling classes, and then progressed to showing her young dog in the breed and winning her first ever CC with Margaret's Min Long Ch Djeata Mountain Ash from puppy.

Emily also showed my mother's Mini Longs and eventually was allowed her first Long in 2005. Emily went into partnership with her grandma on her first top prize-winning dog Ch Frankanwen Sundance to Bronia, whom she also took in the Junior Handling Association and Kennel Club Junior Organisation classes and won the JHA semi-final at Richmond with him.

In 1989, our kennel's top winner was born. James was born into a litter where the mother completely rejected them and no milk was produced. I had to hand-rear the litter and in the end, it was more than just worth it.

There were two males in the litter which I couldn't decide between so I went back to my mentor Margaret Swann for advice. I'll never forget her advice that day: she told me, "Keep the one with the neck!" and she was proved right. She subsequently gave Ch Bronia Conquistador a CC and BOB early on in his career which thrilled me.

I was also involved in Cockers and American Cockers winning my first ever CC with a homebred American, Bronia City Swinger, in 1976. I co-owned a Whippet in the '70s, I showed a Borzoi in the early '80s and a Basset to her title in 1993; all through the years I have always had the Longs.

Latterly mother had French Bulldogs. The boy she retained from her last litter was eventually sold at six months to Adrian Findley in Ireland where he was made up.

Mum, Emily and I have all been on committees, all three of us on both Northern Dachshund Association and North East Dachshund Club and, since the clubs have merged, Northern Counties Dachshund Association of which I am chairman and Emily is treasurer.

My mother was a founder committee member of the Northern Newfoundland Club.

She worked until her early eighties as an osteopathic physiotherapist; she was fully trained in osteopathic manipulation techniques which she used to great effect on many exhibitors. She was also one of the first to register as ACPAT, approved to also treat animals.

I worked in Lloyds Bank as a youngster then ran a grooming parlour within my family's boarding kennel and finally managed to buy my own boarding kennel where it is easier to keep and spend time with our own dogs.

When Emily had finished her studies at university, I gave her a Long bitch for her birthday, Ch Bronia Carmelita, who was in effect her foundation bitch from whom she bred her first champions, owned by her and others, in the UK. This bitch produced her top winner to date, Ch Bronia Lotario.

Emily doesn't have much say on the kennel side of things as she works as a licensed insolvency practitioner which takes up most of her time, along with her daughter Annabel (who is very keen on dogs!).

I have a boarding kennel on site so do the majority of the care during the week, Emily road-working her dogs after work and spending more time at weekends. She also plays ball hockey which has occasionally taken priority over shows.

Emily I think has had a good head start in the world of dog shows. Not only did she have my mum and me, but her godmother was Margaret Swann. She has benefitted from handling lessons from Marita Rodgers when she was through to the junior handling final and growing up around the group ring when Conquistador was in his prime.

When it comes to breeding, we don't always agree on pick of litter (we rarely disagree but there are occasions!) but always take each other's comments on board. I think this helps in improving our kennel as a whole if you can take the honest criticism but I have been known to tell Emily she is far too critical of her own.

We have different lines in the Longs and I breed Mini Smooth while Emily has Mini Longs so each of us can have an outside opinion.

There is a bit of rivalry in the ring, especially at the moment when we are both showing champion males in open dog, but we are both in support of the other's achievements. Not all judges are going to like the same dogs and we show different types at the moment so it's healthy competition.

Between us we have bred and/or owned 60 UK champions, 41 Longs, nine Min Smooths, seven Min Longs, two Min Wires and one Basset. ∎

FRAN MITCHELL

The Sundust SAGA

A great kennel in pictures

Yvonne Knapper-Weijland's Sundust kennel has been among the leaders in American Cocker Spaniels since well before the breed attained challenge certificate status in 1970; indeed she was among the first to introduce the breed to this country when she brought over two from her native Holland when she came to live in the UK in 1964.

Since then she has made up many show champions, home-bred or imported, plus the breed's only full champion of the past 40 years, as well as exporting worldwide.

She says: "I consider myself extremely lucky in that some top breeders in America have trusted me with some truly beautiful dogs.

"In latter years I managed to borrow some top stud dogs as I found out that of course no one likes to part with their very best, but with the temptation of a UK title, which is still highly thought of, I persuaded them to lend me their precious boys."

Like all breeders, Yvonne has had disappointments too: "Yes, I had some fabulous dogs who did a great deal at the time, but then sadly went down with eye problems, so we scrapped that line."

She has never owned more then five adults dogs at any one time, nor bred many litters.

She was also involved in the early days with Cocker Spaniels from the Merryborne kennel and has dabbled with her first love, importing from Sweden a Miniature Poodle Harbovi's Kwik Step to Sundust, line-bred to Ch Lochranza Hells Fire. He became a famous stud dog, producing among others the best in show winner Ch Kertella's Dansarella.

Pictured here are a selection of her best known American Cockers. ■

Yvonne imported her first two American Cockers into the UK in 1964. Here is Belgian Ch Mysica's Little Bit Naughty, imported in 1964.

Also imported in 1964: Just A Belle van de Cockerbox, who had earlier won two CACs and two CACIBs in Europe.

The breed's first classes in the UK were scheduled at a show for rare breeds held at Stevenage in 1967, judged by Catherine Bede Maxwell from the US. Here are Stephanie Hunt Crowley (Chandhara), Yvonne and Rex Knapper and Pat Jones (Mittina). BOB and BIS was Sundust Merryborne Leading Lady (left).

PHOTO SALLY ANNE THOMPSON

[T]he 1967 import from the US, Sundust Artru Sun Blaze, who sired the first UK show [c]hampion, Lochranza News Flash.

A number of Sundusts have made an impact in Scandinavia, including Annalisa Heikkinen's Int/Norw/Fin Ch Sundust Patience (Can Ch Musblaik Morganne's Light My Fire ex Repercussion), number three all breeds in Finland 1977.

PHOTO C M COOKE & SON

The kennel's first UK titleholder and first homebred CC winner, Sh Ch Sundust Extra [S]pecial (Am Ch Sundust Bobwins Did You Ever ex Sundust Promise), made up in 1972.

Sh Ch Sundust Thanks Dur-Bet (Am Ch Dur-Bet's Knight To Remember ex Sundust Ranitas Ebony Mystery), Yvonne's first homebred male show champion and the first to take a group placing. He was sire of six titleholders.

The import Sh Ch Bobwins Sundust What The Hell at 19 months. He won 15 CCs and was BOB at Crufts under Frank Kane.

PHOTO: ANNE CUMBERS

The import Sh Ch/Am Ch Sundust Bleuaires Repercussion, a multiple CC winner from [t]he early 1970s who played an important role in the breeding programme.

The import Sh Ch/Am Ch Kaplar's Kwik-Step to Sundust, Yvonne's first group winner and an influential sire who won the kennel's hundredth CC and was top gundog in 1984.

Pictured winning reserve best puppy in show at National Gundog is Sh Ch Moonmist Persistance with Sundust (bred by Penny and Christine Iremonger by Kwik-Step ex Sh Ch Moonmist Remembrance), who later won the kennel's 200th CC under Rick Beauchamp from the US.

PHOTO DAVID DALTON

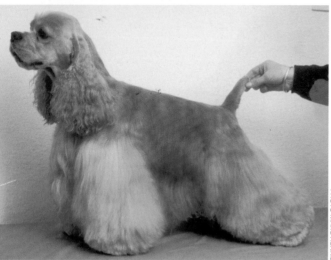

The import Sh Ch/Am/Can Ch Hu-Mar's Hellzapoppin at Sundust, 'one of the nicest dogs I ever had'. Sadly he developed cataract, the scourge of the breed for so many years.

PHOTO MARC HENRIE

Sh Ch Sundust Taboo (Sundust He'll Do ex his dam Sh Ch Kamps' Kopper Kleaner of Sundust) winning a heat of the Pup of the Year competition, one of three Sundusts to do so, the others being Sh Chs Me Black and And Me.

PHOTO JOHN HARTLEY

The first kennel's general and group championship show BIS winner, co-owned with Mike Gadsby, was Sh Ch Sundust Kream Kopper with Afterglow (Hellzapoppin ex Kopper Kleaner), a multiple CC winner including Crufts.

In 1990 Yvonne gave this dog best of variety in California. Later she brought him to the UK – Sh Ch/Am/Can Ch Piperhill's King Arthur at Sundust was a multiple CC winner incliudng Crufts, won a group and sired 11 UK titleholders.

An important brood bitch in both the UK and Sweden: Sh Ch Sundust Thumbelina (Sh Ch/Am Ch Jo-Bea's Diamond In The Ruf ex Taboo).

Littermates by King Arthur ex Thumbelina: Sh Ch Sundust Lancylot at Cosalta, a RBIS winner owned by the Swigciski family, Sh Ch Sundust Tom Thumb, Sh Ch Sundust Guinevere and Sundust Maid Marion of Goldenmist. A brother, Sundust Robin Hood from Saldawn, was an influential sire for Afterglow.

For Lone Wandel from Denmark, Yvonne made up Sh Ch/Int Ch Cavatina's Mustang Sally to become the UK's first tailed show champion in the breed.

...h Ch Sundust Guinevere, who is behind Yvonne's current dogs.

Ch Sundust Me Too (Cotton Quilt ex Sh Ch Sundust Me Black), the breed's first full champion for over 30 years, trained by Pam Wadsworth.

Coals to Newcastle: Bill and Cindy Mixon's Am/Int Ch Sundust Sir Percival (King Arthur ex Kaplar's Sugarplum Fairy at Sundust), a successful sire in the US.

Sh Ch Sundust For Me (Cotton Quilt ex Sh Ch Sundust And Me).

Sh Ch/Sw Ch Sundust From Me To You (by the import Am/Lux Ch Lydgate Latest Issue at Sundust ex Sh Ch Sundust For Me), exported to Anki Johansson in Sweden.

Sh Ch Sundust Black Out (Sh Ch/Am Ch Marshen's Ain't Seen Nothin Yet ex Sundust Dont Stop Me Now), Yvonne's latest show champion. Her crowning CC was the 350th for Sundust.

Yvonne and Hugues Schuh relaxing after Welsh Kennel Club 2015, she with her latest winner Sundust Oh Tan and he with Fin/Lux Ch Very Vigie I Don't Know who had won his third CC and second group from four UK shows. Yvonne had awarded him his first BIS at a spaniel show in France and persuaded his owner to have him shown in the UK.

The Swedish import Sh Ch/Int/Sw/Norw/Dan Ch Point Blanc Cotton Quilt at Sundust (Thumbelina's son by Candelle's Strike It Rich), a multiple CC winner, BOB at Crufts and Yvonne's first owner-handled BIS winner at Welsh Kennel Club under US judge Harry Smith, seen with Esmée Samuel, Trevor Evans and Denys Simpson.

IRELAND

Report and photos
Joyce Crawford-Manton

Certificates galore!

The first event of the year is always the Fosse Data Champion of Champions, sponsored by Happy Dog and hosted by Dublin Dog Show Society, one of the oldest all breed clubs in Ireland. The name of the judge is kept secret until the night for this canine social affair, held in a Dublin hotel with a dinner dance. The judge who was to crown the Champion of Champions 2014 was Denmark's Kirsten Scheel, whose winner was Philip O'Brien, his wife Jarka Poulova and breeder Richard Dalton's Kerry Blue Terrier Ch Dalstar Il Divo, who this year won his UK title. Among his other successes was BIS at Fermoy international.

Judging BIS at the Combined international show was Hitoshi Sayama from Japan who chose the Kerry Blue Terrier, John Weatherhead's UK Ch Hallsblu Fibber Magee, on a rare appearance at an Irish show; he then had eight CCs and was BOB at Crufts, and was top Kerry in the UK in 2013. Stewart Carson represented sponsor Dr Clauders.

In some ways things have not changed greatly on the Irish show scene during the past year, except that the show calendar seems to be expanding with more and more all-breed championship shows and fewer and fewer free weekends!

For such a small country, Ireland had 30 all-breed events including four internationals and next year it will be 31, with the addition, at time of writing, of yet another all-breed show.

The end result would appear to be that, at last, the often predicted fall-off in entries has finally arrived, and many shows during 2015 have found they have been down quite a few dogs, particularly those outside Dublin and the country 'back-to-back' events. Those in the capital seem to have held their numbers, albeit with a captive audience. Even so, up to 50 per cent of entries come from Northern Ireland to support all the shows from one end of the island to the other.

The Irish Kennel Club held two international championship shows back to back in October and next year the IKC Celtic Winners, our original St Patrick's Day Show which used to be the jewel in the crown, will be on the Saturday closest to the 'Saint's Day', the weekend following Crufts, and will be an international event. We hope some of those exhibitors travelling for the Kennel Club's main event will stay on and include a trip to the Emerald Isle in their itinerary.

St Patrick's Day proper, March 17, now sees a 'Discover Dogs' affair to attract the general public and promote responsible ownership.

As mentioned here last year, for the first time since the 'Council' or An Ard Chomhairle was closed back in the '80s, for 2015 it reverted to the original rule laid out by the IKC founders and opened up to all affiliated clubs and societies. The number of representatives therefore swelled the original 90 or so to well over 200, giving a wider spread of views and opinions, something that can only be for the good and in the end affording, hopefully, more democratic decisions.

Whether or not this was the reason for a few changes at the January AGM, we saw three members of the Judges and Green Star Committee voted onto the General Purposes Committee (or board of directors, as the IKC is a limited company), plus one

Best in show judge at Celtic Winners was Joan Walsh whose winner was Ch/UK/Int Ch Grasco's Honky Tonky, the Miniature Bull Terrier being campaigned in Ireland by Ger and Laura Cox, and owned by Moreno Scotton from Italy. He took his first BIS the previous October at the IKC international, and six days earlier took his fifth CC and was group 4 at Crufts.

The Royal Canin/Irish Canine Press Veteran of the Year was Catherine and Tina Broaders' Wire Fox Terrier Ch/Int Ch Crystalwire Solo of Brookside, always handled by young Catherine, and she received the presentation from IKC president Séan Delmar, Mary Davidson of Royal Canin and Des Manton of ICP. His wins were from the veteran stakes at all-breed championship shows throughout the year, and he accumulated the most points to top the Leaderboard.

The final of the Top Irish Showdog Contest, sponsored by Eukanuba, took place in the Crowne Plaza Hotel in Dublin with Manuel Borges from Portugal judging the 40 qualifiers from the 2014 all-breed championship shows. The winner will represent Ireland at the Eukanuba World Challenge in Amsterdam and it was fitting that the winner was Ch/UKCh Tirkane The Big Issue, the Toy Poodle owned by the international partnership of breeders Ann Ingram (left) and Kay Ryan (third left) from Cork, Marlies Morzik (second left) from Germany and Leanne Bryant and Lisa Nelson from England, as he was also the Irish Kennel Club Dog of the Year 2014 by virtue of his six all-breeds BIS wins last year. He is first DOTY for many years to 'do the double' and win this contest.

Rita McCarry-Beattie's choice to top the IKC international day one show was James Newman and Sean Carroll's Papillon Ch/Cz/GerCh Hundebuden's Juno Pondabudens, who had won his fouth group, having been BIS3 at Combined international.

Petru Muntean from Romania was the judge for the Combined Canine Pup of the Year 2014 final and his winner was Stephen Minogue's Japanese Shiba Inu Jiltrain Jackpott, who had qualified at the IKC international day one having won best puppy in show. He has gone on win many groups and top awards including BIS at Hibernian, and currently tops the Gain Petfoods/Irish Canine Press/Dog World group 5 Leaderboard 2015.

At the IKC international day two, June Wall gave top spot to Seamus Magee and Lisa Sweeney's Bullmastiff Ch Bullmeredith Captain Rowlo of Tarbhore, his second such win in the space of a month as he topped the entry at Tralee, the final show of the Munster Circuit.

other, so we also had new faces on the former committee, with fresh ideas which will hopefully in time bear fruit.

Financially, it would appear that the IKC is finally back on an even keel after a couple of worrying years and investment in a new all singing, all dancing website, instigated by the CEO of three years, will one hopes be a considerable aid to improving the number of registrations with easier access for 'Joe Public', money from registrations being the club's main source of income.

A new veteran title was launched at the IKC summer championship show in July. Those entered that day automatically won their title, but in future all others must win veteran with

The sought after title of Irish Kennel Club Dog of the Year is won on points for BIS and RBIS wins at all-breed championship shows. In 2015 the wins were shared around until the end of June when the Irish Setter, Diane Ritchie-Stewart's Sh Ch/UK Sh Ch Glendariff Whippersnapper, having taken BIS at Munster Canine, collected his second BIS at Deise, following on with another at the next event, Bray, giving him a clear lead. He then was RBIS at Tralee and the IKC international two, so with three BIS and two RBIS and just two shows to go, it could be an Irish native breed taking the crown. 'Nilsson' was top Irish Setter in the UK in 2014 and is currently top again for 2015.

Another in line for the IKC Dog of the Year is Kelly, Paul and Jean Lawless' Groenendael Ch/UK Ch Revloch Figo, who took his first BIS of the year in July at the IKC summer show under Brian O'Hara after winning his second group of the year, then collected RBIS at the IKC international day one and BIS at the All Ireland Bull Breeds show at Hallowe'en. He also has eight CCs. With just two more shows to go, he is two points ahead of the other possible contenders, so we will have to wait until the end of the year to see the final placings, as there are a further six dogs who could take points before the season closes just after Christmas.

an excellent qualification on five occasions at an all-breed championship show, so quite a few golden oldies are revisiting their past glories, many still a force to be reckoned with at eight and over.

Add this to titles of champion, Celtic Winner, junior champion, junior diploma etc, and there is a myriad of certificates which may be bought from the IKC once the required qualifications are met.

The education of judges is also moving up a level, with innovation from the Green Star and Judges Committee hopefully improving the standard of those aspiring to adjudicate both at home and abroad. That can only be a forward move, along with other improvements in our system which should be seen to bear fruit for the future. ■

UNITED STATES

Report by
Bo Bengtso

Record lows and record highs

When looking back at what has transpired in the sport of purebred dogs in the US during the past year, it's probably natural if one tries to maintain an upbeat attitude. After all, there's so much to be grateful for that all the griping we dog people do throughout the year may seem petty and almost inappropriate in a review of this kind.

In that vein, here are two examples of why things may not be as bad as they sometimes seem — one illustrating the big picture and the other a small, personal detail.

First, I have been informed that the American public bought about 2.7 million purebred dogs last year. That's a huge number by any standard and means that purebred dogs retain a solid grip on pet-buying dog lovers over here. That's something to cheer at.

If people still like purebred dogs in spite of all the hoopla about 'designer dogs' and mutts, there's hope for all of us. Perhaps more dog lovers are realising the advantages of predictability (in size, coat, temperament, and many other particulars) that come with a purebred dog.

The second example hit close to home in a different way. We were discussing a suitable name for registering a puppy. When an agreement had been reached and the appropriate paperwork was submitted to the American Kennel Club the registration certificate arrive in my computer's in-box LESS THAN AN HOUR after the application had been filed! Surely that's a record of some kind.

The above is proof both that purebred dogs are still popular in the US and that the AKC can function amazingly efficiently on occasion.

In between these two extremes there are, however, a lot of things to worry about, and no year-end review would be complete if they were not mentioned.

Provided that the 2.7 million purebred-puppies-per-year figure is correct (and it comes from a reliable source, in fact from one of the AKC board members), it's worrying that such a small percentage of them are registered with the AKC.

Its registration figures have been dropping steadily since the peak in 1992, when there were over 1.5 million registrations. By 2010, when the AKC decided no longer to make the annual figures public, the total was down to 563,611.

The race for Top Dog all breeds in the US for 2015 is unusually clear-cut. The German Shepherd bitch Gr Ch Locklyn's Rumor Has It v Kenlyn has been number one almost from the start and is now so far ahead that it's very unlikely that anyone can catch up, even though as this is written there are two-and-a-half months and at least a couple of hundred shows left of the show season. Rumor has an interesting pedigree: both parents are grandchildren of Ch Kismet's Sight For Sore Eyes, Top Dog in 2002. Rumor has also done well at specialties, which is not common for a top all-breed winner in German Shepherds: she won select at both the US and Canadian national specialties.

Rumor has been handled from the start by Kent Boyles, who also bred her in partnership with Pam McElheney. They also co-own her with Deborah Stern, Pamela Buckman and Patti Dukeman. Most big American winners have multiple owners to help finance the enormous cost of a top-level 'specials campaign', which usually involves flying to several shows every week all year long in different part of the count She is pictured winning BIS at Hatboro under Kenneth Kauffmann.

The Pomeranian Gr Ch Hitimes What The Inferno is almost sure to be number two all breeds, a respectful distance from the German Shepherd both in BIS wins and in number of defeated competitors but way ahead of everyone else. 'Danny' was born in Canada and was not even meant to be a show dog at first: then he went to Thailand and won big before his present handler Curtiss Smith saw him at AKC Eukanuba in late 2013. He did well 2014, but '15 has been Danny's year: by October 1 he had won 66 all-breed BIS, many more than any other Pomeranian ever in the US. Danny was bred by Joan and Ashley Carcasole and is owned by Bonnie Bird and Udomsin Littichaikun. He is seen taking B at Los Encinos under James Reynolds.

The Royal Canin/Irish Canine Press Veteran of the Year was Catherine and Tina Broaders' Wire Fox Terrier Ch/Int Ch Crystalwire Solo of Brookside, always handled by young Catherine, and she received the presentation from IKC president Séan Delmar, Mary Davidson of Royal Canin and Des Manton of ICP. His wins were from the veteran stakes at all-breed championship shows throughout the year, and he accumulated the most points to top the Leaderboard.

Rita McCarry-Beattie's choice to top the IKC international day one show was James Newman and Sean Carroll's Papillon Ch/Cz/GerCh Hundebuden's Juno Pondabudens, who had won his fouth group, having been BIS3 at Combined international.

At the IKC international day two, June Wall gave top spot to Seamus Magee and Lisa Sweeney's Bullmastiff Ch Bullmeredith Captain Rowlo of Tarbhore, his second such win in the space of a month as he topped the entry at Tralee, the final show of the Munster Circuit.

The final of the Top Irish Showdog Contest, sponsored by Eukanuba, took place in the Crowne Plaza Hotel in Dublin with Manuel Borges from Portugal judging the 40 qualifiers from the 2014 all-breed championship shows. The winner will represent Ireland at the Eukanuba World Challenge in Amsterdam and it was fitting that the winner was Ch/UKCh Tirkane The Big Issue, the Toy Poodle owned by the international partnership of breeders Ann Ingram (left) and Kay Ryan (third left) from Cork, Marlies Morzik (second left) from Germany and Leanne Bryant and Lisa Nelson from England, as he was also the Irish Kennel Club Dog of the Year 2014 by virtue of his six all-breeds BIS wins last year. He is first DOTY for many years to 'do the double' and win this contest.

Petru Muntean from Romania was the judge for the Combined Canine Pup of the Year 2014 final and his winner was Stephen Minogue's Japanese Shiba Inu Jiltrain Jackpott, who had qualified at the IKC international day one having won best puppy in show. He has gone on win many groups and top awards including BIS at Hibernian, and currently tops the Gain Petfoods/Irish Canine Press/Dog World group 5 Leaderboard 2015.

other, so we also had new faces on the former committee, with fresh ideas which will hopefully in time bear fruit.

Financially, it would appear that the IKC is finally back on an even keel after a couple of worrying years and investment in a new all singing, all dancing website, instigated by the CEO of three years, will one hopes be a considerable aid to improving the number of registrations with easier access for 'Joe Public', money from registrations being the club's main source of income.

A new veteran title was launched at the IKC summer championship show in July. Those entered that day automatically won their title, but in future all others must win veteran with ▶

The sought after title of Irish Kennel Club Dog of the Year is won on points for BIS and RBIS wins at all-breed championship shows. In 2015 the wins were shared around until the end of June when the Irish Setter, Diane Ritchie-Stewart's Sh Ch/UK Sh Ch Glendariff Whippersnapper, having taken BIS at Munster Canine, collected his second BIS at Deise, following on with another at the next event, Bray, giving him a clear lead. He then was RBIS at Tralee and the IKC international two, so with three BIS and two RBIS and just two shows to go, it could be an Irish native breed taking the crown. 'Nilsson' was top Irish Setter in the UK in 2014 and is currently top again for 2015.

Another in line for the IKC Dog of the Year is Kelly, Paul and Jean Lawless' Groenendael Ch/UK Ch Revloch Figo, who took his first BIS of the year in July at the IKC summer show under Brian O'Hara after winning his second group of the year, then collected RBIS at the IKC international day one and BIS at the All Ireland Bull Breeds show at Hallowe'en. He also has eight CCs. With just two more shows to go, he is two points ahead of the other possible contenders, so we will have to wait until the end of the year to see the final placings, as there are a further six dogs who could take points before the season closes just after Christmas.

an excellent qualification on five occasions at an all-breed championship show, so quite a few golden oldies are revisiting their past glories, many still a force to be reckoned with at eight and over.

Add this to titles of champion, Celtic Winner, junior champion, junior diploma etc, and there is a myriad of certificates which may be bought from the IKC once the required qualifications are met.

The education of judges is also moving up a level, with innovation from the Green Star and Judges Committee hopefully improving the standard of those aspiring to adjudicate both at home and abroad. That can only be a forward move, along with other improvements in our system which should be seen to bear fruit for the future. ■

The top hound of 2015, the Whippet Gr Ch Sporting Fields Shameless with handler Amanda Giles and judge Michael Dougherty at the AKC Eukanuba National Championship. Co-owners with Amanda are Dionne Butt and Barbara Call.

...mong the year's Top Dogs: the Skye Terrier Gr Ch Cragsmoor Good Time Charlie, seen ...inning RBIS at Westminster, handled by Larry Cornelius and pictured with president ...eán McCarthy, judge David Merriam and chairman Tom Bradley. Charlie was also BIS ... the American Kennel Club Eukanuba National Championship in December 2014. He ... owned by Victor Malzoni, the Cragsmoor kennel and Nancy Shaw.

Records for the past few years are a closely guarded secret, but ...'s known that the annual figures have continued to fall – although ...he haemorrhage appears to have stopped last year.

Those who know aren't telling, but the question is if AKC still is ...he world's largest purebred register', as claimed in the past. Has ...ussia, China or Japan taken over?

Show entries have dropped too, although not as much as ...egistrations. The reason is largely that there are more shows now ...han there used to be: in 1996 there were 1,266 AKC all-breed ...hows with a total of 1,757,856 entries, for an average of 1,389 dogs ...er show. That's not a large sum by British standards, of course, ...ut it's a lot better than the 2014 figures: 1,625 all-breed shows with ...,396,702 entries, or an average of only 860 dogs per show – more ...han 500 dogs fewer per show than in 1996.

Specialty shows have proliferated even more, with an increase ...rom 1,950 shows in 1996 to 2,553 in 2014, yet the total number of ...ntries dropped from 165,333 to 140,645, or an average of 85 dogs ...er specialty show in 1996 against 55 in 2014.

One of the Top Dogs of 2015, the Shih Tzu Gr Ch Hallmark Jolei Rocket Power with judge Francine Schwartz and handler Luke Ehricht, BIS at the Progressive Dog Club of Wayne County. Another of his successes was the group at Westminster. Luke co-owns him with Patricia Hearst Shaw and his wife Diane.

These figures come from the president of one of the ...rofessional dog show superintendents we have in the US, Bobby ...hristiansen of MB-F, Inc. They have been freely circulating in the ...og press, and much discussion has ensued about the reason for ...he decline.

The simple fact is, however, that there's not much to entice new ...og fanciers to compete at the average all-breed show. There's a ...uge shortage of qualified all-rounder judges, and of course no ...reed specialists at all with the small breed entries at an average-...ized show.

As there is no 'grading' and no critique-writing at AKC shows, ...nost novice exhibitors will know as little after a show as they did ...eforehand, except that neither they nor their dogs can hold ... candle to the professionally handled dogs who take the vast ...najority of the top awards. Consequently, there is little incentive ...or them to come back.

Yet there's no question that exhibitors will support a show they ...eel is worth visiting. The national specialties we have in the US ...re the sport's saving grace over here: at their best they are huge, ...ast for days, and incorporate much more than just the regular ...onformation judging.

At my breed's national specialty in April, the American Whippet ...lub hosted lure coursing, obedience, triathlon, Canine Good ...itizen testing, a discussion on the illustrated Standard, the annual ...neeting, a 'parade of honors' and one of rescues, a cardiac study ...ecture and judge's education.

Top sporting dog is the Brittany Gr Ch Rainbow Splash's Ruggedly Handsome, seen with judge Edweena McDowell and handler Clint Livingston winning BIS at San Antonio. Owners are Carolee Douglas, Jim and Alisa Andras, Kathy Hogan and Amanda Cone.

The leading non-sporting dog is the Boston Terrier Gr Ch Sabe's Simply Invincible, BIS at Angeles Canyon Dog Club's Sunday show, with handler Jorge Olivera and judge Jacqueline Stacy. Owners are Joe and Carla Sanchez and Sharon Saberton.

The Canadian-bred 15" Beagle Gr Ch Tashtin's Lookin For Trouble, handled by Will Alexander to BIS at Westminster KC 2015 under David Merriam. On the right is chairman Tom Bradley. He is owned by Lori and Kaitlyn Crandlemire from Canada and Eddie Dziuk.

One of the Top Dogs of all breeds, Amelia Musser's Scottish Terrier Gr Ch Round Town Queen Of Hearts of Maryscot, shown by Gabriel Rangel to win BIS at the Angeles Canyon Dog Club's Saturday show under Polly Smith. She is the daughter of the 2010 Westminster BIS winner Ch Roundtown Mercedes of Maryscot.

There was a special class for altered dogs, a festive Top 20 competition, sweepstakes classes for veterans and futurity classes for youngsters.

We had 562 Whippets making 722 entries, and that doesn't even include the lure coursing which would put the total well beyond 1,000 entries.

We are lucky to have a well-organised, established national specialty in my breed. Like those for most other breeds it moves around from one location to another each year. Entry figures may vary depending on how difficult it is to get to the show, but there are other breeds that have even bigger national specialty shows.

The Golden Retriever Club of America set what may have been a record with 884 individual dogs entered at its national specialty in North Carolina in October 2014. One judge officiated for all the 'class' (non-champion) males, another for the class bitches and a third, Carol Anne Gilbert from Britain, judged the huge 'specials' (champion) class.

Many other breeds have large entries for their national specialties. Labrador Retrievers, Shetland Sheepdogs, Collies, Poodles, Great Danes, Rhodesian Ridgebacks, Boxers, Australian Shepherds, Portuguese Water Dogs, Samoyeds, Bernese Mountain Dogs and Dachshunds are just a few that usually attract hundreds of entries at the biggest specialties. They offer a welcome change

from the run-of-the-mill all-breed shows and have much more to offer overseas visitors than most other events.

There are, of course, a few all-breed clubs that are worth mentioning, although not even the biggest American all-breed shows can compare with those in Britain or Europe for size.

According to AKC's official list of the top 25 all-breed shows for 2014, the largest – the AKC Eukanuba National Championship in Florida in December – had 3,495 dogs in competition. Second largest was the Kennel Club of Palm Springs with 3,097 dogs at its Saturday show in January. This weekend, incidentally, may take the prize as America's, possibly the world's, most beautiful dog show, held on the vast lawns of the Polo Grounds in Indio in California.

Most of the other top shows were held the same weekend as either AKC Eukanuba, Palm Springs or the big Louisville shows in March. However, none of them except the top two had more than 3,000 dogs in competition.

Perhaps the figures would look a little better if AKC did not present totals with absentees deducted. Most of these shows had a couple of hundred more dogs entered than were actually present.

The famous Westminster Kennel Club dog show in New York does not rely on numbers for its status. There were 2,681 dogs entered at the 2015 show, which as usual included an exceptionall high percentage of the top winners.

A victory at Westminster is the ne plus ultra for any serious exhibitor, and Westminster's storied past puts it in a unique category among the world's great dog events. This year David Merriam, the great terrier specialist, had been chosen to judge best in show, a responsibility he conducted with great aplomb. His winner, the 15" Beagle bitch Ch Tashtin's Lookin For Trouble, was a popular choice. She also marked a unique double for the breed, which most recently won in 2008 with Ch K-Run's Park Me In First Both dogs are co-owned by Eddie Dziuk, chief operating officer of the Orthopedic Foundation for Animals (OFA).

This year there was one all-breed show that brought back much of the glory from the past. Old-timers may have heard of the Morr & Essex Kennel Club event that for several decades up to the late 1950s was the biggest dog show in America, for a while even in the world. It was the brainchild of one of America's wealthiest women, Geraldine Rockefeller Dodge, and was hosted each year ii unrivalled splendour at her large estate in Madison, New Jersey.

After a disagreement with the AKC in 1958 Mrs Dodge discontinued the show, but the memory lingered on. At the end o a century the idea to recreate the show for the new century started to take form.

A 'new' Morris & Essex Kennel Club was formed, and it was decided to hold an all-breed dog show that as closely as possible would recreate what Mrs Dodge had wanted her show to be like.

Such a show could not be held every year, but the first attempt in 2000 was followed by others in 2005 and 2010, each with

Dorothy Collier's choice for BIS at Morris & Essex was the Pekingese Gr Ch Pequest General Tso, bred, handled and co-owned (with Nancy Shapland) by David Fitzpatrick. David, amazingly, also won BIS at the 2010 Morris & Essex with General Tso's grandsire, the English import Gr Ch Palacegarden Malachy.

Clay Coady, now retired from professional handling, judged BIS at Montgomery County and found his winner in the Wire Fox Terrier Gr Ch Hampton Court's Monte Cristo, bred and owned by Victor Malzoni of Brazil from two British exports, Ch Travella Starlord and Davwen Sapphire at Saredon, and handled by Leonardo Garcini. With them are Kenneth Kauffmann and chairman Bruce Schwarz.

increasingly smooth organisation and big entries. Guided by club president Wayne Ferguson and supported by a membership that included many of the heaviest names in the sport, the 2015 M&EKC show, held on October 1 in Somerset, New Jersey, became one of the largest one-day dog shows ever held in America.

There was an entry of 4,152 dogs making 4,667 entries, more than most of the 'old' shows and nearly as big as the record (4,456 dogs in 1939), with many of the exhibitors adding a glamorous touch by dressing in period costume. Mrs Dodge would have been proud!

Best in show was to have been judged by Jane Forsyth, the great ex-handler who in recent decades had become equally well known as a judge. With her husband, Bob, she was one of the few married couples to have both won BIS at Westminster. Bob, in fact, judged BIS at the 2010 M&EKC show.

Sadly, Jane died before the show. Her place as BIS judge was taken by Dorothy Collier, widow of the late Westminster KC president, Chet Collier, and a successful judge and past handler in her own right. Many of us will have a hard time waiting until 2020 for another Morris & Essex Kennel Club show, but judging by this year's

version it will be worth the wait!

Morris & Essex's record entry was particularly impressive in that the show was held on a Thursday. As the famous Montgomery Country Terrier classic was held in the same area the same weekend, this no doubt helped the entry totals: Montgomery County had over 1,600 terriers entered, of whom just over 1,200 were also entered at M&EKC. ∎

Winning the herding group at Westminster for the second time, judge Klaus Anselm, was the US' number two dog of 2014, the Old English Sheepdog Gr Ch Bugaboo's Picture Perfect, owned by Ron Scott, Debbie Burke and Colton and Heather Johnson and handled by Colton Johnson. Steward was William Jackson.

Ken Murray gave the sporting group at Westminster to the English Springer Spaniel Gr Ch Wynmoor Sweetgrass White Diamonds, owned by Dr Erin and Billie Kerfoot and Dr Alison Smith and handled by Janice Hayes. Dr Bernard McGivern stewarded.

Canadian judge Shirley Limoges chose the Standard Poodle Gr Ch Dawin Hearts On Fire, owned by Linda Campbell from Canada and handled by Sarah Perchic, to win the non-sporting group at Westminster. William Roberts III was the steward.

Top Dog in the US for 2014, the Canadian-born Portuguese Water Dog Gr Ch Claircreek Impression De Matisse, owned by Milan Lint, Peggy Helming and Donna Gottdenker, was handled by Michael Scott to win his third Westminster group, judge Theresa Hundt. Steward was Barclay Douglas.

The national specialties for many breeds attract several hundred dogs. The Golden Retriever Club of America specialty in late 2014 had 884 dogs entered. BOB was judged by Carol Anne Gilbert from the UK, shown with her winner, nine-year-old veteran Gr Ch Goodtimes Johnny Bee Good, owned by Paula Petelle and Jane Alston-Myers.

Monte Cristo

Our appreciation to Breed judge Mr William McFadden and Group judge Mr Clay Coady

The greatest success is to live the life of your dreams

MBIS MBISS AM GCH Hampton Court's Monte Cristo

Best In Show Montgomery County Terrier 2015

Multiple All-Breed Best In Show Winner

Number One Wire Fox In America

A Top-Ranking Terrier

Breeder-Owner Victor Malzoni Jr
Presented by Leonardo Garcini

CANADA

Canadians dominate at Westminster

Report by: **Mike Macbeth**

Canada's most significant news in 2015 did not occur on home soil but on a cold February day in New York City.

Proving again our strength as a country of top breeders, three of the seven group winners at Westminster, including the best in show winner, were born and bred in Canada, and a fourth had strong Canadian ties, as the group-winning Shih Tzu Gr Ch Hallmark Jolei Rocket Power was bred and co-owned by his handler, ex-pat Luke Ehricht.

The charismatic 15 inch Beagle Ch Tashtins Lookin For Trouble had little trouble winning America's most prestigious show. Bred by Canada's Lori Crandlemire and owned by Lori and Kaitlyn Crandlemire and American Eddie Dziuk, 'Miss P' was piloted by the well-known Canadian handler William Alexander.

The working group was once again won by America's Top Dog all breeds in 2014, Gr Ch Claircreek Impression De Matisse. As reported last year, this outstanding Portuugese Water Dog became only the fifth dog to be awarded more than 200 BIS in the US. Bred and co-owned by Donna Gottdenker, Matisse's dam is the maternal grand-dam of Canada's current number two all breeds, also co-bred and co-owned by Donna.

Westminster's non-sporting group winner, the Standard Poodle bitch Gr Ch Dawin Hearts On Fire, is bred and owned by Linda Campbell of Ontario. After winning BIS at 2014's Poodle Club of America national specialty and becoming number three all breeds in the US, she has returned to Canada for maternal duties. She is a half-sister to Ch Dawin In Hot Pursuit who is currently number three all breeds in Canada.

The current race for Canada's Top Dog in 2015 is led by a breeder/owner/handled Giant Schnauzer. This is the first time in five years that a breeder/owner is successfully challenging the professional handlers for top spot. In fact, three of the top six dogs are owner-handled.

Challenging seems to be the appropriate word when it comes to all aspects of Canada's purebred community. Registrations at the Canadian Kennel Club have declined about five per cent to 47,619, which of course means there are fewer dogs to compete in the shows. Yet entries in all CKC event programmes are up

Canada's current Top Dog, and likely far enough ahead to maintain her position, is the Giant Schnauzer Can/Am Gr Ch Lowdown Remys Girl v Aerdenhout, owned by Linda Low and her breeders Lisa Hawes and Janine Starink, and handled by Janine who first became prominent as a breeder with her grandsire Ch/Am Ch Aerdenhout's Make It So. To date in 2015 'Abbey' has won 53 groups and 34 BIS including two at Canada's largest show, the Alberta KC.

Abbey won BIS for thae second time at the Giant Schnauzer National in the US where she was also awarded two groups, a BIS and RBIS.

slightly (one to four per cent), possibly due to the fact that more and more clubs are receiving permission to hold two limited entry shows per day.

This strategy provides more money to the CKC in recording fees, but both exhibitors and clubs are complaining that there ar too many dog shows. With an entry fee between $25 and $30 per

Currently comfortably in second spot is Gr Ch Claircreek Lusitano Oceano Atlantico, a Portuguese Water Dog owned by Mark Ulrich and his co-breeder Donna Gottdenker. His dam is half-sister to the US' Top Dog of 2014, Matisse, also bred by Donna. Just as Matisse holds the PWD record for BIS in the US (238), 'Oceano' owns the Canadian Porty record for BIS. To date he has 32 of which 27 have been awarded in 2015. This year he has amassed 78 groups.

Currently number three Linda Campbell's Ch Dawin In Hot Pursuit comes from a long line of outstanding Dawin Standard Poodles, and is a half brother to Hearts On Fire, non-sporting group winner at Westminster and number three all breeds in the US in 2014. That year, when Hearts On Fire won the Poodle Club of America national, 'Daniel' was best puppy in variety. His mother Ch Dawin Hot N Spicy was select bitch at PCA in 2012. Daniel has already won 22 BIS and 85 groups.

The race between the fourth, fifth and sixth top dogs is so tight that a single best in show could change the standings At the time of writing, the Papillon Gr Ch Marron's Jimmy Choo holds the fourth spot. 'Jimmy' is bred and owned by Mary Ronald and Lori Chrusciel. Mary and her husband Earle owned 1991's Top Dog in Canada, Ch/Am Ch Telcontars Tahitie Sweetie, who with 52 BIS in a single year broke the breed record. Like many dog people in recent years, the Ronalds have downsized to Papillons.

Jimmy's show record in 2015 includes 12 BIS and 57 groups.

ast year's top herding dog and number five all breeds is currently in the same osition. Owned in 2014 by co-breeder Joe Beccia, the German Shepherd Am/Can Gr Ch Signature's Harry Nile v Kridler was bought by his handler Emily Burdon and er partner Raul Olvera at the beginning of 2015. After winning two BIS in his first five hows this year, Emily learned that 'Harry' was inching toward the Canadian record for BIS, giving her the incentive to continue. The record of 27 BIS was held by another German Shepherd handler from the same small town of Saint Lazare, Quebec.

Harry broke the record in May. As Emily is usually a professional handler, and Harry s the first dog she has actually owned, it was personally an exciting accomplishment. o date he has 35 BIS, 16 awarded in 2015. The exhilaration of Harry's success was dampened in August by the sudden death of Emily's mother, who as an admirer of German Shepherds had introduced Emily to the breed. He is also a top ten GSD in the US in very limited showing.

PURINA.

PHOTO: DOGS IN DESIGN

Just behind the owner-handled German Shepherd is an owner-handled Irish Setter, Am Ch/Can Gr Ch Ex Eltin's Unequivocal Contender PCD RN. 'Quinn' was bred by Manette Jones, a respected trialing competitor who felt Irish Setters can be successful in both the field and the show ring. She offered Pauline Taylor the opportunity to own him, and soon he became a top winning puppy with six BPIS. Now he has won two national specialty BIS and finished in the US in two weekends, taking winners dog at the Irish Setter Club of America national. In Canada he has 14 BIS, including twice at shows where he also won in obedience or rally.

how, an exhibitor could spend $180 on one weekend alone.

The smaller clubs in distant locations are particularly vulnerable. In August, a club in northern Ontario, a four or five-hour drive for most exhibitors, held two all-breed shows a day during the week, on a Tuesday, Wednesday and Thursday. At the sixth show, on Thursday afternoon, the total entry was 58 dogs, with only one dog, a Labrador Retriever, entered in the sporting group, usually any show's largest group. The Tuesday show saw 63 dogs, with three terriers entered. Yet two days before, albeit in a more advantageous location, another show's entry was 326.

But the increase in the number of shows in the first seven months of 2015 produced an increase of conformation entries of 30,000, against 77,000 over the same period in 2014. Only trials and tests are down slightly. The one positive exception is agility which is up about 33 per cent over the same period last year.

To further support the positive trend in performance events, the CKC will be introducing a 'chase ability program' in March 2016. This new event is somewhat modelled after lure coursing with some significant differences; dogs runs on their own as a single, whereas in lure they run in threes and the course is shorter.

The event will provide all purebred and mixed breed dogs a chance to earn a title in a field event. A CKC club approved to hold lure coursing trials will be automatically approved to hold chase ability events.

Close to a million dollars has been reserved to fund a multifaceted 'e-business' plan, a major component of which is an initiative to replace the CKC's outdated 30-year-old computer system. Consultations with members, staff and directors will identify the priorities before selecting and designing a system. These will include faster turnaround for registration transactions and results; more online and self-service options for members; less cumbersome rules and regulations and better access to timely and relevant information. This part of the plan is expected to launch early in 2017.

Elections at the end of 2014 saw a new board of directors for the CKC. 'New' is the appropriate word, as more than half of the 12 member board are directors for the first time. It was somewhat discouraging that five of the 12 directors were re-elected unopposed, indicating that there is a certain amount of apathy across the country. The natural enthusiasm of the novice is balanced by the four returning members from the 2011-2014 board, plus another from a previous board, providing consistency and experience.

The new chairman, elected by the board, is Robert Rowbotham who served on the previous board. He believes the balance of old

and new is positive as 'the new board members bring to the table varied skillsets that are a plus for this organisation'.

One can hope that negotiating is one of these skills. Earlier this year a letter from the Asian section of the Fédération Cynologique Internationale was sent to US judges, threatening them with blacklisting should they judge a non-FCI show in Asia (particularly in China where the FCI and US accredited clubs are in fierce competition).

Inexplicably, the same letter was also sent to Canadian judges, despite the fact that Canada is clearly not the United States of America nor a member of the FCI, and thus governed by neither.

Until a meeting between the AKC, the FCI and the CKC is held, Canadian judges appear to be innocently caught up in the middle of this muddle, with no resolution in sight. ∎

The Standard Poodle Am/Can Gr Ch Crystalton Suspence became Canada's Top Dog of 2014 with more than 13,000 points, almost double his nearest rival. 'Graydon' won 44 BIS (50 in all) and 113 groups, By Canada's number two of 2010, Ch/Am Ch Classique Scaramouche, he is owned by Jerry Harvey and co-breeder Carol Graham and handled by Terry Bernier.

He came out of retirement temporarily to win Canada's largest dog show, the Purina National. Immediately after, he was retired from all Canadian shows.

NORWAY

A stormy year for Norwegian dogdom

Report by: **Espen Engh**

The Pembroke Corgi Ch Siggen's Queen Of Spades, bred and owned in Norway by Rita and Leif Herman Wilberg, won her UK title in 2015. This natural bobtail won her first UK CC with BOB at Crufts after having won the group at Stockholm international. She comes from a litter of five champions and traces back through many generations of the Siggens breeding to their foundation bitch imported from the UK in 1968.

PHOTO LISA CROFT-ELLIOTT

For the third time in eight years a Kerry Blue Terrier owned by Helge Kvivesen is Norway's Dog of the Year. The 2015 winner, the homebred Ch Shyloch Qosmos is a BIS winner in three countries and has been unbeaten in the terrier groups at Norwegian Kennel Club shows during the year. He is a son of Dog of the Year 2012 Ch Shyloch Navagator to Edrus and a great-grandson of the 2007 winner Ch Link To Shyloch Iz Goluboi Legendy.

2015 has been a memorable and stormy year for the Norwegian dog sport for two main reasons; for the first time ever Norway organised a major FCI title show, the European Winner Show. And in the months leading up to the event, the Norwegian Kennel Club (NKK) made worldwide headlines by strongly opposing the Fédération Cynologique Internationale's decision to arrange the 2019 World Show in Shanghai, China.

Norway is unquestionably a country of dog lovers. Purebred dogs have been very popular for many decades. Compared to our human population of merely five million people, the almost 100,000 memberships of the clubs constituting the NKK are disproportionally many compared to most other countries, as are entries of about 6,000 dogs at our annual Oslo international winter show.

After some 80 years as full members of the FCI, it was perhaps high time that Norway staged a major FCI show. Four years after winning the vote in the FCI European section to arrange the event in Lillestrøm just outside Oslo, the show went ahead on September 4 to 6.

With an entry of almost 12,000 dogs at the main event and another almost 6,000 at specialties arranged the same weekend, this was by far the largest dog show weekend ever in Norway. Even more dogs had been anticipated and sadly some judges were cancelled, never a popular decision with the exhibitors, and especially not for an important show like this.

Unusually for an FCI title show, but as usual for Norway, there were a number of British judges and even more for the specialties. The very strong ties between the dogdom in Norway and the UK are obvious in most breeds, including Continental breeds such as Great Danes and Boxers.

The top breed entry was Flat-coated Retrievers with 176, then

Staffordshire Bull Terriers with 176, Bernese Mountain Dogs with 175, 144 each of French Bulldogs and Labrador Retrievers, 140 Golden Retrievers and 135 Whippets. A remarkable 150 Griffons were entered under British breed specialist David Guy, but under FCI rules this breed is divided into three varieties judged separately.

Naturally the largest number of entries came from Norway itself with 5,114 dogs, then our closest neighbour Sweden had 2,123 dogs entered followed by Russia with 1,358 and Finland with 1,062.

In all there were dogs from 52 countries entered, including such unlikely and far-away countries as Laos, United Arab Emirates and even Rwanda! There were 25 dogs from the UK and 30 from the US.

For this show only, dogs who had been legally cropped and

The Pyrenean Sheepdog Ch Angeyja's Aela is among the top winning dogs in Norway for 2015. A consistent winner at both breed club and all-breed shows, she is a daughter of two World Winners, owned and bred by Per Tore Romstad and Gro Mathiesen.

ocked in their own countries were allowed to be shown, as were ogs of banned breeds such as American Staffordshire Terriers, ogo Argentinos, Fila Brasileiros and Tosas. For these breeds his was not only a chance to win the coveted European Winner tles, but their one and only opportunity to become Norwegian hampions. However the entries in these breeds were rather isappointing.

Without critiques, the judging was much quicker than usual and nore dogs could be judged in each ring and under each judge. ven if this was necessary at a show of this magnitude to keep the osts and space requirements down, the no-critique system left a lot f exhibitors totally empty handed, and there are no plans to do way with the individual critiques at other championship shows.

The show provided a unique opportunity to present the even FCI recognised Norwegian breeds to the world. Certainly he internationally best known of our national breeds are the Norwegian Elkhound (grey), followed by the Norwegian Buhund. Much less known, but steadily growing in popularity, is the Norwegian Black Elkhound, more similar to the Buhund for looks, ut sharing the function as a moose hunter with its better known rey cousin.

The unique puffin hunter, the Norwegian Lundehund, has ecently spread out to other countries. The breed is however still onsidered an endangered breed in Norway along with our three ery attractive scenthound breeds, the Dunker, Haldenhound and Iygenhound.

Not being there to enjoy the show, I am unable to report in detail rom the show itself. However, Norway's longest active all-rounder udge Rodi Hübenthal of the Picador Dobermanns, Briards and Pinschers judged best in show. The winners from an exceptionally nternational line-up are pictured separately.

The show unfortunately had its own version of 'Tailgate' as the roup-winning Shih Tzu from Thailand was photographed and ilmed when lifted onto the table by the leash around his neck and by his tail. This caused an outcry on social media and complaints vere made, resulting in the handler being banned from showing he dog in BIS, but the dog being allowed to compete with another andler.

The breed club also reported both the breed and group judge for not having intervened, but both were later acquitted, claiming that hey had not witnessed the dog being carried onto the table.

Another unfortunate incident was that the best in show trophies vere stolen on the final day. It is difficult to imagine how something ike this could happen, and perhaps especially in a country with

PHOTO PAULINE OLIVER

During 2015 Ch Montserrat Caballe, handled by breeder Åge Gjetnes, became only the second Norwegian-owned and bred dog to win the group at Crufts. Co-owned by Åge with Elsa Storesund, the Miniature Poodle won her UK title undefeated.

one of the lowest crime rates in the Western world. What could the motive possibly be? I would imagine that the market for stolen and never awarded dog show trophies must be rather limited!

In November 2014 the NKK AGM voted to ask the board to consider the implications of staying in or leaving the FCI and to present an evaluation and possible recommendations to the 2015 AGM.

The voting majority in the AGM consists of hunting enthusiasts whose interest in and dependence on the FCI is not obvious, to say the least.

The numerically strong hunting clubs have for several years protested against the FCI bestowing the international champion title, CIE, on dogs that have not proven their worth in the field, and this has catalysed their strong opposition to the FCI.

When the FCI general assembly in early June 2015 voted to have the 2019 World Show in Shanghai, China, Norway voted for another candidate, but did nothing at that time to express any opposition to the Chinese candidateship.

When shortly thereafter, social media strongly focused on the Chinese Yulin festival where dogs are severely mistreated before being slaughtered for consumption, the decision to award the World Show to China met with a storm of protests from Norwegian dog people and general animal lovers alike.

Animal welfare already being one of the main priorities of the NKK, the board and the administration wrote a letter to the FCI expressing their disgust and asked FCI to take measures against the festival.

A few days later, the NKK wrote again to the FCI asking for the 2019 World Show to be relocated, questioning measures to improve animal welfare from the China Kennel Union (CKU) and the FCI, and at the same time urging Norwegian judges and exhibitors not to take part in the Shanghai World Show.

The NKK two days afterwards received a reply from the FCI Asia Pacific Section where the section confirmed that a letter has been sent to the governor of the Yulin province to express condemnation of the animal abuse. The section also expressed dissatisfaction with the reaction from the NKK.

The NKK wrote back to the FCI to propose that the FCI should focus more strongly on animal welfare in general, including when allocating the World and section shows. It also repeated the request for the 2019 World Show to be relocated.

On July 2, the NKK received a letter from an FCI attorney where the FCI threatened the NKK with sanctions and possible suspension ▶

PHOTO ROGER SJØLSTAD

The BIS-winning Bracco Italiano Ch Olympos La Mia Maschera A Carnevale, bred by Gitte and John Finnich Pedersen in Denmark, and owned by Irene Krogstad and Eirik Muan, is among Norway's top winning dogs of all breeds in 2015.

PHOTO PER UNDÉN

The Akita Int Ch Estava Rain Only Style Remains is one of several top winners owned and bred over the years by Friedrich Birkmar. He was BOB at the World Show in Milan and is an international championship show BIS winner in Norway and Italy and among the Top Dogs all breeds in Norway for 2015.

Ch Soletrader Trick Or Treat, a Petit Basset Griffon Vendéen bred in the UK by Gavin and Sara Robertson and exported to Anders Tunold-Hanssen after obtaining her UK title, is the top winning PBGV for four years running and among Norway's Top Ten dogs of all breeds in 2015.

The Norwegian-owned and bred Greyhound bitch Ch Jet's Moonlight Serenade won BIS at Windsor and is the top Greyhound in the UK for 2015. She was bred by Espen Engh and the late Kari Engh and owned by the former with Åge Gjetnes.

if the NKK did not go back on its recommendations to judges and exhibitors to stay away from the Shanghai show. The NKK board decided to stick to their guns and informed the FCI about this five days later.

A week later, the NKK sent another letter to the FCI and CKU protesting against gold VIP cards given by the CKU to FCI delegates. NKK returned the cards and proposed that the large amount of money that is intended to be spent on treating the FCI delegates could be much better used promoting animal welfare in China.

The FCI then called for a meeting in Brussels with the NKK, the CKU, the FCI Asian Section and the FCI board in Brussels to try to reach an agreement in the matter. The NKK refused to attend on the grounds that the board had been given a mandate to promote animal welfare and that they felt unjustifiably threatened by the board of the FCI.

The NKK suggested that an extraordinary general assembly of the FCI should be called to put animal welfare firmly on the agenda and to have a new election for the 2019 World Show venue. It also complained to the FCI that FCI board members had made statements on social media that were deemed unacceptable, including calling for blacklisting of judges. The meeting in Brussels was conducted, but without representation from Norway.

On August 3 the FCI general committee sent a letter to the NKK concluding that the club's conduct had been in breach of FCI's statutes and standing orders and giving NKK three options: to remain members of the FCI by revoking the recommendation not to attend the World Show, to leave the organisation voluntarily or by not replying by October 1 to risk being sanctioned by the FCI.

By the time of writing, this letter has not been retracted by the FCI, so presumably the three options may still stand.

On August 19, the Swedish Kennel Club (SKK) made a statement to strongly support the NKK. The SKK found the threats by the FCI to the NKK for voicing an opinion unacceptable, and went even further than the NKK by calling the VIP cards corruption, by deciding not to apply for FCI international shows and initiating a process by which Sweden may possibly leave the FCI through negotiations.

The Finnish Kennel Club followed on August 27 by supporting the NKK's rights to voice their opinion and stating that the FCI and the World Shows have taken a serious blow. Both countries recommended their judges and exhibitors not to attend the Shanghai World Show, but with a somewhat different wording from Norway.

The Nordic Kennel Union (NKU) wrote to the FCI to recommend that the FCI statutes and standing orders are revised in order to make animal welfare and the fight against animal cruelty a significant priority, to make the organization more transparent and to look into a revised voting model. Later the NKU also wrote to the FCI to ask for the threats of sanctions to the NKK to be recalled.

In conjunction with the European Show in Oslo, the FCI European section meeting took place as usual. On the agenda was trying to sort out the China row, and even FCI president Rafael de Santiago attended the meeting.

In short, the NKK proposed that funds within the FCI should be earmarked for health and welfare initiatives, that amendments to the FCI standing orders and statues should be made to reflect these priorities including a minimum level of dog welfare in the statutes of the FCI and for countries hosting the FCI title shows.

From all accounts the meeting was successful and it is hoped that the difficult situation can be resolved without Norway being expelled from the FCI while animal welfare may be found firmly placed on the FCI's near future agenda. ■

PHOTO ROGER SJØLSTAD

Dog of the Year in Norway 2014 was the Pug Ch Analog Ci Nobody's Business, owned and usually handled by Bjørn Erling Løken and co-owned with Christine Sonberg. Although a frequent group winner at international championship shows, the Pug very unusually won the Top Dog of the year award without winning a single international championship show BIS.

THE EUROPEAN SHOW

King rules Europe – again

photos by:
**Paula Heikkinen-Lehkonen
and Harri Lehkonen**

OSLO 2015, Sept. 4-6

Reserve BIS was the 16-month-old Samoyed Cabaka's Happy Go Lucky, from Italy, who also won best junior of his day and was part of his Danish breeder's winning breeder's group. Group judge was Marianne Holmli.

For the second year running the Wire Fox Terrier Ch Kingarthur van Foliny Home, and his Welsh handler Warren Bradley won the Fédération Cynologique Internationale European Winner Show, this time held near Oslo in Norway. Judge was Rodi Hübenthal. Representing the sponsors are Jose Luis Ibanez from Eukanuba and Christian Geelmuylden of Agria Pet Insurance. 'King' is owned by Tony de Munter and Dieny Uiterwijk from Belgium and Victor Malzoni from Brazil.

BIS4 was the Afghan Hound from Russia Ch Amal Salang Coeur D'Coeurs, with group judge Göran Bodegård.

Group winner under Barbara Müller: the Australian Shepherd from Russia, Olga Serova's Seventy Seven Rurikovichi My.

BIS3 was the Petit Basset Griffon Vendéen from the Netherlands Caramel Apple van Tum Tum's Vriendjes, whose son was a UK BIS winner in 2015.

Group winner: the Shih Tzu from Thailand, Wanida Busakornnunt's Smile-Absolute's First Down Ten To. After a 'tailgate' controversy, the Norwegian Kennel Club ordered that he should have a different handler for the final judging.

Group winner under Rafael Malo Alcrudo: the Russian Black Terrier from Russia, Ekaterina Zaitseva's Fine Lady S Zolotogo Grada.

Group winner under Sigurd Wilberg: the Miniature Wire Dachshund from Italy, Valentina Barcella's Queenslord Skinny Love.

Group winner under Claudio di Giuliani: the Weimaraner from Belgium, Edwin Lenaerts, Linda van der Sichel and Tonie Finch's Doc N' Camelot's Heaven Can Wait.

Group winner under Annika Ulltveit-Moe: the UK-bred Flat-coated Retriever who won RBIS at Crufts, Anette Dyrén's Castlerock Simply Magic, from Sweden.

SWEDEN

Report
Dan Ericsson

Winds of change

Anne Reider won the award for Top Breeder 2014 with he Shellrick Shetland Sheepdogs. Her team of almost identic Shelties, often presented on loose leads by a single handler, has been a wonderful sight in our show rings.

The Stockholm show in December 2014 drew an excellent entry of quality dogs as usual and proved to be an exciting finale for the competitions for Top Dog and top breeder, always a hugely popular and much sought-after award in Sweden.

Carl-Gunnar Stafberg of Bombax Border Terrier fame judged best in show and had a splendid line-up. He has been involved in dogs all his life and has been a championship judge for a long time – many felt that his appointment here was long overdue. Exactly 50 years ago, the Border Terrier Ch Bombax Ericus Rex, bred by him, won BIS at the same show, the only Border ever to win BIS here and the judge on the day was breed exper George Leatt.

Carl-Gunnar's final choice was the black Miniature Poodle Ch Kudos Firework, bred and presented by Mikael Nilsson, owned by him with Fredrik Nilsson. This victory also secured his position as Top Dog all breeds in 2014. On the right is group judge Valerio Nataletti.

PHOTO LILLEMOR BOOS

The past year has in many ways been one of many changes for the dog fraternity.

New rules and views on breeding and stricter rules for exporting (yes!) young puppies from a rabies-free country have been implemented and also loud views have been expressed by many of our veterinary surgeons on health in the short-faced breeds, leading to a major upset among senior breeders.

More than 70 vets have signed a petition demanding various health checks and even a total ban for some breeds. The Swedish Kennel Club (SKK) has been adamant in its support for the breeds concerned and will now hold a seminar in February in an attempt to iron out misunderstandings. Breeders, club officials, judges and vets will participate – an interesting project and certainly a long-awaited opportunity for all to discuss the breeds in question.

At the SKK annual (well, not annual any more as it is held every second year) meeting in October there were several changes on the General Committee. Nil-Erik Åhmanson had decided to stand down as chairman and did not wish to be re-elected onto the committee. He had been chairman of the club for over two decades and has steered the club competently; he will be much missed.

Over the years, he has also been involved in the FCI on various posts, more recently as auditor, but he relinquished his post there in 2014 and has since been an outspoken critic of many issues involving the FCI.

Senior vet Pekka Ohlsson was unanimously elected new chairman of the club and he has also been a committee member for several years. Pekka is well known primarily in his role as a vet to many people within the Swedish dog world, but he also has an involvement in the insurance company Agria which has been generous in its support to the SKK.

It will be interesting to see in what direction he and the new committee decide to steer the club which is very active within so many fields. The constant debate on soundness will undoubtedly continue in full force, but there are also many other issues that will be challenging for the club.

Entries at shows has remained fairly stable, also interest in various trials and tests, many of which are now made compulsory for different breeds before any dog or bitch can be bred from. Some of these tests are indeed necessary and this applies to many of our strict health tests, but how much testing is reasonable?

There seem to be more and more companies advertising tests, often DNA-testing, for ailments unknown to many breeders of standing and one sometimes wonders where this will all end.

The SKK has in fact issued a statement advocating restriction suggesting that health testing should in fact only be done when

PHOTO LILLEMOR BÖÖS

...ohan Andersson's Alistair's Bearded Collies have had a good year winning BIS with ...everal homebred dogs. This is Ch Alistair's Rock The Boat, who won at Tvååker. In the ...K Alistairs Ready Made for Malarkey gained his title at Midland Counties.

PHOTO LILLEMOR BÖÖS

Kenneth Edh (right) judging BIS in Eskilstuna in August 2014 putting up Charlotte Sandell's Standard Poodle Ch Da Maya Huffish Copyright Woman, who in 2015 was BIS at Bournemouth and Welsh Kennel Club on visits to the UK, and is currently number four all breeds in Sweden. This was one of Kenneth's last appointments and certainly his last time judging BIS in Sweden.

© Per Undén

PHOTO PER UNDÉN

Currently leading the top dog rankings in Sweden is the Yorkshire Terrier Ch Debonaire's Hold Me Now, owned by Bernice Undén and handled by Sergio Amien from Spain. 'Mike' started his show career and eight months by winning best puppy at the Swedish Yorkie specialty. He has won 20 BIS, four of them at specialties, in several countries. He was fourth in the group at the World Show in 2014 and is the only dog ever to win three consecutive BIS at MyDog, one of the biggest shows in Sweden. He was BOB at Crufts 2015 and will represent Sweden at the Eukanuba World Challenge. Judge here is Swedish ex-pat Liz Cartledge from the UK.

PHOTO ALAN WALKER

Runner-up in the Top Dog table at the time of writing is Anette Dyren's Flat-coated Retriever Castlerock Simply Magic, bred in the UK but by a dog bred by Anette. Among his international successes are RBIS at Crufts and the group at the European Winner Show.

PHOTO ALAN WALKER

Number three in the Top Dog list at the last count was Jessika Junehall Lindberg's Leonberger Ch Namulaan Bling Smack Chap. He was group 2 at Crufts 2015 which was remarkably successful for Swedish dogs.

...here is a clinical problem – sound views indeed and well worth ...emembering by those advocating more and more tests.

Main ring commentator par excellence for 29 years at ...tockholm show, Kenneth Edh, was not there in 2014 as he ...ad suffered a fall, later resulting in a major stroke. He had ...nnounced that he was going to do the commentary for the last ...ime as it would make a nice even number, but sadly this was not ...o be and he was much missed.

We all knew he was seriously ill, but the news was that he was ...aking good recovery, so it came as a shock when he died later in December 2014. He was 66 years old. He was a close friend whom I miss tremendously. He was a popular and knowledgeable judge worldwide. His knowledge of dogs, charm and style, ability to deal with people and his gentle manners with the dogs made him one of the world's much appreciated judges.

His contribution as a mentor to many of our newer judges has also been of particular value and over the years he has been involved in many clubs, always making a positive contribution. The theme for the 2015 Stockholm show will be a tribute to Kenneth, and I am sure that he would have appreciated that. ∎

An 'export' Britain can be proud of

Andrew Brace is Face to Face with Paul Stanton

Now one of Scandinavia's most popular all-breed judges, Paul Stanton is of course British and was born in Whitley, a small village in the Wiltshire countryside.

Paul wasn't born into a traditional doggy family so I was keen to discover where his love of dogs came from.

He says: "I really have no idea where my passion for dogs comes from as my mother and maternal grandparents always had cats and my father loved horses… he was in the Royal Wiltshire Yeomanry during the second world war.

"I have always loved all animals and my parents told me stories of when I was small and had to be kept on a harness as I wanted to pet every dog I met! One time while at a petrol station I climbed out of the car and my worried parents found me cuddling the German Shepherd guard dog!

"While I was very young and still in a pram, our landlord's two Staffordshire Bull Terriers would creep through the hole in the hedge and come and play with me and I remember my mother telling me that Zola would jump up into my pram and guard me so that she could nip around to my grandparents who lived just two houses up the road to borrow or leave something.

"When Zola had a litter of pups with Zag she brought the whole litter through the fence to see us so I suppose I was indoctrinated with dogs without knowing it.

"When I was about five or six years old

Paul Stanton handled Ch Dokham Cavarodossi of Tintavon to make breed history as the first UK championship show best in show-winning Tibetan Terrier, taking this award twice in 1974. Judge here is L C 'Jimmy' James. Paul has now lived in Sweden for many years and is today a world-travelled all-round judge.

the landlords, Mervin and Iris Pocock, had bought a German Shepherd as a guard dog and I can vaguely remember him as he was so kind and gentle and I could ride on his back. His name was Prince.

"My parents were not religious and

actually had a civil wedding but I was very religious for some reason, went to Sunday school, evening Bible classes and I had a great love for Jesus.

"But when I was 14 years old I had what was probably the greatest crisis of my life a

Paul receiving a diploma at the local flower show for a wildflower arrangement.

Paul's interest in grooming started young…

then understood that I was homosexual and at that time (1964) no one talked about 'that' and I really thought I was 'the only gay in the village'! This was such a crisis that I thought irrationally, or maybe it was rational, that 'there is no God because if there was why would he punish me – I was a good boy and loved Jesus' – so from that moment at morning prayers in school I became a non-believer as I do not think I had heard the word atheist then.

"It sounds drastic now but if I had not come into contact with dogs I would probably have taken my life but it was dogs that gave me something to live for. And so my school work suffered as I had no interest in anything but dogs which on looking back was a big mistake as I should have learnt a trade and I think, knowing what I do now, I should have continued my parents' great interest in flowers and vegetables as both my parents were successful at all the local flower shows.

Paul's first pedigree dog was the Shetland Sheepdog Tint of Wytchfields, seen with his parents around 1967. He lived to 17 years.

"It was dogs that gave me something to live for"

Even I showed in the children's classes making miniature gardens or wild flower arrangements, so market gardening or landscape gardening would have been an ideal occupation."

Paul left school at 16 after taking some CSE exams and was determined to work with dogs. He was actually offered a job with the recently deceased Jane Kamp, of Grayarlin kennels and one of the US' most successful professional handlers, before he became Mrs Forsyth, but his parents absolutely refused to let their 16-year-old only child go to the US as this 'thing with dogs was a passing phase'!

But Paul would not be deterred and started looking in the dog papers for a job where he could live 'as family' as he really did not like the idea of being self-sufficient and living in a caravan.

His parents drove him to Wingham in Kent for an interview with Anne Matthews of the Hardacre kennels and to his great joy (and his parents' distress) he was given the job on a one-month trial but actually stayed with Anne for two years. Paul recalls: "I will be forever grateful to Anne who not only taught me so much but opened up a whole new world to me."

In 1963 Paul started going to the local kennels of Mr and Mrs Stevens who had boarding kennels and bred Cockers and Shetland Sheepdogs. He would walk some of their dogs at weekends and he started to bring them home for a few hours and even go to some local shows with them.

The first dog Paul ever handled was a lemon roan Cocker bitch named Celandine but it was the Shetland Sheepdogs he liked best and in 1964 he was offered one of their old stud dogs to whom he had become attached.

Paul continues: "His name was Tint of Wytchfields and he was born in 1959, a rather shy dog with the most beautiful rich autumn colours in his coat. Of course my father said 'no dogs here' and only after a big fight did my parents agree, thanks to Mum of course, that I could have Tint. As you hear he is the first part of my kennel name and the other part is the river Avon as the Bristol Avon runs through Melksham so I have the affix Tintavon, pronounced Tint Avon and not Tinta von!

"While I was working for Anne Matthews

Tintavon Nyima of Showa, born 1969, Paul's first Lhasa Apso.

Paul's first Lhasa Apso champions UK Ch Cheska Gregor and UK Ch Wicherty Thea of Tintavon with Int/Nord Ch Tintavon Burundai (one CC) owned by Marina Reuterswärd, Sweden.

UK Ch Tintavon Goldameir, the first champion bred by Paul and owned by Jim Bainbridge (Botolph).

Int/Nordi Ch Tintavon Sa-Skya, Sweden's third Top Dog in 1975, owned by Marina Reuterswärd and seen with handler Christel Axell.

UK/Int/Nord Ch Tintavon Tsai-Lun, Paul's foundation bitch in Sweden.

who had mainly Basset Hounds at the time and six Labradors (two of each colour) which was her first breed, Anne had started to develop a deep interest in Tibetan Apsos (as they were then named) and Tibetan Terriers and this was the first time I had seen these breeds or even heard of them… there were no photos of Apsos in the *Observer's Book of Dogs* at that time.

"I had two Sheltie males with me while at Hardacre, a sable from Loughrigg and a tricolour from Francehill, but every night I also took the ugliest little grey Apso bitch with me to bed. Her name was Taschi and she charmed me completely. I became enamoured with these very intelligent but stubborn little dogs from Tibet and it must have been destiny that I changed from Shelties to Apsos.

"However there are two reasons for this and one was that the famous Sheltie breeders at that time had no interest in a young man with so many questions while the Apso breeders and enthusiasts thought it was wonderful that a young man was interested in 'their beloved breed' and helped and supported me immensely.

Remember that at that time the Apso breeders were mainly titled or at least higher middle class yet they welcomed the young working class boy with open arms and hearts.

"The second reason was the temperament of these little Tibetan dogs; they annoyed me by not doing what I wanted unless it suited them, you could not bribe them for their love but you had to earn it.

"I remember the evenings when Mrs M as we called her, Jackie Vroome (now Tidmarsh who became famous for her Tambora Beardies) and myself while watching TV would brush and comb the Apsos on our laps while chasing and killing fleas!

"Anne took Jackie to shows for the herding and utility days which often were the same day, then would take me for the hound days and I think this (and looking after around 60 Bassets) cemented the great love I have for that breed.

"Anne also kept ten goats for the milk for the pups, while her son Nicholas was about one year old, so our days were busy and long but without this opportunity I would never be where I am today."

When Paul left Hardacre he went back to his parents and worked as a clerk for the Avon Rubber Company where his father also worked and by this time he knew he wanted an Apso but the breed wa still rather rare, only having had CCs first awarded in 1965.

He could find no pups for sale but Irene Plumstead of Showa fame entrusted him with a bitch on breeding terms. Paul remembers her vividly: "Her name was Tintavon Nyima of Showa, a very pretty white and black who had an excellent front assembly, great body and a very pret head but like many of her time her mouth was not her fortune (to be truthful she was lacking quite a few incisors) but her adorable temperament made up for all he faults.

"A daughter went back to Irene but she also did not develop all her adult teeth either so I bought her back and mated he

Ch Dokham Cavaradossi of Tintavon was a natural showman for Paul, seen in his then trademark white coat.

The legendary littermates as youngsters, Cavarodossi with Paul and Ch Dokham La Calisto with Graham Newell winning under Owen Grindey. Calisto later joined the Antarctica kennel of Ken and Betty Rawlings.

avarodossi and his trophies including that for BOB at
rufts centenary show in 1973.

Ch Tintavon Desdemona winning BIS under American judge Maxwell Riddle at Stockholm International 1979 to
clinch Top Dog in Sweden and the Nordic countries. PHOTO WILHELM DUFWA

o Ch Cheska Gregor whom Frankie Sefton
eft with me as a pup when she emigrated
o Australia. That produced my first
omebred champion, owned by the late
m Bainbridge, Tintavon Goldameir.

"I was then given the opportunity to buy
fabulous young black and white bitch
ho hated showing but the late Thelma
Morgan said 'if anyone can get her to show
hen it's you'… and we did, after much
ocial training.

"Witcherty Thea of Tintavon became a
UK champion, winning six CCs to Gregor's
en CCs but what was so special with
hese two were that they produced great
ffspring including all-breed and specialty
BIS winner Int/Nord Ch Tintavon Sa-
kya owned by Marina Reuterswärd of
weden, top Apso for five years in a row,
UK Ch Tintavon Ariadne owned by Jim
Bainbridge, and my own two specialty
BIS winners UK/Int/Nord Ch Tintavon
sai-Lun and group winning Int/Nord Ch
intavon Kreskin (nine RCCs in the UK).

"Although my big love was the Apsos
was pressured into buying a Tibetan
errier by Graham Newell and Penny
pencer who kept saying 'You present
nd handle your Apsos so well; we need
omeone like you in our breed'.

"My response was 'Well, if ever you mate
h Hlaka Kangri of Dokham with Ch
uneville Prince Krishna then I might be
nterested'. No sooner said than done and
found myself the owner of a gorgeous
ream coloured little bundle of mischief
ho did so much to promote the breed
nd myself.

"Birmingham City was his and my
avourite show as he won his first CC there
s a pup, a year later the breed's first group
in and in 1974 he was best in show having
aken the first ever such win the same year
t Birmingham National.

"I think I was so overwhelmed that when

I think back on that day it just goes to
prove that with hard work, dedication and
some good luck it is possible for novices
to get to the top. This once-in-a-lifetime
dog was not perfect as it was always said
he was a shade long in body but I think
he should have had more hind angulation
and knowing what I do now about coats
I could make him look much shorter as
he had too much coat on his chest and
back end. What he did have was the most
glorious head and expression and superb
front angulation and forechest.

"This immortal dog was Ch Dokham
Cavarodossi of Tintavon. He won 39 CCs,
BIS at the first breed club championship

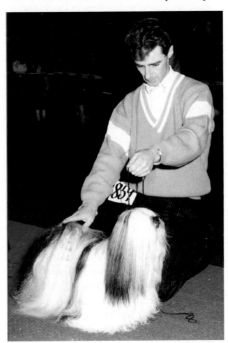

Int/Nord Tintavon The Toreador from Paul's first litter
born in Sweden, winning best veteran in show at
Tonsberg, Norway, in 1985 where his daughter Ch
Tintavon Pandorah won BIS and son Tintavon Perry King
won his Int Ch title. Toreador sired 15 champions and
was top Lhasa 1981 and '82.

show and the dog CC five years in a row at
Crufts! I blush when I think that I showed
a very light cream coloured dog with a
white overall. There was still lots to be
learnt and I am still learning today!

"I met my ex-partner and first real
boyfriend in 1973 and within one month
of meeting Terry Young I had left home
and my secure job and moved up to Hayes
just outside London and with me I took
Gregor, Thea and Cavarodossi who were
already UK champions. This was a very
stormy relationship (as were all of Terry's
relationships); the first two years were just
about liveable but the last two years were a
'living hell'.

"When things became quite unbearable I
knew I had to get away for good. I had three
options and I took the third which was to
leave the country and as I had most contacts
in Sweden through Marina and friends I
had made when I judged at Tibethund in
1975 I decided this was where my new life
would be. Again it was pure destiny as it
could have been any country in Europe if I
had had contacts there."

Paul from a very early age was
acknowledged as being something of a
master groomer, as at the time he was
hitting the high spots presentation was far
less sophisticated than it is today. I asked
him about this great talent.

"I am honoured Andrew that you call
me a 'master groomer' and I suppose I
was ahead of my time as in the late '60s
and early '70s not so much bathing was
done and grooming was kept simple but I
knew then I must find people to watch and
learn from so I watched the Afghans being
shown and how they were groomed for the
shows.

"I probably learnt most about handling
by watching Standard Poodles being shown
and I so well remember Vicky Marshall, of
Vicmars fame, with her orange hair and ▶

Int/Nord ChTraschi-Deleg Kunga, bred by Gerti Bracksiek in Germany, dam of ten champions, seen winning BIS at Tonsberg in 1986, a show where Paul has won BIS three times.

Int/Nord Ch Tintavon Torch Song Trilogy.

UK/Int/Nord Ch Ffrith Smoke Cignal, bred by Glenys Dolphin,'the dog who gave us show temperament and style.'The circle is nearly complete'as here he is winning best veteran in show at the Tibethund show under Iren Plumstead (Showa) who bred Paul's first Apso.

knickers, and Pat Ashwell, of Torpaz note, with her huge pink hairdo, and I seem to remember thinking that they were too much! But they were always winning and you always noticed them and this was when I learnt that handling and presentation were so important.

"In the good old days both Apsos and TTs had correct strong hair and on hot days I would leave Cavarodossi outside to dry in the sun which is something that horrifies me now.

"My favourite product then was Robin Starch Original, it was amazing to soak up any wet hairs and brushed out leaving no trace of powders or feeling 'strange' and sorry, no it cannot be bought any longer as the company changed to Robin Starch Instant then to a spray.

"I think I am proud that I introduced the centre parting on TTs. This was not something I had planned but came naturally as we had partings in Apsos. This was not highly thought of by some of the older breeders who tried to remove the parting while judging (when I would stubbornly put it back in place); now no one would dream of showing a TT without a parting.

"I was lucky enough to start in dogs when 'it was all about type'; we would sit around the benches and discuss – well I mostly listened – about the different dogs, judging, breeding etc. This was the most important aspect to make a good day out but of course if you won then the day was great.

"I hate judging dirty or matted dogs and I do appreciate a well groomed and conditioned dog but NOT at the expense of correct type.

"I think my 'pet hate' is the overdone exaggerated topknots on Shih Tzus in some countries. The exhibitors spend hours just creating a stupidly huge topknot on a tiny pin-headed dog where you can hardly see the eyes. If only they realised that the head looks smaller because of this ridiculously high topknot… and I know you will agree Andrew as I have seen you tell the exhibitors to brush this out or you will not judge or put the dog/s up.

"One thing that really makes me angry and sad is that some judges are so enthralled by these perfectly groomed glamorous dogs and they forget completely what should be underneath the coat. One thing I will not forgive is a hugely coated perfectly groomed dog but without body and muscles! Who is to blame? Groomers who just want to win and judges who just look at glamour… and it also seems that the faster you run your dog the happier the judge is!"

Paul relocated to Sweden in December 1977 with four Apsos – Kreskin, two of his sons and Tsai-Lun – and in February of the following year they were joined by UK Ch Tsangpo Eridanus of Tintavon (a black son of Cavarodossi) and a junior bitch by Eridanus ex Tengrinor Rhona, a Cavarodossi daughter. She had just won the reserve CC at Crufts behind Cavarodossi's illustrious litter sister, Ch Dokham La Calisto, and she was to become the first big Tibetan Terrier star in Scandinavia, Tintavon Desdemona.

Like her double grandsire she was a cream with light golden ears. She was shown only from May to December in 1978 but became third Top Dog all breeds and top female and the first TT to win an all-breeds BIS in Sweden, but 1979 was to be her year as she won Top Dog all breeds in Sweden, Finland and the Nordic countries, finishing off with BIS at Stockholm international under Maxwell Riddle of the US.

I asked Paul how the West Countryman took to learning a totally new language. "I am still trying to learn and the big problem is that most Swedes speak excellent English as it is the second language and they start learning at nine years of age.

"Nothing is dubbed on Swedish TV so you hear the original language which is mostly English or American English and Swedes just love to talk English when they get the chance. I stupidly did not go to school to take Swedish lessons but picked up the odd words by listening and gradually it has gone over to Swenglish which I still speak."

Paul had also been involved with Tibetan Spaniels. "When I moved hastily to Sweden a wonderful lady, Agneta Reis (Nalinas Tibetan Spaniels), whom I had met in 1975, let me stay with her just outside of Stockholm and I helped with the dogs, pigs etc. I also went to help Lisbeth Sigfridsson (now Hagman) a couple of days a week.

"It was Lisbeth who had bought UK Ch Amcross Kam-Dar from Terry and myself and I showed Kam-Dar to his Int Ch title here; I have also bred a UK Tibetan Spaniel champion in Ch Amcross Kai-Tei by Kam Dar out of our Amcross Ta-Rosa (one CC and one reserve CC).

"In 1978 I started handling for the famous Anibes Shih Tzu kennel of the late Anita and Kurt Berggren and I later moved to them to take care of and show their dogs, also to much success as in 1979 when Desdemona was Top Dog all breeds I also handled UK/Int/Nord Ch Bellakerne Sui Sue, an all-breeds and specialty BIS winner to the number two position. At that time they competed in different groups as TTs were in the companion group – a sort of utility-type group – while Shih Tzu were in the toy group as were Apsos."

"I moved to Stockholm at the end of 1979 and my 'fairy godmother', Moa Persson, found me a flat opposite the head

...om the last litter of Lhasa Apsos, Int/Nord Ch Tintavon ...lta Vigo (Multi Ch Whisborne Heatwave ex Int/Nord Ch ...ntavon Black Opal), one of four champions in the litter.

PHOTO EDMILSON REIS

From the last litter of Tibetan Terriers, Braz Ch Tintavon Zenio (Multi Ch Falamandus Jára-ki Khaki ex Tintavon Tosca), one of six champions in the litter.

Whippets have always been Torbjörn's big interest and here are four generations: far right Ch Signum Something Got To Give (breeder Magnus Hagstedt) born at their house, far left is her daughter Ch Tintavon Gail Deevers, centre Ch Tintavon Gail Force Wind and in front Ch Tintavon Espen Keyzerson as a puppy, who is now 11 years old.

...lice station in Stockholm and it was ...iends who decided that Torbjörn Skaar ...nd myself would make a good couple. So ...was in the middle of 1980 that Torbjörn ...oved into my huge flat of 28 square ...etres but we also spent a lot of the time ...utside of Stockholm with another dear ...iend Inga Enstad who looked after some ...f the dogs during the week.

"My first 'real' work was cleaning offices ...here I would start at 5.15 to around 11.30 ...r so and Torbjörn worked in one of the ...ost famous restaurants in the Old City so ...e worked lunch or evenings.

"We were lucky to get a secondhand ...ontract on a three-room and kitchen on ...e outskirts of Stockholm but after one ...ear we did not get the contract renewed ...s it was 'needed' for a family with a child ...ith drug problems and that was deemed ...ore important than the two of us who ...orked and paid taxes so we were forced ...estiny again) to buy a house in Tyresö ...hich is a town of nearly 50,000 just 20km ...om Stockholm. We have lived in this town ...nce then but in three different houses.

"Torbjörn had Great Danes with his ...other when I met him but big dogs were ...st out of the question although that is ...e breed that can get his heart racing fast. ...e has been lucky enough to award CCs in ...e breed at Midland Counties a few years ...ack where he also awarded CCs in Apsos ...nd Whippets. Next year he will judge at a ...hippet championship club show in the ...K. Torbjörn started judging in 1992 and ...now on his final exams to become all-...reeds judge."

The Tintavon kennel campaigned Apsos ...ostly after the success of Desdemona ...nd has owned or bred 14 all-breed BIS ...inners. The first Tintavon Apso litter ...as born in 1978, a result of a Kreskin son ...ated to Kreskin's litter sister Tsai Lun, ...nd this produced probably one of the best ...psos Paul considers they have ever owned ...r bred.

"He had great construction, a most ...eautiful head and expression and the first ...er with 42 teeth and an excellent wide ...nderjaw. His coat was of amazing quality

and grew like weeds but he was a 'plodder'; never dropped his tail but if only he had more enthusiasm he could have won so much more instead of the odd group and specialty wins.

"His name was Tintavon The Toreador and he was also a very good producer; his son Tintavon Torch Song Trilogy was another group winner and specialty BIS winner and our very first World Winner in 1995.

"All our dogs have been produced from these lines until we were given an amazingly well constructed gold sable female from the Traschi–Deleg kennel in Germany. Kunga did not get on well with her owner and handler Gerti Bracksiek in the ring, but again destiny was calling as I had handled Kunga's paternal grandfather Dolsa Marlo Matador, a US import, to BOB from the junior class at his very first show in Europe which was the Amsterdam Winner Show in the very early '70s for owner Annie Schneider Louter.

"I had also judged Kunga's sire and dam and Kunga was line-bred to Matador. Her problem, no, our problem, was that Kunga was also a 'plodder' if she did not want to show but she did become a multiple BIS winner including a BIS2, 3 and 4 at three Helsinki shows in a row.

"We bought a pup from Glenys Dolphin, 'my sister' and daughter of dear Thelma Morgan, but as we had also bought a young male from Jean Blyth we asked Jim Bainbridge if he would have him and he was delighted and worked really hard to get him up and showing. He became UK Ch Ffrith Smoke Cignal, a grandson of one of my all-time favourites UK Ch Cheska Alexander of Sternroc.

"Now we had a showman who would power himself around the ring, sometimes on two legs or all legs up in the air. He also became a BIS and specialty BIS winner but it was when we mated Smoke Cignal to Kunga that we produced one of our greatest stars in Tintavon Isolde, a BIS and specialty BIS winner who had Kunga's construction but with Smoke Cignal's beautiful head and his proud carriage.

Here at last had what we dreamed about – producing an Apso of correct type and construction and with showmanship and style.

"Kunga and Smoke Cignal had two litters together and of the ten pups nine became champions with quite a few winning groups and specialty BIS.

"I think from this you can see that we prefer the British way of line-breeding with an outcross now and again to a dog that is also line-bred. This has always been our philosophy and I suppose I had been lucky starting in Apsos when I did, so had seen most of the very first UK champions. We firmly believe that you must know the good and not so good points of dogs in your pedigrees.

"We did the same with the TTs until we mated Desdemona to a Cavarodossi son we had sold to Sweden. Although they were excellent type the litter was too small and fine so we went to Finland and did complete outcrossing and were extremely happy with the type that was produced. She actually produced seven champions in her three litters.

"It was fate again when our first Whippet arrived in 1985 and she was already an all-breeds BIS winner, Multi Ch Bokellas Marilyn Monroe, owned by Magnus Hagstedt who asked us to take care of her for a few days before she returned to her breeder. Of course that never happened and so we started out with a new breed and have been successful with the very few litters we have had. We usually took one litter from a female and kept a female until the last litter consisting of three males and now we have just Espen left who is 11 years old but also a group winner.

"The Whippets are the opposite to our Apsos and TTs as they are not line-bred as this seems to be more 'the done thing' in this breed and we have listened to the advice of our peers in the breed."

In 1992 Torbjörn and Paul were awarded the Swedish Kennel Club's ▶

Ch Tintavon Gail Force Wind winning BPIS at the famous Skokloster Sighthound Show.

Paul handling Anita Berggren's Shih Tzu Int Ch Formargårdens Q-Ti-Pie to BIS at Mantorp in 1978.

Thai Ch Santos of Palmplace the day after he arrived from Thailand, the first time a Thai Bangkaew Dog had been shown in Europe. He won CAC and BOB at Helsin Winner Show in 2011 under Ichiro Ishikawa from Japar

Hamilton Plaque for outstanding breeding of Lhasa Apsos, the first in this breed so it is something of which they are understandably extremely proud.

The Swedish KC (SKK) holds bi-annual general meetings for all the special breed clubs, group clubs and county kennel clubs and it is there that the plaque and pins are awarded to certain breeders from all breeds. It can be for producing many show winners or for those who breed and are successful in working tests as in German Shepherds or hunting breeds as in Elkhounds.

Paul did not specifically plan to be a judge like many do in Scandinavia, but as he first awarded CCs in the UK to Lhasa Apsos in 1975, then a year later in Tibetan Terriers, when he moved to Sweden he was automatically approved for these breeds along with Tibetan Spaniels.

He remembers his beginnings: "I was then taken into the Swedish judging scheme, starting off with the toy group although I also took Shelties but the first breed I passed my exams on was Yorkshire Terriers in 1981 and then Shih Tzu. I continued to take exams either in the ring, at special weekends covering related breeds or evening exams for related breeds, for example all setters. After passing exams for over 150 breeds I received a letter from the SKK congratulating me on becoming an all-breeds judge back in 1996."

"The Swedish judges' scheme is very thorough although it does sound complicated to those not living in Scandinavia. The first thing that is required is that you have to have passed your basic exams and worked as a ring steward. The next stage is that you have to pass your exams in anatomy and show regulations, and when this has been done successfully you can apply to the SKK to join the next judges' course which are usually held every second year.

"You are given a questionnaire to fill out which includes all that you have done in dogs, like how many litters, champions bred, courses attended and a lot more questions, and you have to write which breeds you want to start judging. This is a minimum of one and a maximum of five and you cannot just choose five from five different groups but you must write why these breeds and what experience you have with them. If I was starting again I would naturally choose the five Tibetan breeds.

"This questionnaire is sent back to the SKK which asks the breed clubs their opinion of you and whether they would support you and also to the county kennel club that you belong to but quite often they do not have a reply.

"If there is more than one person applying then the clubs need to write in which order they would support the applicants – this does not mean that the SKK judges committee will agree.

"The questionnaires are then checked by the group who conduct the course and of around 50-60 who apply around 25 are called for an interview. Of those a maximum of 18 are selected to go on the course.

"The course is usually in May and starts on Sunday afternoon and finishes with the examination on Friday. Every day you are taught how to write critiques, go over dogs, measuring, checking bites, coat quality and of course construction and movement. In this course you are expected to describe what you see and feel and not what you know about each breed unless it is the breeds you are applying for.

"On the first days there are usually a lot of students panicking and saying 'I breed GSDs but I do not know what breed that is'. It is the same with those who want to become judges for toy breeds when faced with going over and describing an Irish Wolfhound. This course is not about learning breed type but learning all the basic skills that are needed to become a judge.

"Often in the evenings there are extra lessons about how breeds have changed, BSI (breed specific instructions) for healthier dogs, question time, becoming a junior handling judge and any other thing that might be of help or interest.

"Friday is examination day where the group is divided in to two and each person is examined by two of the teachers. Usuall they are given three breeds to judge one at a time, of which one must be one of the breeds they have applied for; if the teachers are a little unsure a fourth dog can be asked in to the ring.

"There are usually some complaints that all the students pass but unlike 20 years ago when around 25 were asked to the course knowing full well that at least five would be failed, this was thought (and quite rightly so) to be a waste of SKK money and unfair on those who were expected to fail from the very beginning.

"This new way of thinking was due to Hans Forsell who although not a judge wa a member of the SKK General Committee and he was 'team leader' until 2011 when Carl Gunnar Stafberg (all-breeds judge, famous Border Terrier breeder and forme vice-chairman of the SKK) took over this post.

"There are four and sometimes five teachers for this course and I must say I feel very honoured to be one of them for the last seven or eight courses.

"Now do not think that these students are now judges because they have only received their 'L plates'. They now have to go three times as pupil and twice as student for each of the breeds they have applied for and student judging can only be done under judges from the Nordic countries who have been judging for at least five years and have judged the breed at least five times. When this is completed they can then call themselves SKK judges.

"To continue judging and take new breeds this has to be applied for to the judges committee and with their approval and the breed club's approval for the new

orbjörn helping Sw Ch Khanjai of Palmplace at Tintavon
eo deliver her first puppy of eight in 2012 with Santos
ooking on. This was the first litter of Thai Bangkaew
ogs to be registered with the FCI.

Three Nordic Winner Titles and three new Norwegian champions: the Thai Ridgeback Dog, Nord/Thai Ch Bo Handlers
Chaithai of Tintavon Leo, owned by Renata Johansson and Göran Stanton, and brought to Sweden by Paul; Edgar
with Sw/Norw/Cz Ch Tintavon Leo Ma Muang (from the first Thai Bangkaew Dog litter born in Europe) and Paul with
Santos who was BOS to his daughter.

reeds to be taken. These exams can be
one either by one pupil (mainly to listen
nd learn) and then one student (writing
ritiques and explaining your placings) in
he ring but only under approved judges
r an examination can be held under two
pproved judges (one from the breed
ub's list and one approved by the judges
ommittee who is usually an all-rounder or
roup all-rounder).

"Here, after breed judging has finished
he student must judge a minimum of
ve dogs, grade and give critiques and
lace them in order for the two examiners
agree, or if they do not agree, to ask
uestions why. Of course it is not necessary
have exactly the same opinion as the two
xaminers as long as there are acceptable
easons.

"A maximum of eight new breeds may be
aken each year so this is by no means an
asy or fast way to become an all-rounder
hich is usually a minimum of 20 years."

Like many of us, Paul is so grateful that
is hobby has given him the chance to
ravel around the world as he is fascinated
y different cultures and the incredible
ariety of flowers, trees and shrubs
hich often make him wonder why he
ill lives in Sweden with its long, cold
nd dark winters! He comments: "I love
xperiencing new foods – especially fruits
and value all the wonderful people I have
et."

When I asked Paul about favourite
hows he had to think really hard. "I have
een racking my brains to answer which
re some of my favourite shows and I
hink I will have to divide this in to two
ategories and the first are the shows I
ave been most proud to have judged at,
of course I must choose Crufts in 1981
hen I judged Lhasa Apsos and awarded
axonsprings Fresno her first CC and BOB
om the limit class.

"Sydney Royal in 2002 was a highlight,
s was judging the gundog group at the
latboro (US) show about 12 years ago.
wice judging the New Zealand Kennel
ssociation National, definitely judging
e UK Chow Chow Club championship

show with their trophies dating back to the
1880s which was really memorable.

"In 2008 I was the first non-Asian
judge to have the honour to judge Thai
Bangkaew Dogs at the most important
show of the year where the King's trophy
is awarded, and of course judging group 9
(toy/companion) at the World Dog Show
in Stockholm and the terrier group at the
WDS in Salzburg in 2012 to name just a
few.

"Thinking again, I must mention my first
judging appointment in Russia where I had
the huge honour to judge the Kerry Blue
Terrier national specialty where I was the
first 'non-terrier' judge to be invited, so it
was nearly more of an honour to be invited
for a second national and two regional
specialties.

"I suppose, being English, that any time
I am invited back to the UK to judge at

Paul's first trip to the country which a few years later
became his home was to judge at the Swedish
Tibethund show in 1975. His Lhasa Apso BOB was Ch
Ting-E-Lings Dionne.

club or all-breed shows I find that really
special."

"I think my favourite showground is the
one in Perth that is owned by the members
and where I judged the Western Classic a
few years back. I was also impressed and
amazed by the Pernambuco KC grounds in
Recife, Brazil where they even have their
own dog cemetery.

"For atmosphere and something a
little different I have to say the Split Four
Summer shows are quite unique.

"I always love judging in Asia because
of the friendliness and easy way you are
treated and I still find the continent
very exotic and it is the same with South
America.

"I tend to remember the shows positively
when I meet really nice people who do
their utmost that I will go home with
great memories and this is definitely true
of many of the smaller kennel clubs and
shows. All judges remember good food
and drink and a nice hotel and good ring
stewards more than the overall quality of
the dogs. I love the Italian shows because
of the cuisine and Gibraltar springs to
mind as unique and also being 'very
British'.

"Russia has been one of my favourite
countries for the quality of dogs and the
warmth of its people and the fun and
enthusiasm they have at shows.

"I have wonderful memories from my
visits to Ukraine, Bulgaria, Moldova and
Bosnia and Herzegovina and in fact all the
Balkan counties; maybe that is because I
know so little of these countries and they
are so different from the UK and the
Nordic countries in culture and way of
thinking. Also I learn so much about their
histories and the struggles they have had
or are having.

"I love to visit Israel as being an ex-

Paul judged the Swedish Irish Soft-coated Wheaten Terrier Club's first show, an open show, in 1980.

This young Weimaraner was Paul's group winner at Hatboro, US, in 2000.

Paul awarded the Whippet Am/Can Brushwood's Moxi of Endeavor her last BPIS and her first BIS at the Manitoba CA in Canada in 2003. She went on to win the US national specialty twice.   PHOTO WELLS

Christian I find it fascinating to visit places Jesus was supposed to have visited or preached and the history and incredible places to visit, and I just loved the Dead Sea as I threw myself in to the water knowing that I could not sink, being a typical non-swimmer from England!"

Obviously Paul has seen many outstanding dogs since he became involved with the sport. "I have been asked before about dogs I will never forget and the list seems to change. I think the first dog I really remember being captivated by was the Chow Chow, UK Ch Ukwong King Solomon, he was perfectly presented and handled and the dog always showed so well.

"Another dog that I have lasting memories of was the Swedish Afghan Ch El Khyrias Hazztaffer, a noble dog and always shown in great coat and condition. The Swedish German Shepherd Ch Triumphs Blaze who won BIS two years in a row at the Stockholm international was magnificent to see as he powered around the ring to the roar of the crowd and what was more amazing was he was a working police dog.

"I must mention the two Apsos UK Ch Cheska Alexander of Sternroc and UK Ch Saxonsprings Fresno, both so fantastic for their type."

Paul actually still only has his British passport as for many years having dual nationality was not allowed and he could never think of giving up his British citizenship. He points out however: "From about five years back it is now allowed to have both British and Swedish passports which I would really like but I would need to hand in my British passport for around six months and this is just impossible with the travelling I do."

He says: "The more I travel to faraway places the less difference I see between the British and Scandinavian dog scene. Of course here we write critiques on every dog and grade them which I think is an excellent idea.

"When the grading is used correctly it is a great help to a breed as the pet quality dogs get lower grades and the owners either get better dogs or hopefully stop showing and do not breed from these poorer quality dogs. Unfortunately we seem to be going through a spell where far too many dogs are given the quality 'excellent' but this is much more noticeable when you go to other countries especially in Southern Europe, Asia and South America.

"I also think it is healthy that neither Scandinavia or the UK is swamped with professional handlers; they do have a negative effect on entries as it can be

Paul says it was a great honour to be one of three judges to judge rare breeds at the Tournament of Champions in Detroit in 1990.

"Maybe this is the reason I love primitive breeds?" Paul with a two-year-old male wolf Kolmården park, Sweden.

ather disappointing for owner/handlers to be beaten often by pro handlers who are usually quite brilliant at showing dogs in perfect condition and trained to move and show like a machine but then again everyone can learn to do at least a decent job of handling and presentation.

"I am happy that still in Scandinavia we do not see so many over-exaggerated breeds with way too much hind angulation and this is due to the close bond that Scandinavians have with the British breeders in most of the breeds.

"I was brought up the old British way that type first, then again and again' whereas in Scandinavia it was much more on construction and movement but I quickly learnt we need a happy medium.

"Now we see many judges from all over the world judging for glamour, construction which is not necessarily correct for that breed and moving breeds much too fast and this is where I feel we miss out on the really good British judges who have seen and handled so many dogs of different quality that they know what is acceptable and what is not.

"The Nordic countries had a reciprocal agreement with the Kennel Club to accept one another's judges much more easily as any UK judge who was on a B list could judge at CAC shows. We did not need the approval of British breed clubs as long as we could fill in the forms adequately, which is not so easy for us as we do not have to keep records of our judging as in the UK, but this has changed now that the Fédération Cynologique Internationale has come to an agreement with the KC… but we will have to see how that develops.

"Personally I would like to see more judges from the UK over here; we often see many at club shows but not so many at the all-breed shows unless they award CCs in quite a few breeds so they can judge both days."

So how does Paul see the future of the dog world? "I am really worried about the future of our dog sport and sometimes I wonder if there is a future as we know and love it because the breeding of pedigree dogs is being attacked by PETA, animal activists, green party politicians and the 'non doggy' media who are looking for any scandal to condemn us all.

"I was horrified by the way the KC reacted to the TV media on 'unsound' and 'unhealthy' dogs while in Sweden a group of the most experienced all-rounders sat down and made a list of all breeds we could think of, 46 breeds I think, and this list was sent out to all the breed clubs for them to study. All clubs replied except one and another 30 breed clubs wanted to be added with what the club considered health issues in their breeds.

"This has progressed over the years to be 'a living document' where breeds can be added or taken away and we can see if the

Paul's wedding to Göran in 1999.

health issues in any breed are improving – which they are. This we also do with the help of the veterinary profession and dog insurance companies so if or when politicians want to know what the KC has been doing we can show them detailed documentation. It is even better now that the Nordic KCs all work together on this matter.

"I also think we must work harder to promote pedigree dogs for all the great things they do for us humans. I am definitely not against the real mutts or genuine Heinz 57 but I do hate this infatuation with designer dogs that are being sold for huge amounts. What we definitely do not need is any more of these crossbreeds to be recognised by the FCI, no thanks to particoloured Poodles or black and white Yorkie crosses!

"Why are the US and Russia producing so many 'new breeds'? We must take care of the breeds we have as we see now that many of the old beautiful British breeds are on the endangered lists such as Otterhounds and Sealyham Terriers. One thing is for sure – we must all work together and not spend so much time on Facebook or Twitter slamming other people or dogs."

Paul has led a somewhat unconventional life in many ways, best described by himself: "I believe I am a typical Sagittarian with a great love of animals and travelling and also the fact that, as Torbjörn says, I can fall in shit but come out smelling of roses!

"Only those who really know me know how shy I was and still can be but I have managed to learn how to cover this up and it was through the dog sport that gave me a lot of the confidence I lacked.

"I have always been a great listener and willing to help friends in need and this is how I met my husband Göran who was going through a crisis and we became friends. We talked a lot and he moved in to the house I owned with Torbjörn and yes, I did feel terrible for Torbjörn who said he would give it one year… that was 28 years

ago!

"Göran and I had a civil wedding in 1999 which was then called civil partnership although now it is called marriage and if we wanted we could now be married in church. Göran works for the Swedish police and was one of the founder members of the Swedish Gay Police Association and each year they march in the Stockholm Pride Parade in uniform.

"Göran works with hate crimes and travels a lot all over Sweden and much of Europe lecturing on hate crimes to gay groups, embassies and EU groups so he now has a life away from the dog scene although he handled the dogs in the beginning of our relationship and became an excellent ring steward.

"What was so unique with our 'civil wedding' was that Göran was allowed to wear ceremonial police uniform and we had a guard of honour made up of four gay and four hetero police friends and officiated by the Mayor of Stockholm in the grounds of City Hall.

"On my fourth judging trip to Iceland I judged a great entry of 40 Icelandic Sheepdogs and in the open female class came in a young man with baggy jeans that kept falling down so I told him it would help if he had a belt… then he could concentrate more on his dog who was beautiful.

"In the best female class, I felt this handler, now wearing a dog lead for a belt, was holding his dog back a little so I told him to 'give her more lead' which he did and her movement and type won them BOB and I later gave them the group.

"Next day when I was judging BIS a very smartly dressed young man came in to the ring and he and his dog did perfect teamwork enough to win the BIS.

"I was so happy that a young handler understood what was wanted and was bright enough to change but it was his mother Stefania who contacted me first, thanking me and saying how showing under me and winning meant so much to her son. Slowly Sigurdur Edgar and I started writing on Facebook and having long conversations via Skype about his crises (it was like talking to a young Paul) and his future.

"To cut a long story short I took him with me to WDS in Paris, he stayed with us on a number of occasions, he went with me to Thailand and later worked at the kennels for two months where I had some of my dogs. We showed at the European Show in Brno, Oslo and now in Milan at the WDS but it was about two years ago when Edgar (Sigurdur is very difficult to pronounce correctly) asked if he could add Stanton to his name on FB and I said yes.

"Although we have not officially adopted Edgar he feels like he is the son I/we never had and is definitely a part of our family. His interest in dogs is so genuine and he wants to learn all he can and even when I ▶

Edgar and Göran on Christmas Day 2014 with the Thai imports Ch Bahley, Ch Santos and Ch Khanjai, Ch Ma Muang, Ch Santolino and Thai import Ch Zeright.

Torbjörn with his BIS winner at the 2014 Schnauzer Pinscher Club championship show the Black and Silver Miniature Schnauzer Ch Fixus On Air.

am away he will send photos via FB asking what I think of this or that dog. I am so happy that now he looks for type first and not the glamorous dogs he loved in the beginning. He now understands that for Irish Setters it is not the more coat the better and overangulation is not good in a hunting breed.

"Edgar charms everyone he meets and in Thailand he has a 'Thai mother' in Pakaporn Kae, the mother of the now very famous ex-junior handler Mind Supasin. And he has an aunt in Canada, well it must be his aunt as she is my 'triplet' Dawne Deeley where he has spent this summer, so we will just have to wait and see what the future holds for him."

Paul has over the years developed a special affection for Thailand and I was keen to learn more about his love affair with that country. "I wrote at the beginning that I stopped believing in God in 1964 and I had no religion but considered myself a humanitarian who could help and do good deeds.

"But things changed for Göran and myself when we made our first trip to Thailand in 1990 and we visited a temple high in the hills near Chiang Mai in the north. It was a beautiful hot day with a magnificent view of the city below, bougainvillea flowered and the golden pagoda shone brightly and I felt I had experienced something special.

"One year later we again visited the temple Wat Doi Suthep and I felt exactly like I had the first visit so I interpreted this as 'a sign' and became a Buddhist which is perfect for me as they do not have a God but believe in the teachings of the Lord Buddha who was born 500 years before Jesus although their teachings are similar.

"Göran and I were in love with Thailand, its people, the food, fruit and weather and we could not be there enough. I judged my first show in Thailand in 1991 and have judged there regularly since then."

"I was first interested in the Thai

Ridgebacks and visited the most prominent kennels but at one show around 1999 I was shown two dogs and I was told that they were Thai Spitz although not recognised. In 2003 I judged over 30 of these Spitz without CCs at an all-breed championship show and this is how my interest was awakened in the Thai Bangkaew Dog.

"Through our very good friend and mentor of the two Thai breeds and well known breeder of Pomeranians Somsak Taechapeti we learnt more and more and in 2008 I was invited to be the first non-Asian to judge the breed at the most important show of the year where the King's trophy is awarded and my BIS winner I thought was a stunner. I met this dog on several occasions later and we formed a bond and in 2009 he was given to me…

"But what to do with a dog of a breed that was not provisionally recognised by the FCI although they had CCs in Thailand from 2006? It was not until June 2011 that the FCI recognised the breed and on January 1, 2012 Santos of Palmplace flew to Sweden as we had new import regulations and he was the first of his breed to come to Europe and be registered.

"It would be wrong to say I fell in love with the breed as it was the dog Santos I fell in love with and I have never had a dog who means so much to me and I think vice versa.

"I was very honoured that the FCI, through Renée Sporre-Willes of Sweden who was the chairman of the Standard Committee, invited me to work with the breed Standard and do the breed evaluation which we did in Bangkok in 2010.

"The TBD is a very primitive breed, absolutely devoted to its family, highly intelligent, great escape artists but they are enormous individual characters. When kept as a flock they have the hierarchy of wolves so maybe that is why most are kept singly or in pairs in Thailand. I know I can never be without this breed again."

So what of Paul's future aspirations? He

has achieved an incredible amount as a breeder, handler and judge. "As I wrote earlier I awarded CCs for Lhasa Apsos and Tibetan Terriers in the UK before moving to Sweden and since then I have slowly gained a few more breeds and I now award CCs in Tibetan Spaniels, Shih Tzu, Swedish Vallhunds and Chow Chows judged at club shows and Old English Sheepdogs, American Cockers, Greyhounds, Scottish Deerhounds, Petit Bassets Griffons Vendéens, Rottweilers, Japanese Spitz and Pugs judged at all-breed shows, so 14 breeds in 40 years of judging.

"If I had stayed in the UK I am sure I would have more breeds but I think I would have had more or most from the utility group and probably not Rottweilers; it is difficult to know where I would be had I stayed in the UK but as my interest has not waned for these 40 years I would hope I would be a group judge at least.

"I have been so lucky to have had so many wonderful people support me throughout my career especially those at the very beginning who must have seen 'something special in that young man' and to those who have mostly passed away now I am eternally grateful. I have won so much with my/our dogs that there are no big ambitions left but to continue with our Bangkaew dogs, keep on judging for as long as I can and to help young or new people the way I was helped.

"I have two regrets and they are that I have never been invited to judge Tibetan Terriers at Crufts and also not had the opportunity to judge junior handling at Crufts as it was as a handler, if I may say it, I became famous for as much as it was as a breeder."

Whatever remains for Paul, he has committed himself to a sport for which he has an overwhelming passion and to which he has given so much. I am sure that, had he remained in the UK, he would now be one of our greatest assets. As it is, Britain can just be proud of one of its most influential and respected exports. ∎

DENMARK

Report:
Michael Smedemark Laub

Honouring world class breeders

The Danish Kennel Club (DKK) experienced a dog show year in 2015 with solid progress in the number of dogs shown. All in all at the international shows, there were 30,398 dogs, up from 28,687 in 2014.

This was also the first year of paper-less critiques. Now, all participants get their critiques online or on a text message. The system has been integrated with great success all over Denmark.

At the last show of the year, the Danish Winner Show in Herning, it was also time to celebrate the results of the Dog of the Year competitions. Winner was the Bullmastiff Librrani High Performance Alonso, bred by Mette Libstrup Soerensen and Imran Durrani and co-owned by Vivi Alaluusua.

PHOTO JEFFREY HANLIN

Runner-up was the American Cocker Spaniel Galaksi This is Me, bred and owned by Michael and Ruth Henny Christensen.

The prestigious title of Breeder of the Year 2015 went to the Norwegian breeder of German Shepherds, Tor W Johanssen under the affix Av Quantos. Best Progeny Group of the Year was sired by the Samoyed Cabaka's Kiss The Rain.

Veteran of the Year was the Puli Bubbleton's Hot'n Spicy owned by Marianne Nyman and Stefan Ernstson. Best junior handler for the second year in a row was Marie-Louise Christensen in her last season as a junior handler.

At the Herning show a new award, the DKK's Breeder Award, was introduced, honouring long lasting, world class kennels whose breeders have made solid footprints:

Kennel Blaaholm, top winning kennel of Great Danes established in 1928 by the late Else and Jacob Staunskjaer, and among the oldest active kennels worldwide. Today the kennel is still run by Tove and Camilla Staunskjaer.

Kennel Sieger, top winning kennel of English Springer Spaniels since 1986, run by Jessie and Kaj B Madsen and their daughter Vibe.

Kennel Cabaka, Gitte Morell and Kim Jensen, breeders of top winning Samoyeds since 1994.

While the decision to give the World Show to China in 2019 caused much discussion throughout the dog world in the wake of the 2015 show in Milan, the debate in Denmark has been much sparser and no breed club in Denmark has demanded that the decision be condemned and withdrawn.

From the DKK side, the decision was met with regret as DKK voted for Croatia. However, the club decided to signal respect to the democratic vote. At the same time, a unanimous DKK board decided to send a strong and clear message to both fellow kennel clubs and to the FCI with support to the FCI in general but a call for modernisation.

The DKK is thus content with the fact that after months of intense debate there now is a consensus in the Nordic countries on respecting the decision about calling on FCI to establish a working group to bring forward clear suggestions for a new voting system, more transparency and a more modern FCI at the next General Assembly.

"Now is time to move forward and to further strengthen our international co-operation to the benefit of dogs and dog owners all over the world," said DKK president Joergen Hindse. ■

Third was the Samoyed Cabaka's Kiss The Rain bred by Kim Jensen and Gitte Morell and co-owned by Nana Qvist. He also sired the Best Progeny Group of the Year.

PHOTO GABOR SZALANCZI

The Lakeland Terrier Hi-Kel Terrydale Destiny, owned by Tenna Grenaa, was in fourth place.

FINLAND

When 'rescue' becomes big business

Report and photos
Paula Heikkinen-Lehkoner

Although in many countries the entry figures are going down, not so in Finland! Registration figures have shrunk a little from the peak year of 2010, but this has not had any effect on the number of Finnish Kennel Club members, which is still about 150,000.

We have a lot of shows, and many exhibitors complain that the entry fees are high, fuel is expensive etc, but still they go to the shows. In fact, many shows have been in trouble when the entry has been too high and more judges have to be found at the last minute. There are not many indoor venues large enough for big shows in the whole country, so most of the shows are held outdoors in the hectic summer season, whatever the weather may be.

Most people want a pedigree dog, and usually they buy it from a reliable breeder. However, more and more unregistered puppies are sold, most of them coming from other countries and sold cheaply by dealers. It is strange how this belief about healthier crossbreeds sticks like glue.

Importing rescued street dogs from Romania, Spain or other countries seems to be quite a big, organised business. Animal lovers feel sorry for these abandoned dogs and offer to give homes for them. However, although these dogs may have veterinary documents about vaccinations etc, the papers have not always been very reliable. These dogs have brought in some illnesses and parasites we have never had before, and so our vets are not familiar with this kind of problem. The new owners may have to pay large sums for various tests and vets' bills.

The buyers don't always realise that a dog who has been living on the streets may not make a nice family pet 'just like that'. It may need a lot of time and training to become socialised.

Luckily the fashion for 'designer dogs' has not – at least not yet – reached Finland. At the same time good breeders are frustrated when they have difficulty in finding decent homes for their healthy, well cared for quality puppies. ∎

The current leader in Finland's Top Dog rankings, the Lhasa Apso Int Ch Chic Choix Cleopatra Eurydice, owned by Piia Helistölä-Laurila, has been among the top winners for some years now, not only in Finland but also in other countries. It looks likely that her breeder Juha Kares will win the title Breeder of the Year as he did in 2014. He judges every now and then, and can't exhibit at those shows. However, he doesn't always need to be there himself as the owners and co-owners of the dogs are excellent handlers.

From the Dachshunds there are two top winners in the top ten list, Nina Lehtolammi's Wire Tappijalan Miss Marple, and Stina Selen's Miniature Smooth Naa-Naan Ilotulitus.

There are several other dogs on the list who are in with a chance. Sanna Vartiainen's American Cocker Spaniel Ch Very Vigie Freezing-in-Finland has taken several BIS wins, as has the West Highland White Terrier Ch Gia'Che Ci Sei della Riva d'Arno, owned by Vesa Lehtonen and Juha Palosaari who have guided several Westies and also Wire Fox Terriers to big wins in past years.

There has been tough competition in the terrier group, because the Australian-born Smooth Fox Terrier Ch Optimo Optical Illusion, owned by Sari Laitinen, Molli Nyman and Janice Campbell, and Pia von Koch and Pirjo Hjelm's Airedale Int Ch Big Lady's Iron Duke have had many good days, too.

The Bullmastiff Int Ch Librrani's High Performance Alonso, owners Viivi Alaluusua, Satu Timlin and Imran Durrani, is leading the Danish Top Dog list but has also been actively campaigned in Finland.

The Veteran of the Year is always a very important competition in Finland. At the big shows you can see hundreds of well-kept oldies. It looks as if the current leader, the Afghan Hound Int Ch Agha Djari's Urban Cowboy, owners Salla Suokas and Sami Lyyski, will take the title. He is seen winning at Lahti under Leif Herman Wilberg.

Sari Vottonen and Tarja Rusi-Juusela's Irish Water Spaniel Int Ch A Redriot A'Curly-Co v Alpha Nordic has kept this relatively rare breed in the limelight.

In the top breeders' list the Chic Choix Lhasas are followed by Mirja Lager's Pipperoo Pomeranians and Petri Turunen's Eerondaali Keeshonds, who have often won the breeders' group final with their teams.

In the veterans table, the Afghan is closely followed by Marianne Forssell's Flat-coated Retriever Int Ch Flat Power Criminal Intent and (pictured) Juha Kares and Karoliina Kallela's Lhasa Apso Int Ch Chic Choix Parti Parade, so Juha and his Lhasas could possibly win all three titles, which would be quite unique.

FRANCE

Will new rules raise breeding standards?

Report
Anne-Marie Class

The climax of the show calendar was the French Championship Show at Dijon where 7,613 dogs were entered. BIS was the Chow King Of Egypt de Los Perros de Bigo, owned by Nuria Vigo Navajon from Spain. Huge halls, an excellent welcome to exhibitors at the SCC stand and a nice main ring gave an excellent atmosphere. That it was too hot was the worst point.

It is a challenge to change the location for our championship show each year. It means another organising team, another venue, another town. Many people feel nostalgic about Longchamp, a prestigious outdoor location in Paris. The problem in Paris is that exhibition halls are outrageously costly.

Year after year, the agricultural show, Concours Général Agricole, stands out as the most prestigious event in the show calendar, With 700,000 visitors in one week, it is the best opportunity for breeders and the SCC to show what they do for pedigree dogs. One Nationale CC winner, one champion, one breeders group and one progeny group per breed may compete. There is also a corner for Discover Dogs. Exhibitors received breakfast and, as a gift, a folding armchair. BIS was Lise Durlot and Dimitri Hébert's Basenji Meisterhaus Signet Higher'N Higher.

The economic situation and new regulations about breeding were grounds for anxiety in the 2015 French dog scene.

The orders concerning dog breeding were published in October, a major topic for the French Kennel Club (SCC) which celebrated the 130th anniversary of the LOF, the French stud book, created in 1885.

In fact, the LOF and its role in dog breeding is recognised in the edict. Publishing advertising will be restricted to those declared to be breeders or to private ones who sell registered puppies. 'Private' means not more than one litter a year. From the second litter in the same year, breeders will have to be declared as such.

One can hope it will help prevent people breeding without any controls and in bad conditions. The purpose is to raise standards in dog breeding and to enforce regulations on the sale of pets while recognising the activities of professional or non-professional breeders who produce registered puppies.

It will not be allowed to sell non-pedigree puppies without a registration number or proof that the litter is registered with the SCC. 'Self-service' animal sale is forbidden. Transferring animals free or for payment is not allowed at events not specifically dedicated to animals.

VAT on sale of puppies increased considerably from 7 per cent in 2013 to 20 per cent in 2014 for professional breeders, a problem for many of them. It did not affect registrations; a

The Paris Dog Show is one of the greatest events but in 2015 there was an attempted terrorist attack in the same area the day before. President Marie-France Varlet chose to carry on the show despite the circumstances, saying that 'to cancel would be to prove terrorism right'. The show went off well and nothing happened to disturb the judging. There were only a few absentees from the entry of 3,574. BIS was the Cocker, Sophie Simonelli's Gallinagos All This Time.

BIS at Angers 2015 from 2,165 dogs was Brigitte Moreau's Lakeland Terrier Slicey The Moonshiner.

Montluçon's BIS was Erick Richard's Pekingese Ch Vannjty Guillaume The Conquerant.

record of 218,328 in 2014 was followed by a similar number in 2015.

The identification file, run by I-CAD (Identification des Carnivores Domestiques), is under way.

The DNA genetic identification managed by the SCC is developing well; 26,000 genetic fingerprints are registered on pedigrees. Next step will be predictive tests.

Show entries remained stable. Entries of dogs with cropped ears will no longer be accepted whatever the citizenship of the owners.

The most successful show of the year was Metz with 4,600 entries. In 2016, the French Championship Show will be organised here on the first weekend of June by the dynamic Canine de Lorraine team.

In addition to dog shows, many recreational activities or working trials took place.

Agility is very popular and more than 700 trials were organised in 2015. The French team was very successful at the World Championship in Bologna.

Agility for disabled people is widely held: Isabelle Kerfuric with her Border Collie was Para Agility World Champion. The French team brought back four gold medals and a first place.

Dog dancing becomes more and more popular and the French team took the top places in Milan.

The herding tradition is still living in our country and more than a thousand dogs took part in tests. Among other disciplines, French teams are World Champions in Mondioring and rescue dogs.

Then there are gundog tests – they must have a working title to be French champions. For hounds, 83 tests were organised; 4,139 passed and 157 obtained certificate of working champion). Dachshund and terrier trials are also. All kind of hunts are popular in France which is we have so many hound breeds, 54.

Trials for truffle dogs involved a variety of breeds, as did water rescue events.

The most prestigious hunting event was the Game Fair held in Lamotte Beuvron. It is mostly given over to pack hounds with 6,000 dogs and 100,000 visitors. It hosted Nationales d'Elevage for group 6 and for some pointing breeds, water dogs and retrievers.

The SCC literary prize, for a work which underlines the relationship between man and dogs, was awarded to Jean-Christophe Rufin for his novel *The Collier Rouge*. He is a neurologist, member of the Académie Française, diplomat, humanitarian doctor, journalist, author and dog lover and gave the prize to a charity.

In 2017 Paris will host the third International Dog Health Workshop. President Christian Eymar Dauphin reminds us that the SCC values have stayed unchanged since tits foundation: breeding healthy, fit dogs, true to Standards and welfare. ∎

At the Dachshund Nationale at Chateaumeillant, BIS from 230 dogs was Christine Marion's Longhaired Eliot d'Harcourt.

After Switzerland, Germany and some other European countries, France has recognised the Continental Bulldog, more commonly called Conti. They were exhibited for the first time at the French Championship. The breed is under supervision of the Club Français du Bullmastiff et du Mastiff at whose Nationale there was a presentation of the breed. Temperament and health tests have been developed.

The Dobermann Nationale was won by Pierre Jegou's Halonzo Graf Vivario vom Steinigerweg. Judges were Carole Bard and Hans Wiblishauser.

GERMANY

Report: **Dr Wilfried Pepe**
Photos: **Robert**

Big shows move outdoors

At the international show held with the Europasieger, D
Wilfried Peper chose as BIS the Afghan Hound, Karin an
Lothar Hessling's Agha Djari's Blue Steel.

The VDH Europasieger show in Dortmund was
combined with a cat show. BIS judged by Rony Doedjir
went to the Samoyed from Denmark, Gitte Morell's
Cabaka's Kiss The Rain, who at the same venue later
in the year won BIS at the international show held in
conjunction with the Bundessieger.

In 2015, the general assembly of the German Kennel Club (VDH) with just a hint of progress, an extremely successful Bundessieger show as highlight of a blooming show scene, and no further decline in registration figures appeared to be the topics of major importance.

At the general assembly, held in April, six of the seven members of the board – among them the president and the two vice-presidents – stood again. With only one exception they were re-elected with nearly unanimous votes. The 'new man', as a second representative of the working scene, reflects the current dominating influence of the internationally most successful German working clubs.

As a concession to economic necessities, even in Germany national and international shows may now be organised as open-air shows. The Meisdorf show with its lovely show venue of Meisdorf Castle has been a really encouraging start, fulfilling the high quality standards of the new show regulations.

As the financial conditions for indoor shows are turning from bad to worse, national and international open-air shows will become an attractive part of the German show scene once the necessary investments are done. In this context, better co-operation by the regional organisations of the VDH could be helpful.

In order to prevent the wind of change blowing too fast in Germany, the general assembly voted against the Fédération Cynologique Internationale proposal to pay moderately higher travel expenses per kilometre and daily fees to the judges.

Nevertheless, all international CACIB shows as well as the national all-breed shows kept their high level of entries and visitors – well-recommended shows close to neighbouring countries drew even more of them.

As far as registrations are concerned the poor record of the previous year is unbroken – but 85 registations more than last year means stagnation at a poor level.

Fortunately there is one group of breeds with registration figures of remarkable stability for more than 15 years: the German gundogs. On top is the German Wirehaired Pointer followed by the German Shorthaired Pointer, Small Münsterländer, German Spaniel (Wachtelhund), German Longhaired Pointer and Weimaraner. A breed group solid as a rock – but unfortunately breeders and owners are not very interested in national and international shows. Traditionally, they prefer their specialties. ∎

The German Dog of the Year
2015 was presented at a festival
evening. Out of 49 dogs who had
gained the title VDH-Jahressieger
2014, a team of three all-rounders,
Luis Manuel Calado Catalan , Gisa
Schicker and Chan Weng, selected
a shortlist of six finalists. FCI
president Dr Rafael de Santiago
had the pleasure of judging the
final. His much applauded choice
was the Sealyham Terrier All Abou
Aksel of Cesky Dream's, owned
and handled by Michael Weser.
He will therefore be the German
participant at the Eukanuba World
Challenge in Amsterdam. He
is seen winning a group under
Euheny Kuplyauskas.

Once again the highlight of the German show scene was the Jubilee Bundessieger show, organised as a dog and horse show for ten years. An entry of 9,383 dogs from 34 countries, 123 judges from 23 countries (at this and the concurrent international show), more than 82,000 visitors, perfect doggy entertainment, and top dogs in the finals – a really successful event. Rafael de Santiago gave BIS to the Weimaraner Driftwood's Quik Draw, owned by Josee Salas from the Netherlands.

Offenburg's BIS under Horst Kliebenstein was the Toy Poodle Osmanthus Omnia Noir, owner Bruno Nodalli from Italy.

...atja and Sabine Rauhut's Tibetan Terrier Falamandus ...emastered Edition was BIS at Chemnitz.

Peter Machetanz gave BIS at Neumünster to the Irish Terrier Red Wire Mastermind, owned by Birgitta and Arne Sköld from Sweden.

A Chinese Crested from Russia won BIS at Erfurt, Julia Poluektova's Olivera's The Most Popular.

Bremen's BIS winner under Roberto Schill was Katherina Dabelstein's Portuguese Water Dog Go And Win Golden Eyes Without Boots.

The German Winner Show at Leipzig was won by Noel Baaser's Basenji C-Quest Jokuba Dandy Shandy. Judge was Leif-Herman Wilberg.

...anuela Massing's Neapolitan Mastiff Rio A Castore Et ...olluce won BIS at Hannover.

Kerstin Patzold's Australian Shepherd Energie's Stonepine The Bachelor was BIS at Nürnberg.

Leipzig international show BIS under Stefan Sinko was the Pembroke Corgi Andvol Newsmaker, owned by Irina Gurchenko from Russia.

NETHERLANDS

Protecting the national breeds

Report by: **Haja van Wessem**

SOME OF the Dutch national breeds are not recognised in the UK and the US. This means that puppies born in these countries will not be registered or receive an official pedigree.

As the population of the Stabyhoun and the Wetterhoun is getting dangerously small, the Dutch Kennel Club (Raad van Beheer, RvB) has agreed with the Kennel Club and the American KC that Stabyhoun and Wetterhoun puppies born in these two countries can be registered by the RvB in the Netherlands. Hopefully, in this way the population and the gene pool of the two breeds can increase.

The first pedigrees for a litter of British Stabyhouns have been issued in August 2015 by the RvB.

As from December 29, 2014 it is no longer allowed to export or import dogs under the age of 15 weeks. Before coming into the Netherlands or travelling abroad, a puppy must have had its rabies vaccine at 12 weeks and stay with the breeder for another three weeks before import or export is allowed. These rules apply to the Netherlands, Belgium and Germany.

This government decision met with many negative reactions from breeders, breed clubs and the RvB, because the prospective owner of the puppy is totally dependent on the way the breeder does or does not socialise the puppy.

In reply to questions, the Minister said not to foresee any problems: breeders could well import an older puppy, have their bitch mated in another country or import sperm.

Finland allows a puppy to come into the country provided there is an official document that it has not been in a possibly

The Amsterdam Winner Show in 2014 was a specially festive event because for the first time a European country had the honour of hosting the prestigious Eukanuba World Challenge. The 34 competing dogs were divided into groups and judged by Aramis Lim from Australia, Ronnie Irving from the UK, Damir Skok from Croatia and Leif-Herman Wilberg from Norway. The winner was the Affenpinscher Tricky Ricky from Yarrow-Hi Tech, owned by Jongkie Budiman and Mieke Cooijmans and handled by Tortrakul Chaiyah. He has also won the World Show in Helsinki. With them are Jose Luis Ibañez and Hounaida Lasry of Eukanuba and final judge Jørgen Hindse.

In 2015 the Raad van Beheer will again host the Eukanuba World Challenge. There will be more activities and more trade stands and the show will have an atmosphere of a lifestyle event.

Runner-up in the World Challenge was the Old English Sheepdog from Hungary, Bottom Shaker So Easy To Love, handled by Zsolt Hanó for József Koroknai and Zsuzsanna Vörös. With them are FCI president Rafael de Santiago, section judges Ronnie Irving and Leif Herman Wilberg and Jose Luis Ibañez of Eukanuba.

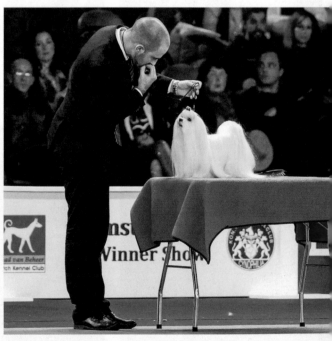

Third in the World Challenge was the Maltese from Italy, Ch Cinecittá Sacha Baron Colen, handled by Javier Gonzalez Mendikote for Franco Prosperi and Stefano Paolantoni. He later won the group at Crufts.

BIS at the Winner was the Saluki Qirmizi Ovation, bred and owned by Niklas and Ingunn Eriksson from Sweden. He had won RBIS at the Holland Cup.

Reserve BIS at the Winner was the Petit Basset Griffon Vendéen Caramel Apple van Tum-Tum's Vriendjes, bred and owned by Gwen Huikeshoven. This internationally successful dog won several groups in 2015, was BIS3 at Rotterdam on the first day and BIS on the second day. He was BIS3 at the European Dog Show in Oslo.

...e Dog of the Year Show, where first, second and third ...aced dogs in the groups in 2014 competed, saw a ...ectacular win for the Shikoku Yuu-Saiki vd Egmato, ...ed and owned by Egitte van Veghel. He won several ...oups in 2014, was top dog in group 5 in 2014 and is a ...orld and European Winner. In 2015 he won three more ...oups and was BIS at Oss.

Runner up to the Shikoku was the multi-titled, group-winning Bearded Collie Beardie Connections Kenji, bred by Ingrid Hectors in Belgium and owned by Rinus and Anneke Otto. He was BIS on the first day at Rotterdam.

On the Friday before the Winner weekend the Holland Cup, a one-day CACIB show, took place. The entry had increased by 200 dogs to 2,300, due to the combination with the Winner Show and World Challenge. BIS was the Pointer Kanix Irene, owned by Christine Sonberg from Norway. It was a truly international affair, the group winners came from various countries and not one of them was Dutch!

...e second championship show for the Dutch Breeds ...as again very successful. There were 464 dogs entered, ...presenting the nine national breeds. BIS was the ...arkiesje Yip, owner Hieke Stelpstra-Metzlar.

...e first Anglo Français de Petite Vénerie has been ...gistered in the Dutch Stud Book. This is a French ...und, medium-sized, used as a scenthound, mostly in ...cks. It was created by crossing French scenthounds ...th Harriers and Poitevins. The name Petite Vénerie ...es not mean that the dogs of the breed are petite or ...all, but that it is used to hunt small game.

The Lhasa Apso Close To Perfection Next To You, bred and owned by Marion Radstock, who was top Lhasa Apso in the UK in 2013, was BIS at Eindhoven and at Goes on the first day.

rabies-infected environment. A request to apply the same rule in the Netherlands has so far been denied.

It has been estimated that around 50,000 puppies a year are being brought illegally into the Netherlands from Eastern Europe. The traders are members of a criminal, mafia-like group, for whom health and wellbeing of the puppies are of no importance. A majority of the puppies die an early death.

As they are in many cases lookalikes of purebred dogs, the effect on pedigree dogs bred by responsible breeders is devastating. To the public they are all one and the same.

It is an eternal struggle for the RvB, breed clubs and breeders to show the prospective puppy buyers that 'cheap' really is expensive. ∎

BELGIUM AND LUXEMBOURG

Report and photos by: **Karl Donvil**

Belgian King conquers Europe

Genk LKV's 35th anniversary show drew 1,724 dogs, a lot for a CAC show, more than many CACIB shows. BIS under Nemanja Jovanovic was the Basenji I Will Survive out of Africa owned by Patrick Daponte.

The Eurodogshow in Kortrijk celebrated its golden jubilee in 2013 with a double CACIB show and that was a big hit. In 2014 it reverted to a single CACIB but the number of entries climbed to a record 3,325. This is probably the most popular Continental show for British exhibitors – 208 were entered – and it was a Crufts qualifier.

It was a double win for our famous Wire Fox Terrier Kingarthur van Foliny Home. On Saturday he won the European Top Terrier Show and on Sunday he won BIS again, judge Norman Deschuymere. He is owned by his breeders Rony de Munter and Dieny Uiterwijk with Victor Malzoni and is handled by Warren Bradley.

This dog is conquering the world with a group and group 2 at Crufts, two groups wins at the World Shows in Helsinki and Milan and two BIS at the European Winner Shows in Brno and Oslo!

Mouscron show keeps on breaking its own record. It drew 2,179 dogs, 71 from Britain. Jean-Jacque Dupas' BIS was the American Cocker Spaniel Very Vigie I Don't Know owned by Mathilde Leonard-Nolle from France and handled by Hugues Schuh. Later he quickly gained his UK title plus two groups and a G4.

Brussels is preparing for the European Show in 2016; it promises to be a memorable event. The 2014 Brussels show drew a record entry of 3,726, no doubt helped by the new Benelux Winner title, introduced together with the Luxemburg and the Dutch kennel clubs. BIS under Damir Skok was the Akita Melodor Heart Of Gold owned by Chris McLean from the UK, handled by Nancy Daponte.

Brabo too increased its entry, by 16 per cent to 2,439. The Crufts qualifier will have played an important part, but the reputation of the show has increased enormously. Jacques Arnold's Cavalier My Little Poppy of Maesllyn was BIS under Diane Degryze.

PHOTO: RBT

…on't mistake the LKV Show in Genk for the Ambiorix Trophy in the same …lls. The Haspengouwse Canine Society is Belgium's youngest and had the …mbition to have its own CACIBs. As that caused a problem for the Belgian …nnel it was decided that the CACIBs be given alternately to each club. So … the first time the Ambiorix show was granted this honour. BIS under Des …anton was the British-bred and owned Australian Shepherd, Angie and …il Allan and Robert Harlow's Allmark Fifth Avenue.

Lommel may be one of Belgium's smallest shows, but certainly one of the cosiest; 1,180 dogs were entered. BIS was the harlequin Great Dane Brisseida Enid von Haus Das Freude, for Roger and Josiane Vanstraelen-Leenen.

Liège's entry dropped to 1,879, but that is still very good. Iuza Beradze gave BIS to the West Highland White Terrier from Germany, Royal Gigolo van Deipen Brook, owned by Bernd, Luise and Tina Deipenbrock.

The Royal Club Canin de Hainaut, organiser of Charleroi show, has had several turbulent years and a few without a show, but now is enjoying a slow and steady comeback. Unfortunately, the date clashed with shows in Germany and the Netherlands and entries dropped to 1,514, though many organisers would be happy with that many. During this show the Belgian Great Dane Club organised the European Championship for Great Danes in a separate hall.

BIS under Luis Pinto Teixeira was the Weimaraner Doc N'Camelot Heaven Can Wait owned by Edwin Lenaerts, Toni Finch and Linda van der Sichel. He also won BIS at Wieze – after a crisis of a few years ago it was doubtful if there would be a future for

…e first Libramont show was held in 2014; in fact it was no new show as it is the …placement for Namur show which was saved from disappearing by Luc Detry. …pectations were high in 2015 for its first CACIB show. Unfortunately, the date had … be rescheduled to September at the end of a busy period. That resulted in 'only' …535 entries which is not bad at all. I think this is going … be one of the most fantastic shows in Europe. It was …victory under Gerard Jipping for multiple BIS-winning …arded Collie Beardie Connections Kenji, owned … Rinus Otto from the Netherlands. He also won at …ogstraten whose entries increased to 2,377 dogs, and …ere was a splendid new layout.

that show. But a new committee brought a new spirit and the success of 2014 was perpetuated. It's 'only' a CAC show, but many will envy their 1,441 entries.

…echelen's entry went up to 1,568. BIS chosen by …an-Pierre Achtergael was the Labrador Leonardo of …gel's Head, owned by Thierry and Nicole Onckelinx- … Smedt.

Luxembourg's spring show was the city's 90th show and drew 5,288 entries. Frank Kane gave top spot to the Chow King Of Egypt de los Perros de Bigo, owned by Nuria Vigo Navajon from Spain.

The Luxembourg autumn show was affected by the concentration of CACIB shows before and afterwards, with a total of 3,944 dogs. BIS under Paul Stanton was an Irish Wolfhound Bourbon Tullamore Good Stuff, owned by Oleg Nalobin and Gregor Nemanic from Russia.

POLAND
A 'World Show' for native breeds

Report: Janusz Opara

Runner-up at the Polish Breeds show was the Polish Hunting Dog Huncwot Klusujaca Sfora, owned by Grzegorz Weron, handled by Aleksandra Szydlowska.

Supreme BIS at the Polish Breeds championship shows was Beata Klawinska's Polish Lowland Sheepdog Akwarela Rawipon.

Both registrations and entries at Polish shows have grown during 2015. A crowded calendar must have made our exhibitors feel spoilt for choice.

The unbelievable 16 international FCI shows plus a no less stunning number of 50 all-breed national events have given more than enough opportunities even to the most greedy collectors of ribbons.

On top of these, we have had countless shows for single or multiple breeds – not many of us could believe there might be any growth in numbers of shows planned for the coming years.

Life has had surprises in store and we were told of the Polish Kennel Club's decision to augment the number of CACIB shows to 19 in years to come.

Another surprise was the FCI decision that Poland will be granted the organisation of the European Dog Show in 2018! We all are happy to have yet another opportunity to prove our worth as experienced organisers.

After our EDS of 2000 and the World Show of 2006 it will be Poland's fourth occasion to host a prestigious FCI event – in 1969 Poland hosted the FCI general assembly with a Pole, Edward Mikulski, as president, and the accompanying FCI Dog Show. At that time it was just an 'international show' as only years later were these FCI General Assembly-combined shows renamed 'World Shows'.

Regardless of the official name, one still thinks with amazement about the invincible determination of the then active dog fanciers. They managed it all under the communists and against their antisocial rules and intolerance towards any attempts of co-operation with the countries from behind the Iron Curtain.

Our FCI events of 2000 and 2006 were held in Poznan, our most renowned show venue due to its fabulous International Fair Centre used for many decades by the experienced crew of the Poznan branch of the Polish KC. These shows were overwhelmingly successful and became a canon for all Polish shows to come.

The EDS of 2018 will be held in a new location – Kielce is a town with population of 200,000 and is one of the most dynamically developing places in Poland. Its International Trade Fair is a modern complex and running a show there will be a challenge for the local branch of the KC, and a chance to expand the Polish exhibition venues with a new one in a completely different part of the country.

Still looking forward to full FCI recognition of the fifth Polish breed, the Polish Hunting Dog, we have tried hard to draw the attention of the FCI, plus international opinion, to this wonderful breed and to the rest of our breeds.

Each Polish breed has its own championship show each year; 2015 was unusual in that all these were run the same weekend at the same showground in Bydgoszcz, home of the Polish Lowland Sheepdog. All were well filled with entries and the finals reflected the situation we have in our breeds – supreme BIS was the Polish Lowland Sheepdog with the Polish Hunting Dog running up. These two breeds have been much stronger than the others both in numbers and depth of quality over quite a long time.

January 2016 will see us run a World Show for Polish breeds – a new idea and a new style of co-operation between our KC and the FCI. The FCI auspices will not only result in the coveted 'World' rank in the show's name but will bring international publicity to help make these breeds known across the world.

They have a super venue at Opole where successful CACIB events have been run over last four decades, and all the knowledge and experience it takes to run a good show. Alongside the show will be a breed symposium with the respective clubs' representatives as lecturers; all have an impressive background as breeders and judges.

BIS at Katowice under Dusan Paunov was Kata Magyar's White Swiss Shepherd Doux of Ice Wine.

The winning breeder's group at the Polish Tatra Dog Club show.

THE WORLD SHOW

Beardie best in Milan

photos by:
Karl Donvil

The Fédération Cynologique Internationale (FCI) World Show took place at in Milan, hosted for the third time by the Italian Kennel Club (ENCI). The show drew an entry of 19,927 dogs of 392 breeds and 68 nationalities for the 184 dogs, plus 9,516 entries at the associated breed club shows.

Held in three enormous halls, the event was generally considered to be a success and judging ran smoothly each day, finishing in good time. The same remarkably efficient results service was used as at the 2014 World Show in Finland. A shadow was cast over the event by the deaths of seven Russians and their 19 dogs in an accident en route to the show.

Best in show was the Bearded Collie Int Ch Ops I Did It Again del Cuore Impavido, owned by Olga Ozimova, a Russian living in Italy, and bred in Italy by Filippo Ripoli. Judge was Francesco Balducci, pictured with the rosette. The cup is presented by FCI president Rafael de Santiago, and ENCI president Dino Muto is holding another of the trophies.

BIS3 was the junior Italian Greyhound Lady Godiva dei Raggi Da Luna, owner Gaetano Caldarone from Italy, who also won the award for best of the Italian breeds.

RBIS was the Black Dwarf Poodle Ch Kudos Firework, owned by Mikael Nilsson from Sweden. Group judge was Roberto Schill.

The Gordon Setter Ch Ludstar Frederick Frankenstein, from Italy, owned by Michele Ivaldi and handled by his wife Ludovica Salamon, was BIS4. Group judge was Barbara Müller.

Highest place for a British-bred dog was a group win for the American Cocker Spaniel Sh Ch Afterglow Dragon Quest, bred by Mike Gadsby and Jason Lynn, and now owned by Attila Csaba. He was Pro Plan/Dog World Pup of the Year for 2012, and was handled by Javier Gonzales Mendikote. Group judge was Paolo Dondina.

Wales'Warren Bradley handled the Wire Fox Terrier Ch Kingarthur van Foliny Home to win the terrier group for the second time at a World Show; he has also topped the European Show twice. He is owned by Rony de Munter and Dieny Uiterwijk from Belgium and Victor Malzoni from Brazil. MORE PHOTOS: PAGE 151

ITALY

The Italian show scene in pictures

PHOTO: ANDREW BRACE

Pro Plan Pup of the Year in Italy for 2014, chosen at the San Remo show, was Maria Lazzavera's Borzoi Jemisse Infanta Esperanza.

A big winner of 2015 has been Luigi Caiazzo's French Bulldog Perfect Lady.

BIS at Italy's Christmas show at Erba was Valentina Barcella's Miniature Wire Dachshund Queenslord Skinny Love, who also won the group at the European Winner Show.

PHOTO: ANDREW BRACE

At the Gruppo Cinofilo Sedrianese show at Milan, BIS was Astrid Conterio's young Bulldog Chewbacca della Ca del Conte.

The Rome show at the end of 2014 was topped by Belamax Budiman's Jack Russell Terrier bitch Granlasco A Beautiful Mind, handled by Alice Varchi. Judge was Hassi Assenmacher-Feyel.

At Alba's first international show, BIS was Barbara Moreschi's Samoyed Cabaka's Bobbie of Storm Cat, a big winner over several years.

At the Vercelli and Biella double shows, BIS winners were Bruno and Paola Nodalli's Toy Poodle Osmancthius Omnia Noir and Fabio Ottaviani's Great Dane Diamante della Baia Azzurra.

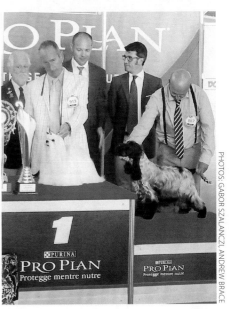

In Italy, a number of societies co-operate in running double show weekends, but in March there was a triple-show weekend with the Piacenza, Parma and Reggio Emilio events. Winners were: Gabriella Lovati's Australian Shepherd Quicksilver Rider del Whymper delle Grandes Jorasses, judge Francesco Balducci; Michele Morganti's Basset Hound Nhabira Kickoff, handled by Federico Sanguinetti (judge Jean Paul Kerihuel); and Franco Prosperi's Maltese Cinecittà Ian Somerhalder (judge Roberto Velez Pico). The Maltese is pictured winning another BIS at Torino under Paolo Dondina. BIS3 here was Angela Francini's Cocker Spaniel Francini's Day By Day, a big winner of the year who had spent some time in the UK in 2014, ending up top Cocker.

MORE WORLD SHOW GROUP WINNERS

Group winner under Carla Molinari: the Dalmatian Int Ch Dalmino Voodoo, owned by Zeljka Halper Drazic and Mihael Drazic from Croatia.

Group winner: the Cane Corso Brutus, owner Marta Garcia Pagan from Spain.

The Wire Dachshund Piumetta del Mio Cappello, owner Annaluce Saletti from Italy and another group winner handled by Javier Gonzalez Mendikote.

Group winner: the Standard Mexican Hairless Zoe, owner Graciela Mendez Galvan from Mexico.

IBERIA
Spain to host the 2020 World Show

Report and photos
Marcelino Poz

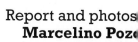

At Talavera autumn show BIS was Alberto Velasco's Lakeland Terrier Chelines Fly Me To The Moon.

Spain

BIS at the Madrid spring show was Nuria Vigo Navajo's Chow King of Egypt de los Perros de Bigo.

According to the RSCE statistics, current undisputed leader in the Dog for the Year table is Tamara Jackson and Ingrid Mayer's Smooth Chihuahua Dartan The Valiant Aladar, a multiple group and BIS winner.

I will begin with the best news: the RSCE, Royal Canine Society of Spain, is celebrating because at the last general assembly of the Fédération Cynoligique Internationale, held in Milan, Spain was elected to organise the World Dog Show in Madrid in 2020.

For 2015, the show calendar included 30 CACIB and 25 CAC shows. The most important shows whose wins qualified towards the Spanish Championship were Talavera autumn international show, the 'flying points' going to Bilbao, and Madrid with the spring international show, where as always Queen Mother Sofia walked around the rings watching the dogs which are her passion.

In second position is a Spanish breed, Felipe Alberto Llano Palacios' Dogo Canario Grando Presa de Casa Goxy.

Current third is the multiple BIS winning Basset Hound, a former Top Dog in Spain, Marta Lucena and Daniel Alvarez's Ch Bombay de Wila-Damar.

a de España

Occupying fourth position is the Japanese Akita Inu Taikou Go Shun'You Kensha, owner Silvia Exposito.

Fifth is the Gordon Setter Fairray Carioca, owners Alfonso Alarcón Vergara and Julia Popova.

Portugal

Portugal's show calendar consisted of 13 CACIB shows and 15 with CACs. Three of them count towards the champion title and two qualify for Crufts, Porto and the Lisbon Winner. Weekends with more than one show are especially attractive to exhibitors.

Once again the Portuguese Kennel Club's Lisbon international show took place during on Friday and Saturday evenings due to the heat.

Carlos Miguel Oliveira Ramos' Basenji Primitive Style Born To Be A Traveler.

Pictured are some of Portugal's top dogs, including José Homem de Mello's Basset Hound Youra dos Sete Moinhos.

Pedro Antonio Ribeiro Café's Grand Basset Griffon Vendéen Et Pour Le Dessert da Terra Quente. Other leading winners are the Bullmastiff GDR Iris and the Portuguese Pointer Fascinio Fatal do Berco do Basalto.

Sonia and Mario Marques' Cocker Spaniel Perchwater Moves Like Jagger.

Gibraltar

In the city of the Rock, the Gibraltar Kennel Club celebrated in September its 42nd and 43rd international shows. As always success was assured, as the events are a meeting point for show dog enthusiasts of southern Europe.

The possibility of gaining a Gibraltar champion title and a qualification for Crufts resulted in 2,177 entries.

In sixth place is Jose Luis Amezcua Dueñas' Afghan Hound Taliban Best Take it All. Following on are another Basset Xanthos de Tres Manzanas, the Dobermann Akira de Lances, French Bulldog Iron County I Gina and American Staffordshire Terrier Karballido Staffs Electra-Natchios.

At the first Gibraltar show Hassi Assenmacher-Feyel gave BIS to the Yorkshire Terrier Heart Breaker de L'Epazeor, owned by Valerie Magoarou.

At the Sunday show under Andrew Brace it was another victory for the Chow King Of Egypt de los Perros de Bigo.

RUSSIA

At last a chance for specialist judges

Report and photos:
Aleksey Kalashnikov

ANY ENDEAVOUR can be successful under the right conditions. This applies to any human activity, including dog breeding, and Russian dog fanciers have been lucky this way.

Firstly, this is because Russia has a population of about 140 million people, which allows for the existence of an independent market and breeders can make money from the sale of puppies.

Secondly, there is an old tradition of having animals as pets. Thirdly, the population has enough free spending money to buy and take care of dogs as pets. Even though we might like to think that having a dog is an absolute necessity of life, in reality this is hardly the case.

Russia has much in common with other countries that have well-developed breeding and show systems, but also has its unique features, which will be mentioned later.

The day after the Eurasia show took place the seventh All Russian Conference of FCI (Fédération Cynologique Internationale) Judges, devoted to presentations on various breeds. It is difficult to evaluate the content as admission was limited and the reports were not published, but this was not a serious blow to dog fanciers as the majority of the presenters had only a faint connection to the dog breeds they were reporting on.

Russia has entered the ranks of the FCI very smoothly and has quickly adapted there, especially when it comes to doing favours in exchange for favours.

Today, noticeable changes are taking place in the composition of judges. For some time it seemed that only all-rounders could work at Russian shows. According to FCI rules, titles are not connected in any way to the number of dogs entered; if a breed has only one entry, then that dog has to right to receive the title of champion. The number of breeds with small representation is so great that it is not feasible for clubs to invite expert judges for each breed.

For this reason and with few exceptions, all-rounder judges (about 80 people) work at all Russian shows. With few exceptions, they are not successful breeders and in general they are just very energetic and adventurous people who are united by the love of travelling. Modern shows sometimes take place in quite exotic places that one probably wouldn't otherwise have the opportunity to visit.

Recently the situation has begun to change and breeders with notable experience over the past 25 years have begun to be invited to judge. For example, successful Cocker Spaniel breeders such as L Moon and Elena Adamovskaya, the Yorkshire Terrier breeder Anna Babaeva, the Dachshund breeder Valeria Bobikova and others have been in demand.

But this is merely a tendency and when you show your dog in Russia you risk receiving your title from a tourist, however pleasant he or she may be.

Fans of working dogs live a completely separate life, and very rarely can anyone combine participation in working contests with the show ring. In February, the sled dog championship took place in the Austrian city of Sharnitz. The third round of medium distance skijoring yielded Maksim Mikhailov from Russia as the winner.

In June the World Championship in Obedience took place in the Italian city of Turin. Galina Fedorova and the Border Collie Wonder Westspasy took the bronze prize in individual competition and the

Crufts' popularity with Russian exhibitors has increased in recent years since it has been shown on television. In 2015, best in show was the Scottish Terrier McVan's To Russia With Love, owned by Marina Khenkina from Russia and bred in the US. She has had many victories, not only in Continental Europe, but in England where she was also BOB at Crufts 2013 and at Windsor 2015. She is pictured after a victory at a past Eurasia show.

This is not the first Russian Scottie to win in England. Other winners have come from the kennel of Valentina Popova including Crufts RBIS Filisite Brash Celebration.

Russian team came in sixth overall.

In the mid '90s in Russia, serious changes took place in all areas related to the Soviet Union, including the system of training working dogs. The persons who called for change were simply the most sure of themselves and not necessarily the most competent or successful specialists in the field. At first, standard norms formulated in the USSR were criticised and then rules, which were not well thought out, were made for conducting competitions. The main element was using the dog against the trainer. Such competitions were called the Big Ring or the Russian Ring as an analogy to mondioring.

Today it seems that working dog fanciers have figured out what's what and now prefer the real training of obedience and agility along IPO guidelines. For those who are the most developed, there is still mondioring, although real success in this sport has been achieved only by one breed, the Malinois.

It is considered that the most apolitical people are found among people who own pets. Such was true for Russia until the Eurasia

The Top Dog of the year is chosen at the end of December at the last show of the year. Until this happens the title of Top Dog is retained by the winner of the most points at the Golden Collar Show of the previous year. For December 2014, it was the Tibeian Mastiff Grand Lioness Ju Akbar, owned by Gennadii Zakhryapin. The second title of Top Dog (under another system) went to the Afghan Hound Amal Salang Coeur D'Coeurs, owned by Denis Shirokov, well known for his wins at Eurasia in 2013 and at the Russia Dog Show in 2014. At the European Dog Show in Oslo he was BIS4.

Top kennel at the Golden Collar show was Norden Liht owned by Inna Yakovleva who has been breeding Smooth Dachshunds successfully for many years.

At the World Show in Milan the Russian entries took second place in the number of CACIB titles awarded with 170 wins. Unfortunately, on the eve of the show a tragedy occurred. In the early morning a mini-van with breeders on their way to Milan went off the road into oncoming traffic and was struck head on. Seven people including the driver and 19 dogs lost their lives. At the session of the General Assembly of FCI, the Russian breeders were honoured with a minute's silence.

The show was notable for both Russian wins and losses. Among the former, the Giant Schnauzer and Poodle kennel Gently Born should be mentioned, as should the Dreamkiss Miniature Schnauzers, Rus Kornels Airedales, Dan-Star-Com Pomeranians, Shafron Sherhi Shih Tzu, Soloviev Borzois and Bon Triumph Chows. And for the first time a dog from Russia won BIS at a World Show, the Bearded Collie, Olga Klimova's Ops I Did It Again del Cuore Impavido.

The ceremony of handing over the FCI flag to the next year's host took place in the main ring and Russia received the flag as the organiser of the WDS for 2016.

PHOTO: YOSSI GUY

PHOTO: YOSSI GUY

The Eurasia show takes place on different dates each year and is slowly being moved closer to summer. In 2015, it took place on March 21-22. BIS on the first day under Marja Talvitie was the Azawakh Azamour Khemosabi, owned by Andrey Klishas, handled by Nicolas Pineiro and seen with RKF president Alexander Inshakov. On the second day under Karl-Erik Johansson, BIS was the Irish Wolfhound Bourbon Tullamore Good Stuff, owner Oleg Nalobin, handled by Gregor Nemanic, seen with group judge Espen Engh. On the first day there were 6,476 entries (200 down on 2014) from more than 200 breeds.

That people who are well off financially are also dog owners is not unique to Russia, but what is specific about Russia is the desire of such people to take part in shows and to win. They do win a lot, from our own Eurasia Show to European shows.

The most prominent of such dog owners include the wife of the vice-premier of Russia, Olga Shuvalova and her Pembroke Corgi Andvol Pinkerton (pictured winning a group under Nemanja Jevanovic, handled by Olga Shilova), and a member of the Federation Council Andrey Klishas who owns the Gran Vencedor kennel which includes French Bulldogs, Bernese Mountain Dogs, Bull Terriers, Russian Greyhounds, Dachshunds, Chihuahuas, Irish Wolfhounds, Akitas and Azawakhs.

In one of her interviews, Mrs Shuvalova expressed her view on dog breeding: "I consider that too many have taken up breeding dogs and there are too few real expert breeders, not only for our breed (the Pembroke). For some reason people think that they can make money selling purebred dogs," this from a person whose official registered earnings are about £30,000 a day. It is difficult to judge the influence Pinkerton has had, but today the Corgi is one of the most popular breeds.

catalogue came out in 2015. On the first page, a large paragraph of the introduction was devoted the life of Ukrainian dog fanciers in the Crimea, which is now under the jurisdiction of Russia:

"It is pleasant to note that starting in April 2015, in the Crimean cities of Dzhanka, Alushta, Fedosiya, Simferopol and Sevastopol, dog shows are now taking place under the auspices of the RKF."

The subject of the Crimea has indeed divided Russian society, but to whom is this introduction addressed? If you don't have time to read the great writer George Orwell, you can see and feel what he wrote about by just visiting Russia. ■

Representatives of two consistently successful breeders: the Giant Schnauzer Gently Born Man Of My Dream, breeder Anna Vlasova, and the Pomeranian Dan-Star-Kom O Urfin Jus, bred by Lyudmila Komyakova.

HUNGARY

A solid, quiet year

Report and photos
Gabor Szalanczi

Runner-up at the 2014 Eukanuba World Challenge was the Old English Sheepdog Bottom Shaker So Easy To Love, owned by Jozsef Koroknai and handled by Zsolt Hano, pictured with Rafael de Santiago, president of the FCI, and Jose Luis Ibañez of Eukanuba.

At the May international shows in Budapest, Friday and Sunday BIS was the Newfoundland Skipper's Aramis, owned by László Kovács and handled by Brigitta Maroti, seen with Dr Tamas Jakkel, main judge of the shows, Nicola Imbimbo, and Andras Korozs, president of the Hungarian Kennel Club. Other Hungarian dogs to win BIS at the country's international shows included Eleonóra Pongrácz's French Bulldog, Vanessa von New Glandorf and József Koroknai's Old English Sheepdog Bottom Shaker Zephyr Dream

For the Hungarian Kennel Club, 2015 was a solid, quiet year with more shows held at home, and moderate success outside.

The year saw held 18 international shows (with an average of 1,000 entries), and 17 national shows (6-700 entries), plus other club shows.

At the World Dog Show in Milan more than 60 Hungarian dogs took junior, adult or veteran World Winner titles.

At the European Show in Norway, Hungary scored just a few modest wins, eight EW titles, and just two BOB. This show was too far away and too expensive for the Hungarian breeders and exhibitors, and only a very small number travelled to Oslo.

There were Hungarian competitors in World Championships in other dog sports, but this year no really big results, maybe next year? ∎

At the World Show, best veteran of the day under Kari Jarvinen was the Golden Retriever Dewmist Silk Screen, owned by Sándor Kozák, and shown by Zsolt Hanó. He also took his third World Winner title.

One of the most successful dogs of the Hungarian breeds, including European (2014) and World Winner (2015) titles, is the Pumi Pilisi Kócos Jóbarát, owned by Dóra Holdampf and Andrea Mesterné Spányik, handled by Virag Mester.

Two Hungarian dogs were runner-up in their junior group at the World Show: the Cocker Spaniel, Aloha Lynwater of La Vie Magnifique, owned by Péter Gombi, and the Miniature Smooth Dachshund Cyberdachs Mini Dior, owned by Tibor Kis. Two Hungarian handlers won groups, Bence Kantor with a Croatian Dalmatian, and Beatrix Fabian with a Spanish Cane Corso.

AUSTRIA

Report:
Maria-Luise Doppelreiter

European Show comes to Wels

Great news: Austria will be host for the Eurodog Show in 2019! The show will be held from June 14 to 16 in Wels, a very nice, spacious showground, with easy access from the motorway.

As the World Show will be held in China that year, this will be something like a 'European World Show' – I hope to meet many friends there!

Tulln is the highlight of the Austrian show year. For many years clubs combined the CACIB show in Tulln with their Clubwinner shows, but in 2015 it was announced at rather short notice that Tulln would be a double CACIB show (all breeds on each day, one day for the Bundessieger title, the other day for the Crufts qualifier) for the first time.

Because of this many clubs had to change their plans; some organised club shows on Friday, some on Saturday afternoon after the judging for the international show, some designated the CACIB winners as the club winners. There are new halls in the Tulln fair centre, and these were used very well with big rings and lots of space around them. In the 'older' halls there could have been more space – I hope this is planned for 2016.

BIS on Saturday was judged by Lisbeth Mach and won by Enrico de Gaspari's Whippet Sobresalto XXX and on Sunday Phyllis Poduschka-Aigner chose Yvonne Weber's Papillon Anton vom Postberg.

We are very proud of our small agility team of Shetland Sheepdogs – they became Vice World Champions!

Our Kennel Club (ÖKV) is very interested in the fact that purebred dogs are also healthy dogs! At every judges' briefing we are reminded to judge not only for type, but also for health and soundness, and in 2015 we also have a vet controlling the BOB winners in the pre-judging ring before they are allowed to enter the group ring.

The last show in Austria is traditionally the double CACIB show in Wels. The competition Champion of Champions was judged a bit differently in 2014. For the first time not just Austrian-owned dogs were allowed to compete, and the event was judged as a sort of knock-out competition. It was nice to watch, although perhaps a bit too long. We'll see in 2015 whether they have changed the regulations to create more excitement.

BIS on Saturday was the Akita Taikou Go Shun'You Kensha; on Sunday the Shih Tzu Blue Diamond.

The first show of the year is traditionally Graz, again a very successful event. With many exhibitors, visitors and trade stands this show is a highlight for all dog fanciers. At this two-day-show we have a 'real' BIS, as the group winners are invited to come back on Sunday and compete for the overall win. This went to the Irish Setter Eirean California Lightyear.

Salzburg's committee headed by Heidi Kirschbichler organised a very nice show as usual. Bests of day were the English Setter Elitiste Mr Rodney von der Guldegg, and Coton de Tulear Nicollass Snezenky z Madagaskaru.

In spite of big problems with floods in the area the ÖKV did its best to organise a great show at Wieselburg. Bests were the Welsh Terrier Terrierix Gorgeous Gigi and Giant Schnauzer Gently Born Light Ray.

At Klagenfurt the Saturday show started in the afternoon, to give exhibitors the chance to enjoy a swim in the Wörthersee. Winners were the Whippet Absolute Mann Betty Boop and Clumber Spaniel Big Boom's Banditos Dex. This was the year's first Crufts qualifier for best junior and CACIB winners.

Oberwart show is held in connection with Szombathelyi (Hungary); dogs can win a combined title if they get a CACIB at both events. Bests were the English Setter Blue Baltic's Lawrence of Arabia and black Toy Poodle Joyful Jeffrey Starring Moravia.

Innsbruck welcomed us for another double show, all groups each day, won by the Siberian Husky Ankalyn Iris Goo Goo and Bouvier des Flandres Hardey from the Dogsfarm.

In 2016 we will again have a full set of shows, plus club shows; for more detail see www.oekv.at. ■

Tulln show also saw the Austrian finals for the Eukanuba World Challenge, which were won by the Miniature Schnauzer Steadlyn Zoomin'in, owned by Maxi Mayer, one of our successful ex-junior handlers, who also owns the runner-up, the Whippet Absolute Mann Never Give Up.

ISRAEL

An Israeli round-up

Report and photos
Yossi Guy

The Israeli Kennel Club (IKC) initiated a lot of different activities during the past year. 2014 ended with the Dog of the Year competition and selection of the junior handler for Crufts.

In January, the IKC held an all-breed CACIB show, followed by other all-breed shows in May, August and October. The number of dogs registered rose as did the number of club members.

Several Israeli dogs attended the World Show in Milan and a few returned with the coveted World Winner titles.

In May, the IKC held its largest show of the year at an agricultural school with expansive lawns, shady trees and a relaxed atmosphere despite the fact that there were over 860 dogs entered. Laurent Pichard gave BIS to Maya Shtirbu's Shih Tzu Ch Blue Diamond who also won in August under Dr Milovoje Urosevic when people flocked to the picturesque northern town of Maalot.

The Dog of the Year competition was judged by Tamas Jakkel, Rui Oliveira and Carlos Quinones. The entry was made up of Israeli champions and the final four were judged as part of a dinner party. Winner was Dorit Dembin and Dor Bazdatny's Cairn Terrier Ch Junior Beit Dembin.

The January show was a two-day affair. The largest entry was in Pomeranians, which have risen to popularity this year, and a Pom from Russia was BIS3. Agnes Kertes-Ganami's BIS was a Bichon Frisé from Russia, Irina Smirnova's Frizzled Life Angel.

The last CACIB show for the year, a Crufts qualifier, was in the desert town of Arad. BIS under Claudio di Giuliani was another Cairn Terrier, Red Beit Dembin, bred by Dorit Dembin and co-owned with the Weinstock family.

A midsummer night show was organised by the Israeli Herding Dog Club, judged by Sean Watson, Katarzyna Fiszdon and Graham Kerr. Graham's BIS was Paz Davidovich's Bearded Collie Ch Firstprizebears Lorne Green. The herding club was joined by several other clubs

The unique aspect of the Israeli Spitz Club show was the venue, the renovated first railway station in Jerusalem, which has become one of the city's trendiest recreational venues. Due to the city's large religious community, few shows have been held there on the Sabbath. Following the election of a secular mayor, more public places are open on Saturday, facilitating this dog show too. Several religious Jews could be seen among the spectators. Winner was Shay Schnitzer and Offer Sheffie's Shikoku Ch Royal Nippon Akitos Ichiban Shku. Following this show, president of the IKC Yossi Kosover announced it would hold two CACIB shows at the same location in October 2016.

Israel's top junior handler for two years in a row and its representative a Crufts 2015 was Paz Chen.

CROATIA

Summer nights' holiday in Split

PHOTO: BORIS GLUKHAREV

The Four Summer Night Shows at Split in Croatia are becoming increasingly popular with the European dog showing community, especially with a number of Britons who combine them with an extended holiday. This time DOG WORLD was one of the sponsors.

Here is the now traditional photograph of the supreme best in show which was judged by Italy's Paolo Dondina whose choice was the Italian Maltese, Ch Cinecitta Ian Somerhalder, a son of the year's Crufts toy group winner. He is owned by Stefano Paolantoni and Franco Prosperi.

With the judge is the famous Croatian singer, Jelena Rozga, who delighted fans by singing in the big ring before the BIS judging while in the foreground are Croatian Kennel Club president Damir Skok, president of the organising committee Ante Lucin and president of the Sporting Dogs Club of Split Zoran Dadić. As is the custom at the shows, 'Emperor Diocletian' was present with his guard of honour.

Ian had won BIS at the two international shows, on Friday and Sunday, under Francesco Cochetti and Hassi Assenmacher-Feyel.

PHOTO: BORIS GLUKHAREV

Thursday's BIS winner under Andras Korozs, and winner of the Interra terrier specialty, was Rony de Munter, Dieny Uiterwijk and Victor Malzoni's Wire Fox Terrier Ch Kingarthur van Foliny Home, handled by Warren Bradley. On the left is group judge Göran Bodegärd.

PHOTO: BORIS GLUKHAREV

BIS at the national show on Saturday at Split under Dinky Santos was the Bearded Collie Ch Ops I Did It Again del Cuore Impavido, owned by Olga Klimova.

PHOTO: GABOR SZALANCZI

Super BIS at the Zagreb international shows at the end of 2014 was the Akita Inu from Spain, Taikou Do Shun'You Kensha, owned by Silvia Exposito Casais and handled by Javier Gonzales Mendikote. Judge was Rony Doedjins.

GREECE

Repor
Lila Leventak

Shows with an island wind ...

Greek dog shows have entered a new era. 2015 saw more shows than ever. We have had shows every month except December and March and in some months more than two.

Two clubs organised shows for the first time: Lamia in January) and Chios in July. It was impressive how Greek exhibitors in the middle of the 'capital control' decided to participate, especially at the shows held during summer on the islands. ∎

Best junior in show on the first day at Syros and RBIS was the Azawakh Magic Pie of Hungarian Diamonds, owners Evi Traggali and Yiannis Karaantonis, seen with judge José Homem de Mello.

During the summer two important national shows were held on the island of Chios Island (six or seven hours by boat from Athens) and for the fifth year on Syros island (three hours).

They were very well organised and the clubs promoted their shows well. Chios Canine Society (www.kynochios.gr) is having a show at the end of July 2016 and Syros CS (www.syroskc.gr) at the beginning of July 2016, the weekend after a triple CACIB show in Athens.

At the Syros show it was impressive that the 80 per cent of the entries were junior dogs. Both days BIS, under Arne Foss and José Homem de Mello, was my 15-month-old Shar-Pei Precious Hug Bigger Than Life, son of the famous Ch Precious Hug True Secret Of Life. He was also best junior in show the second day and runner-up the first day.

At the time of writing we do not know who will be Top Dog for 2015. The Akita will certainly be in the final ten as will be another UK-bred dog Ch Reenano Rave Revue, Tsikalakis Constantinos' Standard Poodle, son of the famoys Ch Afterglow Maverick Sabre, and the Bulldog Ch Soul Guardian Atlas, owned by Manos Matsakis.

An important show was organised by the Greek Kennel Club (www.koe.gr) in Octobe Rafael de Santiago judged in Greece for the first time and Carla Molinari for the fourth. Other judges were Roberto Velez Pico, Erwin Deutscher and Janusz and Krystyna Opara. BIS on the last day of the triple show under Rafael was Vasilis Panopoulos' UK-bred Akita Ch Mynyddhaf's King Of The Ring, Top Dog all breeds in Greece for 2012 and 2014.

SOUTH AFRICA

**Photos:
Showdogs**

Show stars from South Africa

Best in show at the Kennel Union of Southern Africa championship show was Rossana Joubert's Siberian Husky Ch Kamchatka Razzmatazz, seen with judge Jaime Ganoza and Greg Eva.

Sita Vosloo's French Bulldog Carpe Diem Bulldog Malawi of Blommeland was best puppy at KUSA championship show under Ekarat Sangkunacap.

Goldfields Dog of the Year was Heidi Rolfes' Maltese Ch Winds Of Fortune Valentina's Magic, who was also RBIS at the Goldfields show.

USA National Dog 2015 was Riekie Erwee's Shih Tzu Ch Midnightdream Thril'F Victory, pictured with judges Ekarat Sangkunacap and Elizabet Caminade-Lavault. Another success for the Shih Tzu was BIS at Goldfields show.

Winner of the Supreme Dog award was Leon van Tubbergh and Carien Rootman's Irish Wolfhound Ch Pitlochry's Moon Walker of Supermoon.

AUSTRALIA

At Sydney Royal BIS under Simiko Ikeda was Lea and Ne[...] Rushforth's Smooth Fox Terrier Sup Ch Wyninebah Lex L[...]

Apathy rules out national unity

Report by: John Bryson

Six states and two territories form the Australian National Kennel Council, an umbrella organisation made up of either one or two delegates from each state, depending on size. National regulations are set by the ANKC, and most states have their own variations on these, on issues as important as judges training schemes.

In early 2015 Professor Brian Corbitt took to social media lamenting what he described as the 'inefficiency, inconsistencies and lack of cohesion' in the Australian dog scene and calling for 'a single governance' body for Australia. He found many supporters, in fact there were very few naysayers from among the rank and file membership.

I estimated from the response to Professor Corbitt's plan for the future that the majority of Australia's dog world would like to have seen it implemented.

However the plan did lack detail on how to achieve the end result and what we were faced with was a lot of reasonable ideas which required a great deal of work. The laconic Aussie laid-back image we have is still happily present in the general community, but in our dog world it unfortunately seems to translate into apathy.

In this instance the main stumbling blocks identified by those who spoke to *Dog News Australia* were firstly assets and secondly the aforementioned apathy. Some states have acquired their own grounds, including structures, and are very well off financially, while others have comparatively little such as, surprisingly, New South Wales.

South Australia's beloved David Roche left them in a very healthy situation and they have managed their finances well. Victoria own their own grounds but costly legal battles with some of their members have cost them dearly in the past five years. Basically the wealthy would like to maintain their autonomy and don't see why they should share with the poor!

So the reality of one national organisation will sadly elude us for many years to come, I fear.

Watching the on again, off again blacklisting of judges and muscle-flexing between the Fédération Cynologique Internationale Asia and the Pacific Section, the FCI itself and the American Kennel Club had already changed the average Australian's view of the FCI.

Combined with the fallout from the over-publicised debates about the World Dog Show in China, but primarily because of the changing

Winner of the Top Dog Australia title for 2014, the competition held in Canberra in February 2015, was the Kerry Blue Terrier representing Queensland, Sup Ch Chaduna Blu Hellraizer, owned by Shane Avery, Tiffany Ross and Kerry Lee. Pictured are John Bryson from Top Dog Media, Cara Hawkins from Royal Canin, and judges Charles Trotter, Patricia Craige-Trotter and Laurent Pichard.

PHOTO: PEDINI

At the Royal Melbourne Show BIS went to Lorraine and Malcolm Boyd's Standard Poodle Ch Picardy PS I Love You. Judge was Rui Oliveira.

PHOTO: INGRID MATSCHKE

Brisbane Royal's BIS, judged by Manuel Borges, went to Mel Brown's Australian Shepherd ArticIvory Watch Ur Back, handled by Belinda West.

PHOTO: INGRID MATSCHKE

Ann Ingram's BIS at Adelaide Royal was the UK-bred Kerry Blue Terrier Ch/UK/Ir Ch Forum's Calico Jack at Irisblu, owned by Jon and the late Cheryl LeCourt, Keith Brown and Robbie Gray, and handled by Simon Briggs.

PHOTO: CABAL

BIS at Canberra Royal under Laurent Pichard went to the Hungarian Puli Ch Rustufarion Indelible Ink, owned by Royson Valore, Patrice Smith and Courtney Spencer.

PHOTO: ANIMAL IMAGES

BIS at Perth Royal selected by Sylvie Desserne was the Great Dane Ch Rorlyn Working Class Man, owned by Lyn and Rory Booth.

of Tibetan breeds' country of origin, the move to join as a full member of the FCI, which had begun to gain momentum, has been severely set back among the rank and file of this country.

Australia continues to suffer from the huge numbers of 'designer crossbreed' breeders, with the inevitable puppy farms which authorities seem unable to shut down. According to Galaxy Research data from last year, crossbred and unregistered puppies made up about five times more of the puppies sold yearly to Australian consumers than did ANKC-registered pedigree puppies.

However the fight to promote purebred and pedigree puppies continues and on a happier note membership of the ANKC increased to 33,118 in 2014. It has come as welcome news to its state member bodies!

On the show front I am very pleased to report that the show scene Down Under has fared well in 2015. Most shows are maintaining figures or slightly up and the effort being put into Australia's flagship royal shows is exemplary.

Sydney and Melbourne continue to raise the bar when it comes to spoiling exhibitors, from free breakfast to free coffee and the now famous 'after parties'. Both royals were rewarded with entry levels up on 2014 figures.

News just to hand is that Australia's biggest one-day show, Sunbury Canine Club, which coincides with the legendary Melbourne Cup Race, is also up with entries in the vicinity of 2,500 dogs. ■

NEW ZEALAND

Report by
**Rosemar
Hubric**

© supashots.com

Junior handler Alysha Judson was selected at the National Show as NZ representative at the Crufts international final in 2016.

The 2015 Eukanuba Challenge Winner, who will represent New Zealand at the final in Amsterdam, is the Australian Shepherd Gr Ch Sutter So It's Karma, owned by Mark Harvey, Lucy Lynch and Lindy Dawkins.

PHOTO: SUPASHOTS

A final goodbye to docking?

As with other parts of the world, the preoccupation of the New Zealand Kennel Club over the past 12 months has been with government interest in the health and welfare of animals.

Animal welfare legislation has moved up the order paper rapidly and a new Animal Welfare Act has been introduced, empowering the Minister of Primary Industries to add new regulations and protocols.

One of the first areas to be regulated will be the docking of dogs, along with the temporary housing of dogs and the transportation of dogs. Further down the work plan, breeding strategies will be targeted – so the focus for the New Zealand Kennel Club will be very much with advocacy work on dog-related issues, with both central and local government politicians. These challenges are not unfamiliar as they confront dog communities throughout the world.

As a result a big part of that focus is on education and advocacy, first to ensure that NZKC members not only have best practice at their fingers tips, but are in fact committing to implementing these codes of practice. NZKC is also talking publicly about what is being done.

Earlier this year the club introduced a code of ehthics for all breeders to support its Accredited Breeders Scheme (ABS) and will soon introduce criteria for those wishing to establish registered breeding kennels.

Other new initiatives foreshadowed in NZKC's strategic plan include its major events strategy, incorporating its National Dog Show, National Dog Obedience Assembly, National Dog Agility Championship and a Discover Dogs Event. The other area of focus is on youth development programmes.

It seems we are near the end of what has been a lengthy and challenging process – that government will shortly ban the docking of dogs, leaving the door open for vets (and/or veterinary students) to dock for therapeutic reasons only and effectively closing the door on the docking of dogs.

NZKC and the Council of Docked Breeds will support our current accredited banding scheme (whereby litters may be docked by banding, done by approved people), but having polled both politicians and government officials NZKC has long since seen the writing on the wall. Based on a survey of member

National Show BIS under Adriano Bosa was Julie Walden and Linda Jury's Bernese Mountain Dog Ch Schallenberg I Am Giant.

The Eukanuba Supreme Dog Show Contest was held in Christchurch and was won by Debbie Hull's American Cocker Spaniel Ch Ebonn Tis Back In The Black. Runner-up was Nigel and Robyn Trainor's English Springer Spaniel NZ/Aus Sup Ch Arawhiti Mr Farenheit.

opinion, the majority of NZKC members do not support docking.

NZKC works to upgrade its image and status in all doggy matters – to rebrand under the banner 'Dogs New Zealand' and become the 'go to' place for information for all dog owners. A strategic plan has been drafted to demonstrate how NZKC/Dogs NZ can remain relevant in today's changing times.

NZKC continues to move towards a more democratic mode, so that more members may vote for the executive council. Postal voting for the council began in 2015 with more clubs permitted to vote. Clyde Rogers was returned as president.

Participation in conformation shows continues to decline, obedience remains steady, and agility participation has increased steadily.

Winner of the Dog of the Year Contest was the Pointer NZ Sup Ch/Aus/Am Gr Ch Chesterhope State of T Art, owned by Diane and Jordyn O'Neil. She had been BIS at the 2014 National.

I am pleased to say that 'casual membership' for breed and group conformation shows has at last come to pass. This permits non-members to enter their pedigree dogs at a breed or group show, on payment of a fee for the day. Breed clubs particularly can increase their show entry this way and the newbies may enjoy the experience – taste and try, we hope to attract more participants. ∎

JAPAN

Report by: **Mai Ozeki Hirai**

All isn't equal for the top dogs

Mai Ozeki Hirai and Minoru Kato's Borzoi bitch Belisarius JP My Sassy Girl, handled by Shota Hirai, won BIS at Japan's biggest show, FCI Japan International Dog Show, under Ramon Podesta (BIS) and Kari Järvinen (breed and group) from over 2,500 dogs entered. Because of the restriction on supreme dogs she was in the US during the summer and was awarded best sighthound in show under Dick Meen and best foreign bred in show under Dana Cline and Jason Hoke at Santa Barbara. Despite the restriction, she is number one all breeds at the time of writing. 'Lucy' will be campaigned in the US in 2016.

The Japan Kennel Club has a rule that any foreign-bred dogs with any foreign champion titles are not eligible to be shown at local club shows. They are eligible to be shown only at FCI shows and big regional big shows.

Therefore, those foreign-bred dogs with foreign champion titles have the opportunity to be shown only once or twice a month on average, while we have dog shows almost every weekend and on national holidays.

It has been years since JKC introduced the restrictions on foreign bred dogs. This year, it added a new restriction even for Japanese-bred dogs: those who have won big awards (best in show, reserve BIS, best in specialty show, best of opposite sex at the specialty) five times will be called 'supreme champion dogs' ▶

and are now not eligible to be shown at local shows, just like foreign-bred dogs.

This is certainly one of the major reasons for the entries dropping. Some of the top ranked dogs are either foreign-bred champions or have won more than five BIS so they have to face this restriction, while some of them are not categorised in either restriction so they get to be shown every weekend and build up the points.

I believe all the dogs should have the same opportunities to be shown and I hope this rule will be cancelled for the sake of all the exhibitors and for the sake of equality.

As for the 2015 rankings, we cannot tell which dog will be all-breed number one until the end of the year as several dogs have been winning at the same level so far. Pictured are some of the dogs who would possibly be within top 20; another is the French Bulldog Le Bijou Andra, owned by Yuko Tamamura, and handled by Yoshinori Sato. ■

The Smash Poodles have done amazingly well as usual; among their achievements in 2015 were that Smash JP Beauty And Beat won BIS at Poodle Club of America with owner-handler Mizuki Murakami. Smash also won best and reserve best at the specialty held with the European Winner Show. Here is Toshi Omura handling the Toy Smash JP Careless Whisper, owned by Kana Tasaki.

Among Japan's top dogs: the Boxer Abel of Tribute JP, owned by Yoshiaki Matsunaga, handled by Katsuyoshi Kanezuka.

PHOTO: MARI NAKASHIMA

Another big winner of 2015: the Pyrenean Mountain Dog Vi'Skaly's Hippy Hippy Shake, imported from Sweden, owned by Kazue Osato and handled by Masakazu Kamiyama.

A leading winner of 2015: the Standard Poodle Gioia of Achan JP, owned by Masayo Sano, handled by Shigeru Kato.

Also among the main contenders: the Labrador Legend of Mikuni K-Russky JP, owned by Miyoko Tamagawa, handled by Akira Miyake.

PHOTO: TAOW

Among Japanese dogs shown overseas, we must mention the Pembroke Corgi Balmy Winds JP Jake. He was number two all breeds in 2014 in Japan and has been shown in the US on a limited basis in 2015. He flew to Milan for the World Show and won World Winner under Andrew Brace out of 91 dogs.

HIGHAM PRESS
THE 'BACKBONE' OF YOUR SHOW

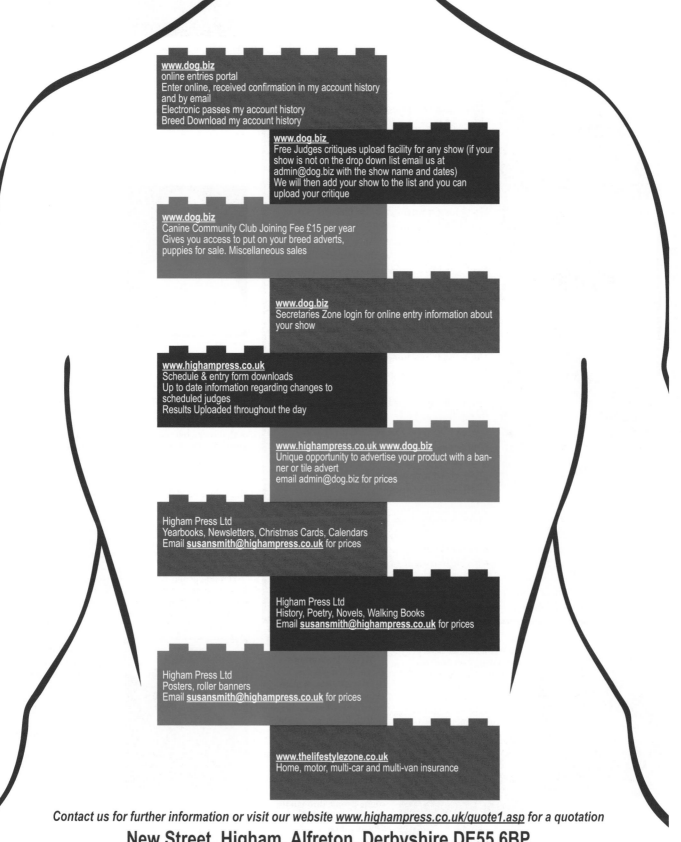

www.dog.biz
online entries portal
Enter online, received confirmation in my account history
and by email
Electronic passes my account history
Breed Download my account history

www.dog.biz
Free Judges critiques upload facility for any show (if your
show is not on the drop down list email us at
admin@dog.biz with the show name and dates)
We will then add your show to the list and you can
upload your critique

www.dog.biz
Canine Community Club Joining Fee £15 per year
Gives you access to put on your breed adverts,
puppies for sale. Miscellaneous sales

www.dog.biz
Secretaries Zone login for online entry information about
your show

www.highampress.co.uk
Schedule & entry form downloads
Up to date information regarding changes to
scheduled judges
Results Uploaded throughout the day

www.highampress.co.uk www.dog.biz
Unique opportunity to advertise your product with a banner or tile advert
email admin@dog.biz for prices

Higham Press Ltd
Yearbooks, Newsletters, Christmas Cards, Calendars
Email susansmith@highampress.co.uk for prices

Higham Press Ltd
History, Poetry, Novels, Walking Books
Email susansmith@highampress.co.uk for prices

Higham Press Ltd
Posters, roller banners
Email susansmith@highampress.co.uk for prices

www.thelifestylezone.co.uk
Home, motor, multi-car and multi-van insurance

Contact us for further information or visit our website www.highampress.co.uk/quote1.asp for a quotation

New Street, Higham, Alfreton, Derbyshire DE55 6BP
Tel: 01773 832390 ● Fax: 01773 520794
Dog.biz enquiries to: admin@dog.biz all other enquiries to: mail@highampress.co.uk

Obituaries

As ever, we have had to say goodbye to all too many of the people who contributed for many decades to the world of dogs – breeders, exhibitors, judges, administrators, welfare officers and more.

We pay tribute to some of them here, and sadly there are many others that space does not permit us to mention – to their relatives, friends and colleagues go the thoughts of all our readers They will not be forgotten.

Nora Down.

Anne Matthews.

FEW BRITISH dog people have had the style and charisma of Pamela Cross Stern (left) who achieved so much as breeder, exhibitor and judge.

Daughter of terrier man and all-round judge Fred Cross, she grew up within the world of dogs, then spent some years in the US before returning to the UK with some Miniature Schnauzers whose progeny made a big mark. Her Lhasa Apso, Alexander, made breed history as the first BIS and Crufts group winner and she owned and bred top class dogs of a wide variety of breeds including Chihuahuas, Griffons, Bouviers and Lakelands. But it was Japanese Chin which made the biggest impression with many Sternroc champions including Dikki, a BIS winner and Top Dog all breeds.

Always perfectly groomed, she was a painstaking and charming judge and eventually awarded BIS at Crufts. She did things her own way – not always the easiest way, as when she lost her Kennel Club committee seat for subtracting a few years from her age – and added colour and glamour to the show scene.

An equally unforgettable but quite different personality was Maureen Micklethwaite (above), a truly down-to earth 'dog person' in the old tradition. She produced champions in all three colours of Scottish Terriers under the Glenecker affix, judged the terrier group at Crufts and was passed for best in show.

'Mrs Mick' was in her element with club work, for breed clubs, for National Terrier of which she was president, WELKS where she held the same office and Three Counties where she was given the title 'honorary chairman emeritus'. She had strong views and a kind, generous heart.

several toy breeds, sharing the Weycombe affix with husband George and his Staffords. They made a popular judging team; he did BIS at Crufts and she the toy group there as well as the Pup of the Year final. She enjoyed a stint as president of the LKA.

June Minns.

June Minns was one of Britain's most experienced sighthound authorities. Daughter of one of the pioneers of the Finnish Spitz, she had champions in that breed but was best known for Greyhounds, Whippets and Italian Greyhounds, being the only UK breeder to produce champions in all three, as well as Borzois, using the Juneric, Exhurst (in partnership with Francis Willey) and Hellomy affixes. A brilliant handler, she judged the group at Crufts.

Few dog people can have been more universally loved than **Olga Bullock**. With her husband Ken they had the Konelga Miniature

versatile breeders was **Anne Matthews**, who enjoyed success in a wide variety of breeds, particularly Bassets and then Lhasa Apsos and Tibetan Terriers in which her Hardacre lines were extremely influential, providing a firm foundation to many other breeders and acting as mentor to several who reached the heights in the dog world. Health was a priority in her breeding plans, too.

Heather Ridley bred the Moonseal Pomeranians and her group-winning Havanese Paloma was a great ambassador for the breed but she will perhaps best be remembered for her expertise in helping breeder solve problems in rearing newborn puppies.

Vet **Mike Findlay** was well known throughout the dog world for his publications and broadcasting, and as the last chief executive of PRO Dog

The **Duke of Wellington** died at the age of 99; he was a vice-president of the Kennel Club and a regular visitor to Crufts. He was passionate about preservation of the countryside and had owned field trial champion Labradors with the Stratfieldsaye affix.

The death, far too young at 39, of Afghan and Pomeranian exhibitor **Melissa Hills**, not long after that of her mother **Carol**, touched a nerve among dog people who recalled her courage and her enthusiasm. Friends got together to raise money for cancer charities by taking part in a gruelling 'Spartan Sprint'. Afghans also lost **Di Kearon** (Shechem).

Maureen Osbourne (Braego) owned a number of breeds, notably Petits Bassets Griffons Vendéens and English Springers, while **Eileen Mayne** had the Eastport Bassets.

Norman Field, whose late wife Mollie had the Houndsmarks, served Beagle and hound clubs well. **Barbara Webb** bred the Woodbarn Beagles and Golden Retrievers.

Esmée Samuel.

Esmée Samuel contributed enormously to the Welsh and British dog worlds, supporting her husband David in his long stint as secretary of

Meriel Hathaway.

the Welsh Kennel Club, then taking over after his death and later becoming president. She had also been a member of the Kennel Club's Crufts sub-committee, and acted as mentor and inspiration to many friends.

Meriel Hathaway's charm and diplomacy won her the affection of many people beyond her and husband Fred's main breed, Golden Retrievers, in which they bred the Melfrickas. She put an enormous amount into breed clubs and to Birmingham National, of which she was president, and encouraged countless young people through the then Kennel Club Junior Organisation.

'A real lady' was everyone's reaction when they met **Nora Down**, who died aged 97. She produced champions in

Olga Bullock.

Poodle but their great contribution was to Leeds show of which Ken was secretary for several decades. After his death she fittingly became president.

One of Britain's most

osemary Spafford was
ne of the Beagle breed's
haracters and specialised in
mall ones.

Gina Rose bred some
eautiful Borzois, notably
ebastian, under her
onebar affix.

One of the triple-
eneration kennels featured
this Annual is Ralines,
nown for Smooth and
Iiniature Longhaired
achshunds. It was founded
y **Peter Lockett** and his
te wife Freda, and carries
n with their daughter and
randdaughter.

Jean Matthews of the
anastre Min Smooths and
Vires was a popular figure
Dachshund shows. **Nora
Vinterbourne** bred the
fluential Maundowne
Iiniature Longs, **Joanne
Vilson** the Coleacres in that
ariety, and **Delia Edwards**
ed the Danward Longs.

Veronica Trim will
e remembered for her
mmaculate Verwill Wires,
hile **Harry Boyle** was part
f the family who campaign
e Zarcrest Longs, Min
ongs and Whippets. **Jeff
Iunt** was a great support
o his wife Betty with her
mous Pipersvale Min
mooths.

Jean Dyson and her
usband **Brian**, who died
n the day of her funeral,
nowed the Blison Wires
nd Min Wires but were best
nown as super stewards
nd for helping run many
nows in the Midlands. **Joe
Ilan** was a familiar figure
round the Dachshund rings
Ireland and Scotland
ith the Auchans of several
arieties.

Diana Allan, who died in
car accident, and her late
usband Ken did much for
ne Saluki as breeders (with
Crufts group winner),
dministrators, authors
nd editors of a spectacular
nagazine.

Vi Nichols contributed
normously the Norwegian
lkhound world, both
hrough the breed club and
s a clever breeder of the
mous Barlestones. **Ron
Iughes**, too, served the
reed well over many years.

Whippets lost **Susan Ellis**
Railfield), **Patricia de
acey Munday** (Whipowil)
nd **Ian Middlemiss**
Normainia), a long-
tanding committee member
f Border Union.

John Digby had the
lsziv Vizslas, and formerly
wned Gordon Setters; his
ogs were very much dual-
urpose.

Des McGarry was one
f the outstanding figures
f the Pointer world, not
nly making up many

Des McGarry.

Toberdoneys but proving
their worth in the field too.
A great character, he was
happy to pass on the breed's
lore and traditions.

Malcolm Kent, along
with wife Yvonne, did well
with the Lokmadi Pointers
and latterly Min Smooth
Dachshunds.

Pauline Perriam had
the Elaphill Irish and Irish
Red and White Setters and
served the breed clubs with
distinction. **Ray Hurll** bred
the Carramore Irish Setters
with his wife Maureen and
both did much for setters in
distress.

Along with his late wife
Audrey, **Peter Forster** had
the influential Wizardwood
Flatcoats, and was equally
keen on show and working
sides and working tirelessly
for the breed. In Goldens
George Hennessy bred,
with his wife Lynne, the
equally important Ritzilyns,
Di Dale the Mindaros,
Margaret Scott the
Gunmarshs and **Margaret
Carnie** the Chebulas.

Margaret Thorpe of
the Rockabees had been a
stalwart of the Labradors
since the 1950s. **Geoff
Harvey** bred the Glenarveys,
Christine Harris had the
Rooklane Labradors and
Irish Water Spaniels, and
Lou Neal the Amberstope
Labradors.

Alan Fowlie bred the
Wydillon Clumbers.

The Lynwater Cocker
Spaniels of **Elizabeth
Maclean** included a Crufts
group winner and she
also bred some significant
Pointers, while **Jane
Halkett** (Wiljana) was part
of the family who owned a
Crufts RBIS-winning Cocker.
George Leckie (Thornlea)
did much for the English
Springer in Scotland.

Iris Haverson
(Woodgay) was involved
with several spaniel breeds
and bred a famous Field
stud dog. **Jenny Park** had
the Parkanine Fields and
wrote breed notes for DOG
WORLD. The Goldsprings
Welsh Springers were bred
by **Barbara Ordish**.

Anne Stone bred the

Wipfel Weimaraners. An
accident took the life of
Charles Rayner – there
had been a number of
Brownbank titleholders
and he was a very talented
photographer of the breed.

Barbara Holland, who
was 91, had owned Airedale
Terriers since the 1940s,
her most famous being

Barbara Holland.

BIS winner Ch Tanworth
Merriment. She wrote breed
notes for DOG WORLD for
31 years.

In Australian Terriers
Beryl Jones bred the
Berijons. **Brian Emsley** had
the Hilldyke Bedlingtons
with his wife Alice and
served the breed well.
Mary McErlean bred the
Barnsnaps.

Betty Dickinson's
Badgerholme Border
Terriers were campaigned
enthusiastically throughout
Britain and Ireland, while
Heather Wing-Mitchell
(Kelgram) was instrumental
in founding the East Anglian
breed club.

In Bull Terriers **Maureen
Bell** (Geham) had been
a fearless exhibitor for

Maureen Bell.

many decades and was a
redoubtable personality, still
judging until not long before
her death at 93.

Cairns lost **Pat Jeffery**
(Sandaig), **Pat Bunting**
(Spirecairn) and **Barbara
Whittaker** (Daleletty).

Eileen Geddes (Gedstar)
was a stalwart of the Smooth
Fox Terrier and **Charlie
Pollard** (Lynphen)
produced several famous
Irish Terriers.

Pauline Rodgers' Laroc
dogs made a mark in both
Lakeland and Welsh Terriers.
Manchester Terriers lost **Ian**

Beales (Brenandi).

Kathy Farr (Salette) bred
a CC-record holding Norfolk
Terrier. **Mary Ferguson** was
another great enthusiast for
the breed and had worked
for Vetzyme for many years.

Pat Roberts was once
well known in Scottish
Terriers for the Aberscots.

The sudden death of
Clare Lee came as a
particular shock to DOG
WORLD as she was our
conscientious, helpful
breed correspondent for
Staffordshire Bull Terriers.
Her father Nap Cairns was
one of the most successful
breeders in the breed's
early years with CCs, and

Clare Lee.

she and husband Tony
carried on the Constones
line very successfully as well
as promoting the breed's
interests in every way.

Lewis Barnett (Boggarts)
had owned Staffords for
over 60 years and he too
worked hard for clubs and to
encourage newcomers. **Vira
Berry** owned one of the
breed's famous champions.

Barbara Hammond
(Greenshire) was a long-
term supporter of the West
Highland White Terrier.
Dutch-born **Jane Kabel**
lived in England in the '70s
and '80s, becoming a partner
in Barbara Graham's Lasara
kennel. She returned to the
UK in 1999 and she and Ida
Bouwhuis enjoyed further
success, this time as Llasara,
contributing much to the
breed.

Joyce Briggs (Brigwood)
owned many important
Boston Terriers and was a
major force in the Northern
club. Her famous Cheyenne
was bred by **Wendy Miller**
(Wenlyn), who also died
during the year, while
Sheila Borthwick (Lorece)
did much for the breed
in Scotland. **Maureen
Broadhead** (Lendor) was
another loss to the Boston
world. **Ron Carson** had
the Carsvale Bulldogs while
David Scully (Sardav) from
Ireland died young in a
tragic accident.

Chows lost **Dorothy
Trick** (Jowtrix), **David Ross**
(Chanako) and **Tom Lynch**
(Tomukoo).

Betty Neath and her
family achieved tremendous
success with the Buffrey
Dalmatians and was she
secretary of Evesham CS
for 28 years. **Joan Curtis**
(Sydon) had been a stalwart
of the Dalmatian scene for
several decades. **Brian Levy**
(Motek) was another hard
worker for the breed.

Long-time French Bulldog
enthusiast **Leta Ogwen-
Junes** (Brithmel) died at 103
after a fascinating life.

Pat Beard's Wyndlee
German Spitz had a big
influence on both varieties.

Sylvia Scroggs bred
many famous Keeshonds,
including a BIS winner and
a CC record holder, and her
Ledwell bloodlines made a
dramatic impact. She worked
hard for the breed in every
way. **John Randall** and
his late wife Mary bred the
Candymay Keeshonds, and
Joan Partridge was another
long-time stalwart with the
Bergaritas.

Rob Richardson
campaigned his family's
highly successful Belazieth
Lhasa Apsos.

Renee Smith, along with
her daughter Diane, enjoyed
much success with the
Renwin Miniature Poodles
including the famous
Rappelle. Her first love,
though, was the Toy variety.

Norman Butcher's
Tuttlebees kennel of Toy
Poodles was of major
importance to the variety,
shared with his wife Miriam
who died in 2014. They
were joint secretaries of the
Poodle Club for an amazing

Norman Butcher.

50 years. Norman was one of
those people with a real eye
who should perhaps have
judge more breeds than he
did. They bred champion
Afghans and Griffons too.

Joan Falconer-Atlee
(Coelegant) had champions
in all three sizes, while
Bob Ratcliffe's Acecliffe
Standard Poodles made their
mark in the agility world
as well as being shown with
success.

The Franhowil kennel
of Schipperkes made an
enormous impact on the
breed in its day; it was owned ▶

with David Short by **Francis Howard-William**s who died in 2015.

Douglas Wilkinson (Brentella) had been involved with Miniature Schnauzers for more than 50 years. Stanley Burke founded the Lichstone kennel of this breed and **Pat Stewar**t bred the Trawests.

Dee Harper, along with son Michael, enjoyed great success with the Harropine Shih Tzu, including a BIS winner and CC record holders, and owned a number of other breeds too.

Irene Chamberlain bred the Chobrang Tibetan

Irene and Stuart Chamberlain.

Terriers and then turned equally successfully to Lhasa Apsos, and contributed TT notes to DOG WORLD. She was a keen fundraiser for health issues in the breed. Her husband **Stuart**, who served as show manager of Windsor, survived her by just a few weeks.

Virginia Stenner (Clashaidy) was a well known personality of the Bernese Mountain Dog world.

Sagra Tonkin and family bred the Tonantron Boxers, including two BIS winners, one of them the immortal Glory Lass. **Jeanne Harris** (Mixonne) had been involved with Boxers since the 1950s, and more recently with Griffons. **Margaret Buck** had the Sherras affix.

Alan Rostron, with his wife Mave, did very well with the Graecia Bullmastiffs.

Dobermanns in Wales lost **Alan Mulholland**, while **Mike Wright** (Kamroyal) contributed much to the Dobermann world.

Roy Tripconey (Pentroyic) did a great deal for the Great Dane in Wales.

Peter Tugwell was partner with Richard Thomas in the Bredwardine Mastiffs which made such a big impact on the breed, and they also owned French Bulldogs and other breeds and types of livestock. In latter years they had lived in Spain.

Liz Guy-Halke did much to promote the interests of the Leonberger.

Kay Gibson (Laphroaig)

worked hard for the Newfoundland breed while **Fiona Gibson** of the Merasheens must have been one of the few former 'page 3 girls' to be immersed in the dog scene.

Joyce Radley shared the Intisari Rottweilers with husband Peter and **Joe Watt** had the Rolencos in Northern Ireland.

A popular Irish personality was **Seamus Oates** of the Oatfield St Bernards who became a

Seamus Oates.

much travelled all-breeds judge, and was always keen to encourage younger enthusiasts. Back in the UK **Michael Wensley** was noted for the Swindridge kennel, and especially for his champion smooths.

Derek Stopforth's Davealex Bearded Collies can be found at the back of many pedigrees. He and his wife Jean also made a mark with Irish Water Spaniels.

Old-timers may remember that singer and TV presenter **Cilla Black** was among the early exhibitors of Briards.

In Rough Collies, **Chris Black**'s Chrisarions produced a number of champions, as did **Elsie Westwood**'s Westlynns, while **Ron Telford** had the Glenbowdenes, **Tom Dent** the Denleas and **Pat Cooney** the Lingwells. **Betty Cockcroft**'s Leecrofts are in countless pedigrees.

Barry Nelson was partner of Mike Gilchrist in the Silkata Pulis and Tibetan Terriers.

Pam Cock (Featwella) was an early enthusiast of the Lancashire Heeler.

Jim Hamilton handled his and his wife Carole's first Samoyed Ch Hurkur Jingles to record-breaking wins and so started their famous Zamoyski kennel. Jingles was bred by **Jim Dougall** who also died in 2105. He bred just four litters but these included six UK champions. **Gordon Tomlinson** was a long-time supporter of the breed and also served as chairman of Driffield dog show.

Derek Stott (Stevlyns) was a loss to the Shetland

Sheepdog world, as was **Janet Sycamore** (Shelbrook) who was only 57.

Corgis lost **Margo Parsons** (Deavitte) whose kennel produced champions in both Pembrokes and Cardigans and who was known for encouraging a new generation of enthusiasts. Her son Simon edits this Annual. **Nancy Mortimore** (Halesmore) was another great character who owned both breeds.

Nancy Fenwick was never a breeder or exhibitor, though she regularly attended Windsor show. But she made her own special contribution in looking after the Queen's Corgis whenever their owner was away, and caring for the Windsor litters. The model of tact and discretion, in her own right she also had a soft spot for the Tibetan Spaniel.

One of the dog world's most gracious ladies was **Susan Burgess** whose Crisdig strain of Cavalier

Susan Burgess.

King Charles Spaniels was one of the most influential the breed has known. Among her many honours was the presidency of WELKS.

Bob Brampton was a toy group judge with a background in Chihuahuas, in which his daughter Shelda Hornby has more recently made such a mark. **Margaret Greening** (Hamaja) was a real character of the Chihuahua world and could often be found on the mic at WELKS. **Sheelagh Christison** was devoted to the welfare of the breeds.

Marie Hall (Pindanett) kept English Toy Terriers, Great Danes and Miniature Pinschers.

Jenny Kearney served the Griffon world well, notably as a historian, and **Dave Dorward** had the Dajelas in Scotland.

Until she died aged 104, **Freda McGregor** retained her interest in the Lowchen breed in which her Littlecourt affix had been borne by many of the breed's early winners, including the first bitch champion.

Freda McGregor.

Ted Fearnley was partner of the great all-round judge and Papillon breeder Ellis Hulme, supporting him in every way and was himself a respected judge of toys.

Barry Offiler, with his wife Ann, bred the successful StSanja Pekingese, and will also be remembered for his breed club work and for being prime mover for the spectacular breed show at Goodwood. The Bramblefields line of **Phil Jones** also made a significant mark on the breed, and **Pauline Seed** bred the Jywantees.

The sudden death at only 58 of **Lindsay Pemberton** was a big shock. As well as breeding the Lynbank Pekes she was a talented

Lindsay Pemberton.

administrator of breed and group clubs, and was treasurer of UK Toy.

Eddie Hurdle shared the Sunsalves with partner Terry Nethercott and was the most unflappable of stewards at countless breed shows.

Daphne Hillman was one of the characters of the Yorkshire Terrier world and correspondence from her

Daphne Hillman.

was invariably fascinating. She bred the long-established Yorkfolds and

also continued the importan[t] Johnstounburn line.

Sweden lost **Kenneth Edh** who will best be remembered for organising and judging BIS at the 2008 World Show in Stockholm.

In Belgium Whippets lost **Dominique Delabelle** (di Mahana), whose dogs made mark in Britain as well as on on the Continent.

Jack Peden (Denorsi) was a successful exhibitor of several breeds, notably Beagles, Whippets and Bostons, plus a Pup of the Year winning German Shepherd, before emigratin[g] from Scotland to South Africa where he remained a prominent figure in the dog scene.

From Germany, **Rudi Dettmar**'s The Joker Bull Terriers made a worldwide impact, while **Stefania Savini** from Italy had many UK successes with her Star Pride Fox Terriers.

Jackie Perry (Vonklebong), based in Thailand, was world-respected as a Dobermann expert and all-breed

Jackie Perry.

judge, and a tremendous ambassador for her region.

In the US, **Jane Kamp Forsyth** was one of the dog world's legends, as a supremely successful handler, then as a judge and mentor. She and

Jane Kamp Forsyth.

husband Bob both won BIS at Westminster, she with the breed she was best associate[d] with, the Boxer. Her visits to judge in the UK were truly memorable occasions.

Gloria Reese campaigned some of the all-time great dogs, includin[g] the Greyhound 'Punky'.

20 Year Club

The 20 Year Club

As always, we would like to thank the Annual's advertisers for their continued support. Those on pages 174-178, 180-262, 264-265, 274 and 481 are members of the 20 Year Club, having first advertised here in 1996 or earlier.

80 years ago

GIRALDA · FARMS

MADISON   NEW JERSEY   USA

Dog World Annual 1976

JOKYL TERRIERS

SEASON'S GREETINGS AND GOOD WISHES
from the owners OLIVE and GEORGE JACKSON
FRENSHAM MANOR, FRENSHAM, SURREY GU10 3ED and
Manager, Mary Swash

40 years ago

30 years ago

TUSSALUD PAPILLONS

…years ago

SEAGIFT WHIPPETS & GREYHOUNDS

Owned by: MRS. D. F. WHITWELL, Kirkholme, Great Ouseburn, York.
Phone: Green Hammerton 252

Ch BOHEM LA TRAVIATA (left) and Ch BOHEM LA BOHÈME

20 years ago

A *Superlative Variety* Kennel
The "OF BOKRA"
At BEAN, near DARTFORD, Kent

70 years ago

HERNWOOD

THE FABULOUS FOUR NOW ALL SEMI RETIRED.....

© N. Keens

AM GRAND CH HERNWOOD MAGIC FORMULA - 1ST UK GORDON TO BE A GRAND CHAMPION

SH CH HERNWOOD DIAMOND ROCK JW SHCM - 1ST EVER GORDON QUALIFY FOR PUP OF YEAR FINAL

SH CH HERNWOOD INDI GIRL AT TOGIPOTO - 1ST SHOW CHAMPION FOR THE JACONELLI FAMILY

SH CH HERNWOOD TALLADEGA RAGER JW SHCM - ONLY ALL BREED BIS WINNER - YOUNGEST GROUP WINNER FOR THE BREED

WERE HISTORY IS MADE & GENERATIONS PROGRESS

Gordon Setters

IN THE USA

AM GCH BLACK ANVIL RAMPANT LION

BLACK ANVIL SEALED WITH A KISS

Am GCH/ CAN Ch WINCREST TRAVELIN PRAYER & AM GCH HERNWOOD MAGIC FORMULA

AM CH WINSOMES MUSIC MAKER & AM GCH HERNWOOD MAGIC FORMULA

No 1 OWNER / HANDLER SPORTING GROUP 2015

1ST TIME OUT - WINNERS BITCH & AWARD OF MERIT.

AND OVER IN IRELAND......

J. Lawless
Our Dogs Ireland

R SH CH HERNWOOD CHANGE OF THE GUARD   HERNWOOD TUATHA DE DANNAN

BOTH GROUP WINNERS IN IRELAND

HERNWOOD

THE UK TOUR

©Hilary White

| SH CH
HERNWOOD
CALYPSO
GODDESS | SH CH
HERNWOOD BOB
DYLAN OF
PRAIRIEDAWN | SH CH
HERNWOOD
CAUSIN A STORM
FOR TOGIPOTO |

MEMORIES ARE MADE & DAYS ARE NEVER FORGOTTEN

PHOTO CREDITS - H WHITE, R HORLER, N KEENS, C LEWIS, W HARRIS, SUTHERLAND

Gordon Setters

WAITING IN THE WINGS

LIBBY   KELLIE   DI   ADAM

TOMMY   ROCKY   HARRIS

LUNA   FABLE   EVIE   ROBBIE
               BOSTON   ARCHIE

S
T
A
R
G
A
N
G

photo Ian Seath

OUR STAR OF 2015

CH LOKMADI SEA HOLLY AT STARGANG

Holly is Top Miniature Smooth Dachshund 2015 having been awarded 13 CCs, [17 in total] 11 BOBs. Hound Group 4 and

BEST IN SHOW
Eastern Counties
Dachshund Association
RESERVE BEST IN SHOW
Great Joint Dachshund Association

Very proud of our young
B/T Brindle boy

STARGANG TIGER FEET
2 CCs and 2 RCCs
Sire Ch Stargang Avenger
Dam Twilight Ot Mariny
Kuranovoy at Stargang [imp Rus]

photo Fay Hutchings

STARGANG SUNSHINE
2 CCs and 2 RCCs

STARGANG DACHSHUNDS
CONTACT
ellen@stargang.org.uk
or shardagang@sky.com

GLENIREN
International Show Dogs
Presents...

ACE

AL-DAHNAS ALOUANN ACE OF HEARTS GLENIREN (IMP)

SIRE: INT CH XCITING RATTLE N' HUM   **DAM:** NOR CH AL-DAHNAS VITAE VICTORIA

Owned by: Glenn Robb & Iain Pritchard   TEL: 07711 247468   glennrobbfitness@gmail.com

Many thanks to Ace's breeders Al-Dahnas Kennel

Travis

BEST IN SHOW - EAST OF ENGLAND CH SHOW 2015 – RODNEY OLDHAM
THANK YOU TO ALL OF THE JUDGES WHO HAVE THOUGHT SO HIGHLY OF OUR
SPECIAL BOY AND MAKING 2015 A YEAR TO REMEMBER.
IRENE ROBB, GLENN ROBB AND CAROLYN ROE

Shoots for the stars

27 CC 23 BOB

- ALL BREED CH SHOW BIS WINNER
- MULTIPLE ALL BREED CH SHOW RBIS WINNER
- 7 X GROUP 1 WINS IN 2015
- MUTIPLE GROUP PLACEMENT WINNER

- MULTIPLE BIS BREED SPECIALTY WINNER
- MULTIPLE RBIS BREED SPECIALTY WINNER
- EUKANUBA CHAMPION STAKES FINALIST 2015
- JUDGE: CLARE COXALL

KINGROCK

est 1975

Jet's Greyhounds

702 homebred champion titles

UK/Int/Nord Ch Jet's Moonlight Serenade

Top Greyhound in the UK 2015; BIS Windsor & The Greyhound Club, RBIS Scottish Kennel Club

Bred by Espen Engh and the late Kari Engh, owned by Espen Engh, Åge Gjetnes and Pauline Oliver

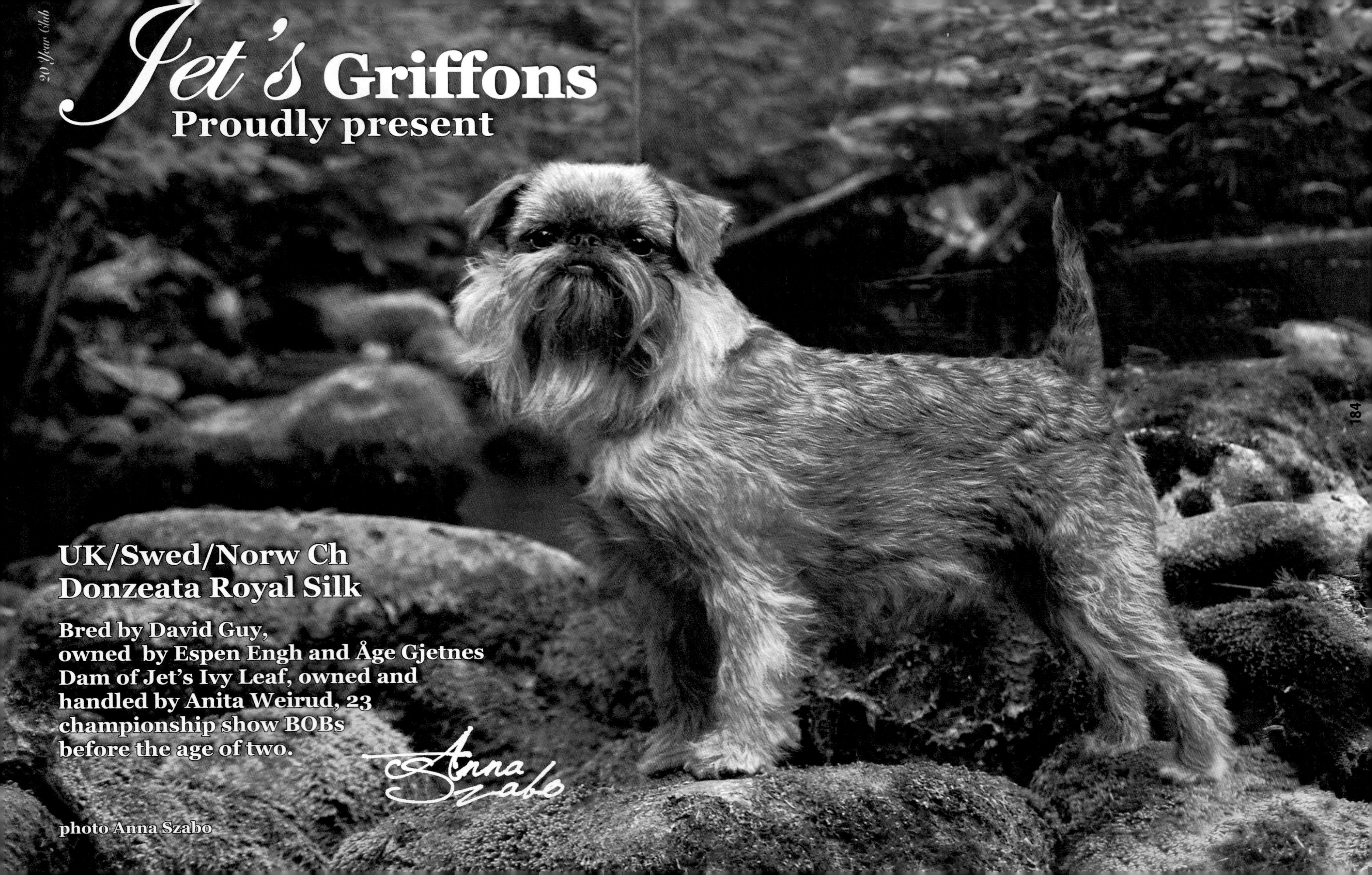

Jet's Griffons
Proudly present

UK/Swed/Norw Ch
Donzeata Royal Silk

**Bred by David Guy,
owned by Espen Engh and Åge Gjetnes
Dam of Jet's Ivy Leaf, owned and
handled by Anita Weirud, 23
championship show BOBs
before the age of two.**

Anna Szabo

photo Anna Szabo

Group victory at Crufts 2015, fantastic!

UK/Am/Int/Nord Ch Montserrat Caballe

Int Ch Sandust The One
ex Int Ch Fidel Andalucia

Breeder-owner: Åge Gjetnes, Norway
Co-owner: Elsa Storesund

HOTdog Magazine
international 2015

STUANE

Ch Stuane Kings Sword (AI)

Ch So What Excalibur ex Ch Stuane Florette

In limited showing Jack has won **12 CCs and several Group placements**

His sister **Ch Stuane Sword Dancer (AI)**
Is the SIXTH generation female CHAMPION in direct descent

Stuart Plane
01915 812200   stuart.plane@virgin.net

DONZEATA

Still looking to the future

© LC-E
unretouched

In very limited showing
Ch Donzeata Royal Gem
has added to her collection of CCs

David Guy
david.donzeata@virgin.net   07889399756

OMG
WHAT A YEAR!

Dialynne Beagles did the double at the two LARGEST SHOWS IN THE WORLD

Double at Crufts 2015
BISS CH IT CH Dialynne Electra ww15
BoB Crufts
12cc multiple group placings

BISS, BIS CH Dialynne Maximus
4th Crufts CC at 10 years old
Crufts 2008 group winner
20+ CC's

CH IT CH Dialynne Breaking News ww15
rDCC Crufts
winner of 6 cc's
BOB WDS 2015

Thank you to judge Christine Lewis for an amazing Crufts

Double WORLD DOG SHOW 2015
Carmen took rbb at club show and best bitch at WDS

Bracken took rbd Club Show & BOB WDS
Shortlisted in the final 8

Ch Dialynne Musketeer
Top Stud dog 13/14/15

Dialynne
Top breeders 13/14/15

Carmen
BISS CH IT CH Dialynne Electra

Max
BIS BISS CH Dialynne Maximus

Bracken
CH IT CH Dialynne Breaking News ww15

Afterglow

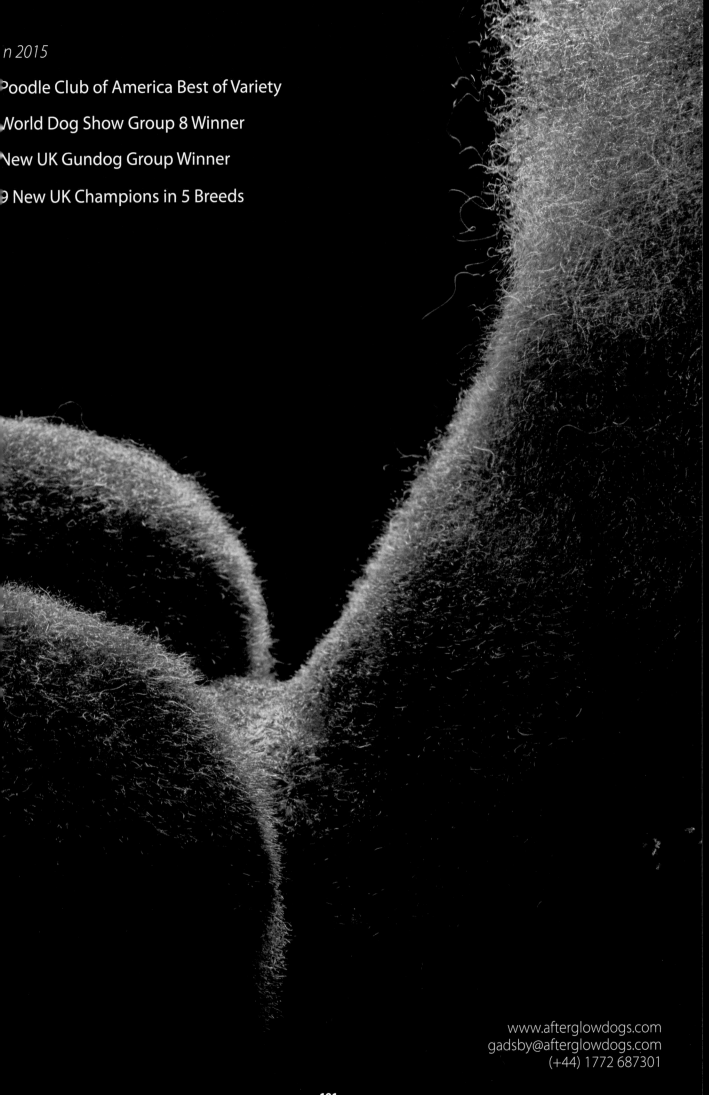

n 2015

Poodle Club of America Best of Variety

World Dog Show Group 8 Winner

New UK Gundog Group Winner

9 New UK Champions in 5 Breeds

www.afterglowdogs.com
gadsby@afterglowdogs.com
(+44) 1772 687301

Wildax French Bulldogs

Wildax Dusty Springfield

2 CCs, 3 RCCs

Dusty is the daughter of the illustrious
Ch Wildax Miss Moneypenny;
we look forward to
campaigning her in 2016

Ann Wildman   Tel: 01744 631190   Email: annwildman19@hotmail.com

192

BYQUY

KEESHONDS & SCHIPPERKES

This year we have concentrated on our fantastic litter of Keeshond puppies out of our English bred bitch **Byquy Willma** 1 CC to last year's top breed winner **Ch Klompen's Who's Your Daddy (imp Can)** grandson to last year's Top Stud 'Ferris'

CH BYQUY LILLEY THE PINK
Top Coloured Schipperke Club Show 201
Judge: Dr Janusz Opara (Poland

photo Walker

Alan V Walker

BYQUY BAM BAM
1 CC, 2 RCCs
4 Best Puppy in Breed
Darlington Puppy Group 2

Loved by all at BYQUY

BYQUY WILL YOU BE RICH
1st Post Grad Dog and
Best Puppy Dog
Midland Counties '15
Loved by Angela Reed and
Antonia Atkinson

BYQUY PEBBLES AT KWAJONGEN

1 CC
2 Best Puppy in Breed
Bournemouth Puppy Group 3

Thank you Geraldine Clark for taking on Pebbles and all the hard work you have put in

Alan V Wal

PITSWARREN

20 Year Ch...

23 SHOW CHAMPIONS   Breeding for quality not quantity   **Over 170 CCs**

IN 2015 WE CROWNED TWO NEW HOMEBRED SHOW CHAMPIONS SH CH RAFAEL AND SH CH SIROCCO

SHOW CHAMPION PITSWARREN RAFAEL OUR 22ND SHOW CHAMPION

**SHOW CHAMPION
PITSWARREN SIROCCO**
Our 23rd Show Champion

**HUBERTUS HUNGARICUM
ADAL AT PITSWARREN**
Best in Show at both the HVC and HVS 2015
breed club shows
Championship Show Group Winner.

PETER and LIZ HARPER
pitswarren@btinternet.com   www.pitswarren.co.uk

THE KENNEL CLUB
ASSURED BREEDER SCHEME

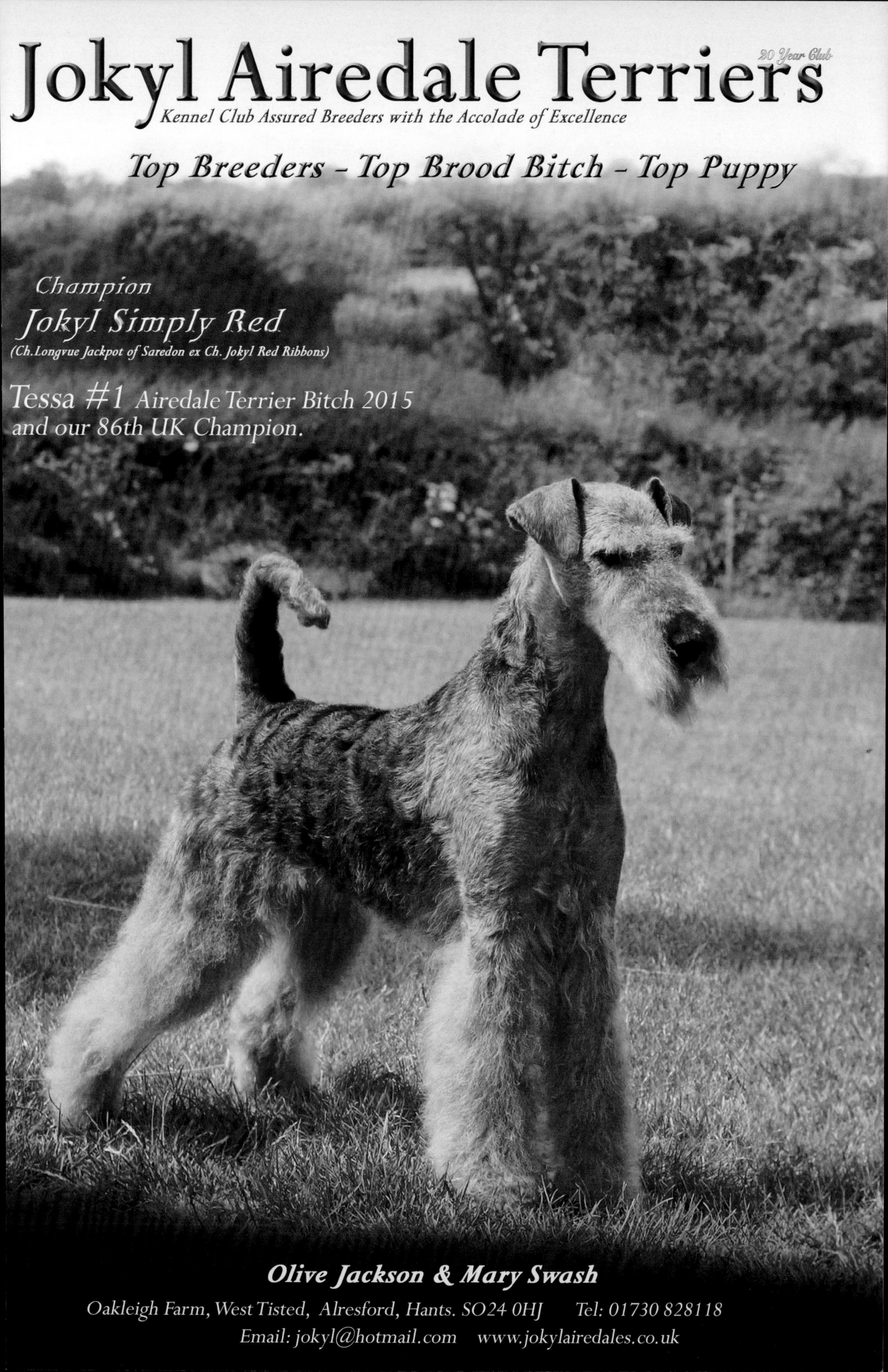

Jokyl Airedale Terriers
20 Year Club
Kennel Club Assured Breeders with the Accolade of Excellence
Top Breeders - Top Brood Bitch - Top Puppy
Champion
Jokyl Simply Red
(Ch.Longvue Jackpot of Saredon ex Ch. Jokyl Red Ribbons)
Tessa #1 Airedale Terrier Bitch 2015
and our 86th UK Champion.
Olive Jackson & Mary Swash
Oakleigh Farm, West Tisted, Alresford, Hants. SO24 0HJ
Tel: 01730 828118
Email: jokyl@hotmail.com
www.jokylairedales.co.uk

photo Ann Middlemiss

Our Pointers enjoying their natural environment.
Still maintaining true breed characteristics.
A combination of show and field stock.

Cicely A Robertshaw
Tel: 015396 20316
Email: crookrise@tesco.net

Helga Edmondson
Tel: 01282 545919
Email: helgaedmondson@outlook.com

www.crookrise.com

Fashionista
& Toydom

Ch Solnes Black Night Ipomoea
at Fashionista (Imp DNK)

CC and BOB Richmond Ch Show 2014 | CC WELKS Ch Show 2015
CC Three Counties Ch Show 2015 | 10 Reserve CCs

Our thanks to Mrs J Cort, Mr L Cox and Mr M Cocozza; his breeder Mrs Solveig Naess and
Mike Gadsby and Jason Lynn for campaigning him

Congratulations to his winning progeny in 2015: Afterglow La Lupe 2 RCCs
Afterglow Maleficent Grayco | Vanitonia Sumthin To Say

We look forward to introducing his daughter out of Ch Vanitonia Life's Too Short

Yvonne Rawley MBE and Adele Summers
T: 020 8685 0371   E-mail: adelesummers1@gmail.com

Feorlig & Cavalli

'Flurry'

'Kiss'

'Arthur'

'Twiz'

'Rona'

'Harvey'

'Dolly'

'Marley'

Cavalli Here Comes Winter Ir Jun Ch
RCC winner ~ 3 Green Stars

Lightly shown in 2015 but watch out for her & her daughter,
Cavalli Beautiful Life, 'Niamh' in 2016.

Caemgen's Element of Truth at Feorlig ShCM
CC & BOB - East of England - Judge: Mrs Jacque Bayne

CC & BIS - Joint Irish Setter Clubs' Ch Show - Judge: Mrs Carole Coode

Multiple Group & BIS winner at Open Shows ~ Bred by Sjored Jobse (Sweden)

Amantra Regius of Feorlig
3 RCCs from Junior

Best Dog & BOB - East of England

Best Dog & BOB - Belfast ~ Open Show Toy Group winner

Roguaie Kisses at Midnight at Feorlig JW
Won her 1st CC at Blackpool Ch Show
under Toy Specialist Mr Rob Sansom

Ch Feorlig Arthur Sixpence
Won his 3rd CC with BOB at Leeds Ch Show
under breed doyenne Miss Muriel Bailey
Numerous RCCs

Feorlig Romantica
1 CC ~ 2 RCCs

Daughter of
Ch Feorlig Arthur Sixpence &
Ch Feorlig Something Wicked

Ir Ch Jolaireg Harmony at Cavalli
RCC winner

Sadly passed away early 2015 and
is sorely missed.

Ch Ir Int Ch Chawell Brando at Cavalli
4 CCs ~ 3 BOBs
G3 Manchester 15

Only Charlie to place in a Toy Ch Show group in 2015

Jenny & Kirsty Miller - Feorlig
01455 220330 - feorlig@sky.com

Evan L Ryan - Cavalli
00353516418107 - Cavalli@live.ie

We would like to thank all judges who have thought so highly of our dogs and made 2015 such a wonderful year for us!

JAFRAK

AFRAK MUCH OBLIGED

FRENCH BY DESIGN BULLY BY NATURE

JAFRAK@BTOPENWORLD.COM   WWW.JAFRAK.ORG

ROSSUT

Can still cut the mustard

Making up 3 new champions this year

CH ROSSUT
ELSBETH

CH ROSSUT
MEMORY OF
PAKOWHAI J.W

Miss P.A. Sutton.
01252 703304
sutton23@btinternet.com

SHOW / CH ROSSUT
FOUL BY WIZARD

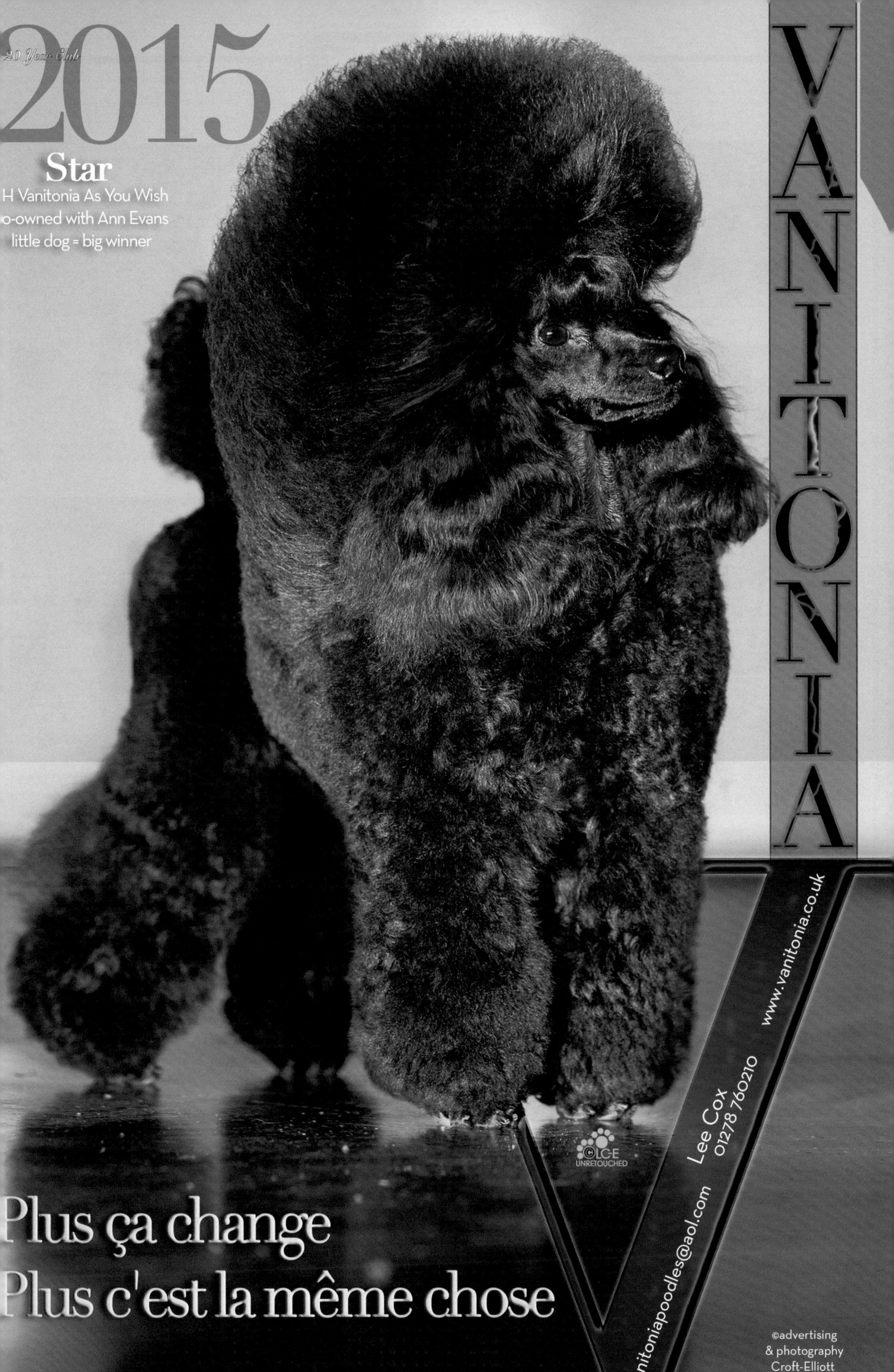
20 Year Club
2015
Star
H Vanitonia As You Wish
o-owned with Ann Evans
little dog = big winner
VANITONIA
Plus ça change
Plus c'est la même chose
Lee Cox
01278 760210
www.vanitonia.co.uk
Vanitoniapoodles@aol.com
©LC-E
UNRETOUCHED
©advertising
& photography
Croft-Elliott

1965.

1972.

1975.

1979.

290 Ch owned/bred

1965. The foundation Pugs, fr. l. **Int Ch Blaezer** b. 1965, **Int Ch Cobby's Apricot Amber, Int Ch Vina of Martlesham, Int Ch Ember of Martlesham** and **Int Ch Colombine of Martlesham**. 46 homebred Pugs became champions.

1972. **Int Ch Melonberry Moonflower,** the foundation Norwich Terrier who was also the breeds first BIG winner in Sweden. 163 homebred Norwich Terriers are champions.

1975. **Int Ch Martlesham Bronson** won BIS at the Stockholm Int. Dec show only 16 month old. Judge was Judy de Casembroot.

1979. **Int Ch Cobby's July's Thunderstorm & Int Ch Cobby's Julie July** of Copplestone strain were littersister & brother and the breeds top winning male & female in 1979.

Renée Sporre-Willes, Villa Björklunda, SE 178 38 Ekerö, Sweden
Tel 46-8-560 326 28. E-mail: info@cobbys.se and **www.cobbys.se**

COBBYs
NORWICHTERRIER

1995.

2007.

2015.

2015.

61 with CC, 67 BIG

1995. Cobby's introduced the first Lagotto to Scandinavia. Fr. l. **Ch Cobby's Clotilde, Ch Cobby's Innovatrice** and **Ch Cobby's Clemente**. 28 homebred Lagotto became champions.

2007. **Int Ch Cobby's High Stakes**, one of many with winning offspring in the UK. Four other homebred are champions in England.

2015. **SE Ch Cobby's Roaring Chase** (Top Stud in UK 2013) was handled by Marita Hillström when he won BIS at the SNT Clubs celebration of the breed's introduction in 1965. Pioneer Siv Jernhake judged the 50th anniversary.

2015. **Cobby's Joint Venture**, our hope for the future is by Am & Eng. Ch Ascot Sunour at Yarrow ex. SE Ch Ragus Comfort and Joy, sister to the famous "Merry Gentleman".

Renée Sporre-Willes, Villa Björklunda, SE 178 38 Ekerö, Sweden
Tel 46-8-560 326 28. E-mail: info@cobbys.se and **www.cobbys.se**

Alan V Walker

Coppergold Simply So Solo at Claymurf

Coppergold Simply So Solo at Claymurf (Dusty to his friends) is loved and owned by Joanne Barclay.

Thank you to Kath and Julie Glynn for all their help and support over the last 18 months but most of all for letting me have Dusty

My life wouldn't be complete without Dusty.

Westmorland Res Best in Show

LKA Best Puppy

Stockport Canine Reserve Best Puppy in Show

Boston Terrier Club
Res Best Dog and Best Puppy in Show

Coppergold Simply A Swagman (Joss) RCC winner Crufts – Judge Wendy Miller, East of England – Judge Mr A Hamilton

Toptuxeudo Rocket Supremo at Coppergold – RCC winner BTC of Scotland – Judge Mr Ian Millar

coppergoldbostons@ntlworld.com

TYTORRO
FRENCH BULLDOG

**Norcairn
Dark n Debonair
at Tytorro
JW ShCM**

1x DCC AND BOB
AT LKA 2014

4 x RDCC
1x RBD

**Vaghnas
Brigadeer at Tytorro
JW ShCM**

Tytorro Voodoo Child

1ST MPD WKC 2015
CRUFTS QUALIFIED AT 6 MONTHS

Tytorro Biba Amoureuse

1ST MPB PAIGNTON 2015
CRUFTS QUALIFIED AT 6 MONTHS

OWNED AND ADORED BY
JANE MORGAN & GED LING
EMAIL: JANE.MORGAN9@AOL.CO.UK
TEL. 07985-675387
TEL. 01268-424748

GUNALT

TO ACCOMPLISH GREAT THINGS

20 Year Club

The UK's top Weimaraner kennel in the history.

Proud holder of all breed records, including top brood, top cc winner, and top breeder with over 80 UK champions & 2 new SH.CH. in 2015

WE MUST FIRST DREAM...

... THEN VISUALISE

THEN PLAN

BELIEVE...

ACT!

Enquires about the breed, puppies or stud dogs or for any of the breed books by Patsy please feel free to contact us.

Stephen & Patsy Hollings,
Gunalt Weimaraners
Carlton Hall Farm, Carlton, Yeadon,
Nr. Leeds, Yorkshire LS19 7BG
Telephone 01132505113
Mobile 07968985582
www.gunaltweimaraners.co.uk
www.facebook.com/GunaltWeimaraners

209

©advertising & photography
Croft-Elliott

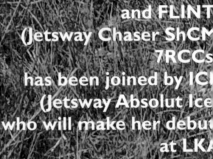

Sh Ch Ferndel True Story with Chanangel

'Naughty Nettle'

Alan V Walker

Proudly owned by:
BONNIE SCOUGALL (Shannas) and
ANGELA CHANDLER (Chanangel)

213

BLACKPARK
Papillon, Maltese and Dobermann

CH LAFFORD PHOTO FINISH AT BLACKPARK (ZEROX)

(5 CCs and 2 RCCs) now a "yummy mummy" to a litter of three bitch puppies in Sept 2015 by Multi BIS's and Multi Ch Affair White Star Of Eternity (DEU) (FENDI)

Above: **Ch Lafford Photo Finish at Blackpark** and **Lafford Bewitched at Blackpark** (both bred by Carol Lees) – Crufts Qualified.
Below: **Obsession White Star Of Eternity (Imp Deu)** – BPIS Winner and 1 RCC Stud Book Number – Crufts Qualified (Bred By Sabrina Scheffczyk).

All coats conditioned and prepared using products supplied by HUB International

At the time of going to press "Zerox" is: Current Top Maltese Bitch 2015.
Bitch CC: Three Counties 2014, judge: Albert Easdon.
Bitch CC: UK Toydog 2015, judge: Sharon Johnson-Love.
Bitch CC: Birmingham Dog Show 2015, judge: Chris Ripsher.

Bitch CC: Blackpool 2015, judge: Val Bloor.
Bitch CC: Windsor 2015, judge: Tom Mather.
Best of Sex in breed (1 CC on offer) Midland Counties 2014. judge: Albert Wight.
Best of Sex in breed (1 CC on offer) Driffield 2014 judge: Geoffrey Davies
Res Bitch CC: Driffield 2014. judge: Geoffrey Davies
Res Bitch CC: Manchester 2015. Judge: Sue Tyler.
Res Best of Sex in Breed (1 CC on offer) Midland Counties 2013. Judge: Chris Ripsher.

CAC – Excellent. S.E.C Liege Golden Fog Trophy 2015. Judge: Luza Beradze.
CACIB + BOB – Excellent SEC Liege Golden Dog Trophy 2015. Judge: Luza Beradze.
RCAC – Excellent. World Dog Show Maltese Raduno 2015. Judge: Paolo Dondina

BIS-4 South Eastern Counties Toydog 2015. Judge: Mike Gadsby.
RBIS, Group 1 and Best AVNSC Toy: Thames Valley all breeds Open Show 2015, judges: Bethan Sarah and Mervyn Evans.

Also a Group 2 and Group 3 at Maidenhead and Henley on Thames (Rivermead in Reading) and quite a number of Res Best of Sex in Breed at Ch Shows where no CCs were on offer for the Maltese breed.

Owner: Cathy Urquhart
Peppard Farm, Peppard Common, Henley On Thames RG9 5JU
Email: Cathyurquhart@Icloud.Com
Tel: 01491-629553.

'at time of going to press

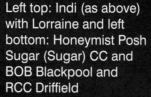

CH KINSRIDGE TOP TIP
DOB 5.10.13

'Martha'

photo Anne Johnsen

19 CCs, 5 RCCs, BIS Three Counties, Group 1 Southern Counties and numerous other top honours

Sincere thanks to all the judges who have thought so highly of Martha and have made 2015 a very special year for us, and all our friends for their tremendous support.

Not forgetting Kinsridge Back Chat (Rafa) 2 CCs with BOB, 4 RCCs, many BPIB and Puppy Group places, all before 18 months.

Di Jenkins Kinsridge Norfolks
01889 270398 – kinsridge@madasafish.com

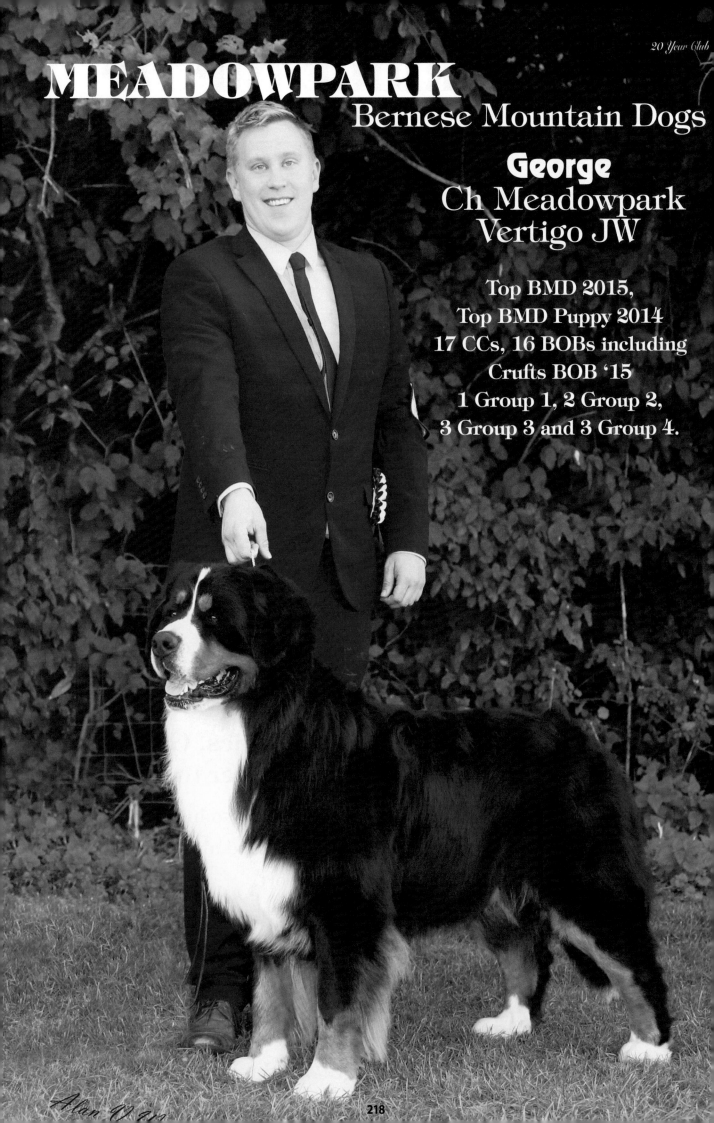

MEADOWPARK
Bernese Mountain Dogs

George
Ch Meadowpark Vertigo JW

Top BMD 2015,
Top BMD Puppy 2014
17 CCs, 16 BOBs including
Crufts BOB '15
1 Group 1, 2 Group 2,
3 Group 3 and 3 Group 4.

Ch.Jasmine of CanerikieJW

Mina

Mina's first litter is
planned for this winter

*Proudly owned by
Barry Mansell & Jocelyn Duddell*

*Beautifully handled by
Luke Johnston*

RBIS SOUTHERN COUNTIES 2015
HOUND GROUP1 BLACKPOOL 2015
HOUND GROUP3 THREE COUNTIES 2013

6 BOB'S
10 CC'S

Artwork & photography: PAULINEOLIVERFOTOS

Muriel, Carol & Melanie Harwood
Photo's by Carol Harwod & Will Harris
www.minarets-poodles.com
Design by Minarets

CC & Multiple RCC Winner
reetano lipizzaner at minarets

ch minarets out of the blue
First BLUE CHAMPION in the UK for over 35 years

minarets nobiz like showbiz
Multiple BPIB Winner

ch minarets no more secrets
Multiple CC Winner, Specialty BIS Winner

Our fabulous new edition.. BPIB Winner
mischtikals manhatten at minarets

OVER 60 CHAMPIONS WORLDWIDE

Clynymona Clarchien & Havanese Stars

years of careful
iminate breeding
aking all records
e breed in the UK
P BOLOGNESE
since 2008

**GIB jCH Little White
Wonder Othello Matteo**
Top Puppy in breed
Top Rare Breed Puppy
Joint Top Toy Puppy

Clynymona Jo I'm Alone
Top Puppy 2014

TOP DOG
2008/9/10/11/12/13/14/15
TOP PUPPY
2010/11/12/13/14/15
TOP STUD
2009/10/13/14/15* to date
TOP BREEDER
2011/12/13/14/15

**All dogs eyes
tested and clear**
We breed purely to
produce good quality dogs
with excellent temperaments

**Multi Ch Bolognese Star Donald
at Havanese Stars**
Top Bolo 3rd Year running
RCAC WS Club Show
Multiple BOB winner

**Multi Ch Bolognese Star Audrey
at Havanese Stars**
Record breaker for the breed in the UK
Vet Toy Gp Winner (1st ever Bolognese)
World Veteran Show Winner 2015

Working together...
... Keeping the Bolognese
community talking Globally

Virginia Dowty, Kathryn Begg & Marguerite Seeberger
Isle of Man, UK, Gibraltar & Switzerland
vdowty@yahoo.com, kath.begg@me.com
+44 (0) 1624823539 answerphone

Oadvertising & photography Croft-Elliott

Ransley Greyhounds

20 Year Club

Ch/Ir Ch Ransley Simply Bewitched 3 CCs 5 RCCs
This year Daisy became our 13th Ransley champion when winning our 88th CC
Rita and Paul Bartlett 01233 500667 www.ransleygreyhounds.com

Lee Nichols, The Hollies, Aldham, Hadleigh, Suffolk, IP7 6NS - 01473 827620

Quality

Bouvier des Flandres

Cersei

Mina & Tyne doing what kids and pups do best - play!

N. Cersei - 2CC's & 8 res CC's, 2 BIS at Club Open Shows, 1 res BIS Club Ch Show & res BIS Sheringham DKA.

Irish Ch & Irish J Ch N. Tyrion at Davdeir (McKenna) numerous green stars, 5 group 1 placings & BIS 3 at Belfast.

Irish Ch & Irish J Ch N. Osha at Wispafete ShCM (Jones & Gibbons) 9 green stars, 2 CC's & 2 res CC's.

Dover - N. Tanzanite at O won veteran bitch at LKA 14', Crufts, B'ham Nat, both club open & ch shows. In mixed classes she was 2nd to her older half brother N Aquilla (Partner) at Windsor & NWPBA. She has 1CC & 1 res CC.

Ceiley - O. Elusive (owned by Lee) won her 2nd res CC at LKA 14' beating her mum Tanzanite.

Tyne - N. Terrell at O finally made her debut at the club Ch Show & won minor puppy bitch.

Tyrion

ANTOC
Rough Collies and Welsh Corgi Cardigan

photo Alan Walker
Taken at Belfast 2015

Atendus Erasure wins our 160th Challenge Certificate

Bred by Gill Browne, he is pictured here winning Dog CC and BIS at the Irish Collie Club Ch Show from Judge Joan Fryer-Clarke. The next day he took the Dog CC and BOS at Belfast Ch Show from Richard Kinsey and followed this by winning the Reserve CC at Midland Counties.

He carries lines to many Champions but interestingly through his dam can trace his lines back 19 generations to the Antoc Kennel's foundation bitch purchased in 1953.

Although owned and shown by Carole, he is actually "Mum, Aileen Speding's" house dog along with our Veteran Cardigan "Bridget", a daughter of Ch Antoc Double-O-Seven for Salvenik, sire of 7 Champions and who is a son of Ch Antoc Audacity winner of 23 CCs.

During 2015, we have successfully attended a few shows but can record 2 new KCSB wins in Collies, along with BIS at Collie Club of Wales with our latest sable bitch, Antoc Soul Diva who also, through her dam's line, goes back to the same foundation bitch

This small but very select kennel is owned by Aileen Speding and Carole Smedley and has housed 29 UK Champions in 4 separate breeds, Rough and Smooth Collies, Cardigan Welsh Corgis and much earlier in Shetland Sheepdogs. There have also been numerous Overseas titled "Antocs". A few of our past Crufts wins include either the CC or CC and BOB in 1972, 1974 with Reserve in Group to eventual BIS winner. CC wins in 1988, 1990, 1994, 1995, 1999, and 2003. In 2016, between us both, we will have judged Crufts on 8 separate occasions!

Aileen Speding and Carole Smedley

Brook Cottage, Ripley, Christchurch, Dorset BH23 8EU Tel: 01425 672424 Email: ca.antoc@btinternet.com

Kulawand

20 Year Club

Kulawand Caruso JW 1 Res CC

SIRE: Ch. Bournehouse Winter Sky of Kulawand
DAM: Lanwickleaze Parade of Kulawand

Kulawand

www.kulawand.com

Kulawand

Kulawand Konquistador JW 1 Res CC

SIRE: Ch. Kulawand Love To Remember
DAM: Sh.Ch. Kulawand In No One's Shadow JW

Tel: (+ 44) 01564 82 38 38

Bob & Sandy Lane &
Penny Lane-Ridyard

INGLEDENE

Dignity Elegance Type Temperament Sound Health

INGLEDENE SPIRITS ARISE

'Clint' at 11 months
Had a great start to his career
with numerous BP, BPIS,
RBIS with RCC and Puppy
Group 2 at SKC

Ch Ingledene All Dressd In Blue JW

'Frieda' returned to the
ring after producing a
beautiful litter and quickly
gained her title with BOB
on each occasion.
Thanks to Judges - Bath
Mrs M Wildman - Windsor
Mrs C Smedley - NWPBS
Ms L Pettitt
for appreciating her many
outstanding qualities.

**Currently Top Collie
(Rough) 2015**

Owned, loved, conditioned and presented by

VALERIE and JOHN GEDDES

ingledenecollies@btinternet.com

Tel : +44 (0)1938 811846

'at time of going to press

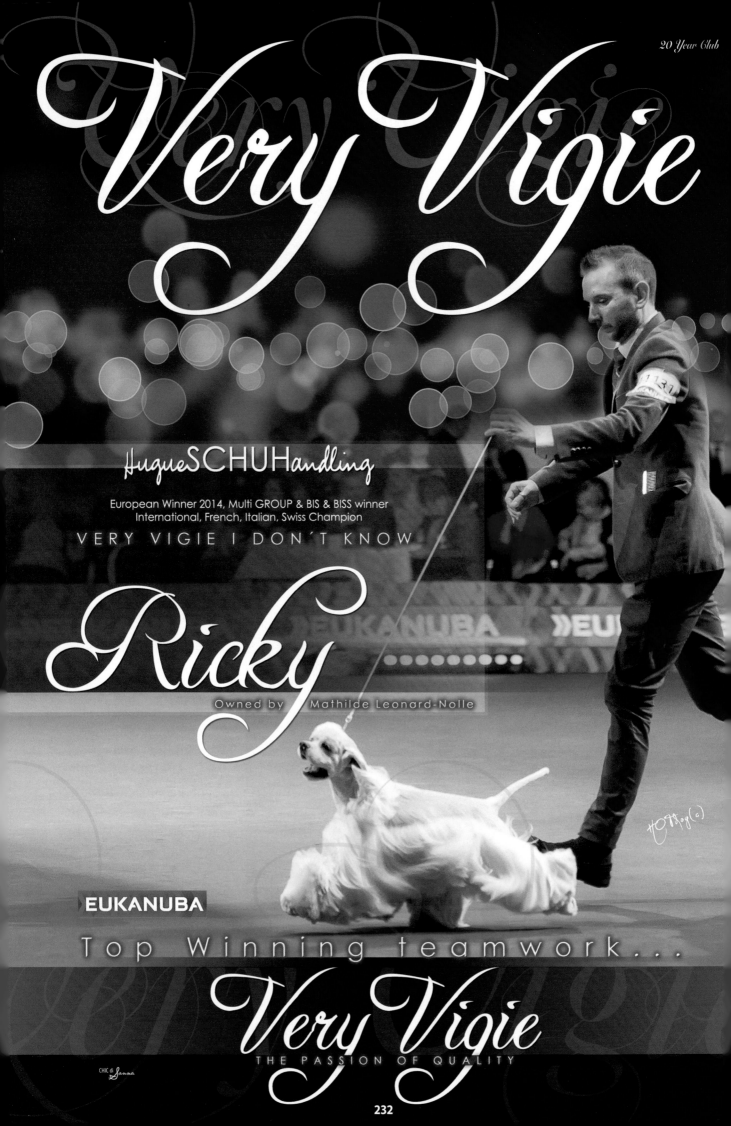

Ch Neradmik Family Affair with Lekkerbek
Brody
Bred by Jean Sharp-Bale

The latest champion from
BIS, BISS, Ch, Am, Can Ch Kemonts Skyline's Game Boy HoF, RoMX (Imp USA)
Ferris – currently Runner-up and Top Utility Stud Dog all breeds (October 2015)
Breeder Mrs Jan Corrington, USA
and
Ch Lady Godiva's Guilty Pleasures with
Neradmik (Imp FIN) Tallulah – currently
third overall Top Brood Bitch all breeds
(October 2015)
Breeder: Mrs Annamaija Tuisku, Finland

4 CCs, two with Best of Breed, 4 Reserve CCs

Owned by Joan Miles and Sarah Dean
75 Chalvington Road
Chandler's Ford SO53 3EF
023 8026 1621
email JAD@barton.ac.uk

photo Photocall

Other Ferris and Tallulah offspring winning CCs this year were:
Ch Neradmik Uptown Girl Deminiac
Neradmik All About the Boy for Watchkees
Neradmik Sunday Lovin' Morvania
Neradmik High Society at Skathki

The next generation

photo Walker

Ch Samkees With Love to Neradmik*
Freddie
bred by Victor Gatt in Malta

By: Am GGCh KJ's It's Nothing Purrsonal HoF (Chubbs)
Ex: Ch SLO JNR Ch MLT Ch Neradmik Late Night Love (Sheva)
Owned by Jean Sharp-Bale, Joan Miles and Victor Gatt

Freddie has had a wonderful puppy career, being awarded:

3 CCs by the age of 12 and a half months
10 Best Puppy in Breed, 2 Reserve CCs
2 Best of Breed, 4 Puppy Groups
2 Reserve Best Puppy in Show
Shortlisted to the last 7 at the Pup of the Year Final

Many thanks to all the judges concerned

*subject to KC confirmation

Jean Sharp-Bale
Wiggs Cottage, Plumley, Near Ringwood BH24 3QB
01202 824368 neradmik.kees@yahoo.com

BANNONBRIG SPINONI

20 Year Club

Established 1982
Carole, Mike & Nicola Spencer
Top Breeders 2010-2013

Celebrating Decades of Success

www.bannonbrig.co.uk

Champions around the World

WINUWUK

We were pleased to make up our 27th champion this year, who also went on to win a 4th CC and Group 2 at Midland Counties **Ch Diceulon Gin Fizz at Winuwuk** is sired by the 2014 Top Boxer and Crufts BOB winner Ch Winuwuk The Outlaw

However, we are always looking to the future, just like this very promising five month old from the Winuwuk stable.

Julie Brown and Tim Hutchings

t: 01453 511303   e: winuwuk@btinternet.com   w: winuwukboxers.com

Charney Japanese Spitz

Our latest champion for 2015

Ch Enfloyz Quinton the Snow Prince with Charney (SWE IMP)

Our thanks to Ewa and Helene for entrusting us with this lovely boy

'Keeley' is now retired from the ring, enjoying the success of his son Charney Precious Gift with Kumiko with thanks to Adell and Kennedy for campaigning him so professionally

**We aim to breed sound dogs who are typical of the breed with good temperaments and who make excellent companions.
Assured Breeder with accolade of excellence
*Japanese Spitz rescue centre***

www.charney-kennels.co.uk
charneykennel@btconnect.com   01367 241063

WORLD CLASS WHIPPETS FOR 55 YEARS

Bohem Whippets continue to exert a strong influence worldwide. Three champions bred here or sired by a Bohem dog were among the Top 20 in the U.S. last year, and more than half of the total descend close up or further back in their pedigrees from Bohem. This is in spite of a modest breeding program consisting of only approximately 40 litters since 1961.

Although not numerous the offspring of Bohem stud dogs include current BIS and SBIS winners in the U.S., Canada, Russia, Italy and Norway.

The single bitch in the only litter bred here in the last 10 years, **GCh. Bohem Swan Song**, continued to win Groups early in the year but was diagnosed with oral cancer in May. Following surgery and chemotherapy she's doing well but will not be bred or shown again. "Rosa" and her handler/co-owner Scot Northern raised over $10,000 to benefit cancer research at the Animal Health Foundation during the summer!

GCh Bohem Swan Song

The puppy **Snow Hill Beyond Blonde at Bohem** was acquired from Susanne Hughes, DVM this fall. "Kylie" will be shown occasionally in 2016. She descends from Bohem far back in her pedigree but is basically an outcross. She lives in Palm Springs with co-owner Scott Mazer and Rosa's sire **GCh. Counterpoint Painted by Bohem, SC**. He continues to sire excellent puppies: seven champions in his first three litters with more on the way.

Ch. Bohem Final Act earned his title in 2015.

Final Act racing.

photo Nikki Russ

Snow Hill Beyond Blonde at Bohem.

Bo Bengtson
PO Box 10, Ojai, CA 93024, USA
email bobengtson@impulse.net
www.bohemwhippets.com

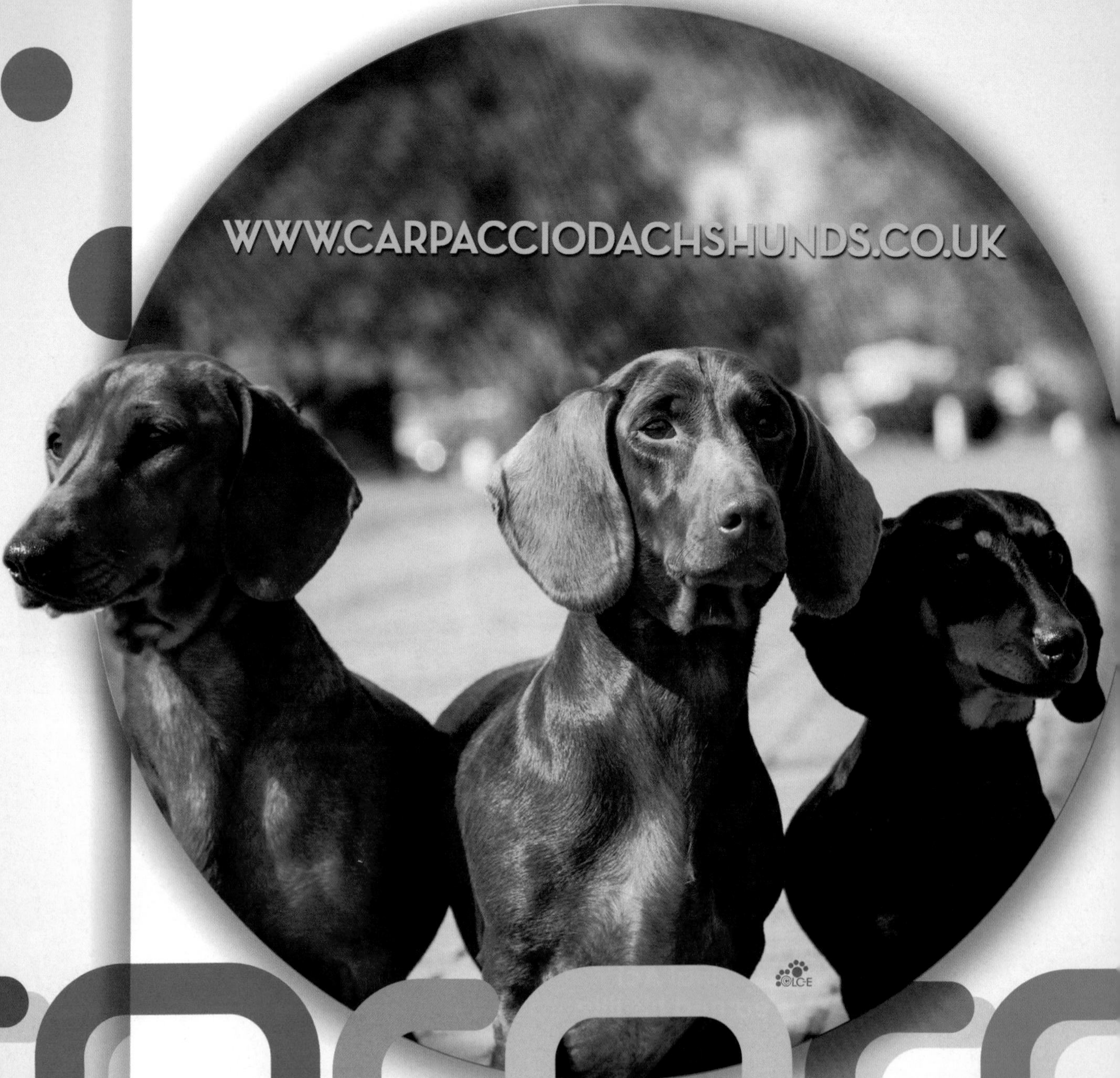

WWW.CARPACCIODACHSHUNDS.CO.UK

©LC·E

CARPACCIO

Jason & Susan Hunt

+44 01793493212
carpaccio@sky.com

CH Sontag Shanda Lea
Top Smooth 201
Bred by the late Mrs E coope

CH Cwmdarhian Hogan
Hero at Carpacci
Top Smooth Dog 201

Carpaccio Casablanc
Top min smooth Puppy 201

TUSSALUD

Breeding and showing top Papillons since 1972

Tia

CH* & IR CH Tussalud Story Tales

Toy Group 1 and 4 CCs in 4 shows since returning to the UK from Ireland

CC, Best of Breed & Toy Group 1, Welsh Kennel Club August 2015
(Mr E Whitehill, breed and Ms A Oliver toy group)

CC, South Wales Kennel Association October 2015 (Mrs J Banfield)

CC & Reserve Best in Show, South Wales Papillon Club October 2015 (Mrs L Bartram)

CC & Best of Breed, Midland Counties October 2015 (Mr G Davies)

Our grateful thanks to the judges and to Sean Carroll and
James Newman (Denemore/Belliver International Papillons) for caring for and handling
Tia to 13 green stars in 13 consecutive shows during summer 2015 in Ireland with best of breeds and
group placings.

Dam: CH Denemore Story's Echo at Tussalud (12 CCs)
Sire: CH &Fin CH Siljans Ragge JR Connection at Tussalud (16 CCs)

Owned and bred by Kay Stewart and Kirsten Stewart-Knight
01582 881 223 / kirstenstewartknight@h tmail

SILHILL SHEREX

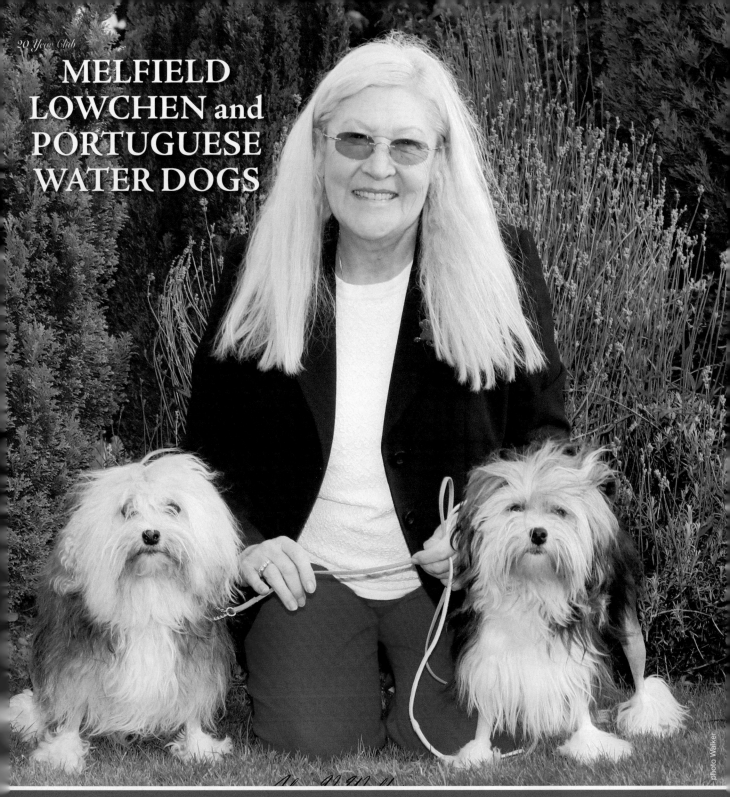

MELFIELD LOWCHEN and PORTUGUESE WATER DOGS

20 Year Club

photo Walker

Windswept naughty 1/2 sisters of Ch Melfield Angel In Black
Ch Secret Angel (Dolly) and Bella Trix (Bella)

Jocelyn Creffield
Tel 01449 744250 email melfieldk9@btinternet.com
KC Accredited UKAS Inspected Breeder

Elusive Emerald consistent winner in puppy classes, now co-owned with Andrea Hobbs

50 years on

Michael Braysher
Braypass St Bernards
22-24 High Street, Orwell,
near Royston, Herts SG8 5QN
044 1223 207278

Glenauld Boxers and Boston Terriers
currently home to

Boxer and 3 Boston Terrier UK Champions | British BC Top Kennel 2014 | Top Boston Terrier Breeders 2014

Glenauld The Entertainer

(7 months)

5 BPD
BPIS Trent B/C

Glenauld Trudy

(10 months)

2 BPIB
Two Puppy
Group 2

photo Humphries

Paula Hamilton

Glenauld Tasmin JW

(10 months)

3 RCC
4 BPIB
One Puppy Group 1

photo Photocall

Ch Glenauld Jackie'O
4 CCs 4 RCCs
Currently Joint UK
Top Bitch 15

Glenauld Gabriella
2 RCCs

Ch Glenauld Nevada JW
6 CCs 5 RCCs
UK Top Puppy 2014
UK Top Boston 2015

**Ch Glenauld
Gianfranco JW**
11 CCs 6 RCCs

photo Photocall

Glenauld Olly Murs
10 months
4 BPIB BPIS NBT Club

Glenauld Rita Ora
10 months
3 BPB

Janice Lynn and Suzanne Mair glenauld@aol.com
FB Glenauld Boxers and Boston Terriers

Field Spaniels

Top Breeder 2012 '13 '14 '15*
Assured Breeder with Kennel Club
Accolade of Excellence

Est. 1980

Sh Ch Nadavin Julianna JW ShCM
2002–2015
40 CCs
25 RCCs
and 26 BOBs
The Breed Record Holder

Thank you "Olivia" for giving
us so many amazing memories.

Crufts 2009 BOB

Sh Ch Nadavin Thistledown JW
"Tianna" gained her crown at WKC 2015 under Judge Dr Ron James
Thank you to all who have paid her so many lovely compliments

Jill and Charles Holgate

Tel: 01282 865705 email: jill_holgate@yahoo.co.uk www.nadavin.co.uk

* at time of press

CHANDHALLY DALMATIANS and ITALIAN SPINONE
EST 1989 and 2010

Looking to the future with new ambitions and many more adventures in UK, Europe and Scandinavia

Norwegian, Danish, Mediterranean & International Ch Redrue Cherriecola to Chandhally

w/o 15/1/2011 (Adone del Feriiia ex Crieda Tamarin to Redrue)
bred by the late Ms H McKie to whom I am forever grateful.
1 BOB, 1 BCC Judge Dr G Mentasti (Ita) Birmingham DSS May 2015
2 RBCC Judges Mrs S Whittingham at 3 Counties Agr S June 2015 and
Mrs A Hardy at Richmond Sept 2015

Lola 3rd in group 7 at Tvaaker Int Ch Show (SW) 2015
(photo Mr N Fleming)

(photo L Coldwell)

Chandhally Limon Cino

w/o 7/11/2014 (Caldocani Cesario ShCM,JW ex
Norw/Danish/Med& Int Ch Redrue Cherriecola to Chandhally)
BP and BPIB at her first Ch Show at 6 months and 3 days old under Italian Spinone
breed Specialist Dr G Mentasti Ita) Birmingham DSS May 2015, BP and BPIB at SWKA
Oct 2015 Judge Mr K Groom

2 BPIB Sweden, 2 BPIB France.

Our aim is to breed for conformation, movement, temperament and health. We are well known for our dogs' friendly and outgoing nature.
We have had tremendous success in the show ring at home and abroad for many years with our Dalmatians and now also with our Italian Spinone, winning top honours across the board and consistently placed at Ch shows attended here at home. Our dogs win on their merits not by who or what we are.
I am a Kennel Club's Assured Breeder and UKAS certification and as recommended by the KCAB Scheme we hip and elbow score, do all the relevant health tests, vet checks, 1st Vaccinations, all our Spinoni puppies CA test, the Dalmatians are BAER tested,

Gone but not forgotten

Ir Ch DALREGIS SHOOTING STAR OF CHANDHALLY
L/B (HK Ch Dalrannoch Citizen Kane to Chandhally (imp Aust)
ex Dalregis La Serenata)

Ir & Int Ch CHANDHALLY CHANTILLY LACE B/B (Ch & Ir & Int Ch Truthful
Tango at Kilndandy ex Ir Ch Dalregis Shooting Star of Chandhally)
UK & Irelands first Multi Country Int Ch

Norw Ch CHANDHALLY SNOW QUEEN B/B (Ch Washakie Chief As Great As
JW ex Ir & Int Ch Chandhally Chantilly Lace)

At home
CHANDHALLY CUVEE DU PRESIDENT B/D 2/11/2007 (Fr Ch Troilus de
Puech Barrayre ex Norw Ch Chandhally Snow Queen) Consistently placed at Ch
Shows. He is the first Dalmatian to qualify for the Irish Pup of the Year. He won
numerous BOB's & winner of Utility Groups and RBIS. Retired from the show
ring – available for Stud .

at Home Hall, Riva and Lola
photo Mrs NR Fleming

Italian Spinone Puppy and Dalmatian Stud enquiries welcome.
Very proud Owner, Breeder, Handler and Slave of the above,
I judge all breeds, CCs in Dalmatians

MRS NINA R FLEMING
CAE BACH HOUSE, CAE BACH, MACHEN. CAERPHILLY
CF83 8NG SOUTH WALES, UK
TEL (00 44) 01633 440371 EMAIL n.fleming27@btinternet.com
www.chandhally.co.uk

Champion Bobander Too Kool For Skool JW

"Happy days"
continue for
'Fonzie'

TOP BICHON*
Multiple Group
finalist
16 BOB
15 CCs
5 RCCs

Our sincere
thanks to all
those judges, good
friends and most
sporting fellow
exhibitors who
have supported us
so enthusiastically
throughout the
year!

Chris and Bob Wyatt
www.bobanderbichons.co.uk
Home of 13 Champions

*at time of going to press

SOUSKA and SWANSFORD
Tibetan Spaniels and Longhaired Dachshunds

CH SOUSKA DEVOTION

(Kiiramanna Royal Salute, Imp Fin, ex Souska Be With You)
4 CCs Including Crufts 2015, Group 2 at East of England
and RCC at the TSA
Owned by Janet Rice

photo Emily Guy

CH SWANSFORD KESTADOR

(Swansford Vanador ex Swansford Dipsydora)
Best in Show at the Dachshund Club Of Wales
Championship Show
Brother to Swansford Warrador and Ch Swansford Whoopydora

CH SOUSKA MOVING ON
TO DANDYDAYO

(Ch/Int Ch Mango's Pentagon ex Souska Evighet)
3 CCs and 7 RCCs, gaining his Title doing the
double with Ch Devotion
Owned by Andrew Roberts

CH SWANSFORD
NIGELLADORA DARSOMS

(Swansford Warrador ex Darsoms Zsimone of Swansford)
Top Longhaired Bitch 2015.
Best In Show at the Southern Dachshund Assoccation
Owned by Cindy Dare

In 2015 Our Tibetan Spaniels have done well for ourselves and others. Our Royal Salute gained his first CC and BOB with his son Pauline Bevis' Souska Empty Room at Starlance gaining his first CC along with 3 RCCs.

Ch Souska Dance Alone (BOB Crufts 2013) produced four super puppies that remain with us.

In Dachshunds Ch Whoopydora produced some exciting puppies and went BIS at The Longhaired Championship Show for the second year running. Our golden oldie Ch Burburydora won the Veteran Stakes at Manchester and Best Veteran In Show at both the Southern and Dachshund Club of Wales Championship Shows making us top breeder so far for 2015

International Stud dogs, Puppies occasionally and advice
IAN BLACKSHAW and DANIEL ROBERTS*
Swansford Kennels, Cannock Road, Stafford ST17 0SU 01785 664461
souskatib@hotmail.com   daniel@swansford.co.uk
*Dog World breed note writer for Longhaired and Miniature Long Haired Dachshunds

BYMIL

Sarah's

CH BYMIL SMILE PLEASE

by Ch Belroyd Pemcader Cymro ex Ch Bymil Picture This

Daisy now has **ten CCs**, three during 2015 including Crufts and **Best in Show** at the South East Corgi Association championship show

photo Will Harris

Sarah, Diana and Simon's

CH OREGONIAN RAISE AN EYEBROW

by Barwal Brave Beau ex Oregonian Fay Wray

Little shown during 2015, **Rufus** won his **seventh CC** at Darlington.

photo Will Harris

With thanks and gratitude to Margo Parsons, who started it all in 1965. An inspiration to each of us...

OREGONIAN

+ BYMIL
+ BIMWICH
+ DEAVITTE

Diana and Sarah's new male puppies, by Nireno Luke Skywalker ex Oregonian Snow Queen, have made an exciting start.

OREGONIAN SNOW LEOPARD

Best puppy, National Working and Pastoral Breeds

Best puppy and Reserve CC, Midland Counties

photo Alan Walker

OREGONIAN SNOW TIGER

Best puppy in show, West of England Corgi Association

Best puppy, Darlington

SARAH TAYLOR
bymil@btopenworld.com

DIANA KING
bimwich@btinternet.com

SIMON PARSONS
wortencottage@hotmail.co.uk

MOCHRAS BASSET FAUVE DE BRETAGNE

Mochras Marzipan NUch-EUW-15, (pictured) a much admired hunting bitch (arctic hare) who can win CACIBs too! Eurowinner 2015, "Miss" will be shown at Crufts 2016. Her brother Ch and Irish Ch Melchior sired Blewwfls Ivan Idea, a group 6 winner before his first birthday (Killarney '15).

Our Jerome du Rallye des Ramondens is full younger brother to the winner of the bitch CAC at the 2015 Elevage and was res best dog at the BfdB club championship show 2015.

Mochras Marc has had a winning puppy and junior career. My thanks to everyone who has given him BOBs and 30 first prizes at open and championship shows.

Liz Thornton   mochrashounds.co.uk   mochrashounds@gmail.com   tel: 01264 790720

NASAILLEEN
TIRKANE
&

Ann Ingram
Kay Ryan
Lisa Nelson
Leanne Bryant

07989 965056
Tirkane@hotmail.com

Nasailleen Tabloid Tal

Kyle

Runner Up Top Toy
Poodle Puppy 2015

3 Puppy Grp Winner
BPIS & RBPIS Awards
(Belfast & SKC Aug)

Puppy Grp 2 & 4

POTY Qualifier

Nasailleen Notorius at Tirkane

Mick

2 CCs

Top Toy Poodle Puppy 2015

BPIS London Home Counties Poodle
Speciality Ch Show.

Irish POTY Qualifier

Photos by
Will Harris

NASAILLEEN

&

AMERICAN COCKER SPANIELS

Lisa Nelson
Leanne Bryant
Beverley Morris

07989 965056
leannebryant@live.co.uk

**Sh Ch (IR)
Mycalleys Bartholomew
at Nasailleen**

Bart

In the UK
2 CCs - 6 RCC

In Ireland
2 x Group 1
Group 2
Group 4

**Sh Ch (USA) Silhouette
Troubling Nasailleen at
Mycalleys**

Trouble

Made up from 6-9 class in
America.
Now living in the UK

2 Best Puppy Dog Awards

DW/Eukanuba POTY 2015
Heat Winner

Hilary White

Gorthleck

Shamquin Ivoire De Chine for Gorthleck

(Desperado de la Caverne Des Anges ex Shamquin Eden Rose)

Breeders: Mesdames B Quinio and J Thomas
EVIE is owned by **CUSH MACNALLY and PAT PIPER**

20 Year Club

Waterley Lushuslips

Waterley Strictly Glitz
owned by
Markus Gisslén (Sweden)

Waterley Worththewait
owned by
Markus Gisslén (Sweden)

Waterley Make A Mark
owned by Kristina Forsberg
(Sweden)

Mark James and Glenn Davies Email: waterley@f2s.com Tel: 01536 762111

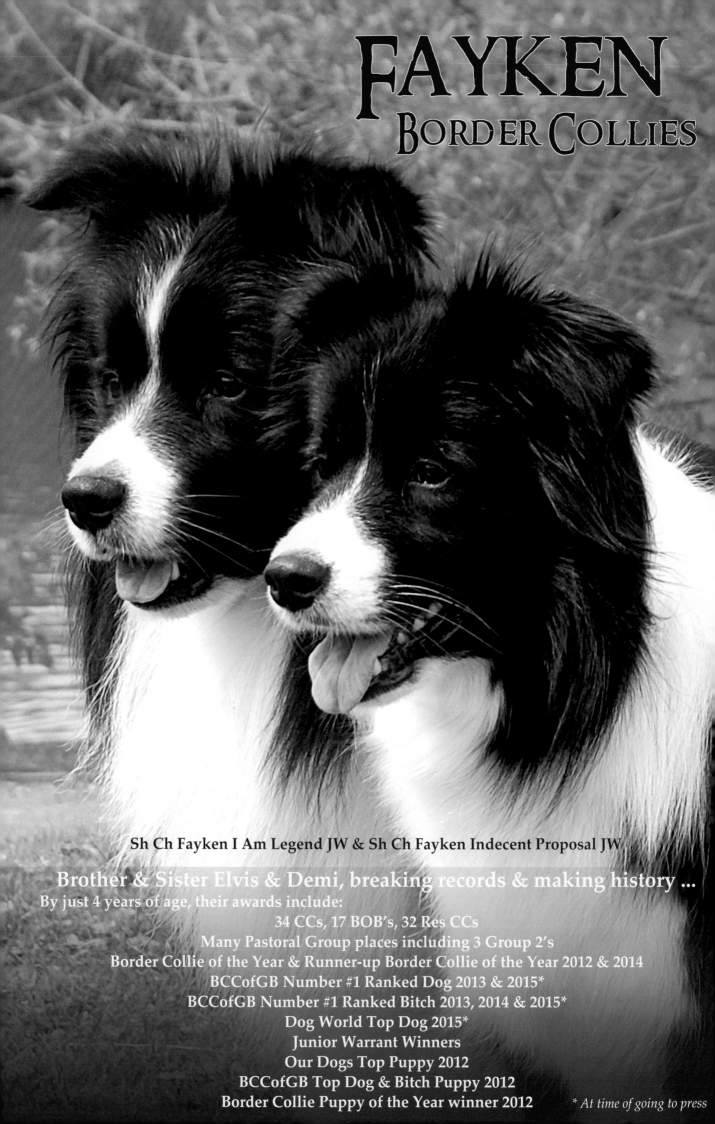

FAYKEN
BORDER COLLIES

Sh Ch Fayken I Am Legend JW & Sh Ch Fayken Indecent Proposal JW

Brother & Sister Elvis & Demi, breaking records & making history ...
By just 4 years of age, their awards include:
34 CCs, 17 BOB's, 32 Res CCs
Many Pastoral Group places including 3 Group 2's
Border Collie of the Year & Runner-up Border Collie of the Year 2012 & 2014
BCCofGB Number #1 Ranked Dog 2013 & 2015*
BCCofGB Number #1 Ranked Bitch 2013, 2014 & 2015*
Dog World Top Dog 2015*
Junior Warrant Winners
Our Dogs Top Puppy 2012
BCCofGB Top Dog & Bitch Puppy 2012
Border Collie Puppy of the Year winner 2012

At time of going to press

Arrodare

"Timeless Quality"

➤ *Our Dogs Top Breeder 2015** ◄
➤ *Dog World Top Border Collie Brood Bitch 2015** ◄
➤ *Dog World 8th Top Brood Bitch 2015 (All Breeds)** ➤

Sh Ch Altricia Lady Grace by Arrodare JW, 8 CCs, 9 RCCs with daughter Arrodare Devil In Disguise JW, 1 CC & BOB, 1 RCC; and son Arrodare Hear Me Roar (see below).

Arrodare Fuel To The Flame "Dolly"

Sire: Sh Ch Fayken I Am Legend JW

* * Coming in 2016 * *

Arrodare Hear Me Roar "Dexy"

Sire: Sh Ch Sashdan Smokin Joe (Imp Aus)

BPIS winner
Puppy Group 3 - Paignton 2015

www.arrodare.co.uk

* Correct at time of going to press

Sh Ch Arrodare It's Now Or Never JW

Sh Ch Fayken I Am Legend JW x Sh Ch Altricia Lady Grace by Arrodare JW

4 CCs, 2 BOB's, Puppy Group 1 SKC 2014

" Mr Lennon"

" I believe in everything, until it is disproved" - *John Lennon*

**"Lenny", my first Show Dog & my first Show Champion.
Titled at Bath 2015, - aged just 21 months.**

Looking forward to 2016 with his baby brother, Arrodare Sex On Fire, - "the Edge".

Nick Smith - nicksmith2511@yahoo.co.uk

Sh Ch Arrodare Moody Blue (Subject to KC confirmation)

Sh Ch Fayken I Am Legend JW x Sh Ch Altricia Lady Grace by Arrodare JW

Jana Hnátková
www.JANA-PHOTO.cz

**"Rori" spent just 10 weeks of 2015 in the UK, and in that period amassed an
incredible 3 CCs, 2 BOB's & 2 Res CCs.**

Owned & loved by Lenka Svobodova, Czech Republic.

www.gaskoprim.websnadno.cz

Arrodare Good Luck Charm

Sh Ch Fayken I Am Legend JW x Sh Ch Altricia Lady Grace by Arrodare JW

2 CCs, 1 BOB, Pastoral Group 1 SKC 2015

"Vienna", although selectively shown, has had a fantastic 2 years in the show ring.
We are very excited for the future.
Proudly owned & adored by Gillian Gorley
www.willosyam.com

Arrodare Just So

Altricia Mister Consistant x Altricia If You Wish for Arrodare

Reserve CC Winner

"Rocco" has been very lightly shown, with much success.
He will be campaigned selectively in 2016.
We are looking forward to a fabulous year to come.

Owned, loved & handled by Lavinia Crompton
07812 734757

"Freddie" has multiple Champ Show awards; looking forward to campaigning him selectively in 2016. Owned & adored by Lesley Atkin - 07976 641347

www.arrodare.co.uk

Dalguise Dream On

Sh Ch Sashdan Smokin Joe (imp Aus) x Aus Ch Tehya Just Like Me At Dalguise (Imp Aus)

"FULL Australian breeding"

⚡ BOLT ⚡

"Bolt" has made a fantastic start to his show career, being a multiple Champ Show winner.

Bolt was bred by Pam Alcorn (Dalguise) and is proudly owned & presented by Lesley Atkin, Ross Green & Jo Ratcliffe.

www.foxkon.bordercollies.co.uk

Cotonkiss Moonrock

Top Puppy 2015
#2 Top Coton 2015
Group 4 Leeds Championship Show 2015

Owned, loved and adored by
Tommy and Anne Craig, handled by Matt Garnham

PUMIDEN
PIONEERING PUMI IN THE UK

Cseri-Subas Mali to Pumiden
Top Puppy
Handled by Matt Garnham

2015 saw Hungarian Pumi gain recognition on the Kennel Club's Import Register and the breed has been eligible to be shown in Import Register Classes since 1st June. Pumiden Pumi have pioneered the breed in the UK and have achieved a number of significant milestones including the first litter of Pumi born in the UK to be KC registered and the first bitch to win a class at a UK Championship Show.

We are currently 2015 Top Breeder, including Top Dog and own the Top Puppy. We have bred show and agility winners across the country with all dogs shown Crufts qualified.

Pumiden Button in the Ear
Top Pumi
Owner Lesley Caines

Baraquiel Pumida to Pumiden
Best Dog Midland Counties,
his first show aged just 6 months!

We have carefully selected and imported from a number of kennels around the world to ensure a wide genetic base as our foundations for this fabulous breed in the UK. A team of well bred, health tested stud dogs are available at limited stud and we are expecting some interestingly bred puppies in 2016.

Many thanks to Matt Garnham and Hazel Gill for all their help with Team Pumiden

MARGARET HARVEY

MARGARETEHARVEY@HOTMAIL.COM   TEL. 07876 390876

Romainville Glen of Imaals
Presents Top Dog of the Year

Champion **Romainville Billy Whizz**
BOB Crufts 2015
5 CCs and multiple RCCs

photo Walker

Crd3 Clear
Sire: Bailielands BB Ben
Dam: Romainville Rhian

Champion **Romainville Ellie**

photo RBT

Crd3 Clear
Sire: Feohanagh Bryan at Romainville
Dam: Briar Rose at Romainville

Romainville Jazz Man
Res CCs

Photo: RBT

Crd 3 Clear
Sire: Bailielands BB Ben
Dam: Champion Romainville
Miss Moneypeny

Romainville Fade to Grey
CC

Photo: RBT

Crd3 Clear
Sire: Grizzlemarsh Digby
Dam: Romainville Rhian

2015 has been a very good year for all the Romainvilles making up two more champions, with Romainville Gracie (co-owned by Matt Garnham), gaining a CC, Romainville Annabelle RCC, Romainville Rock on Ruby a RCC and gaining BOB at the club show. Thanks to Matt for all his hard work and handling of the dogs and to Jo for all her help. Thanks to all the judges who thought so highly of our dogs. Congratulations to other Romainvilles gaining top awards with their owners R Uptown Girl waiting on 2 CCs, R Fast and Furious gaining a CC and R High Flyer gaining her champion status in Finland. Our dogs are at limited stud to approved and tested bitches only.

Enquiries for top winners and promising puppies to:

Kathy George 01432 880819 Email **kathy@romainvillegsd.freeserve.co.uk** Website **www.glenofimaalterriers.co.uk**

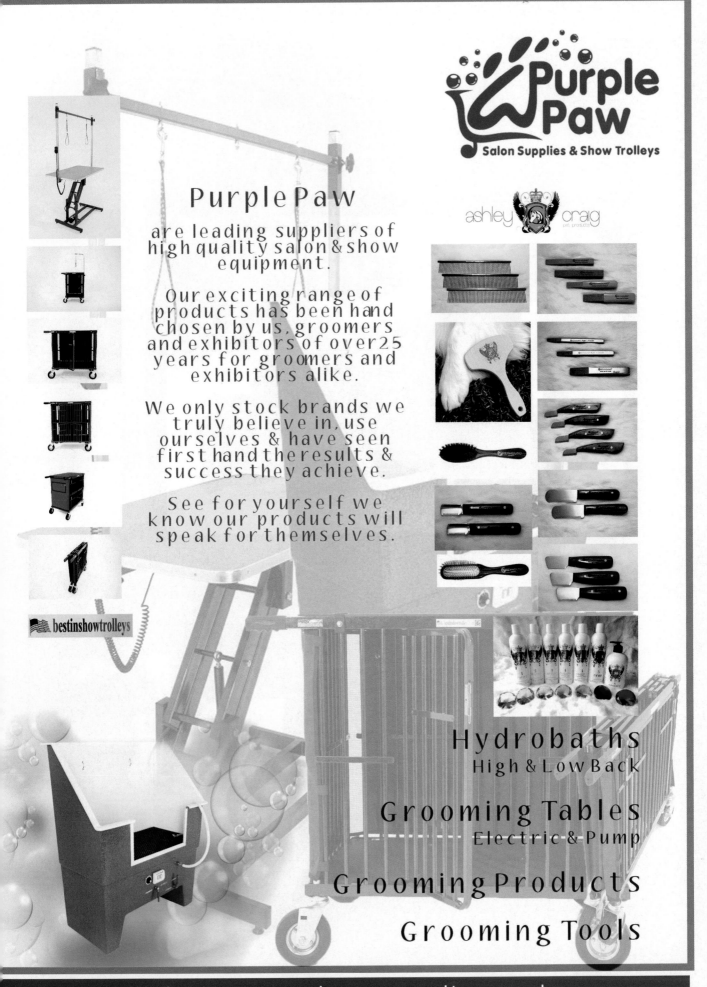

Purple Paw

are leading suppliers of high quality salon & show equipment.

Our exciting range of products has been hand chosen by us, groomers and exhibitors of over 25 years for groomers and exhibitors alike.

We only stock brands we truly believe in, use ourselves & have seen first hand the results & success they achieve.

See for yourself we know our products will speak for themselves.

Hydrobaths
High & Low Back

Grooming Tables
Electric & Pump

Grooming Products

Grooming Tools

Chester

Am Ch Silverhall Flyin' High Flipside

Chester has been shown on a limited basis throughout 2015.

He has **1 CC & 3 RCC**.

His outstanding movement and conformation speaks for itself. We look forward to getting him back out and about in 2016.

Icon is our exciting young buff male currently being campaigned by his breeders Bonnie & Wilson Pike in the USA.

Icon is royally bred, with the greatest of the greats adorning his pedigree.

He stepped out in style at his first show and picked up a **5 point major** in strong competition.

We look forward to seeing him shown at the Flushing Spaniel show in January and eagerly await his arrival in 2016.

Tel: + 44 (0) 7767 292199
Web: nujaxshowdogs.com
eMail:
nujaxshowdogs@aol.com

Silverhall Social Icon

Icon

Jaxson & Amy Manser

Abby

Ch Nortonchase Look N Fabulous

*Number One
Miniature Schnauzer

9 CC - 4 RCC - 5 BOB
Group 3 & 4

BIS - Miniature Schnauzer Club of GB.

Owned by Ronni Tierney

Handled & Presented by Jaxson & Amy Manser

Kudos

Blomendal Catch Me If You Can

2 CC - 2 BOB 2 RCC

Co-owned with Mr & Mrs Ensell

Isa

Ch & Int Ch X-tra Beauty Saltus Ze Zahrabske at Nujax

*Number One
Schnauzer Bitch

5 CC - 3 BOB - 3 RCC

Co-owned with Ms Chandrani Chapman

Thank you to all the judges for thinking so highly of our dogs and making 2015 a great year!

Nujax

*at time of going to press

Bregantia

Jimmy

Ch/Bel Ch Rarjo For Your Eyes Only

All time top winning PWD in the UK
15 CCs 10 RCCs 19 Best of Sex
3 RBOS 29 BOB 4 CACs 4 CACIBs
3 RCACs 2 RCACIBs
1 GR1 3 GR2 4 GR3 2 GR4
Breed Record Holder
Top PWD 2013 and 2014
Halfway Leader 2015

Coco

Winterkloud Coco Chanel at Bregantia

2 CCs 2 RCCs 1 BOB
4 Best of Sex 8 RBOS
3 CACs 3 CACIBs
Crufts 2015 BOB winner

Thank you Breeder Sarah McGill

and Rarjo

Bregantia

Blossom

Tamlin Spring Blossom at Rarjo

**1 BOS 2 RBOS 1 BPIB
(Championship Show)**

**1 BP PG1
(Open Show)**

*Thank you breeders Thelma and
Brooke Taylor*

Connor

Kingrock Morticon

**1 BPIB (Championship Show)
BP Kortrijk International Show
2015**

*Thank you breeders
Chris Thomas and Graham Godfrey*

and Rarjo
Byron Williams Handling

Byron has been given some great opportunities this year to handle some beautiful dogs. The wins below are what Byron has handled them to. Byron thanks all the owners for their trust in his handling of their dogs.

BISS Can Gr Ch Am Mex Nor Swe It UK CH Hi Seas Dr Romeo MacDuff

Owned by Glenda Newton (Canada)
**3 CCs 3 RCCs 7 BOB
2 GR1 2 Gr2 2 Gr4 Top PWD 2015**

Zimorodek Next Germanika (imp) and Winterkloud Liquorice Wand at Tamlin

Owned by Thelma Taylor
Placed in classes

Winterkloud Kola Cube

Owned by Sarah McGill
Placed in classes

Jaybeim Voo Doo at Potterspride

Owned by Violet Slade
1 CC and 1 RBOS

Neron Kontaktas of Potterspride

Owned by Violet Slade
2 RBOS and many class wins

Kincroft Cromar Tyross

Owned by Sheena and Huw Stalker
BOB Leeds Championship Show

Afterglow Kinky Boots

Owned by Sandra Stone and Jason Lynn
Best AVNSC and GR2

Thank you to all the judges for a fantastic year

Rachael Reddin, Byron Williams and the Late Ruth Bussell
rachael-reddin@supanet.com

BIRKCROS
BORDER COLLIES

BREEDER OWNERS:
ANDREW BIRKETT
DAVID MCDOWELL
ROBERT HARLOW

TIME HOLDS THE PROMISE
OF MANY GREAT TIMES

RHARLOW@BTCONNECT.COM
+44 1900 65722
MOBILE 07899665051

MBIS MBISS CH
Allmark Fifth Avenue

TIFFANY

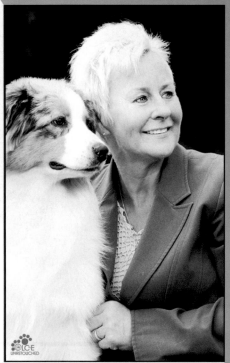

The Top-Winning
Australian Shepherd
Of All Time In The UK
Breed and All-Breed

Breed Record Holder

Multiple Best In Show Winner

Crufts Group winner

World Dog Show Group Winner

Breeder Owners
Robert Harlow & Neil Allan
Presented By Angie Allan

ALLN

www.allmarkshowdogs.com

Top Breeders of All Breeds 2014
ARK
OLC-E UNRETOUCHED
©advertising & photography Croft-Elliott

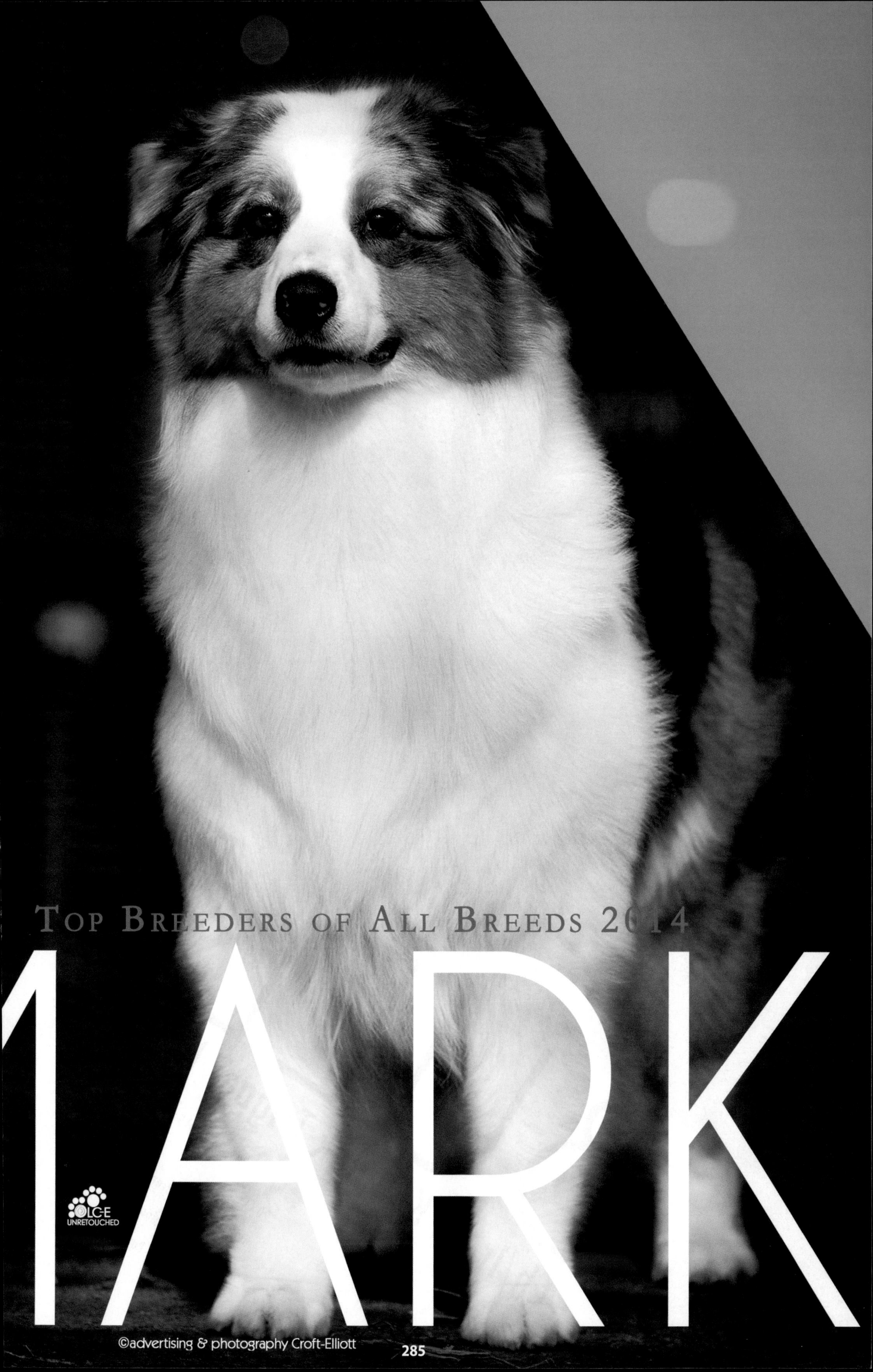

BULLET

Ch/Ir Ch Kebulak Trigger Happy

Top dog 2014 and 2015

20 CCs.

multiple group placements

Eukanuba Champion stakes finalist

Campaigned by Paul wilkinson

©advertising & photography Croft-Elliott

Top brood 2015 - Kerries and Welsh
Top stud 2015 - Kerries and Lakelands
Top Welsh bitch 2015
Top breeder Kerries 2011, 12, 13, 14, 15
Top breeder Welsh 2014, 15
Top breeder Lakelands 2013

www.kebulak.com

KENZO

LORENZO

Ch Kebulak Lady Killer

Top brood 2015 - Kerries and Welsh
Top stud 2015 - Kerries and Lakelands
Top Welsh bitch 2015
Top breeder Kerries 2011, 12, 13, 14, 15
Top breeder Welsh 2014, 15
Top breeder Lakelands 2013

Top male 2014
6 CCs
Mulitiple group placements
Owned by Dr Richard Young
Campaigned by Geoff Corish

"every picture tells a story…"

Presents...

Ir Ch Nikolaev Osha of Wispafete ShCM Ir J Ch

R O S I E

Austrian Dream Be Well Suited Of Wispafete JW ShCM Ir J Ch (Imp)

A C E

ACE

Owned, loved and handled by:

Haley Jones

and

Sarah Gibbons

Rosie has had an amazing year adding her Irish Champion title to her junior title. She also gained her Show Certificate of Merit, 2CC & 2RCCs. Results: YKC Stakes final Qualified '15 & '16, 2 CCs, 2 RCCs (inc 1 at BDF Club Championship Show), 2 BAVNSC W, 11 BB, 1 BOB and 5 BOS Irish Championship Results: 1 CACIB, 9 GS, 1 BOB, 4 RGS

Following on from Ace's successful puppy career in the last 12 months he has taken his Junior Warrant, Irish Junior Champion title and Show Certificate of Merit. He also took 3rd YKC Stakes Pastoral Final '15 he has a BIS and RBIS at open shows. Results: YKC Stakes qualified '15 and '16, Junior Warrant Semi-Finals qualified '15, RBD, 6 BPIBs Irish Championship Results: G3, 3 BOB, 4 GS and 5 RGS.

SVEN

CASPER

Sarah handled Australian Shepherd Ch Allmark Spirit of St Louis ShCM to take YKC Stakes Dog of the Year '15 which is held at Crufts.
Sarah and Casper have attended only one IKC Ch show together and took GS, BOB, G1 and BIS 4
Results: G2, 2 G4,13 CCs, 6 BOBs and 11RCCs 1GS,1G1 and BIS4
Owned by Mr P and Mrs J Longhurst, Mrs N Gregory and Miss S Gibbons

Gerwazy Bouvi-Buzi with Wispafete (Imp)

(Pictured left)
Sven is the new recruit who in his short show career so far has already secured himself
Top BDF Puppy '15 along with a RDCC and a RBPIS at an open show.
Results: RCC, BD, BOS, WPG4, 6 BPIB (2 with no CCs on offer) and RBPIS (open), 3 BBPIB (IKC)
Owned, loved and handled by
Haley Jones and Sarah Gibbons

Wispafete Kennels
Haley Jones and Sarah Gibbons
www.wispafetekennels.co.uk
wispafetekennels@hotmail.com
07930485587

To see our results with Bayard Beagles and Silkcroft Soft Coated Wheaten Terriers. Please visit pages 21 & 295.
Also see Paige Spencer's section on the Wispafete Juniors page to find our new recruit

Wispafete Handling Presents...

Fernwood Presents...
Zube

Rohantia Nikolai at Fernwood ShCM

In 2015 Zube made breed history by being the first Russian Black Terrier to win a group at a UK Championship Show. He is also believed to have more BOBs at Championship shows than any other RBT. He is Current Top Rare Breed(time of print) and RBT 2015, to add to being Top RBT 2013 & 2014 and Top Working Rare Breed, 3rd Top Rare Breed & 5th Top Working 2014.

Results: WG1, 2 WG3, WPG2, 33 BOB, 3 BAVNSC W, 36 BD, 15 RBD and 8 BPIB

Irish Championship Results: G3, 3GS, 9 RGS and 3RCACIBs

Owned by: Mr L and Mrs M Smith

Handled by: Sarah Gibbons

Groomed by: Beth at K9 Cuts

Coming soon is puppy Diego, Phoenix Kontaktus at Fernwood who will be joining the Fernwood/Wispafete show team in 2016.

Springhaze Ice Cool at Pendower

Ice has only had a short showing career of just 9 shows, so far he has been awarded... 6 Best Import Registers 7 Best Dogs 1 Reserve Best Dog

Owned by: Anne Barry

Handled by: Sarah Gibbons

Breed: Greater Swiss Mountain Dog

Pendower Presents...
Ice

Wispafete Kennels
Haley Jones and Sarah Gibbons
www.wispafetekennels.co.uk
wispafetekennels@hotmail.com
07930485587

Wispafete Juniors Presents...

PAIGE SPENCER

Paige has had a fantastic 2015...

At Cruft 2015, Paige won the YKC 6-11 Working and Pastoral class with Bernese Mountain Dog, Archie. At BUBA Ch Show Paige met Miniature Schnauzer, Finn on the day and went on to take 4th in the JHA Utility Semi-Finals. Then at UK Toy Dog Ch Show Paige met Lowchen, Ashley only 30 minutes prior to the JHA 6-11 Toy Semi-Finals class, they went on to win the class and earn their place at the JHA 2015 Finals. Paige has qualified numerous times for the JHA Semi-Finals and YKC Crufts Final 2016.

In the breed ring Paige has handled lots of different breeds with great success. She has achieved BOB and group placings at Open Shows with both her Bernese Archie and Skye, took BOB with a German Shepherd and a group placing with a Siberian Husky. Paige has handled a number of breeds some of these are Shetland Sheepdogs, Newfoundlands, Bouvies Des Flandres, Australian Shepherds & Soft-Coated Wheaten Terrier (SCWT). She loves to handle new breeds and considers this as being an important part of learning all aspects of showing and handling.

Also joining Paige's family of dogs is Australian Shepherd, Dream. Dream will mainly be shown by Paige and is co-owned by Haley and Sarah.

TAMSIN BLYTON

Tamsin is often in both the breed and handling ring and has enjoyed amazing success in 2015.

Tamsin's greatest achievements with Boxer Yogi are gaining a RGS at Tralee, winning the JHA semi-finals in both 2014 and 2015 as well as multiple BOB's, JHA and YKC class wins and winning the YKC Working Stakes at City of Birmingham, qualifying for the YKC Stakes Finals held at Crufts '16 .

Tamsin has also handled a number of other breeds, some of which she has only worked with for a small amount of time before entering a class with the dogs. Tamsin met Havanese Honey at UK Toy Ch Show where they went on to take 2nd in the JHA Toy 6-11 Semi-Finals. At the JHA Terrier Semi-Finals held at National Terrier, Tamsin handled SCWT Bryson to take 5th in the 6-11 class.

One of Tamsin's favourite companions is Bullmastiff Stanley, their biggest achievements together are winning the first YKC class they ever entered together, multiple JHA class wins, retaining her BJH title at the British Bullmastiff League as well as multiple BOBs and gaining G1.

Tamsin has enjoyed outstanding success in the handling ring winning 98 classes so far and winning Best Overall Junior Handler more than 25 times!

Wispafete Kennels
Haley Jones and Sarah Gibbons
www.wispafetekennels.co.uk
wispafetekennels@hotmail.com
07930485587

SILKCROFT
Soft-Coated Wheaten Terriers

Cheryl & Chris Satherley
01827 382186
enquiries@silkcroft.co.uk
www.silkcroft.co.uk

Team Silkcroft - Passion Personified
What A Year It Has Been!

© Silkcroft Photography

Millie
Current Top SCWT
(UK Breed Club)
and Top Bitch 2014
Handled by
Harriet Billingham

UK CH Silkcroft Colour of Magic ShCM

15CCs, 9RCCs, Group 3 Bournemouth

© Silkcroft Photography

TzinTzin – New UK Champion
UK/INT/SWE/IT CH Modny Style
Loverboy at Seamrog (Imp)
4 CCs, 5 CACIBs, 6 GS, 2 RCCs
Handled by Sarah Gibbons

© Silkcroft Photography

Perri – Junior Warrant at 13 months
Silkcroft One Step Closer JW
1 BIS UK Breed Club Show,
1 RBPIS, 1RCC, 1 RGS
Handled by Cheryl Satherley

© Silkcroft Photography

Lola – First UK Bred Irish JCH
Silkcroft Sky Full of Stars ShCM Ir Jr Ch
1GS, 2 RGS, 1 RCC, 2 RBIS, 1 BPIS, 3 RBPIS
Handled by
Harriet Billingham / Cheryl Satherley

© Silkcroft Photography

Beckett – First show out BPIS
Silkcroft Crests of Waves
(owned by Ms N Meister and Dr J D Brooks)
1 BIS UK Breed Club Show, 1 BPIS, 1 RCC
Handled by Cheryl Satherley

© Silkcroft Photography

Lottie – Continuing her winning ways
Silkcroft World Explorer
Top Puppy 2014
1 RCC, 1 BPIS UK Breed Club Show
Handled by Haley Jones

VAUCLUSE

Hungarian Pulis since 1976

Winnie

Ch Zaydah You Win Again for Vaucluse

Winnie is the first and only female Puli to wi
BIS at a general championship show in the
UK. Huge thanks to Mrs Val Foss (breed), M
Gordon Rual (group) and Mrs Jill Peak (BIS
at the City of Birmingham 2015.

She has 10 CCs, 7 BOBs, 11 RCCs, 3 CACIF
3 CACs, G2 at Maastricht 2014, G2 Windso
2014 and G4 Leeds 2014. She was Top Puli
Bitch UK in 2014 and current leader 2015.

Leo

Ch/Int/Lux Ch Zaydah Don't Stop Me Now at Vaucluse WW10

Leo is the only Puli to win BIS three
times at the Hungarian Puli Club of GB Ch
Show. He is an FCI International Champion,
winning in Denmark, Luxembourg, Holland
and Belgium. He is 10 years old and gained
his best UK win at Leeds 2015, winning the
Pastoral Group under Mr Stuart Mallard. He
has 15 CCs, 9 BOBs, 20 RCCs, 4 CACIBs and
CACs, G1 and G3 and was Top Male Puli UK
in 2013.

Our grateful thanks to all the judges who have thought so highly of our Pulis, to our friends at home
and abroad for all their support and to Jacki and Pete Evans for providing us with two special Pulis.

John and Mary Whitton
'Vaucluse', 10 Abbeyfields Drive, Studley, Warwickshire B80 7BF
Tel: 01527 850570   Email: john@vaucluse.co.uk

JOJAVIK

DOBERMANNS
JACKIE AND VICTORIA INGRAM

#1 **DOBERMANN** 2015 AT TIME OF PRINT
BITCH 2014

THE JOINT YOUNGEST
D O B E R M A N N
C H A M P I O N   E V E R

18 CC's, 13 BOB's
6 BIS's, 5 GS's, 11 RCC's
GROUP 3 - Darlington 2015
GROUP 3 - Limerick 2014

Viva CHAMPION
JOJAVIK POISON IVY JW SHCM

Designed by *Winkdreama Design*

CH Chancepixies Locomotive X CH Tronjheim Belladonna From Jojavik JW ShCM

#1 DOBERMANN PUPPY 2015

Hanna
JOJAVIK PENELOPE PITSTOP JW
CH Chancepixies Locomotive X CH Tronjheim Belladonna From Jojavik JW ShCM

#1 DOBERMANN BREEDERS 2014 & 2015

In 2015
10 BPIB All Breed CH
2 BPIS Specialty CH
PG 1 & RBPIS - Windsor
PG 1 - Three Counties & PG 2 - Bath
PG 3 - Southern Counties, Paignton & Belfast
BIS & BPIS Clacton Open Show
THE YOUNGEST JUNIOR WARRANT WINNER

Billy
UK/IRISH CHAMPION
JOJAVIK MIDNIGHT EXPRESS JW SHCM
CH Chancepixies Locomotive X CH Tronjheim Belladonna From Jojavik JW ShCM

RUNNER UP DOBERMANN 2014

THE YOUNGEST UNDOCKED
UK/IRISH CHAMPION

9 CC's, 7 BOB's, 7 BIS's,
7 GS's, 11 RCC's, 1 CACIB
GROUP 1 - LKA 14
GROUP 2 - Windsor 14
GROUP 1 & RBIS - Tipperary 14
GROUP 4 - Combined International 15

Don't be Jel...
...be JOJAVIK

Gino **NEW CHAMPION**
JOJAVIK ELITE MAFIA

CH Italo Elite House (IMP POL) X CH Jojavik Bella Mafia JW

5 CC's, 2 BOB's, 2 BIS's, 3 RCC's, 1 RGS
GROUP 3 - NW&PB 15

Zak
JOJAVIK SWEDISH HOUSE MAFIA

CH Italo Elite House (IMP POL) X CH Jojavik Bella Mafia JW

1 CC, 1 BIS & 2 RCC's

Theo
JOJAVIK BULLETPROOF BOMB

H Chancepixies Locomotive X CH Tronjheim Belladonna From Jojavik JW ShCM

In 2015
1 BPIB, 2 BPIS's & 13 BPD

Harlie **CHAMPION TRONJHEIM**
BELLADONNA FROM JOJAVIK JW SHCM

CH Jojavik Mafioso JW X Jojavik Save The Last Dance

#1
DOBERMANN BROOD BITCH
2014 & 2015
WWW.JOJAVIK.COM

Designed by *WindstreamDesign*

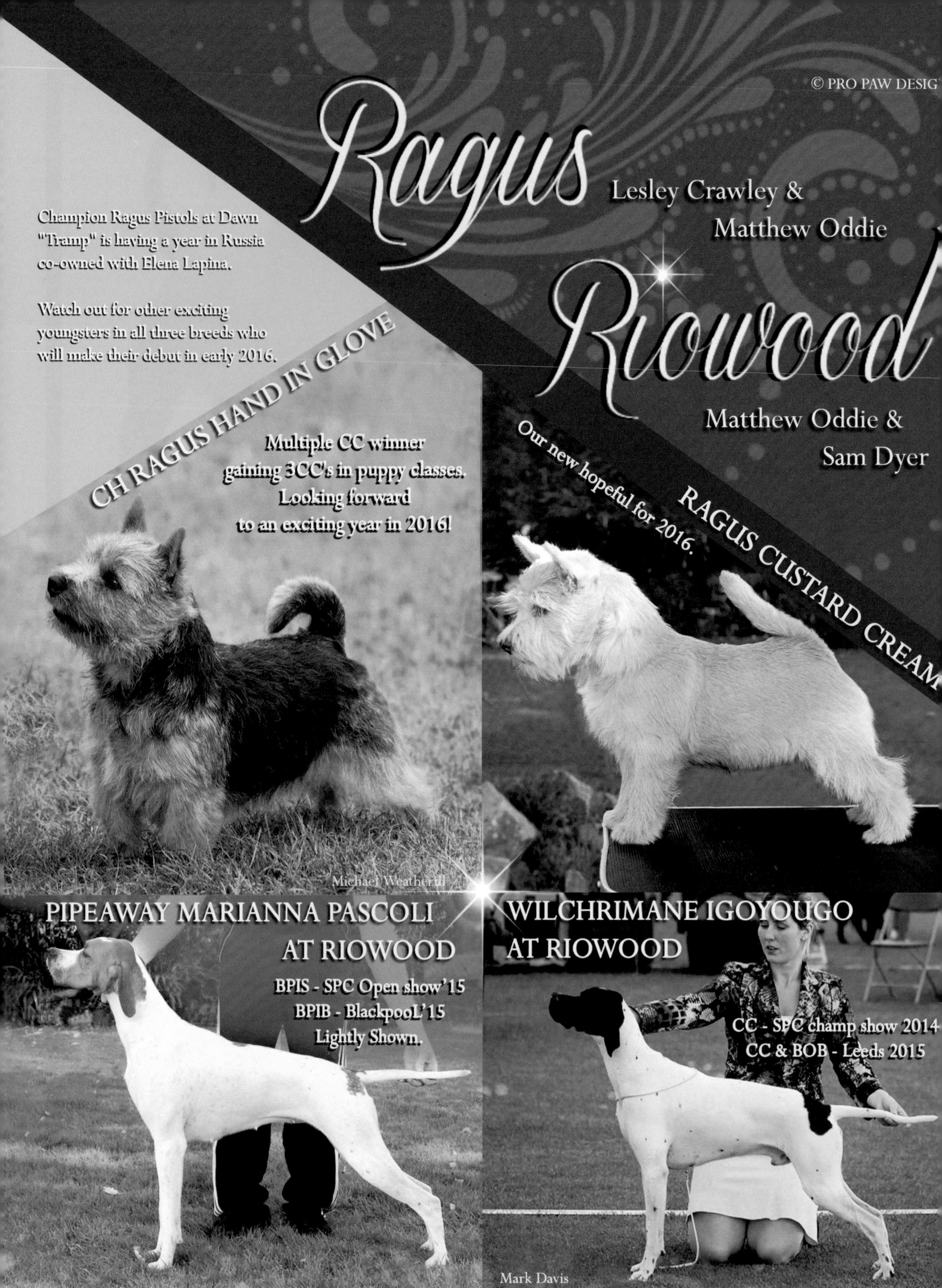

Ragus

Lesley Crawley &
Matthew Oddie

Riowood

Matthew Oddie &
Sam Dyer

Champion Ragus Pistols at Dawn
"Tramp" is having a year in Russia
co-owned with Elena Lapina.

Watch out for other exciting
youngsters in all three breeds who
will make their debut in early 2016.

CH RAGUS HAND IN GLOVE

Multiple CC winner
gaining 3CC's in puppy classes.
Looking forward
to an exciting year in 2016!

Our new hopeful for 2016.

RAGUS CUSTARD CREAM

Michael Weatherill

PIPEAWAY MARIANNA PASCOLI AT RIOWOOD

BPIS - SPC Open show'15
BPIB - BlackpooL'15
Lightly Shown.

WILCHRIMANE IGOYOUGO AT RIOWOOD

CC - SPC champ show 2014
CC & BOB - Leeds 2015

Mark Davis

Ch Pencader Thunderball (NBT)

We are pleased to feature our latest bobtail champion, the fourth made up here and the third homebred!

Our thanks to the judges, Mr Graham Hill, Mrs Annette Green and Mrs Karen Gilliland for his CC and BOB on each occasion plus Mr Peter Jolley and Mr Tegwyn Jones for his two Group 4's – the only Pembroke this year to be placed in a General Championship Pastoral Group.

Magnus joins his full sister later litter in the upper house – Ch P Bobbi Sox has taken time out to produce a litter by our and Allan Taylor's import from the USA, Nebriowa Skidaddle with 5 out of 6 being bobtails ! We feature one of the babies below.

302

Pemcader Spectre

Featured here is our new hopeful for 2016, "Yogi" is also a natural bobtail out of our 3rd bobtail champion Pemcader Bobbi Sox and sired by Nebriowa Skidaddle (imp USA) – our grateful thanks go to Tim Mathiesen and Tomm Dedini for allowing Eddie to come to the UK. We also hope to campaign a tailed bitch from the same litter, P Posh Totti.
We currently have 3 males at stud, Ch P Thunderball, Swed/Dan Ch Pemcader Jensen Button and Nebriowa Skidaddle.

Kevin Dover and Lars Saether
01989 750362   kevindover57@hotmail.co.uk

photos Lars Saether

303

CASSOM Cocker Spaniels

'Vinnie'

photo Eva Cernohubova

SH CH VERATEY VINCENZO AT CASSOM JW

Sire: Sh Ch Lindridge Star Quest   Dam: Veratey Verona at Cassom

19 CCs, 15 BOBs and 5 RCCs

Gundog Group Winner Leeds 2015 – Judge Mr M Gadsby (Afterglow)
Gundog Group 3 SKC (August) 2015 – Judge Miss S Pinkerton
(Bareve)
Gundog Group 3 Midland Counties 2015 – Mr A Brace (Tragband)
Best In Show Cocker Spaniel Club Championship Show 2015 – Mr M
Parkinson (Dillonpark)
Dog World/Arden Grange Top Cocker 2015 and The Cocker Spaniel
Club's 'Cocker of the Year' 2015
Dog World/Arden Grange 3rd Top Gundog 2015
(at time of going to press)
Our Dogs Cocker Puppy of the Year 2014 & Cocker Spaniel Club
Puppy Of The Year 2014

A massive thank you to the judges and also to our friends for making 2015 such an amazing year.

Vinnie is available at stud along with his grandsire Cassom Rock Star (RCC) and Sh Ch Cassom Hey Jude JW

All three boys are hereditarily clear for PRA and FN, hip scored and have clear results for KC/BVA eye tests.

photo Bernd Smith-Vornsakul

photo Katie Nuttall

Also winning well for their owners are these three youngsters. all have been consistent winners with numerous top awards between them:

CASSOM SKY ROCKET AT CANDYKE JW

1 RCC

(Owned by

Mark and Joyce Collins)

Sire:

Sp Ch Bencleuch Bollinger

Dam: Cassom Skyfall

photo Shel Cowles

CASSOM FAST AND FURIOUS AT OLIBOND

1 RCC

Sire:

Sh Ch Charbonnel Life 'N' Times

Dam: Cassom Bridget Jones

(Owned by Mick and Jane Bond)

CASSOM HOPES AND DREAMS AT MANLINSON

(Owned by Mandy Edwards and Mike Wildman)

Sire:

Sh Ch Charbonnel Life 'N' Times

Dam: Cassom Bridget Jones

SARAH AMOS-JONES

TEL: 07950 117361 sarah.cassom@gmail.com

Jessica

Charnell Jessica at Glebeheath JW
(Ch Pascavale Jamie (re-imp) ex Charnell Imagine)

1 CC, 1 RCC and BP Crufts '15

Proudly owned and loved by Julie Guvercin
01793 763987

Glebeheath

Ch Glebeheath Tea n Tiffers

Tiffers gained her title at 19 months having attended just a few shows and becomes my **11th UK Champion**.
Her progeny will debut late spring '16.
Congratulations to Nicki Smith, Fencho Border Terriers, Australia on gaining titles for
Aus Ch Glebeheath Name That Tune – 2 RCCs and BP Crufts '14
and Aus Ch Jump Ship to Glebeheath.

A new addition to the team in

Charnell Jessica at Glebeheath

Bred by Sandra Ireland (Charnell) Jessica has had a fabulous start to her show career winning
1 CC, 1 RCC and Best Puppy Crufts 2015 along with many championship show firsts.
She becomes my **17th CC winner**, *but 1st Cavalier.*

HERONSVIEW

Tibetan Mastiffs
The All Time Top Winning Kennel in the UK

Tibetan Mastiffs were awarded Championship Status for 2015 with 7 sets (14 CCs), of these 9 were awarded to Heronsview owned or bred dogs.

As well as the 5 CCs awarded to Champion Sierras LL Cool Jay at Heronsview (imp USA), the following dogs were in the cards:

**Heronsview Buni
Bea For Madire**
(owned by Pat and Mark Leak)
CC – Crufts – Terry Munro
CC – Darlington – Pam Jeans-Brown

**Heronsview
Kiesha Queen**
CC – NW and PB – Lyn Hall

**Kehl-Sang Amrita At
Heronsview (imp Rom)**
CC – TM Club Show – Sandra
Marshall

**Int/Lux Ch Chodak-Druk
du Domaine de Toundra
of Heronsview (imp Fr)**
RCC – Welsh Kennel – Ron James
RCC – TM Club Show – Sandra
Marshall

**O'Billie Jean Mahatma-La
of Heronsview (Imp Pol)**
RCC – TM Club Show – Sandra
Marshall

**Heronsview Don't Mess
With Me at Sobarna**
(jointly owned with Andy Briggs)
RCC – NW & PB – Lyn Hall

Richard Gardiner
Glasfryn Kennels, Water Street, Margam, West Glamorgan SA13 2PN
Tel: 01656 740588 / 745313   Mobile: 07770 500058

HERONSVIEW

Tibetan Mastiffs.

Champion Sierra's LL Cool Jay at Heronsview (imp USA)

The first ever UK Tibetan Mastiff Champion

My grateful thanks to the following judges for L's CCs in 2015:
Keith Baldwin – Birmingham National
Peter Radley – Scottish Kennel Club
Dr Ron James – Welsh Kennel Club
Pamela Jeans-Brown – Darlington
Sandra Marshall – TM Club Championship Show.

Also thanks to the following judges who awarded "L" Best of Breed at non-CC Championship Shows:
Working and Pastoral Breeds of Wales – Jackie Stubbs
Bath – Marion Sargent and Jeff Horsewll for the group shortlisting
Three Counties – Andrew Brace
Blackpool – Zena Thorn-Andrews
Birmingham City – Adrian Bicknell

"L" was awarded Best In Show at both the Tibetan Mastiffs Club Open Show in April, by Tim Ball, at 14 months - his very first show, and at the Clubs first Championship show in September by Sandra Marshall.

"L" was bred in the USA by Kristina Shirling (dob: 12th February 2014) Am Ch Sierra's Kat Rgyal – Am Ch Chenpowrewa Hum Helena) arriving in the UK on Christmas Eve 2014.
I will be forever indebted to her for trusting me with this very special boy.

Richard Gardiner
Glasfryn Kennels, Water Street, Margam, West Glamorgan SA13 2PN
Tel: 01656 740588 / 745313   Mobile: 07770 500058

BART

BIS BISS
RBISS BJISS
CH CHAYO
MY PREROGATIVE

NUMBER ONE MALAMUTE 2014 & 2015

NUMBER TWO WORKING 2015

A TOP TEN DOG ALL-BREEDS 2015

4TH TOP UK DOG ALL-BREEDS 2014

BREED CC RECORD HOLDER

WORKING GROUP ONE
CRUFTS 2015

311

CLOVERWOOD DANDIE DINMONT TERRIERS

German Dandies' Terence Hill at Cloverwood

(Cloverwood Driving Force ex Int Ch German Dandies' Rebecca)

Crufts BOB at 14 months, Southern Counties Group 4

Thank you to Manfred and Monika for sending us this beautiful Dandie

Mrs Joan Glen Tinsley

joantinsley@aol.com

Arnscroft Norwegian Buhunds

TOP PUPPY 2013
TOP BUHUND 2014 and 2015*

Over 150 Challenge Certificates
won since 2001

CH/IR CH ARNSCROFT DI TO BE A SAILOR IRJCH (Sirius)

Really eye catching with strong ring presence Showed non stop:
Liz Cartledge

I was told once the only way to get a perfect dog is to draw it yourself. If I could draw, it would be this boy: Gail Hussey

The star of the day. Outstanding mover. A dog who could win in his home country: Espen Engh

This confident Showman went beautifully covering the ground, so typey, fit and masculine: Jane Lilley

Not only is he great to look at he moves with elegance and drive: J Deacon-Cobb

BIS Working and Pastoral Ch Show 2015 Mr Jeff Luscott BPIS Bath Ch Show 2013 Mr Vic Salt.
12 CCs, 12 BOBs, 17 Green stars, 17 BOBs, hips 5;4 BVA clear eye cert.

Harmonious in outline an excellent breed representative. Showing his socks off: Stuart Mallard

Alf and Shirley with Sirius.

Masculine male of lovely breed type, super head and expression, excellent mover:
Elina Haapaniemi

(The Dog Star) making history for the breed...

BPIS Bath Ch Show
Top Buhund Puppy 2013
Top Buhund 2014
Top Buhund 2015 (current)
Group 1 W&P Ch Show 2015
Group 4 Windsor Ch Show 2014
Group 3 W&P Ch Show 2014
Group 4 Driffield Ch Show 2014
BIS NBC Ch Show 2014
Group 1 W&P Ch Show 2015
Group 4 Leeds Ch Show 2015
BIS W&P Ch Show 2015
Group 4 Darlington Ch Show 2015
Dublin International Group 4
BIS NBC Ch Show 2015

Perfectly well balanced picture standing. He really scores in type and movement:
Renée Sporre-Willes

Top quality lad with the exuberance and overall balance. Going round the ring with attitude and purpose. to me the performance of the day:
Jeff Luscott

One gets the feeling early on in the class if something special is put in front of you:
Mike Vines

We are so proud and cannot believe the year we have had. We thought nothing could top last year but once again he has just changed the breeds history. We are now both in our eighties, founder members of the Norwegian Buhund Club of the UK and did not expect to have a dog like this in our Autumn years. Thank you Di for allowing us to be part of his story. We are so proud to be owners and to watch him go to the top time after time at Championship Shows. The wonderful support for him around the big ring is so heart warming and the good opinion of so many top judges just makes our hearts swell with pride.
Alf and Shirley Dobson.
Sirius is bred, trained, handled and lives at home with Di and all his Arnscroft family

Di Stirling www.arnscroft.co.uk. KC Assured Breeder Arnscroft@aol.com 0044 1724 732398

Arnscroft Norwegian Buhunds

Top Breeder 02-03-04-05-06-07-08-09-10-11-12-13-14-15
Top Kennel 02-03-04-05-06-07-08-09-10-11-12-13-14-15
Top Buhund Dog/Bitch 03-04-05-06-07-08-09-10-11-13-14-15
Top Brood Bitch 02-03-04-05-06-07-08-09-13-14-15

See the kids at
WWW.ARNSCROFT.CO.UK

Every year we Show you all our kids in working mode as champions in this country and abroad but this year I wanted to Show you them at home and on hols just chilling. I am very proud of all my dogs from the Breed Record Holder Mia, history making Sirius, Top Pastoral Brood Bitch Dinah, to our multiple group winners here and abroad and all our champions and non-champions. The only Buhund kennel who have qualified for the finals of Pup of the year, Junior Stakes and Champion stakes finals. My kids have shone for me and for their owners in the UK, Norway and the USA. So here they are MUCKY WET AND HAVING A BALL...

Please note, win or lose, Arnscrofts are loved and cherished from cradle to grave – if this is not the way you see owning, showing or working please do not contact us.

To all Arnscroft owners and helpers, thank you for your friendship and for loving my babes. I could not do it without you and our success is down to you and my kids and the judges who have been kind enough to reward the quality of the kennel.

DI STIRLING   Arnscroft@aol.com   01724 732398   www.arnscroft.co.uk

AMICA

PROUD BREEDERS OF GENERATIONS OF CHAMPION SIBERIAN HUSKIES & DOBERMANNS

Caroline Friend-Rees

And Ellis Rees

Carolinehrees@aol.com

01656 - 865919

Dedicated to breeding healthy
happy Siberian Huskies
that are fit for function
and fit for family

RANGALI

Rangali Quinnie Buzz

Junior Irish Champion. 4 green stars at just 18 months old.
Owned and loved by Vy Mochan.
Midland Counties Champ Show 2014, 1st Minor Puppy Bitch
Catrine Canine Club Open show, Best Hound Puppy
West Lothian Canine Club, Best Hound Minor Puppy and Best Minor Puppy in Show
Greenock and District Best Hound Puppy.

Ir Ch Rangali Jam Roly Poly over Wildan

(Uber Shiroblam (Imp Fra) ex Ir Ch Brequest Brettany Avec Rangali)

Belvoir is loved by and lives with Carol Johnson
Contact: caroljohnson99@live.co.uk

Rangali Rockstar at Laserna

Proudly owned by Mr A Jones and Mrs L Jones
Hugo, our little rockstar at only 11 months old.

4 Best Puppy in Breed, Res Best Dog at Three Counties
Puppy Group 3 at Bath and Res Best Puppy in Show Hound Club of East
Anglia.

We would like to thank all the judges who have thought so highly of him

Rangali Little Ted

Owned and loved by Adrian and Louise Walder.
RBIS Guernsey Kennel Club Autumn Show 2015
BOB, GP1, 2 RDCC, 2 BD and numerous BP awards

RANGALI

Top Fauve, Top Puppy and Top Stud 2015
Gaining a group 2 and group 4, puppy group 2 and two puppy group 3,
12 CCs and BOBs and 5 RCCs in 2015,
Ch Rangali Oh La La gaining her title at Crufts 2015 and was BOB, our fifth champion

Ch Hirondelle Rangali (imp France)
Top Fauve 13/14
Breed record holder 20 CCs

Ch/Ir Ch Brequest Bailee Basler
Top Fauve 2015 at 9 years old
Dog CC record holder
with 13 CCs

1 Group 2 and 2 Group 4

Heidi Allenby with **Ch/Ir Ch Brequest Bailee Basler and Ch Hirondelle Rangali (imp France)**

Ch Rangali Magic Moment
4 CCs
BIS at Club Championship Show 2014
Now proudly owned and being shown by Maisie Allenby

Rangali Roses
Top Puppy 2015
1 RCC, 2 Puppy Group 2 and 1 Puppy Group 3
Daughter of Hirondelle and Basler (above)

Tibetan Spaniel
SuSu

Handled &
owned with passion
Claire Cooper
07855255287

Dedicated To Don't Waste Time
2 xrcc, JW, Jw'14, Njk'15

Dedicated To Sensational White
xrcc, BjwLu'14, LuxJCH'14

Amcross Going Dutch
BPIS Nothern Tibetan Spaniel Club
Co owned: Lynne Ellingford

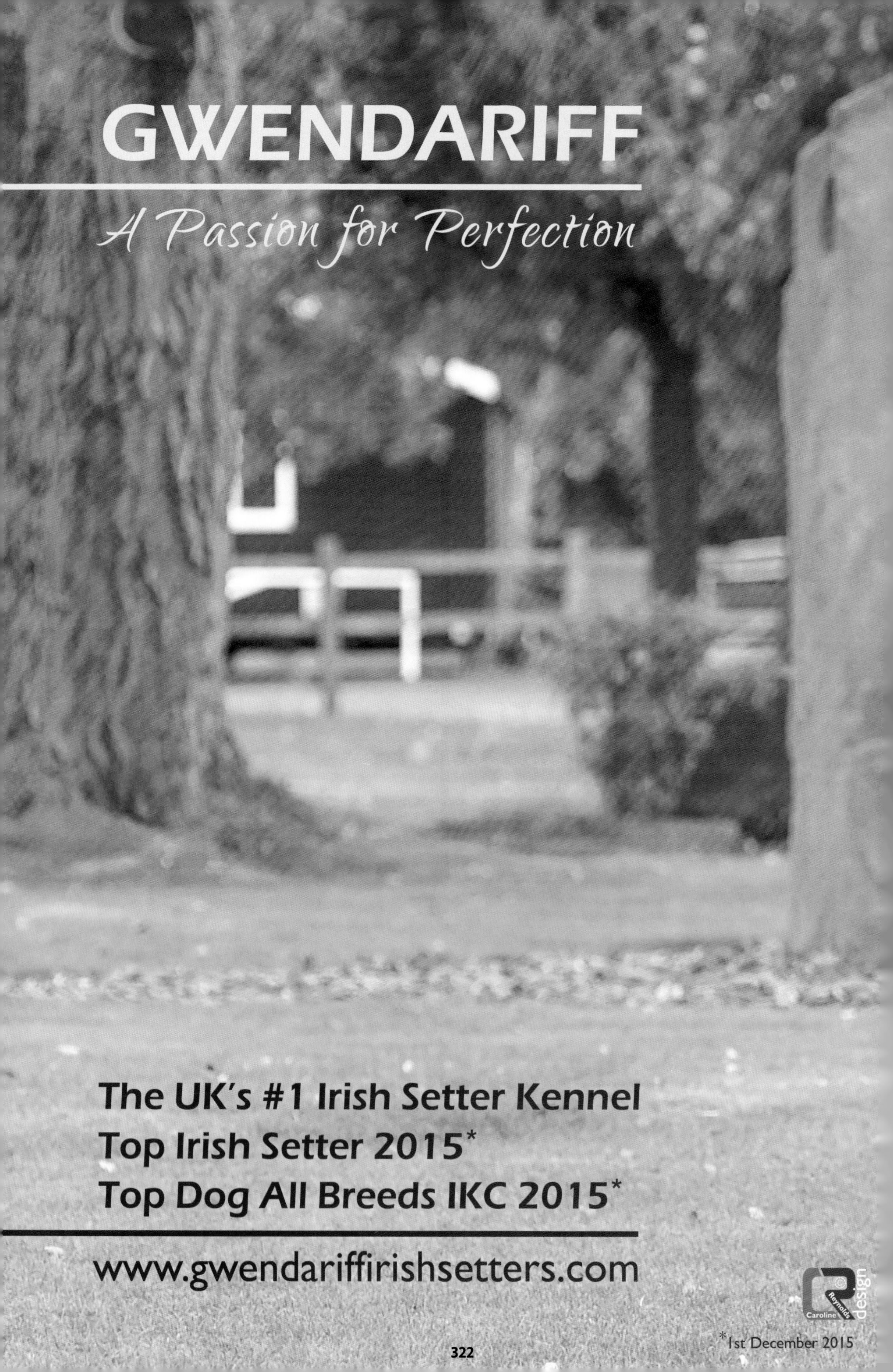

GWENDARIFF
A Passion for Perfection
The UK's #1 Irish Setter Kennel
Top Irish Setter 2015*
Top Dog All Breeds IKC 2015*
www.gwendariffirishsetters.com
Caroline Reynolds design
*1st December 2015

©Will Harris

324

HANNAH WAYMAN

BERNARD
CH SUPETA'S RAZZALICIOUS JW SHCM
3 CC'S, 7 RCC'S & 1 BOB
EUKANUBA CH STAKES FINALIST '13

TEDDY
SUPETA'S BREAKING DAWN
2 CC'S & 3 RCC'S

DR SPEED

PEPPA
CH SUPETA'S BOOTILICIOUS BABE SHCM
7 CC'S, 3 RCC'S & 4 BOB'S - 1 x GP 2 - TOP BROOD '15 *

RENE
SHINY SENSATIONS SPIRIT OF LOVE
FOR SUPETA (IMP NL)
1 CAC, 3 VDH CAC's, 1 CACIB, EUROPASIEGER '15
MULTIPLE UK CH SHOW CLASS WINNER

KORIFEY DOBERMANNS

PHARELLE
SUPETA'S FEELING FROSTY FOR PHAREAL
EUKANUBA PUPPY STAKES DAY HEAT
WINNER PAIGNTON CH SHOW '15

HARVEY
SUPETA'S JACK FROST AT TRONJHEIM
MULTIPLE BPIB WINNER AT OPEN SHOWS
QUALIFIED FOR HAMPSHIRE TOP DOG

FYNN
SUPETA'S POLAR EXPRESS
BPIB DRIFFIELD CH SHOW '15

Green Star Winner

GEMMA
SUPETA'S ICED GEM AT AILESBURY
BIS WINNER AT THE ACOI OPEN SHOW '15
GREEN STAR BITCH KILLARNY & DCC CH SHOW '15
IRISH PUP OF THE YEAR FINALIST

THE WHIPP CLUB
www.the

GINNY
SUPETA'S BLACK MAGIQUE OF VEREDON
RBPIS NIWC CH SHOW '14
MULTIPLE CLASS WINNER AT CH SHOWS

EFFY
CH SUPETA'S DAZZALICIOUS JW SHCM
4CC'S, 2 RCC'S & 2 BOB'S - 1 x GROUP 4

SAMANTHA WEBSTER

EVA
SUPETA'S ICE ICE BABY OF FREEHAMELT
MULTIPLE BPIB & HPG WINNER AT OPEN SHOWS

264

GRACE
SUPETA'S HOCUS POCUS
MULTIPLE CLASS WINNER
LITTER PLANNED FOR 2016

New kids on the block...

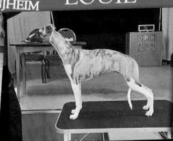

PETER   SUPETA'S SO SNAZZY AT TRONJHEIM   LOUIE   SUPETA'S SO STRIKING

SUPETA'S SO SUAVE   SQUIFFY   SUPETA'S SO SQUIFFY   BEN

CHARSON BRIARDS

SEISO ▶

AM GCH UK CH STORMFIELD SEISO AT CHARSON

UK Top Briard 2009&2010

BOB Westminster 2012

Multiple Best in Specialty Winner

Multiple Group Placings

Multiple Group Winner

DCC Crufts 2013

The 1st Briard to become a British and American Champion

We would like to thank all judges who have thought so highly of our dogs and look forward to 2016 !

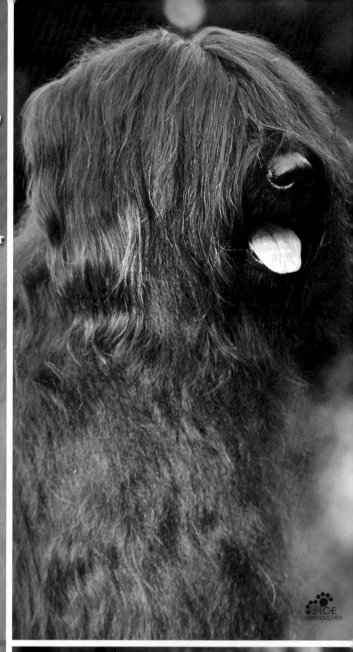

NEYO ▶

UK CH SENDERO HERE WE GO AT CHARSON (IMP USA)

The 1st American Bred Briard to become an English Champion

Multiple Group Placements at CH Shows

Best Dog Briard Association Open show 2015

Bred by Merry Jeanne & Tommy Millner

Owned by Sonya Hillier & Merry Jeanne Millner

Owned and Bred by
Sonya Hillier & Adam Gardner
07793 980541 – 07545238980
charsonbriards@gmail.com

YOLO ▶
CHARSON HOT GOSSIP 1CC (YOLO)

Bitch CC Southern Counties 2014

Best Bitch Three Counties 2015

Owned by Sonya Hillier & Adam Gardner

DEXTER
CHARSON YOLO AMERICAN DREAM 2RCC

RDCC Paignton 2014

RDCC Bournemouth 2015

Owned by Sonya Hillier & Loraine Peters

▼

MOJO
The newest member at Charson!!!
Dorany Dorainblue Pon P'zaz our Polish Lowland Sheepdog

327

100%
Poodle

CH Pitfour Piperwhyte
PITFOUR ALIX

Maud

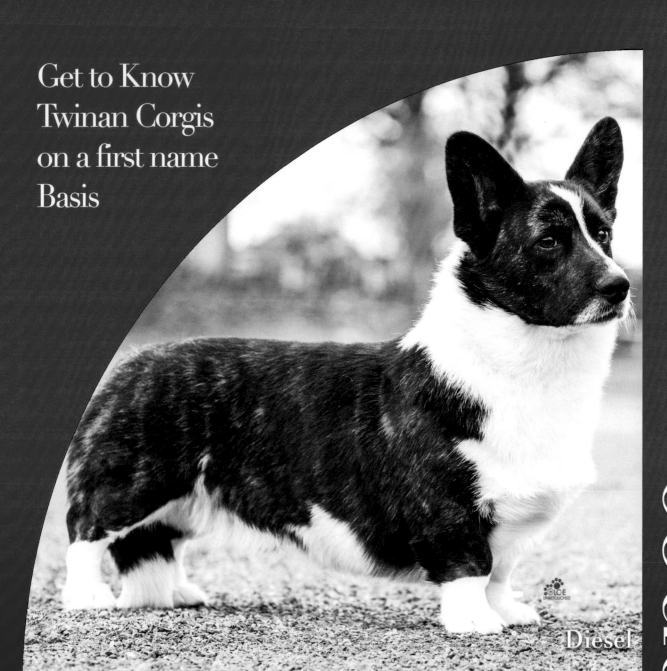
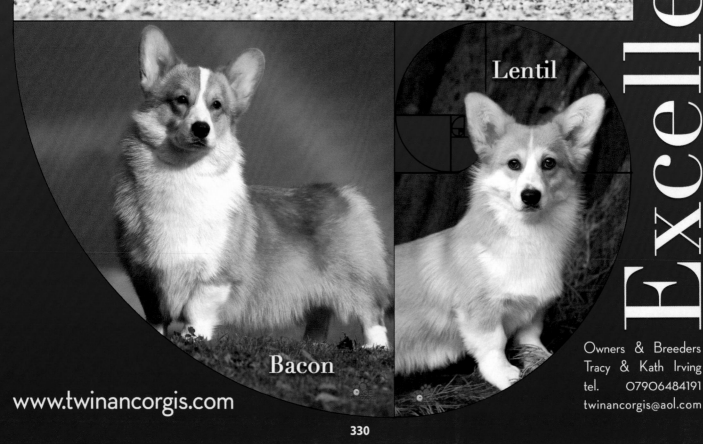
330

Get to Know Twinan

Winners of:

Multiple Bests In Show

Multiple Best Puppy in Show

Multiple Bests In Specialty

Multiple Groups

Winners of
over 90 CCs

...is
never an
accident.

Butter

Twinan

Ketchup

Lettuce

EUKANUBA
BREEDERS CLUB

www.breeders.eukanuba.co.uk

©advertising & photography Croft-Elliott

Yennadon Dual Purpose Gordon Setters

Colin N Waddell

Ch Yennadon Time For Daisy

Yennadon Reiss

Yennadon Carrick Field Trial award Winner

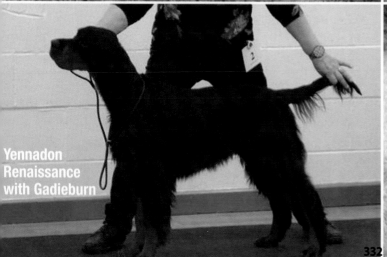

Yennadon
Renaissance
with Gadieburn

Yennadon
Lochan at
Rubymoon JW

332

Nicky Ackerley-Kemp 01822 870215 Yennadon@hrsupportconsultancy.co.uk

Yennadon Malin

Yennadon Reiver

Yennadon Lexie

Ch Yennadon the Druid

Yennadon Fortes at Rubymoon

333 Yennadon Fairisle at Clacorick

Eternalpride Bullmastiffs

CH ETERNALPRIDE CALISTRA

Our latest Champion Paws has 4 CCs , 4 RCCs and 1 BOB

Introducing

Eternalprides Dark Secret

1st MPD and BPD Bullmastiff World Cup

Eternalpride Beauty

CONCHUR
Dachshunds and Boston Terriers

'REBA'
Lady Godiva v.d. Mibaf's Hoeve at Conchur (Imp NLD)

Bred by Lammy Hamelink

We fulfilled a long-held ambition to re-introduce the dappled Standard Smooth Dachshund to the UK. Reba was imported from Holland on 1st January 2015 and made her debut later in the year. Reba was bred using a clever mix of European lines – giving us the colour, ground clearance and temperament – combined with the wonderful type of her British-bred dam from the renowned Carpaccio kennel. She's now maturing nicely and has won classes at Championship level and more recently gained her stud book number (a first for a dapple standard smooth for a number of years) with a RCC at the Great Joint Dachshund Association.

Joining the team in 2016…

'PEBBLES'
Conchur Keela

CONCHUR
Dachshunds and Boston Terriers
'ALFIE'
Ch Bronia Gregorio JW ShCM

PRA Clear   Bred by Fran Mitchell

©Dom Santoriello

4 CCs   5 RCCs   4 BOB
Hound Group 1 – SKC August 2013
RBPIS and Puppy Group 1 – Southern Counties 2013

During Alfie's break from the ring in 2015, he was busy filming after being chosen as the new star of the Vitality TV adverts, including multiple appearances with the national teams for the Rugby World Cup. He has since resumed his successful ways with Best of Breed at Richmond 2015.

Alfie is available at stud to approved bitches.

Mark Smith and Lee Connor, Barnstaple, Devon
www.conchur.co.uk   mark@conchur.co.uk

Llaremeth

Boston Terriers

Tim & Dawn Rathmell +44 (0) 1422375635
Email: Dawnrathmell@btinternet.com

Danadri & Llaremeth

Mlt Ch/Jnr Ch Yogi Bear
Dos Sete Moinhos

Owners: Hili & Rathmell   Email: danadrikennels@yahoo.com

Satchmo

BE, NL Ch Grafmax Louis Armstrong ShCM
(Int, Lux Ch Aritaur Histabraq ex Cosajoro Nina Simone at Grafmax)

1 CC, 4 RCC.
8CAC, 7 CACIB.
BOB and group
shortlist Crufts 2013
vWD clear,
PHPV clear,
Hips 5:4

Velvet

Taevas Black Velvet at Grafmax JW ShCM
(Fr Ch Gangster-Dandias de la Villa Valiano ex
Ruzuna Precious Princess at Taevas JW)

1 CC, 1 RCC. 1 CAC/IB, 1 RCAC/IB,
Benelux Junior Winner
vWD clear, PHPV clear, hips 4:4

Boris Grafmax Rudolf Nureyev   *Kiki* Grafmax Ninette de Valois

GRAFMAX DOBERMANNS

Elegance with strength

© Heidi May Photography

Satchmo & Velvet at home with Sue . Litter planned 2016

Nina 2004-2015

Sue Thorn
suejthorn@yahoo.co.uk
07545 330851
www.grafmax.org

Amanda Carter (Afilador) and Roberta Hozempa (Amahte) present our boy

Amahte Runnin On Jamaican Time (imp Can) JW ShCM

Bolt

Nick Carter

Bolt has continued his winning ways at both open shows and championship shows, winning RDCC at The National, and BD and BOS at Bath and Windsor.

Bolt has also won Reserve Best in Show at Exonian, qualifying for the Top Dog of Devon competition.

Bolt presents his latest litter out of my Amahte Bewitched IMP "Tabitha"

Tabitha has produced 3 Boys ("The Boltlets") and 5 Girls ("The Tabblets") on the October 22, 2015

To read more please visit www.afilador.co.uk or follow us on Facebook.

Afilador show team

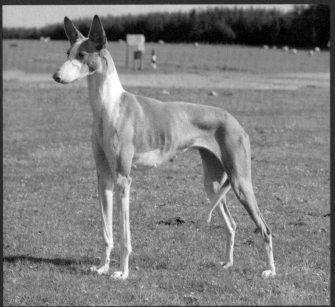

Diecisiete Mandarina at Afilador ShCM
Kalusha

Kalusha is now 10 years old, and is still doing well in breed competition at open and championship shows.

She won BVIS at SWHC open show, RBVIS at the first Duchy open show, and BVIS at HDoAE show for the 3rd time!

Afilador A Hint of Jasmine
Jazmine

Jaz is now 7 years old and, is doing well in veteran competition at both open and championship shows, winning BVIB at the Hound Association show.

She is handled by her co-owner Caitlin Channon.

Afilador Thunderbolt
Torran

Torran has been making progress in the ring this year handled by Nick. He is maturing slowly, and has won at both open and championship show level.

Puissance Adore
Molly

I have again this year had the great pleasure of handling my God-daughter "Miss Molly Mouse" for her owners/breeders Maria Martin and Christina Vanstone.
She has won well at open and championship level winning Post Grad Bitch at Paignton Ch show which qualified her for Crufts 2016!

Thank you to all the judges who have made all this possible, to my army of handlers for all their help and support, and to everyone who has given me the opportunity to handle their dogs. Long may this continue.

Silmoralbion Eurasiers (all 2015 only)

BECh, Lux CH, DUCh Asimov's Beaufort

2015
Midland Couties BOB
Dortmund Germany 1st Champion Class
Rotterdam 2 BOB, 2 CACIB, 2 CAC,
Zwolle 2 BOB, 2 CAC, 2 CACIB,
Milan BOB
Luxembourg CAC and RCACIB
Windsor 1st Open Dog RB Male
Crufts 2nd Open Dog
Manchester BOB
Boston BOB
Group 3
gained his Luxembourg Championship
and became the first UK-born and bred
Eurasier
to become Dutch Champion

Owned by Olwen Watkins

Silmoralbions Euphoria at Yarwen
results Championship and Open

14 BOB
2 BOS
3 BB
1 Group 3
1 Group 4
11 BPIB
2 Puppy G1
1 Group 4

Owner Wendy McKean

New Champion
Silmoralbions Arya JW15

Dutch Champion
Multi BOB
Muli CAC in Belguim and Holland
Multi CACIB Holland
Owned by Inga Cleas

**Congratulations to other Silmoralbion Championship
Winners and Crufts Qualifying:** Silmoralbions Calidora,
Silmoralbions Firework at Yarwen, Silmoralbions Whichapi,
Silmoralbion Born To Be Wild and Ch Silmoralbion Aqurius

Olwen and Stephen Watkins
silmoralbioneurasiers@gmail.com   www.silmoralbion.co.uk

346

Albionspitz Eurasiers

JCH Silmoralbions Kitti

Results at Championship and International Shows:
Junior Luxembourg Champion
1 CACIB
1 CAC
1 Best bitch
1 RB Bitch
2 1st in Intermediate
1st in Post Grad
3 Best Junior Wins

JDCh JLCh Albionspitz Mercury

Junior Luxembourg Champion
Junior Dutch Champion
Best Puppy in Breed Crufts 2015
4 Junior CACs
3 RCAC
Puppy Group 1
Puppy Group 3
1 Best male
6 R-Best male
7 Best Junior
8 Best Puppy in Breed
8 Best Puppy Dog
Unbeaten in Puppy Class in UK

Crufts Qualified UK Championship Winners

Albionspitz Bedazzed, Albionspitz Tyler, Albionspitz Darkness at Yarwen, Albionspitz Augustin at Qiqein, Albionspitz Kato, Albionspitz Tanzinite, Albionspitz Darkness at Yawren, FRCH WW08 7 WW11 Albionspitz Aerin, Multi Ch Albionspitz Aragon

Awards won by Albionspitz affix

Best of Breed Winner 2015	Norwegian Champion
Crufts Best Puppy in Breed Winner 2015	Czech Champion
UK Show Certicate of Merit	Junior Czech Champion
Top Norwiegian Top Junior Eurasier 2014	International Champion
	Irish Champion
TOP UK Eurasier Breeder 2010,2013,2014	Irish Junior Champion
Top UK Brood Bitch 207,2010,2014	Irish Annual Champion
Top UK Puppy 2009,2010,2013	Swedish Champion
Top Stud 2010	Norwegian Champion
World Champions 2008,2011	French Champion
Celtic Winners 2006,2010,2011	Greek Champion
Celtic Junior Winner	Belguim Junior Champion
European Winner 2010	USA Rare Breeds Champion
Junior European Winners 2010	Canadian Champion
Winster Winner	UKC / INT Champion
Nordic Junior Winner	Luxembourg Junior Champion
Nordic Veteran Winner	Luxembourg Champion
Norwegian Junior Winner	Eurasier Breed Specialty Holland BEST PUPPY IN SHOW
Norwegian Vetrain Winner	
Dutch Junior Champion (awaiting confirmation in post)	USA Breed Specialty BEST IN SHOW
	UK Open Show BEST IN SHOW

Albionspitz Beloved

Best Bitch and Best of Breed Crufts 2015
RBB Richmond
BB Welsh KC
RBB Windsor
BOB and Best Bitch Southern Counties
BOB and Best Bitch WELKS
RBB Boston
Owned by Susie Reynolds

Albionspitz Topaz

UKC & INTChampion
Multi Group Winner
Best puppy In Show winner
Best Rare Breed BIS Puppy
Owned by Colleen P LaFleche

Albionspitz Zephyr

Canadian Champion
Owned by John McRoberts

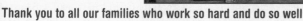

Thank you to all our families who work so hard and do so well

Stacey Watkins
www.albioneurasiers.co.uk
albioneurasiers@gmail.com

INTERRA
WINNER 2015
**MONAMOUR
WALK OF FAME
MUSASHI**

FCI JACK RUSSELL TERRIER
Monamour JACK RUSSELLS SHOW TEAM
Since 2001
Breeder KAO MIICHI
Specially conditioned by HIROSHI TSUYUKI (JAPAN) /
JOVANA DANILOVIC (Croatia) / GREG STRONG (USA)
clumberup@gmail.com   +81-80-1226-2612 (Japan)

LOCHEIL *Jack Russells*

We are delighted to have KC registration and look forward to showing our Jacks in 2016

We would like to thank the following breeders who have helped us with our foundation stock, giving us world class bloodlines. Marianne Raister Dunne (Krisbos), Christina Areskough (Ducklings Kennel, Sweden), Monica Fonzo (Alljacks Kennel, Italy), Simon Mills and Ann Knight, Australia, Geoff Corish (Sealaw) and Mrs Hetherington (Jarot).

Ducklings JR Just Non Stop (Nova)
C-JW 15 Jnr Champion,
5 Green Stars

Krisbos Flint (Finley)
Siring wonderful puppies

Jarot Here to Stay (Sushi)
Lots of Baby Puppy wins

Alljacks Unusual (Winnie)
Many Best Puppy wins

Jarot Aim For The Top (Monty)
Owned by Christina Areskough
Best Baby in Show, Limerick Intl. Show

Heather Turner . Audrey MacDonald . Julia Alexander

locheilbordercollie.com   locheiluk@gmail.com

JACK RUSSELL TERRIER
In Sweden
Kennel Ell-Ell's

'JONAS'
Ell-Ell's Just Me
Sire: CIB, Dk UCH, SE UCH, Siegers Body Tequilla Dame: Duckling's Jr Just Card
Owner: Tony and Jean Barker, UK

www.ell-ells.se
Lena and Martin Lovdahl Fasth

Dr Candace Lundin and Frank Zureick
DBF Russsell Terriers, Virginia, USA
candace@DBFRussellTerriers.com

Jack Russell Terriers

GCH DBF Stanley Cup

Junior World Winner 2014

Select Dog, Westminster 2015

2nd-Exc Champion Class, WDS 2015

Owned by Peggy Jackson and Candace Lundin

Kennel Hunterhawk

JACK RUSSELLS TERRIER IN NORWAY FOR COMPANION, SHOW AND SPORTS.

photo Helga Hallestad

"Sally"

photo Monica Tellnes

"Marlow"

photo Jouni Heikkinen

"Toffer"

BIS WINNER HUNTER HAWK ULTIMAT COUNTESS CORONA

BIS WINNER HUNTER HAWK ZIP IT MINISTER

FIN NUCH NJW12 MON AMOUR JP MR ENERGIZER

Maria Huseby
fophei@online.no
www.kennelhunterhawk.dk

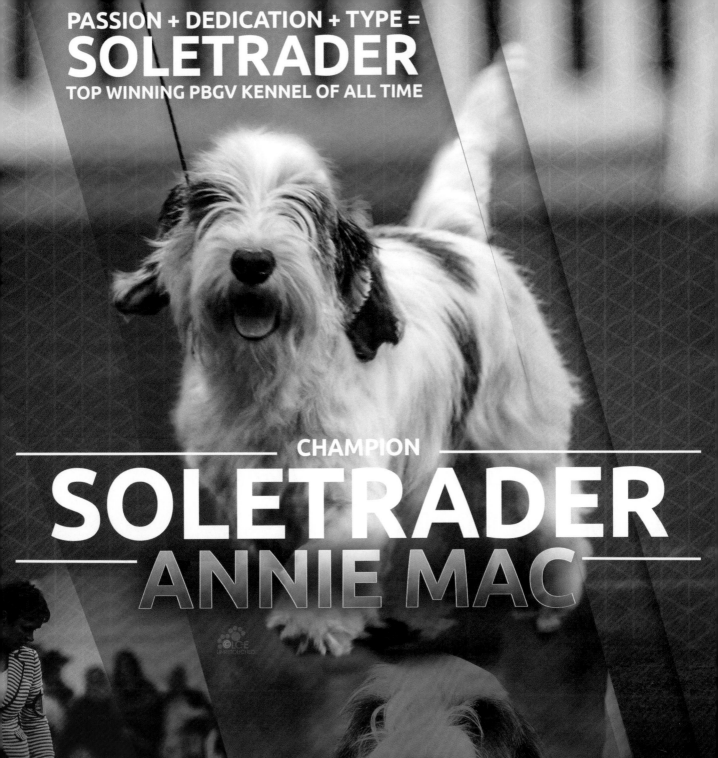

PASSION + DEDICATION + TYPE =
SOLETRADER
TOP WINNING PBGV KENNEL OF ALL TIME

CHAMPION
SOLETRADER
ANNIE MAC

owners
SARA ROBERTSON, WENDY DOHERTY
AND RON & DEBBIE SCOTT

EXCLUSIVELY HANDLED BY SARA   www. **SOLETRADERPBGVS** .com

Optimus
Bullmastiffs

"Looking A Head"

Ch Old Manila's Whisky Mac For Optimus JW

\# 1 UK Top Working Dog 2014
\# 2 UK Top Dog 2014
\# 1 Bullmastiff 2013 & 2014
34 CC • 31 BOB
8 x Group 1
1 x BIS • 2 x RBIS • 9 x BISS
Multiple Group Placings

Mac Is Proud Of His Daughters

Ch Optimus Rhondda JW

World Champion 2015
Italian Champion
Top Bullmastiff Bitch 2015
13CC • 2 x BOB
BPIS @ SKC 2014

Optimus Seven

RBPIS
City of B'Ham 2015

Multiple
Best Puppy Awards

Peter Myers & Deborah Morgan
www.optimusbullmastiffs.co.uk
optimus@blueyonder.co.uk
Tel : 07711814129

Eardley Beagles
what a *Stewpendous* Year with *Berry* good results

Champion Eardley Stew Pendous JW

Pup of the Year Overall Winner 2014
Group 2 at Bath, Three Counties and Belfast

Eardley Merry Berry

Top puppy in breed 2015
BPIS Paignton
with many Puppy Group placings
Pup of the Year
overall Runner-Up 2015

We are proud of our kennel's achievements this year and thank all the judges who have thought so highly of our hounds

Tim Jones and Steve Jepson   www.eardleybeagles.com

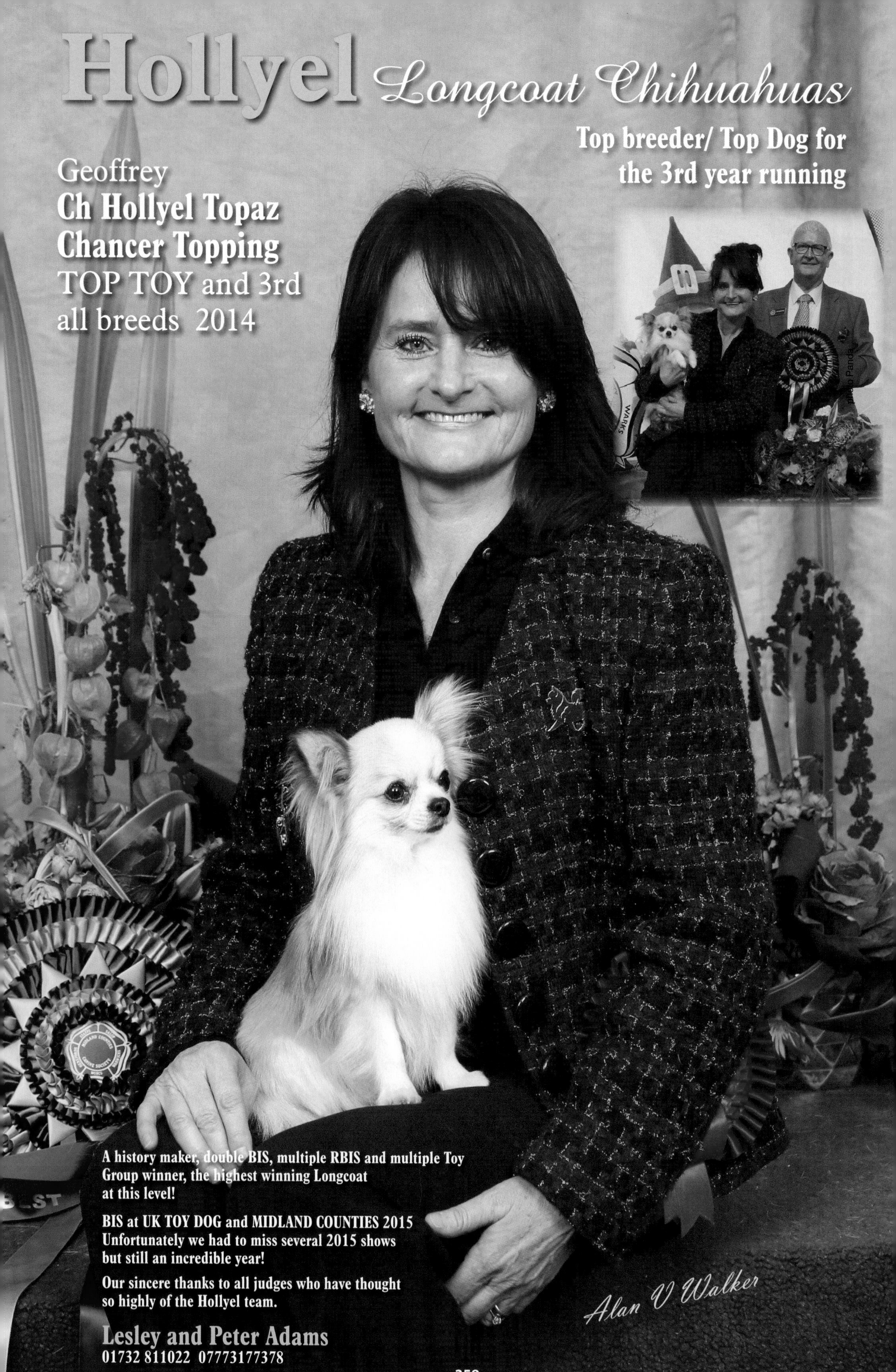

Hollyel Longcoat Chihuahuas
Top breeder/ Top Dog for the 3rd year running
Geoffrey
Ch Hollyel Topaz Chancer Topping
TOP TOY and 3rd all breeds 2014
A history maker, double BIS, multiple RBIS and multiple Toy Group winner, the highest winning Longcoat at this level!
BIS at UK TOY DOG and MIDLAND COUNTIES 2015
Unfortunately we had to miss several 2015 shows but still an incredible year!
Our sincere thanks to all judges who have thought so highly of the Hollyel team.
Lesley and Peter Adams
01732 811022 07773177378
Alan V Walker

Gunalt Fansome of Allenie (ai)
Richard Bott & Anthony Allen

Sh Ch Bardonhill Please Don't Tease Quensha
Richard Bott, Anthony Allen & Angela Morgan

Allenie & Quensha

AM Ch Tampa Bay and Snobo Gusty Seas Batten Down the Hatch
Anthony Allen, Linda Hess & Emily Elliott

Sh Ch Ember Red Hot Chilipepper of Quensha
Richard Bott, Anthony Allen & Angela Morgan

Thank you to all of the judges who thought so highly of our show team in 2015

Anthony Allen & Richard Bott

01757 611265

www.allenie.co.uk

Silken Windhounds (uk)

Breeding For Quality & Performance in the UK

BISS- Kent UKSWC 2013
ESWC Res Winner Dog Germany 2012 & 2014
UKSWC Res Winner Dog Scotland 2015

The Next Generation

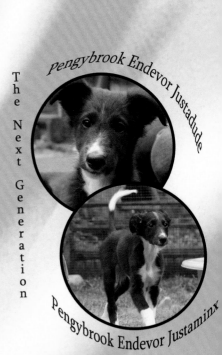

Pengybrook Endevor Justadude

Pengybrook Endevor Justaminx

Ch Firesmoke Spirit of Endevor
The 1st UK Bred ISWS Champion

Endevor Prince of Thieves

Kushbudar Reel Around the Sun

Overall BSFA Lure Course
Winner 2015 Silken Programme

Kushbudar Cloudsong at Endevor

Kushbudar Chu Chulain

Best Puppy, Best Junior & Res Winners
Bitch Norfolk 2014
Fastest Bitch Scotland 2015

Best Junior 2015 UKSWC Scottish Shows
Overall Winner Scottish Track Event 2015
Winner on Both Hill and Flat Straight Sprints

Kushbudar Whispering Winds

Winners Bitch-
UKSWC Scottish Specialty Show 2015
Res Winners Bitch -
UKSWC Lothian Specialty Show 2015
Puppy BISS- ESWC 2014

at Variare

Sue Lewis - Pengybrook- susilken@aol.com

Joy Middleton - Variare - joy.midds@outlook.com - 07927 809 672

Silken Windhounds (uk)

Endevor

Bred by Francie Stull
UKSWC Kent 2012- Supreme Best Match
UKSCW Kent 2013-Res Winners Dog
ESWC Baden 2014- 1st Open Dog
UKSWC Scotland 2015-Best American Bred

Kristull Barndance of Endevor

Allagante Winsome Riviera

ISWS & UKC CH
BISS UKSWC Lothian Speciality Show 2014
Overall Winner 2014 for:
Oval Track: Straight Hill Sprint, Straight
Flat Sprint, Scottish Silken Derby

The American Boys

BISS- UKSWC Scotish Speiality Show 2014
American Bred Dog ESWC Germany 2014
Puppy Class Winner, Slikenfest 2014
BOB Lure Coursing BSFA 2015
BISS and BOW Scotland 2015

Kushbudar

Morgendell Tioga

ill Grist - Endevor - gill38endevor@yahoo.co.uk
ilary Tringham - Kushbudsr - hilary@moupik.fsnet.co.uk

Wilholme and Bessalone

Another good year for team Wilholme and Bessalone.

In Spinone, Afterglow Hashtag Scandal at Bessalone became the youngest ever Show Champion in the breed at 13 months old as well as being Top Puppy in breed for 2015.

He has also picked up 4 Green Stars in Ireland as well as qualifying for the Irish POTY Final. His kennelmate, Sh Ch Liattch Mister Mister at Bessalone picked up his 3rd CC at Paignton, so making up two new Show Champions in 2015. Sh Ch Cobbets Rock 'N' Roll Party at Bessalone got his final Green Star to take his Irish title. The GSP's have also had a good year, Wilholme Sharp 'N' Smart at Bessalone winning 2 CCs, a RCC and 3 Green Stars in Ireland. Wilholme Saucy Brown JW CW 15, picked up the RCC at the GSP Association show in the biggest entry of the year of over 140 GSPs as well as her Celtic Winner title in Ireland and Wilhome I Gotta A Feelin for Bessalone has won well both in the UK and on his visits to Ireland.

Wilholme Sharp 'N' Smart at Bessalone

Afterglow Hashtag Scandal at Bessalone

Wilholme – David Shields sand Irene Glen wilholme28@gmail.com 07774 973723

Bessalone – Sue and Sally Knowles and Irene Glen bessalone@hotmail.com 07914 430918

Valentisimo *Spanish Water Dogs*

'A tradition of quality in looks and function'

Top Breeder All Breeds 2015*

We have had another proud and unforgettable year with our team of homebred dogs showing and working with great success across Europe and Spain. We are also very pleased to see our friends achieving excellent results in the show ring with their Valentisimo dogs. We would like to sincerely thank all the judges who have thought so highly of our dogs and look forward to doing the breed proud in 2016.

TOP SWD and 3rd TOP GUNDOG 2015*

Valentisimo's Castro

This year alone 'Castro' has added another 15 BOBs to his ever growing record along with 1 Group 2 and 3 Group 4 placements. BIS at the SWDC UK Open Show and also winning the Open Male and RCAC at the Monografica and Open Male at World Dog Show 2015.

'Castro'

TOP SWD BITCH 2015*

Valentisimo's Pacopilik

Our sweet girl 'Tica' has proven her worth by amassing another 13 BB's including BOB at Crufts this year. Also winner of BOS at the Club Show held in conjunction with the World Dog Show this year. She was also World Champion Bitch 2015 at the Champion of the World contest in Ubrique

'Tica'

'Pinnto'

TOP SWD PUPPY 2015*

Valentisimo's Gran Pinnto

The new kid on the block! 'Pinnto' has had an amazing start to this year winning 6 BPs, 1 BOB, 1 PG2 (Ch Show), 1 PG2 (Open Show) and 1st PD at Madrid. We hope he continues to fulfil his promise in the future.

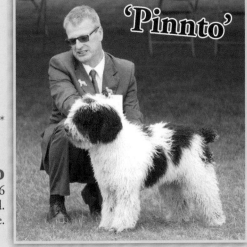

TOP SWD STUD DOG 2015* and
TOP SWD BROOD BITCH 2015*

'Paco' (Int/Swe/Sp Ch Curioso del la Ribera del Genil del Valentisimo) and 'Vida' (Leonneusg de Ubrique del Valentisimo) are both enjoying a happy retirement in our home and are so proud of their progeny's successes.

Many thanks to our handlers for this year: Hanna Wiseman, Fleur Walker, Lizzie Greenslade and James Newton. We couldn't have done it without you all! And never forgetting our dear friend Jose Haro Haro

Nigel, Jenny and Ben Egginton

email nigel@spanishwaterdog.net Telephone: 01246 888081 www.spanishwaterdog.net
or follow us on Facebook:www.facebook.com/spanishwaterdogs

SERENAKER

SERENAKER v2015
THREE NEW CHAMPIONS

Serena Parker &
Graham Stevens

CH SERENAKER OTHELLO
Owners: Cuthill Parker & Stevens

CH SERENAKER FASHION
Breeder Owners: Parker & Stevens

CH IR CH SERENAKER SIROCCO
Owners Parker, Stevens, Carota & Sipperly

SERENAKER@GMAIL.COM

WWW.SERENAKER.CO.UK

07792570307

BITCON & FERNDEL
Show team 2015

Almanza Final Impact
2 CCs and 4 RCCs

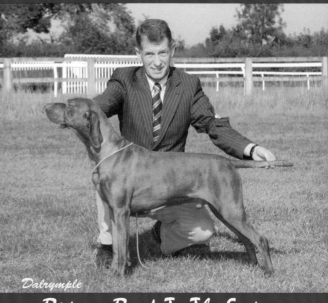

Bitcon Back To The Future
1 CC and 4 RCCs

Sh Ch Ferndel Aeron Magregor
Lightly shown during 2015 but continuing his winning ways

Sh Ch Bitcon Witchcraft
5 CCs, 1 RCC, Group 2, 3 and 4

Also campaigned during 2015

Sh Ch Ferndel Folly to her title, now retired for maternal duties.

And the Flat Coat **Bitcon Carefree** to Top Puppy award.

Once again both kennels have achieved the Top Breeder award in Hungarian Vizslas and Welsh Springers, with 6 different Vizsla CC winners and 7 Welsh.

We would like to thank and congratulate all the owners of our breeding who have helped us achieve this award.

Puppies available early 2016 in all 3 breeds.

Moray Armstrong
01228 674318

ferndel@jthirlwell.fsnet.co.uk

John Thirlwell
0191 4887168

Byermoor

Ch Queens Maid

No hype
just Type !

Ch Princess

Ch Masquerade

ROB SANSOM
byermoor@googlemail.com

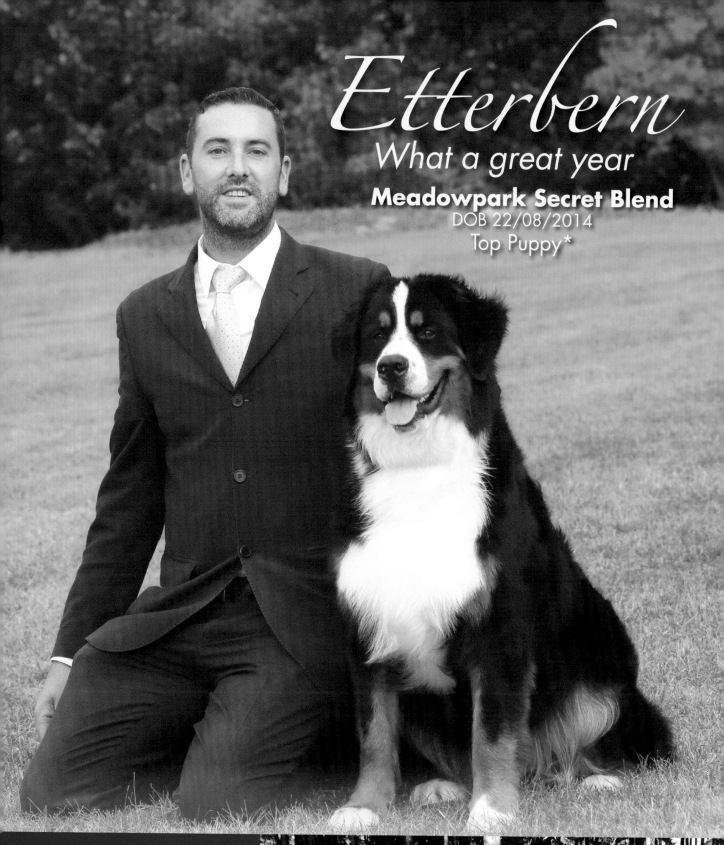

Etterbern
What a great year

Meadowpark Secret Blend
DOB 22/08/2014
Top Puppy*

Etterbern Rosinha
DOB 01/09/2014

Lee Reynolds
07776 431225

*at time of press

367

Westaway
of Norway

photo: HAP FOTO

99 homebred champions

pictured running are Norw Dan Sh Ch Westaway The One And Only and Chetruda Secret Asset for Westaway

picture right

Norw Dan Sh Ch Westaway The One And Only
by Norw Sh Ch Westaway Black Jive
ex Norw Sh Ch Westaway Moment of Magic

Number 1 English Springer Spaniel in Norway 2015

picture below

Norw Sh Ch Westaway Stop Press
by Norw Sh Ch Westaway Good News
ex Westaway Best Foot Forward

Number 2 English Springer Spaniel in Norway 2015

picture below right

Norw Sh Ch Westaway Beggars Belief
by GB Sh Ch Ferndel Aeron Magregor
ex Norw Dan Sh Ch JWW-08 Westaway Reds Have More Fun

Number 2 Welsh Springer Spaniel in Norway 2015

Photo: M B Kjellevold

Design: westaway.no

Stig A Kjellevold & Frank W Bjerklund • Kleven Cottage • Kleivaveien 138 • NO-3178 Våle • Norway
www.westaway.no • westaway@online.no • Telephone 00 47 33 06 20 90

SH CH GUNALT DE ICE AT STRIDVIEW

'ICE'
A true dual purpose gundog – fit for function

City of Birmingham Championship Dog Show

RESERVE BEST IN SHOW

Alan V Walker

TOP WEIMARANER 2012/13/14/15

44 CCs
BIS at Belfast 2014
BIS at National Gundog 2015
RBIS at City of Birmingham 2015
7 Group 1
Numerous group placings including twice at Crufts
Ranking in the Top 10 dogs all-breeds

Handled by **Jacqui Ward**

Owned by **Karen Whitehead**

Bent Hill Farm, Hazelwood,
Bolton Abbey BD23 6JL
Telephone: 07802 472795
Email: karenben1@hotmail.com

Ice is also a working gundog

369

AMSCOT GORDON SETTERS
'TRULY DUAL PURPOSE'

'Dallas'

Colin N Waddell

AMSCOT REBEL WITH A CAUSE (AI) JW

AM Dual Ch Sun-Yak Spellbound Heaven Scent (ET) ex Amscot Unbeliva Belle

3 Reserve CCs 4 Field Trial Awards

Hip Score 6/4 - DNA CLEAR for PRA and Cerebellar Degeneration

Dallas is the first male Gordon Setter with show awards to win an OPEN FT Stake in 60 years!

A 'Dallas' Niece

'Raina'

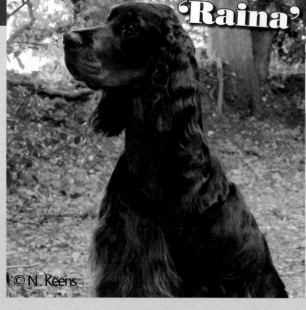

© N. Keens

Storskogens Amor Joy of Amscot (Imp Swe)
1 CC and 1 RCC
Hip Score 5/6 PRA Clear

Raina was the BGSC Top Gordon Setter Puppy for 2014 and has now added a CC before reaching 2 years of age. A litter is planned for 2016 from our lovely girl.

A 'Dallas' son

'Barclay'

BLACK MYSTERY PHANTOM OF THE OPERA BY AMSCOT (IMP CHE)
ON A COVEY OF PARTRIDGE.
2 RCCs. Hip Score 4/4 PRA Clear

'Trisca'

photo Ridley

DUAL CHAMPION AMSCOT IRRESISTA BELLE

1995-2010
THE FIRST DUAL CH
SETTER IN UK HISTORY

OUR BOYS ARE AVAILABLE AT STUD TO APPROVED BITCHES (AI AVAILABLE)

THE AMSCOT TEAM ARE HANDLED BY JAMES NEWTON, JOANNE HOAD, AND CLAIRE LEWIS.

JEAN COLLINS-PITMAN

AMSCOTGORDONS@AOL.COM
+44 (0) 7877 286702

Cúboglach   Irish Water Spaniels

Sh Ch Cúboglach Petite Wave (Hips 0:3, Elbows 0)

The Top IWS for 2015 | Fourth Top Gundog* | Top Vulnerable Breed*

**CHAMPIONSHIP GROUP 1
MIDLAND COUNTIES AND
EAST OF ENGLAND**

**GROUP 2
BATH, DARLINGTON AND
RICHMOND**

**GROUP 4
GUNDOG SOCIETY OF WALES**

**2 BESTS IN SHOW AT
ALL BREED OPEN SHOWS.
12 CHALLENGE CERTIFICATES
(2 RESERVES), 17 BOBs.**

**WAVE IS MY 8TH GENERATION,
UNBROKEN BITCH LINE.**

photo Walker

Cúboglach Speckled Beauty

photo Craig Koshyk

**3 TIMES A
FIELD TRIAL WINNER
14 FIELD TRIALS
AWARDS
AND A GROUP 8
WINNER**

Whether working in the shooting field or in the show ring, Cúboglach IWSs excel.
The Top Dual Purpose Kennel for 4 decades.
31 Field Trial Awards with 5 different dogs, including 4 wins!

In Champion Cúboglach Rosy Rustic, Fen Rustic and Speckled Beauty, Martyn has bred, trained and handled the most successful IWSs in both retriever and spaniel field trials in UK breed history. Martyn is the UK's the only owner, breeder and handler to have won Field Trial awards in both spaniel and retriever trials with IWSs.

Martyn Ford, Eastbourne House, Tregarn Road, Langstone, Gwent NP18 2JT.
01633 416682/07719 490092 martyn@martynford.co.uk www.irishwaterspaniels.biz

*at time of going to press

371

Tameron & *Layways*

4 Dogs, 3 Groups, 2 Owners, 1 Year

Linda and Helen Howard
01623 812062

www.tameron-layways.co.uk

Shaun and Samuel Layton
01246 856555

Eric
Ch Tameron Mr Red Edition JW

Top Puppy 2014

BPIB at Boston '15
and Puppy Group 2

BPIB at Manchester '15
and Puppy Group 1

6 CCs, 4 BOBs, 8 RCCs
Utility Group 3 and 4

Cilla
Tameron Miss Black Opium

Top Puppy 2015*

11 x Best Puppy In Breeds

3 CCs, 1 BOB, 3 RCCs

Res BPIS at Bournemouth and
5 Puppy Group 2s

Bradley
Layways Silent Night At Tameron

CC at Border Union 2015
CC and BIS at SYWC
2 RCCs

Lana
Layways Lana Del Rey JW

POTY Qualifier 2015,
BPIB at Crufts
BPIB at Manchester
and Puppy Group 2
2 CCs, 1 BOB, 4 RCCs

Thank you to all the judges
who have thought so highly of
our children.

372

KELLTARA

Where breed history is made, home to TOP DOG 2008-2015

BISS Friponne Du Pic D'espade Kelltara

Friponne adds, to her already impressive show career, Best in Specialty Show 2015.

2 Best in Specialty Show
7 Championship Group Places
3 Crufts Bests of Breed
Top Dog UK 2013, 2014 and 2015
Top Dog France 2014
Championnat De France in Angers 2014
BOB, CACIB, CACS and 2nd in Group
Always graded excellent in France
25 Bests of Breed

*Thank you to all of the judges who have
rewarded Friponne*

Owned and loved by **Pat Phillips**
Handled by Steve Phillips
Bred by M N Gainche
www.kelltara.co.uk / 01782 325032

KELLTARA and SEACOURT PYRENEAN SHEEPDOGS

SHOW CHAMPION
Farnfield Topo Gigio (AI) JW ShCM

Top Labrador UK 2014

All enquiries: owner / breeder Richard Stafford
rsfarnfield@aol.com

LOCHEIL *Border Collies*

CLASS WINNER 2015

Locheil Keep Your Promise, our new hopeful, seen here at 6 months old winning **Best Puppy in Show** at the Scottish Border Collie Club Ch. Show. Judges, Kate Duncan & Peter Simmons.

Swimming buddies, Lola and Maisie.

Sh Ch Irish Ch Locheil Ooh La La, owned by Audrey MacDonald. Lola now has 10 CC's and a Group 1 and a Group 2 at Irish International Ch. Shows and UK Group Placings.

Heather Turner & Julia Alexander

locheilbordercollie.com   locheiluk@gmail.com   Tel: 01670 518195

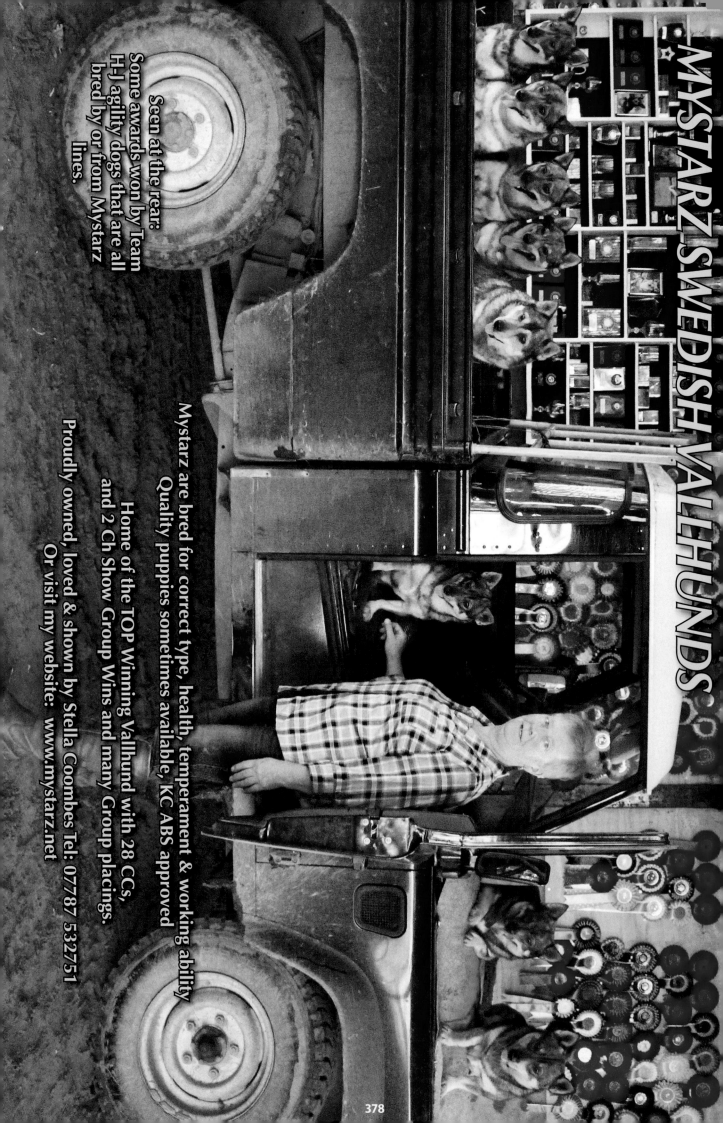

RIDANFLIGHT

Pointers and Miniature Wirehaired Dachshunds

photo A H Brace

Ch RIDANFLIGHT RICARDO

PRA and Laforas Clear

Ricky has had a fantastic 2 years winning 15 CCs in 2015 taking his total to 24 with 15 BOB & 7 RCCs

Some of his significant achievements :
Top Miniature Wire Male 2014
Top Miniature Wire Male to date 2015
No 2 Hound and then Joint No 1 Hound at the half way mark 2015
Best in Show Miniature Dachshund Club Ch Show 2015
Res Best in Show Lancashire and Cheshire Dachshund Ch Show 2014
Res Best in Show Midland Dachshund Ch Show 2015
Group 1 LKA 2014
Group 3 Birmingham National 2014
Group 4 Three Counties 2014
Group 2 WELKS 2015
Group 2 Southern Counties 2015
Group 3 Birmingham National 2015
Group 3 Paignton 2015

RIDANFLIGHT RHONWEN

Ronnie has had to take a back seat to Ricky this year but she has achieved

Group 3 City of Birmingham 2014
2 CCs, 1 BOB and 5 RCCs

We would like to congratulate all owners on their successes with all Ridanflight connected stock which are currently Top Puppy and Joint Top Puppy in both breeds

We are hoping to have a litter early 2016 from Ridanflight Rhianna (1 RCC), litter sister to Ronnie

Alan V Walker

STEVE AND PAM ROSE
WWW.RIDANFLIGHTPOINTERS.COM
STEVE.RIDANFLIGHT@GMAIL.COM
01639 885062

379

DAVRICARD

CH DAVRICARD HARRISON, reflecting on a great year during which he won 12 CCs, group 3 and was a Eukanuba Champion Stakes finalist.

MOONLIGHT gained her 2nd CC at the Beagle Association Ch Show. The new youngsters, litter brother and sister **BRANDON** and **BALLAD** won consistently, including a number of BPIBs/ BPIS and puppy group placings, and both are reserve CC winners.

DAVID CRAIG
Tel (01325) 285485
davbeagle@hotmail.com

LCE
UNRETOUCHED

JANMARK Bedlington Manchester Terriers

2015: another great year, two New Champions and one Top Puppy...

Barney

Talanors Diamonds N' Dreams avec Janmark JW

br. Knight

Mo

Ch Janmark Jkay JW ShCM

Wilma

Ch Digelsa Diva avec Janmark JW ShCM

br. Oxley

Wilma was only shown lightly in 2015, gaining her crowning 3rd CC. Our 1st Manchester Terrier Champion. Now on maternity duties.
Thanks go to her breeders Mick and Gill Oxley.

Mo finished 2014 as Bedlington Terrier Top Puppy Bitch and continues her winning ways in 2015, finishing Bedlington Top Bitch.
Midland Bedlington Terrier Club, Best in Show
National Terrier Open Show Pup of The Year, Winner.
Pontefract, Consett and Newton Aycliffe Shows –
3 Reserve Best in Shows.
Bath, BOB.
WELKS, Windsor and Welsh KC – 3 RCCs
Birmingham Nat, CC and BOB
Southern Counties, CC
Midland Bedlington Terrier Club, CC and RBIS.
Leeds – CC and BOB.

Barney, what a puppy career he has had, finishing Top Manchester Terrier Puppy. 2 BPIS, Ripon and Pollard. Reserve Best Puppy in Show, Northern Counties Sporting Terrier and BMTC.
Best Puppy in Breed at 14 Championship Shows – Birmingham National, SKC, Bath, Southern Counties, Blackpool, Windsor, Leeds, Paignton, Bournemouth, WKC, Birmingham City, Richmond, Driffield, Midland Counties.
BP AVNSC Border Union.
Puppy Group placings at Championship Shows, Group 1, Paignton. Group 4, Bath and Southern Counties.
Pup of the Year Competition. Day Winner and Overall Runner Up Bath & Richmond.
RCCs, SKC and Richmond.

Thanks go to his breeders Gill and Clive Knight.

We are particularly proud of our youngsters results through 2015 and look forward to next year. Many thanks to all the judges that have thought so highly of our dogs & have rewarded them with top honours.

Mark and Jan Walshaw

Tel 01287 652860

www.janmark.co.uk

Teckelgarth Otterhounds

Top Otterhound 1996-2007, 2009,2012-2015, Top Breeder 1996,1998,2000-2009,2011-2015. Top Stud Dog 2014, 201

photo Robin Alner

We are very proud of our 20th and 21st homebred Champions made up this year
at Southern Couties by Hound expert Mrs Marianne Nixon, Maximus (on left, jointly
owned by S, A and E Smith), who now has 5 CCs, is also Top Otterhound 2015,
and Iolanthe (right, jointly owned with K Smith).
Having gained her title, Iolanthe is now the proud mum of 8 puppies.

Ch Teckelgarth Horus
jointly owned with J Court
has continued his winning
ways this year and now has
20 CCs, 19 BOB, 13 RCCs
1 Group 3

Ch Jollity
jointly owned with C Scott
has won 2 CCs, 1 BOB
and 1 RCC this year

We also won RCCs with
T Jouster,
T Myrtle,
T Maeve and
T Roman,
who also had
5 Best Puppies

Mercury has won 1 CC and BOB this year

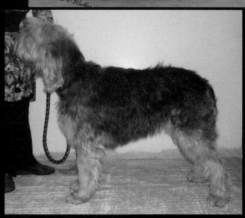

Ch Mimi jointly owned with M Cairns has
won 3 CCs, 2 BOB and 2 RCCs this year.

My deepest gratitude to all the Teckelgarth team for all their support at Championship shows, Game Fairs and with
looking after our beautiful puppies.
We can be contacted though our website www.teckelgarh.org

at time of print

Introducing
Troy

**Royal Pack Ukraine
Victory for Glastyle**

*Beaglee Hope In My Pocket
x
Arctic Kiss Spotty Friend*

SCW Photography

Gladstyle
Beagles

and his Son

Google

Gladstyle Google Me
out of
Gladstyle Mad About Me

Jim & Dawn Coates
www.gladstyle.com

JARKO

ZELDA

ELVIRA

EVANGELINE

Top Stud 2015*
*Also grandfather
of Rigpa Atisha*

JARROD

Top Tibetan Spaniel Breeders UK 2010, 2013, 2014, 2015*

Avigdor

THE
WELSH KENNEL
CLUB

**GROUP
4**

Alan V Walker

New UK Ch – Griffon Bruxellois

GB & IR.CH. Vanity Fair Corsairey Casch

GB. & IR.CH. Sommerlyst's Rigpa Atisha

<u>UK</u> 12 BOB's, 12 CC's, 5 Res CC's (Including Crufts '15).
BIS TSA & Northern TSC '15, Group 3 Windsor '14,
Group 3 SKC '15, Group 4 WKC '15.
Currently Top TS UK
<u>In Ireland</u> BIS TSAI'15 , GP1, GP4,
Champion Stakes Winner

Tony Moran & Lionel Prouve, www.avigdor.eu

Frenbosen Boston Terriers

frenbosen@yahoo.com

Tel: 07957642157

Bred, handled and cherished by Bron Ward
BPIB and Group Placings
Best Puppy Bitch Driffield Ch Show 2015
Judge Colin Reed
Best Puppy Bitch Midland Counties Ch Show 2015
Judge Irene McManus

Frenbosen She's So Fancy

- Denise Hardy & Trish Hallam Present -

Tokaji

Mattie

Mattie is Ch/Am/Can Ch Klassics
Girl with a Curl (Imp USA)

6 CC'S 4 RCC's 2 group 2s. Owner Dee Hardy, Trish Hallam, Sue Kite and Jeff Gillespie, bred by Sue and Jeff. Top Basenji 2015.

9 CC'S 4RCC's owners Dee Hardy and Trish Hallam, bred by Moray Armstrong currently Top Hungarian Vizsla 2015, Top Puppy 2014, youngest ever Sh Ch Vizsla. Special thanks to Liz and Gaz Phillips & to his reserve handlers and fans.

Trigger

Sh Ch Bitcon Sirocco
at Tokaji JW

- Denise Hardy (07963157866) & Trish Hallam (07496033409) -

TALLOWAH BEAUCERONS
Steve and Jackie Barnes
www.tallowah.org.uk
L:R –
Int/Ir Ch Jupiler du Regard Mordant
Cot 4, CSAU, CANT, Top Beauceron
2014 and 2015
Ir Ch Haureole des Feux de l'Ange
Tallowah Eden Hazard (at 9 months)
Miss Scarlet du Regard Mordant
Top Beauceron Bitch 2014 and 2015

JENSON
CH JANEYJIMJAMS JENSON JW SHCM

- Arden Grange/Dog World Top SCWT 2015, 2014 and 2013

- 28 CCs and 24 BOBs

- Terrier Group 1 Boston 2015
- Terrier Group 1 Manchester 2015

- Owners: Mike and Alison Fallon
- Handled by: Alison Fallon
- Breeder: Jane Charleton

SH CH FELDKIRK FASHION
GB Sh Ch Nu Ch Su Ch Covenstead Ambassador (imp Nor) ex Rosy Beauty

A really memorable moment for us when 'Fashion' took the bitch record in July with her 36th CC
and to go on and finish the year on 41 CCs
41 CCs, 28 BOB, 11 RCCs, 4 G2, 1 G3 (Crufts), 1 G4
Youngest Champion in the breed gaining her title from Junior

Top CC winning bitch for the last 4 years
2 years Top Flatcoat, handing over to her brother, our Blake,
2 BIS at Breed Club Shows, BIS United Retriever, 2 times BOB Crufts
Winner of Scotland's Top Gundog competition 2014

An all-round special 'Flatcoat' and Honoured to have won the 'Becky' trophy
donated by the late Pat Chapman

Very proud that in this time we also had great success with her brother 'Blake' Top Flatcoat 2014, has 15
CCs, 2 G1, RBIS National Gundog, 1 G3, BIS, United Retriever also, and two other siblings, MacKenzie
and Sarina who both gained their titles and also won Group places.
(MacKenzie also Group placed at Crufts)
Top Hungarian Vizsla also with 'Asia' also Group placed and BOB Crufts

Tom H Johnston and Frank H Whyte
North Lodge, Mosseknowe, Kirkpatrick Fleming, Lockerbie, Scotland DG11 3BE
Tel (0044) 01461 800372 email tomstjohn17@yahoo.com

394

GLENCHESS

Ch Glenchess Ilolas

Winner CC under Finnish Breed specialist Tapio Kakko, Club Championship Show 2015

Owned and bred by STEVE and ELAINE SHORT

Tel: 01746 862323

HARVESTBANK FIELDS OF GOLD JW ShCM
(Flo)

2 RBCC at only 20 months

Best Puppy Bitch in Breed 2014

Fourth generation of Harvestbank Bernese Mountain Dogs

Breeding for Temperament, Type and Conformation

Owned, bred, handled and very much loved by
TRISH GOODYEAR
07766 880162

Alan V Walker

Tony

photo Ashburn

Ch Tudorhurst Commodore

**Top Male King Charles Spaniel
with limited showing**

with litter sister Ch Tudorhurst Pearl and breeder
Julia Pennington, did the double twice this year

Chinart Yuunagi

**'Archie' at 6 months
Bred and entrusted to me by Peter Van
Baaren-Grob and
Lorraine Gillhespy**

Dr A G Schemel MRCVS

Jodak

Ch Jodak's Passion In
Black 4 CC's 2 rcc's.
Paige

Dimara Roll The Dice for
Jodak. Crufts RCC. BPIS
winner.
Jonty

Jo House & Mark Hinchliffe

LAino
Bichons

Calvin
Alizo Sahara

Best Puppy Dog Crufts 2015
BPIS Northern & Midland BF Club
CC & BOB Southern Counties
rCC WELKS.

Owner: Richard Smith
smithrichard36@aol.com

©advertising & photography Croft-Elliott

BRONABAY PROUDLY PRESENTS

CH BRONABAY CHERISH THE MOMENT JW
TOP PUPPY 2009, 9 CCs, 6 BOB and 6 RCCs

That's my boys!
Both boys are proven studs and available to approved bitches only

Champion at 21 months
Ch Bronabay Troopin The Colour JW
DOB 13.11.10 Dog World Top Dog 2012
6 CCs, 4 BOB and 5 RCCs
Sire – Ch Highworth Northern Lights over Pendrell JW
Dam – Ch Bronabay Cherish The Moment JW

Champion at 21 months
Ch Bronabay Cannonball JW
Current Leader Top Dog 2015
DOB 25.9.13
6 CCs, 1 BOB and 4 RCCs
Sire – Ch Pemcader Belroyd Zeus JW
Dam – Ch Bronabay Cherish The Moment JW

Our sincere thanks to the judges who thought so highly of them!
Proudly owned, bred, forever loved and adored by KC Assurred Breeders
Misses L A Weedall and N A Bogue 01606 550402 lorraineweedall902@btinternet.com

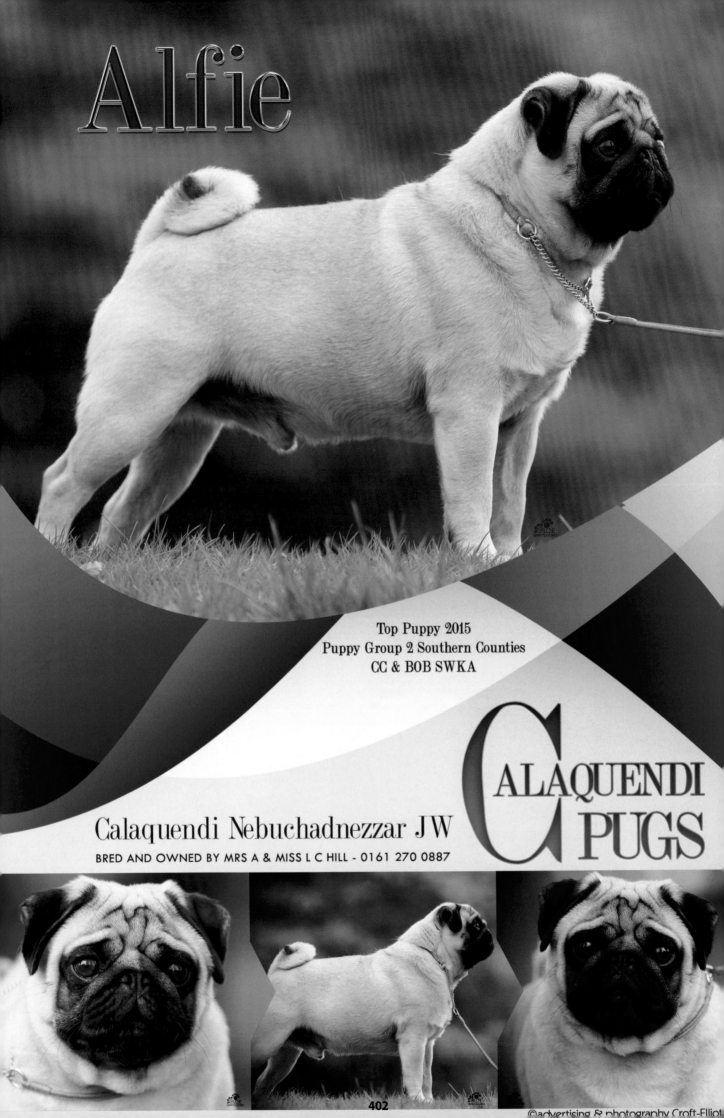

Alfie

Top Puppy 2015
Puppy Group 2 Southern Counties
CC & BOB SWKA

CALAQUENDI PUGS

Calaquendi Nebuchadnezzar JW

BRED AND OWNED BY MRS A & MISS L C HILL - 0161 270 0887

©advertising & photography Croft-Elliot

CH LOUISIANNA TROUBLEMAKER

7 CC
8 RCC
G3
2 G4
PG2

Currently Res Top Dog

Top Brood Bitch
Ch Vanitonia Takin Back My Love at Louisianna

Top breeder

CH LOUISIANNA GIFT OF THE GAB

6 CC
7 RCC
Top bitch '14

Handled by Gabriella Stafford

LOUISIANNA BICHON FRISE
Louise, Gabriella and Thea Stafford 07739 321699

Int CH. Ir CH. Lux CH. Bel CH.
Haia da Casa de Loas em Bamcwt ShCM (Imp Port)

Joining the team for 2016
PT CH Odi da Casa de Loas em Bamcwt (Imp Port)

Bamcwt Estrela Mountain Dogs
Continuing to lead the way

Proudly owned and shown by
Louise Bermingham & Sue Kendrick

www.bamcwtestrelas.webs.com

Int CH. Ir CH. Asterel Sabugeiro of Bamcwt EJW'11
Top Estrela 2013, 2014 & 2015

(c) Will Harris

Charibere Simply Magic at Chezanna

(c) Alan Seymour
Charibere Simply A Dream at Chezanna
Top Puppy 2015

Already making their mark in the ring

Chezanna Pyrenean Mountain Dogs
It's all in the name

Owned and loved by Christine Kenyon,
Arthur Ward & Louise Bermingham
Bred by Linda Marston

www.chezannapyreneanmountaindogs.com

CH Charibere Simply Special at Chezanna JW ShCM
Top Pyrenean 2014 & 2015
Breed record holder for Championship Best in Shows and Group Wins

CHAMPION
Boughton Brigadier

Loved by Andrea Spurr

Thank you Clare Boggia
for entrusting this special boy to my care

ANDREAJSPURR@ME.COM

Brandon makes breed history

KYNOWEB — Raad van Beheer Dutch Kennel Club — OUR DOGS

Netherland Champion Minaelea's Black Mambo JWAW13

5 CAC, CACIB
5 BOB
1 Group 2
Amsterdam Winner
Holland Cup Winner

Dogshow Rotterdam 2015

UK Champion Minaelea's Black Mambo JWAW13

18 CCs
16 BOB
Crufts Group Winner 2014,
Paignton Group Winner
3 Group 3, 3 Group 4

Robert and Donna Taylor would like to thank
all judges who thought so highly of our boy

Remesca

DOBERMANNS

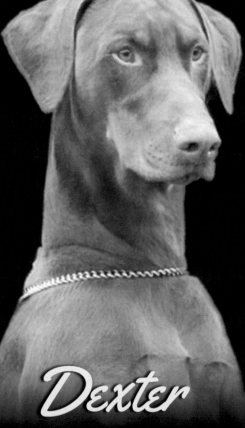

Dexter

REMESCA'S ROSINNI JW SHCM

GREEN STAR DOBERMANN CLUB OF IRELAND 2015

RESERVE CC CITY OF BIRMINGHAM 2014

Owned by Zarina Brough

Reeva

REMESCA'S RIVE GAUCHE

RESERVE CC DRIFFIELD 2015

Owned by Karen Brannan & Carol Smith

Frieda

REMESCA'S REET PETITE

CRUFTS CLASS WINNER 2015

MULTIPLE CHAMPIONSHIP SHOW WINS

Owned by Ruth Robinson

CH ARITAUR CARDINAL RED AT JODASEEN SHCM
X CH REMESCA WHAT EVA JW

Carol, Karen, Zarina and Ruth would like to thank all the judges who have appreciated the quality of the Remesca siblings.

For further information:
EMAIL: remesca@aol.com

© Photos by Will Harris and Sam & Lynne Jones

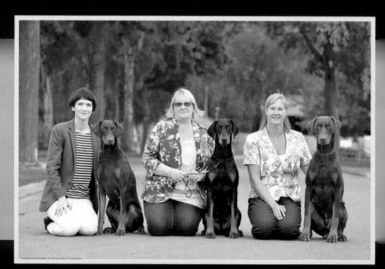

Tidemill Pugs

Established 1978

© Will Harris

DELWIN'S BLACK REBEL AT SALDAWN
Bred by Grace Godwin, owned by Joyce Grant, shown by Nigel.
Siring quality black puppies.

CHAMPION YORLANDER RONALDO AT TIDEMILL JW
Bred by Mrs Kath Hindley
22 CCs
Top Pug 2009. Top Stud Dog 2011, 2012, 2013 and 2014

Congratulations to Ronnie's Champion children and CC winning progeny

CHAMPION DYLVILLE LILYBETH AT TIDEMILL (IMP BEL) JW
Bred by Ingrid and Jan Mylemans
Hoping to pass on her qualities to her offspring.

CHAMPION SIMOS DELIA DELIGHTS TIDEMILL
Bred by Kamini Agrell – a cracker from the early 90s!

Tidemill King Charles Spaniels
Blasts from the past

CHAMPION TIDEMILL SERENA
a home bred stunner!

CHAMPION JENTIKI CAMILLA
Bred by Jennie Baker

TERRY PURSE and **NIGEL MARSH**
Tel 023 8086 4963 Email nigel@tidemillpugs.co.uk www.tidemillpugs.co.uk

Kay Woodward

Jubliana Eterna
Flame for
Cwsscwn
Res CC

Laura

Ferndel Silhouette
of Cwsscwn JW
1 CC, 1 Res CC

Sh Ch Ferndel
Butterkist
Cwsscwn JW

Top WSS 2015 *

15 CCs   14 Res CCs

Grp 2, 3 x Grp 3, Grp 4

Cwsscwn Calico
Res CC

*Christine Morgan
&
Chris Schofield*

* at time of going to press

BELLEVILLE

Snooker

2 RCC's 3 PB
BPIS Grantham &DCS
PG3 Darlington
Belleville Just For Effect

Radar

**Ch Belleville Seduction
Crufts BOB '15 & '14**
Photo Michael Mawson Photography

Ch Hooligan Song for Belleville)
Ellie is the youngest PWD champion at
16 months 4 x CC's

Her Litter brother Mikko
Hooligan Sing To Finland From Belleville
Both Bred in Finland by Arja Koskello

Ellie

Mikko

Ellie

Cathy Thompson-Morgan & Ed Morgan www.bellevillenorfolkterriers.co.uk

ELNAJJAR SCHNAUZER

Home of Schnauzer (Pepper and Salt) and Miniature Schnauzer (Black and Silver) Home reared with a priority for health and temperament

New Irish Champion Cleopatra's Charm Of Daiquincy at Elnajjar (Imp HUN) (DCM: tested clear)

"...well balanced and with quality. Nicely proportioned head, pleasing eyes, elegant but powerful neck, firm backline, well sprung ribs and moderate angulation throughout. Sound and steady mover. PGB (1)" judge Mr A H Brace (Three Counties Championship Show)

Sire Rapid Reflex Alarm Beskyd
Dam Int Ch/HJ/H/Hsch, H GCh All That Magic of Daiquincy **(DCM: tested clear)**

BOB and Reserve Best in Show at The Schnauzer Club of Ireland 2015

Whisper Of Wind Divinebell at Elnajjar (IMP POL)

"A really tidy sturdy built 7 month old puppy bitch, a little gem with attitude, lovely feminine head, alert expression, correct mouth, darkest of eyes, good length of neck, well laid shoulder, good front, ribs well sprung, good rear angulation, moved soundly and just did not stop showing off. BOB, BP, PG1, RBPIS" judge Mrs N Fleming (The Royal Cornwall Agricultural Show)

Sire Int Ch/Pl/Dt/LT/J/PL Ch Whisper Of Wind Amaro
Dam Ch/PL/J/PL Ch Whisper Of Wind Grasant

Amin O'Carroll (Elnajjar Schnauzer) Rosnannon, Bodmin, Cornwall PL30 5PJ UK
+44 (0) 7850 510915 aminocarroll@yahoo.co.uk

Scarletfair Stars

Spotty
SPEYMALT NORTHERN STAR JW

OWNED BY HANNAH
1 X RDCC
8 X CHAMP SHOW FIRSTS
MULTIPLE BEST PUPPY WINNER
RBIS & RBPIS MWC LIMIT SHOW

George
**COBYCO CHASING STARS
AT SCARLETFAIR JW**

15 X CHAMP SHOW FIRSTS
BIS SOUTH WEST WHIPPET 2015

Teddy
**SPEYMALT SEE THE STARS
AT SCARLETFAIR JW**

6 X CHAMP SHOW FIRSTS
BIS EVESHAM & DCS
RBIS TAUNTON & DCS
MULTIPLE BEST PUPPY WINNER

HELEN, JOAN & HANNAH WAYMAN
Helenscarletfair@Yahoo.co.uk   www.scarletfairwhippets.co.uk
DESIGN © PROPAW DESIGN

SHOW CHAMPION
LACEWAY PHAAROS
BY BRITTEB
4CC/1RCC

OWNED BY PATRICIA DAY   HANDLED BY RACHEL SPENCER   BRED BY HANNAH FAWCETT

pattemplewood@aol.com

Roanjora

Giles

Roanjora Montepulciano

Roanjora Pinotage ShCM 2CC 3RCC

Nina

Irish Red & White Setters

Jasper

Roanjora Castelao JW 1RCC & JW Semi Finalist

Owned and Loved by Ray, Debbie and Roxanne McDonald

Also home to

Bree (Sh Ch Courtdown Summer Breeze over Roanjora ShCM)

Darla (Roanjora Chianti JW)

Janey (Roanjora Tsarine Tzarina)

www.roanjora.co.uk
roanjora@roanjora.co.uk

Collypins Miniature Pinschers
Cindy Collinson & Shirley Dare www.collypins.co.uk

(Kilmuir Celtic Cross Among Collypins ex Keljantzi Pretty Pindora At Collypins)
DOB- 20/09/2009, Ch Collypins Lickety Split ShCM, 16 CC's,13 BOB,10 RDCC.
"Alfie" retired in style at SC's 2015 with a BOB & GRP 4 under SuzanneSantoriello and
Sigurd Wilberg. along with BIS at Club Open Show under Linda Benton Taylor
Sincere thanks to all judges for his accolades throughout our amazing journey.
He is and always will be our **"DOG IN A MILLION "**.
Photo kindly supplied by Alan V Walker.

(Ch Estivals Airbourne Magic JW ShCM ex Ch Collypins Whats Occurring JWShCM
DOB -29/09/2012 Ch Collypins Tayla Maid JW ShCM.
9 CC's, 4 BOB,12 RBCC, Top Puppy 2013, Top Dog Of Devon 2014,
We are incredibly proud of "Foo" who has certainly made her presence
known this year collecting a futher 5 BCC's to date.
Photo taken by Michele Farleigh

Introducing the third generation
(CH Valetta Alexander JW ex Collypins Lil Miss Pink Among Minihays)
D.O.B: 25/11/2014

Collypins Vive Le Rock 3 RDCC
"Jeffo" is owned by ourselves and is Top Min Pin Puppy 2015.
BPD- SC's 2015- Suzanne Santoriello, RBPIS-Min Pin Club Open Show 2015- Linda Benton-Taylor
BPIB & RDCC- Windsor 2015- Annette Oliver, BPIB & RDCC- Paignton 2015- Jill Peak
BPIB- Bournemouth 2015- Keith Baldwin, BPIB- C of B 2015- Espen Engh
BPIB & RDCC- Richmond 2015- Mervynn Evans, Photo taken by Dom Santoriello

Collypins Livin Is Easy.RBBC
"Mouse" is owned by ourselves and exhibited by Ria Watts.
BPB- Bournemouth 2015- Keith Baldwin, BPB- C of B 2015- Espen Engh
BPB- Richmond 2015- Mervynn Evans, BPIB & RBCC- Darlington 2015- Di Stark
BPB Midland Counties - Frank Kane

Thank you to all the judges for appreciating our team throughout 2015

Collypins Let It Be Me At Valetta
"Trudy" is owned by Val Dunn & Sue Bayliss
BB, BPIB, PG1 & RBPIS -Three Counties 2015
-Mark Cocozza, Jane Lilley & Ann Arch
BPIB-E Of E 2015-Jane Lilley, BPIB-WKC- Mr A Easdon
RBPIS-Miniature Pinscher Club Championship Show
- Mr B Hernandez, Photo kindly supplied by Alan V Walker

Collypins Hashtag Yolo
"Tag" is owned by Sue Davies
BPIS- Miniature Pinscher Club Championship Show 2015
- Mr B Hernandez

Collypins Chances Are
"Olivia" is owned by Chris Brown.
BPIB- Blackpool 2015-Dr Goran Bogarde (Sweden)
BPIS- Harrogate & District CS 2015 -Rodney Oldham.
photo supplied by Simon Jones

418

Laurelhach
Gordon Setters With Personality Plus

Crufts 2015
Laurelhach Encrypt 'Moon'
1st Puppy & Junior Dog

His sister
Laurelhach Entrapment JW 'Remy'
1st Puppy Bitch & BPIB

~~~~~~~~~~

Later this year their dam became
Sh Ch Laurelhach Legacy JW 'Lacey'
& now has 4 CCs

~~~~~~~~~~

Moon is now living in Germany & gained
his hunting qualification under the care &
guidance of Dr Uli Muskat.

Moon & his sire, Triseter Celtic Link
With Laurelhach, are available at stud to
selected bitches

~~~~~~~~~~

www.laurelhach.co.uk

Lignum Gordons

lignumgordons.co.uk

Simply the future

A TOP WINNING KENNEL FOR OVER 25 YEARS
Owned, bred, handled over 20 Champions accross 3 different breeds

Donut

Magregor Shneeball
The new kid on the block!
Winning regularly at Championship Shows:
5 x Best Puppy In Breed, inc. GSP Club Champ Show
Gundog Puppy Group 1 - City of Birmingham '15

Pod

Sh Ch Magregor Schokolade
BOB Crufts 2014
BIS GSP Championship Show 2014

Magregor Three's a Crowd at Pothouse JW
Owned by Anne Burns & Rob Brown
Morris has done exceptionally well in his 16 months,
winning countless classes at Championship Shows, and
a Reserve Challenge Certificate.

Morris

Sh Ch Magregor Fluffernutter
7 x CC's
1 x Group 2 - Border Union
Champ Show '15

Fluff

We would like to congratulate
John Thirlwell on his sucess with
Welsh Springer
Sh Ch Ferndel Aaron Magregor
54CC's

Also at home:
Sh Ch Magregor Chocolossus
At Stud to approved bitches.

Photo's by Chris Wilson

Magregor
German Shorthaired Pointers

Both are Gundog Group Championship Show Judges.
Gordon also awards CC's in toy breeds.

Gordon Haran & Marion Waddell
01505 - 685539
email: magregorgundogs@aol.com

vert by Nicola Maddox

ZANDVOORT
KEESHONDS

We said Goodbye to
Am Ch Lasers Tuxedo Junction of Zandvoort (imp USA)
19.09.02 – 02.03.15
2 CCs including Crufts 2008 and 1 RCC
Top Veteran 2014
Top Stud Dog 2011 Both Clubs
Sire of Top Dog 2013 Ch Hunnivoles Woody
Valentine JW
13 CCs 7 RCCs Top Puppy 2011
Puppy Group I Birmingham National

His Son
Ch Zandvoort
Dream Machine Wolfie
3 CCs, 1 BOB and 6 RCCs
Veteran Group 4 Birmingham National
2015 Mr Bert Easdon
Veteran Group 4 Darlington Ch Show 2015
Mr J Horswell

Tux's grand daughter
Ch Vanstrand
Quantum Of Solace
Bred by Mrs Francine Battram
6 CCs, 3 BOBs, 2 RCCs
BIS North of England Keeshond Ch Show 2013
Utility Group 3 Birmingham National 2015
Mr Rodney Oldham
BOS/RBIS at North of England
Keeshond Club Ch Show 2015

BRIZEWOOD - TREVARGH

NOVA SCOTIA DUCK TOLLING RETRIEVERS

THE BOYS JUST HAVING FUN

"VINNI"

GLENDERMACKI FOX CRAGG

AT

BRIZEWOOD

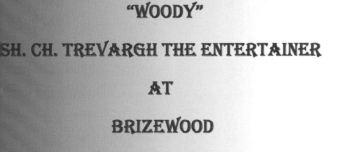

"WOODY"

SH. CH. TREVARGH THE ENTERTAINER

AT

BRIZEWOOD

PROUDLY OWNED BY

BABS HARDING & ELAINE WHITEHILL

uk.toller@btinternet.com

WWW.BRIZEWOOD.ORG.UK

Ashoka Tailor Made JW

ADAM

CH Pamplona Bring Me Sunshine X CH Arthlorn's Let's Go Girls At Ashoka

Bred, Owned, Loved,
Prepared and Presented
by David & Sue Walklate

Top Bichon Puppy 2015

**Puppy Group One Windsor 2015
& Birmingham National 2015**

**Puppy Group Two Border Union
Junior Warrant Before First Birthday**

HUNDWITH & RUTILUS

Weimaraners - Gordon Setters - Pointers

Sh Ch Lourdace Fulcrum JW

Top Gordon Setter 2015 and #3 Gundog*

Winner of Championship Show BIS and RBIS,
3 Gundog Groups (inc BIS GBAS 2015), 2 G2, and 21 CCs
– all BEFORE the age of four!

We have enjoyed a successful 2015 as we gained a SGWC
with Beck, making her the third FULL champion for Hundwith,
the second homebred.

Sh Ch Hundwith Duty to Sireva JW continues to sire
promising youngstock, including the youngest ever full Ch in
the breed, Ch Sireva Skype (group winner) and many other
titleholders and those on their way.

Sh Ch Afterglow Bare Face Lie at Kanix ShCM, liver
and white Pointer, added yet another CC to his collection from
only two appearances in 2015!

All enquiries to
David Crowther and David Alcorn

crowther1001@aol.com
davidralcorn@outlook.com
www.hundwith.webs.com
www.rutilus.org
07719 407621

Sh Ch Hundwith
Duty to Sireva JW

*joint at time of going to press

Hella`s Zigne

DKV-13-14 NV-14 NORDV-14 NV-15
Ignaheim`s Betty Boop

N DK UCH DKJV-14 NJV-14 NORDJV-14 NV-15
Hella`s Yndis

HELLA

Eva og Kent Pedersen
Tangenveien 62, 1914 Ytre Enebakk, Norway

www.kennelhella.net - eva@kennelhella.net

Weimaraner - German Wirehaired Pointer - Wirehaired Dachshund

Clint

SH CH KILLARY'S GRAND VENTURE WITH VANDERS AND ROMAUNT (IMP USA)

Owned by Julien Barney & Jackie Howatson
Juilen.barney@talk21.com
vanderssetters@hotmail.co.uk

ON HIS WAY TO MAKING BREED HISTORY
✦ YOUNGEST EVER SH CH ✦
✦ 1ST USA BRED SH CH ✦
✦ TOP MALE CC WINNER 2015 ✦

Breeders: Peterson, Zawikowski & Harrison

Dora

B Isadora JW ShCM
Owned by
Carole and Barry Canty
Puppy Group Bournemouth, 1RCC

Darcey

B En Vogue JW ShCM
Owned by Carole and Barry Canty,
1CC, 1RCC,
BiS Retford, Newark & North Lincs

Lola

B Tosca JW*
Owned by Claire and Nigel Wallis
Puppy Group Windsor

*subject to KC confirmation

Millie

B Carmen
Owned by Gemma Gibson
RBPiS Honley

Just a few of the 'family'
we are so proud of at

Bargemon

01636 892310
Carole and Barry Canty

bargemonbeardies@
hotmail.co.uk

Molly

B La Napoule
at almost 13 years old
Owned by Pam Hall 1RCC,
numerous BViS

Fletcher

**CH B Baryshnikov of
Barkenbear JW, ShCM**
Owned by Barbara and Ken Handley,
9 CCs, 6 RCCs, Group 3, Top Bearded Collie
2013 (DW/Arden Grange Points)

Ziggy

**B Beauford Tourer at
Barkenbear ShCM**
Owned by Barbara and Ken Handley

And Ella the Briard

Hartswelin Counting Stars for B
Owned by Carole Canty and Pam Hall,
1RCC

Porsche

B Boadicea JW
Owned by Pam Hall
1 RCC

MINFAA
Shih Tzus

Champion Minfaa Lavolta
Matsonic Sunshine Buddy
ex Minfaa Flying Solo

Champion Minfaa Jitterbug JW
Easy Rider Huxlor
ex Minfaa Disco Dancer

Minfaa Disco Dancer
Harropine Chicago Star at Minfaa
ex Minfaa Dancing Queen

Minfaa Scaramanga JW
Minfaa Zorro
ex Minfaa Disco Dancer

Champion Minfaa Labamba at Miracey ~ Top Brood Bitch*
Showing soon: *Minfaa Fly Me To The Moon*
Sire Ch Popeye's Quick On The Trigger at Huxlor Ex Casamays Clamaty Jane at Minfaa

Bred by **Jenny and John Quick** | jennyminfaa@aol.com | 07929 000236

430

*at time of going to press

TRIXHUND

TRIXHUND EUPHORIA JW ShCM

CC AND BOB
THE DACHSHUND CLUB
CHAMPIONSHIP SHOW
BOB
BATH CHAMPIONSHIP SHOW
BIS
PEMBROKESHIRE AGRICULTURAL
SOCIETY OPEN SHOW
BIS
MEIRIONYDD AGRICULTURAL
SOCIETY OPEN SHOW
RBIS
PONTARDULAIS AGRICULTURAL
SOCIETY OPEN SHOW

© Emily Guy 2014

Alan V Walker

TRIXHUND TALKING OBSESSION JW ShCM

BPIB
BLACKPOOL CHAMPIONSHIP
SHOW
BPIB & PG4
WINDSOR CHAMPIONSHIP SHOW
RBPIS
NORTHERN SPRINGER SPANIEL
CLUB CHAMPIONSHIP SHOW
BPIS
ABERYSTWYTH, LLANDYSUL &
NEWTOWN OPEN SHOWS

OWNED, BRED AND HANDLED BY
MICHAEL LEWIS AND JASON BULLOCK
TRIXHUND@BTINTERNET.COM   01570 470533

433

Ch. Janfrey Randal Upon Rundle JW ShCM

Our first Champion

SIMON

Multi CH. Zeppeline AL CAPONE x Multi CH Aryakas Rolingview Elektra

A r y a k a s SIMONIDES At Beauvallon

dob: 05th March 2014

All the way from winning BPIB at Crufts 2015 to
BOB and Group Two at Midland Counties 2015.
(with very limited showing)

A big thank you to all the judges concerned, both "Breed Specialists" and "All Rounders"

MRS. DELLA OAKES	MR GEOFF CHERRY
MR. JEM SWATKINGS	MS ANN INGRAM
MR. ANDREW BRACE	MRS J. WILKINSON

Bred by Mr. Nikolas Kanales, ARYAKAS OES
Owned by Mr. Gareth & Mrs. Helen Harris, BEAUVALLON OES
Handled by Mr. Matteo Autolitano, AIRZEPPELINE OES

"a long lasting relationship
based on our mutual love
for this amazing breed"

435

Melview Gordon Setters

Melview Moving Time 'Poppy'
7 BPIB
including 2 breed club shows

Melview Just in Time
'Winston'
Numerous BPB wins

Melview Falling Leaves 'Pebbles'   **Melview Russet Leaves** 'Barney'
Have taken a back seat this year to allow the youngsters to come out

LINDA HALL   01202 824004

History in the Making
LEAMAP GREAT DANES
CROWNS TWO CHAMPIONS IN 2015

CHAMPION
LEAMAP WHISKEY GALORE JW
Owned and bred by Pam Price
leamap@onetel.com

CHAMPION
LEAMAP BLACK SABBATH WITH SARAWEN
Owned by Sara Pepper, bred by Pam Price
sarawen@btinternet.com

438

Abinvale

Frank, Bette & Emma Archibald
Tel: 028 2766 5797
e-mail: abinvale@hotmail.com
www.abinvale.com

Kennel Club
5 Challenge Certificates
1 Reserve Challenge Certificate
Best in Show Joint Breed Club's Ch Show

Irish Kennel Club
32 Green Stars
2 All Breed Ch Show - Best in Show
1 All Breed Ch Show - RBIS
8 Group Wins

Middle: Sh. Ch. & Ir.Sh. Ch. Abinvale The Aviator An Ch 12 ShCM (Denver)
(Sh Ch Shardanell Talk O' The Town at Ipcress JW x Gunhills Blue Secret at Abinvale)

Left: Ir. Sh. Ch. Abinvale Mystic River Jun Ch (Tegan)
(Sh Ch Shardanell Talk O' The Town at Ipcress JW x Gunhills Blue Secret at Abinvale)

Right: Abinvale Levanto (Cody)
(Sh. Ch. Telkaro First Look JW x Ir. Sh. Ch Abinvale Mystic River)

439

LESANDNIC
WIRE HAIRED DACHSHUNDS

Ir Ch Lesandic Lil EeTee
having a well deserved rest!

©T Morgan
Animal Photography

'Elliott' started 2015 by winning Northern Ireland's Hound of the Year competition, and ended it as Ireland's top Wire haired Dachshund. He had tough competition from our sensational L Snow Fairy, BIS-3 at Sligo Ch Show while still a puppy, our consistent Ch & Ir Ch L Sea The Stars who won his 6th CC and BOB at the WHD Club (and RDCC at Crufts!), Great By Lucky Dalmacia, our lovely Hungarian import, who won her Irish title and the RCC at SKC, and his group winning sister Ir Ch L Lilla. Many thanks to all who have helped us have a really enjoyable year!

Lesley Patton – Dromore, Northern Ireland
00442892 688350 lpatton@lesandnic.fsnet.co.uk 00447736 431090

441

Trebettyn

SOX

Kevin

Bwthyn Headliner
Owned by Bethan Williams & Jen James

Top Cardi Puppy
Multiple BPIB at Champ Shows
& 2 RCC's from puppy

Spellcast Talk To Da Paw
at Trebettyn ShCM
owned by Bethan Williams

Catsun
Est:1979

443

French people do love foreign exhibitors and invite you to

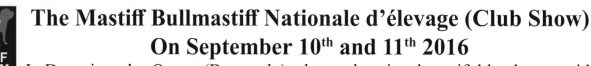

The English Bulldog Nationale d'élevage
(Club Show)
on May 7th and 8th 2016

in Chicamour Castle with a beautiful surroundings in the French countryside.
More than 250 bulldogs are expected.
Information : heldenis@aol.com
www.clubdubulldog.fr

The Mastiff Bullmastiff Nationale d'élevage (Club Show)
On September 10th and 11th 2016

In Dompierre les Ormes (Burgundy) a huge place in a beautiful landscape with
easy access and facilities. Camp site and lodges a cable's length away.
Judges Holly Scott (USA) Albert Hope (UK) Sylvie Flamme, Pierre Renard (F)
Information : amclass@aol.com
www.mastiff-bullmastiff.com

The Championnat de France
June 4th and 5th 2016

The French all breed Championship Show in Metz
To enter online : www.cedia.fr/2016

The Metz International Meeting
November 4th 5th and 6th 2016

Mastiff Bullmastiff Bulldog
Metz CAC and CACIB Specialties
Information : heldenis@aol.com
amclass@aol.com

SEB

CH ITALO ELITE HOUSE
TOP DOBERMANN 2014
TOP STUD DOG 2015

Who's the daddy!

ZAK

ZIGGY

JOJAVIK SWEDISH HOUSE MAFIA

Northern Ireland Dobermann Club - CC and BIS
Birmingham & District Dobermann Club - RDCC
Midland Counties Championship Show - RDCC
Owned by May Michael and superbly
handled by Penny McIlroy Stracey.

STORMHOLD ENIGMA FROM DIEGO JW

1CC & 4 RCC's
Still only 21 months old
Seb & Ziggy are owned, loved
& handled by Tracy Feeney

CH KNECHT MAREK

3CC's, 5 RCC's & 1 x Group 3
Owned & Bred by Robert Downie
Tel: 01324851474

CH JOJAVIK ELITE MAFIA

5CC's, 2 BIS's, 2 BOB's, 3 RCC's,
1RGS, Group 3 - NW&PB.
Owned & Loved by Tony & Linda Fisher

BEST IN SHOW

Border Union Agricultural
Society Canine Section

THE STIG

GINO

THE ELITE TEAM

AcreGate Gundogs

"Ralph"

Melverly Desert Strike over AcreGate JW.
ShCM

DOB 08.08.12
(1CC, 1RCC & G3 at WELKS)
Fully health tested and clear,
Proven Sire,
Frozen Semen available,
Bred by Mr Ray Smith

"Arthur"

Sh Ch Meadowdale Alabama Slammer at
AcreGate ShCM.

DOB 03.09.08
(5CC's, 6RCC's)
Fully health tested and clear,
Proven Sire
Frozen Semen available
Bred by Steve & Jane Eyeington

Acregate are Assured Breeder stud dog owners. Both the boys are fully health tested.
Both Arthur and Ralph are available at stud and are proven sires.
www.acregategundogs.co.uk   jennie@acregategundogs.co.uk
Contact Jennie for more details or information 07833 663738 or 0151 428 8990

THE KENNEL CLUB
ASSURED BREEDER SCHEME

The "Boys" are owned and adored by Jennie Tracz

Glenbrows
Welsh Springer Spaniels

We take great pride in presenting 3 generations of CC winners; firstly the young son of Sh Ch G Rainman JW, our stunning Glenbrows Trademark JW. At not yet 2 years of age, this young male has had a phenomenal career to date, CC and BOB, RCC and Best in Show at WSSCSW.

photo Joy Hartley

His mother, the beautiful Sh Ch Glenbrows Tribute to Weslave JW; and her father the evergreen Sh Ch Glenbrows Picture This JW ShCM

Sh Ch G Tribute, taken ringside, an untouched photograph by Joy Hartley, and Sh Ch G Picture This, in the ring captured forever by Kay Woodward.

Many thanks to all concerned for making 2015 another memorable year!

Tim and Honor Harrison

01332 701559   www.glenbrows.co.uk   glenbrows@live.co.uk

Maudaxi

CH Maudaxi Jimmy Choo

CC Driffield '15 Mr B Reynolds Frost

CC East of England '15 Mrs S Ergis

CC & BOB Bournemouth '14 Mr M Cocozza

photo Walker

photo MacCormack

CH Maudaxi Chewy Vuitton

CC & BOB Richmond '15 Mr P Marks

CC SKC '15 Mr J Luscott

CC Crufts '15 Mr R Buche

CC East of England '13 Mrs J Betts

Maudaxi Ja Maica Me Crazy

CC & BOB Bournemouth '15 Mr J Walton Haddon

7 BPIB at Championship Shows 2015

RBPIS Hound Association Open Show 2015

photo Walker

Jimmy, Elvis and Jamaica are all homebred out of Maudaxi Cosmopolitan.

Top Brood Bitch 2014 and current leader 2015

Ir Ch Algernon Prince

Current Top Import Hound Group '15

10 Best Dog Import Register 2015

7 BOB Import Register 2015

CAC/CACIB & III Group VI Kortrijk '14

Trezeguet Plum Crumble at Maudaxi

4 RCC

3 BB at Championship Shows

Maudaxi Tommy Holedigger

RCC Paignton '14 Mr A Mease

BD & BOB Leeds '14 Mrs S Hewart Chambers

BD & BOB Border Union '15 Mrs E A MacDonald

Philip and Dianne Reid

maudaxibgv@gmail.com

01235 831217

maudaxibgv.co.uk

OVERBECKS

CH OVERBECKS CHEDDAR GEORGE ShCM

"George"

4 CCs, 4 RCCs

OVERBECKS ISN'T IT IRONIC

"Ronnie"

Aged 6 months and 1 week

RCC and BP Driffield 2015

Thanks to judge Ben Reynolds-Frost for thinking so highly of Ronnie

BP at SWKA 2015

Owned by LYNNE SCOTT and JOAN PUCKETT

OVERBECKS ARTIE FISHEL ShCM

"Archie"

**1 CC WKC 2015 - Frank Kane
4 RCCs**

Bred and often handled by Lynne Scott
Owned and loved by Joan and Stuart Puckett
Tel 01305 782648 email joanpuckett@hotmail.co.uk

SOLETRADER AIN'T ACTIN UP AT OVERBECKS ShCM

"Milli"

**1 RCC at SWKA 2015
Numerous Open Show Group
placings including BIS**

Bred, owned and loved by **LYNNE SCOTT**
Tel 01258 452620 Email lynne.scott@overbeckspetits.co.uk

Marunnel PGBVs

Ir Ch Maudaxi Coco Chewnel from Marunnel IrJCh

BOB Midland Counties
2014

2 CCs

4 RCCs

Graded Excellent at
Nationale Elevage 2015

Culdaws Diesel from Marunnel

BOB Midland Counties
2015

RBIS Hound Association
of Ireland 2013 and 2014

3 RCCs

Reached final 6 dogs in
Open Class at Nationale
Elevage 2012

Graded Excellent at
Nationale Elevage 2012
and 2015

Owned and shown by Ceri McEwan cerimcewan@gmail.com

L'End Melissa Blu Flower at Fralex JW

Awards:

Windsor Championship Show Judge: Sharon Ames	Bitch CC
SKC Championship Show Judge: Martin Phillips	**Res. Bitch CC**
Three Counties Championship Show Judge: Jane Graham, Group Judge: Bill Browne-Cole	**BOB and last 8 in Terrier Group**
Southampton + DCA Judge: Viv Phillips, Group Judge: Cara Davani	**BIS** (nearly 1,000 dogs)
Marlborough & District Open Show Judge: Barry Day	**BOB and Terrier Group**

Best Minor Puppy/Puppy in Breed Awards:

Richmond Championship Show	Judge: Tom Johnston
Darlington Championship Show	Judge: Peter Kiernan
Driffield Championship Show	Judge: Pam Morton
Bedlington Terrier Association Championship Show	Judge: Eileen Needham
Midland Counties Championship Show [also Best Junior B]	Judge: Roger Thomas
Manchester Championship Show	Judge: Julien Barney

Stakes Awards:

Richmond Championship Show	Higham Press Yearling Stakes Winner
WELKS Championship Show	Open Stakes Winner
Birmingham National Championship Show	Higham Press Post Grad Stakes Winner
Bath Championship Show	Petplan Junior Stakes 2nd
Three Counties Championship Show	Higham Press Junior Stakes Winner
Darlington Championship Show	NES Yearling Stakes Reserve
Richmond Championship Show	Higham Press Yearling Stakes Reserve

Fralex Culibre Seymour

Awards:

Eurodogshow, Kortrijk, Belgium 2015	Best of Breed Best Junior in Breed
Birmingham City Championship Show Judge: Jenny Miller	Best Puppy in Breed
Richmond Championship Show Judge: Tom Mather	Best Puppy in Breed
Driffield Championship Show Judge: Roger Crooks	Best Puppy in Breed
Bedlington Terrier Assoc. Champ. Show Judge: Tony Waller	Best Junior
Midland Counties Championship Show Judge: Carlos Saevich	Best Minor Puppy in Breed

Stakes Awards:

Birmingham City Championship Show	Eukanuba/Dog World Puppy Stakes Reserve	Judge: Ben Reynolds Frost
Midland Counties Championship Show	Eukanuba/Dog World Puppy Stakes 2nd	Judge: Peter Jolley
Midland Counties Championship Show	Fosse Data Junior Stakes last 6	Judge: Renée Sporre-Willes

Champion Fralex Culibre Pharos

5 CCs
2 BOB Belgium
2 CACIBs
2 CACs
Best Puppy Eurodogshow, Belgium
Best Puppy – Kortrijk

Mr A and Mrs J Hurley B Phil MA
Fralex, Middleton Road, Winterslow Wilts SP5 1QL
Tel: 0044 (0)1980 862600
Email: jacqui@fralex.co.uk

457

Sobers Yacob

Sire: Sobers Galileo   Dam: Azrams Secret Desire

pictured at 11 months old

- Donaueschingen Sighthound Speciality 2015
  Puppy BOB & Puppy BEST in SHOW III
- Tulln, Bundesjugendsieger 2015
- Hungarian Junior Champion 2015

- 1 x Puppy Best in Show
- 1 x Res.Junior Best in Show
- 3 x BOB, Multi Group placements
- 2 x Crufts qualification for 2016

Photo: Gábor Szalá

Owned and loved by Adrienn Urban, Hungary
Breed by Bitte Ahrens Primavera & Pierluigi Primavera
Handled by Attila Schlosser
markanti.2@gmail.com   Phone: +36305516871

Manlinson

Mike Wildman ICMG
+ 44 (0) 7793 755905

Mandy Edwards
+ 44 (0) 07986 550006

TJ

SH CH & IS SH CH
Travellers Joy of Malpas

4 CC - 2 RCC

Co-Owned by Mike and Mandy Edwards

Winner of The Cocker Spaniel Club Veteran Challenge 2015

Photo: Fairbairn

Zac

Sh Ch It Sh Ch Lindridge Ticket to Ride JW

20 CC's - 12 Rccs

Co-Owned by Mike & Edith Fowles

Phoebie

Cassom Hopes
and Dreams at
Manlinson

Co-Owned
by
Mike &
Mandy Edwards

©TMorgan
Animal Photography

Norris

*Ch. Daddy Cool at Manlinson
* Subj to KC Conf

3 CCs - 5 RCCs

Best In Show
British Toy Poodle Ch Show 2015

Sire: Clopton The Man in the Brown Suit
Dam: Vanitonia You Think So

Norris is Co-Owned by Mike Wildman and Mandy Edwards.
Prepared and handled by Mike Wildman and Philip Langdon

Will Harris

Zara Boyle design.com

459

LIWANG BASENJIS

 SULLA LIWANG

MULTIPLE BPIS AT GENERAL CHAMPIONSHIP & INTERNATIONAL SHOWS
FIRST OUTING IN JUNIORS — BEST JUNIOR & CRUFT'S QUALIFICATION

SKILLFULLY HANDLED & EXPERTLY SPOILED BY DOROTA MÜLLER

KRYSTYNA & JANUSZ OPARA   LIWANG@WP.PL   WWW.LIWANG.PL

**INT NORD DK UCH NJV-12 SEV-13 HEV-13 NV-14 NV-15
XI Av Larhjelm**

**NORD FI UCH DKJV-13 DKV-13 NJV-13 NV-13 SEJV-13 HEJV-13
EUW-15 Absint Av Larhjelm**

**INT NORD UCH N VCH NV-13 NORDV-14
Visvas Av Larhjelm**

Larhjelm

Lars Hjelmtvedt - Odderudveien 20 - 3089 Holmestrand - Norway
Tlf +47 416 60 485 - www.larhjelm.net - lars@larhjelm.net

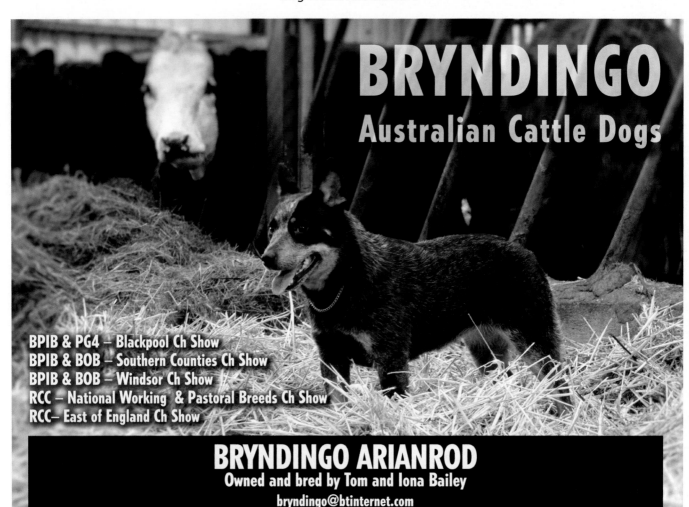
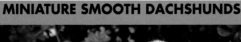

OBERITZ
Finnish Lapphunds

Oberitz Silmänilo
2 CCs, 1 RCC

(Photo Xenia Kosla)

Ch. Oberitz Onnetar
4 CCs

Oberitz Rumpai
1CC, 1 RCC

(Photo Sammy Cooper)

Glenchess Nallukka By Oberitz
5 RBD in 2015

Ch. Oberitz Rillumarei
3 CCs, 1 RCC

Aramis Des Calaban Of Oberitz
(Imp USA) - 5 BPIB

Niki Allison   01939 232556   oberitz@aol.com   www.oberitz.co.uk

2015 - A GREAT YEAR FOR THE GIRLS

Pamela continued to make history in 2015...

This multiple Best in Show winning bitch added to her long list of achievements by becoming the first Supreme Champion Harrier in Australia, and added to the list of 'firsts' by taking out BEST in GROUP at Sydney Royal.

Pamela has won under International panels at some of Sydney's biggest Shows, this year adding to the tally Runner Up to Best in Show at North of the Harbour (twice), and Best in Group at the Dogs NSW Spring Fair.

Presented by: Brigette Bryson

Owned by: Brigette, Celeste & John Bryson
Foxhunt Kennels Australia

Bred by: Paul & Fiona Danaher

PAMELA
SUPREME CH FELLHUNTERS LOVE HER MADLY

Monday is still the only Siberian Husky to hold both Aust Supreme & NZ Grand titles - a history making achievement at 3 years of age. Monday has won 40 Best In Shows including BISS & RUBISS one of them under world renowned Breed Specialist Kim Le Blanc (Snowmist Siberian Huskies).

At just 5 years of age we are so very proud of this sensational Siberian Husky and her latest achievement
Best In Group and
Best In Show 4th at the
2015 Melbourne Royal.

Presented by: Cherie Bryson Karam

Owned by: Cherie Bryson Karam, Pauline Suhr, Tamzin Letele & Sarah Halliday.

Bred by: Tamzin Letele & Sarah Halliday

MONDAY
SUPREME CH & NZ GR CH ALYESHKA LITTLE MISS PERFECT

BETWEEN THEM THE GIRLS TOOK OUT BEST IN GROUP AT AUSTRALIA'S 2 MOST PRESTIGIOUS ROYALS, SYDNEY & MELBOURNE IN 2015, MONDAY GOING ONE STEP FURTHER TO BIS4!!!

A winning team...

Photograph: David Paton

©Zhaggari

Palamedees Tallon JW

Ch Guillaume Du Menuel Galopin JW x
Palamedees Shahmilah

BPIB Crufts 2015
Judge: Espen Engh

Multi BPIS

Winner Junior Dog Stakes
Bournemouth Champ.
Judge: Jeff Luscott

Proudly owned by
Joseph Lee-Brown, Anouska Simpson
and Angela Lee-Brown (breeder).

Incalux Xplorer
with Anouskarn

Ch. Alilah's Xtra Well Dressed at Waterley
x Incalux Lady of the Nyte

BCC - Border Union 2015

Danjubet Special
Beginners Trophy

1x CC
3x RCC

Thank you to the breed specialists
who have thought so highly of her

Proudly owned by
Anouska Simpson, Joseph Lee-Brown
and Marjorie Barber

Bred by Barbara Stringer

Photograph © Joseph Lee-Brown

Anouskarn
Afghan Hounds \ Tibetan Terriers

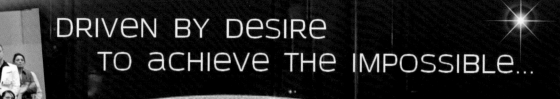

Bushwacker Captain Courageous at Ruskinite ShCM

 Owned and Loved by Jenna Cocking and Peter Barnaby
Bred by Julie and Ashleigh Frost
Handled in the Show Ring by Jenna

Spencer had an excellent year in 2015 gaining 2 CC`s

and increasing his Reserve CC total to 9

(including the Reserve CC at Crufts 2015)

Bushwacker Thriller

Owned and Loved by Jenna Cocking and
Peter Barnaby
Bred by Julie Frost
Handled in the Show Ring by Peter

Lightly shown in 2015 but consistently

placed well in classes, looking forward

to Veteran debut in 2016

Photos kindly taken by Aino Vayrynen at Crufts 2015

We would like to thank all judges that thought so highly and placed our

dogs in 2015 and look forward to campaigning both boys in 2016.

jenna.cocking@gmail.com / peter.barnaby@icloud.com

HAVALAG HAVANESE

Introducing TELAZARO BLAZE OF GLORY FROM HAVALAG

Our fabulous red/gold brindle bitch puppy from Serbia. At her very first show, City Of Birmingham CH Show, (judge Ann Horan), just a week after arriving in the UK, aged 6 months on the day, "Glory" was **Best Puppy in Breed**. At South Wales Ch Show (Judge Elaine Waddington), 7 months on the day, "Glory" won her second **Best Puppy in Breed** and took **Reserve Best Bitch**. One week later at the Havanese Club of GB first championship show (Judge Zena Thorn-Andrews) "Glory" won **Best Puppy Bitch** and then went Best Puppy In Show.

At Midland Counties Ch show, where she was second in her class, judge Robert Hitchcock wrote "another very lovely puppy here, correct all through for type, shape and style, her front was superb and her topline also correct. I liked her feminine head and expression, very pretty with dark eyes & good muzzle, her rear was correct and complemented the front to give a well-balanced outline. Younger than the winner and not quite the coat yet, but one to watch certainly, a very nice puppy indeed, she was sound and true on the move with her light happy gait".

We look forward to campaigning our stunning "Glory" in 2016.

Waiting in the wings to accompany "Glory" in 2016 are **Behike's Maestro from Havalag** (Reserve Best Puppy dog at the Havanese Club of GB Ch Show), **Behike's Nadja From Havalag** (Best Puppy at Coventry (Foleshill) Open Show), both Polish imports, **Amazing Dance Skye At Havalag** (Spanish import) **Sandra's Venezia Vienna at Havalag** (German import) and **Kendry Maiko Havana Wild Angel Havalag** (Czech import).

Not forgetting out lovely veteran bitch **Australian Ch Torza Colour O'Love for Heronsbridge** – Top Veteran Havanese for the second year running.

Philip Grocock – 01945 450923 www.havalag.com

wratthembray
basset & griffon fauve de bretagne

2015 UK	2015 International
2 CCs	1 CACIB
1 RCC	BOS World Dog Show
1 PG4	Junior World Winner
BP Crufts	Italian Junior Champion
2nd in AV KC GCDS Stakes Houndshow	Celtic Winner & Celtic Junior Winner
and Paignton Championship Shows	Benelux Winner

UK	International
4 Best Imported Register	7 CACIB | 1 G3 | 2 G4
	World Winner
3 BOS Imported Register	Benelux Winner
	Ir Annual Champion 2014
	Celtic Winner 2014 & 2015
	Ir Junior Ch

HIBECK PAIN AU CHOCOLAT AVEC WRATTHEMBRAY

We are grateful to our friend Jean McDonald-Ulliott for entrusting us with "Brompton" (Basset Fauve de Bretagne) and to all who have supported his first year of showing.
Thank you... Barry Jones and Matthew Gregg

IR/BENELUX/LUX CH LILLIE BEATRICE FOR WRATTHEMBRAY

We are grateful to our friend Jean McDonald-Ulliott (Hibeck) for introducing us to the breed and to all who have supported and helped to handle "Beatrice" (Griffon Fauve de Bretagne).
Thank you... Barry Jones and Matthew Gregg

Sh Ch Ferndel Justin Time ShCM

Group 1 WELKS

Group 3 Blackpool

6 CCs

8 Res CCs

1st Champion Stakes Midland Counties 2015
Owned by Ian & Kay Douglas www.santallina.co.uk

Ferndel Comander of Bethersden ShCM

2 CCs

6 Res CCs

Ferndel High Society To Bethersden

Owned by Gil & Shelagh Tolladay
bethersden@sky.com   01977 604205

Keep Your Temper Caballero Pedoro

Clayard Stady Lady at Labayamesa

Tiny Lady By Labayamesa

OUR
CHAMPIONS

Labayamesa
Havanese

www.labayamesa-havanese.com

TIVALAKE JINGLE BELL ROCK
ShCM, RL2

TOPAZ

Mary Coe

Titovets

Kathrine Gunstad

CC Windsor 2015
RCC WKC 2015

Working Gundog Certificate 2014

Picking Up Working Dog
Numerous Open Show BOBs
and Group Awards

We look forward to welcoming Topaz's
puppies in the show ring next year.

We also hope to see Monae's
(Tivalake Cover Girl, top picture, right)
puppies debut in 2016.

Handled by Marina Scott
Proudly bred, owned & adored by
Yvonne & Nick Burchell

www.tivalake.co.uk

MAINTAINING THE STANDARD

www.ridleyceskyterriers.com

Sheila Atter

Abby Webb from Southend, Essex

Started showing back in August 2013 with her first Tibetan Terrier, Ciel (Abelenus Black Ice Ciel). Since then Adalia, (Abelenus Delta Alysia), who is half sister to Ciel, joined the team. They have had two wonderful years competing in breed classes, junior handling, YKC classes and competing in the Young Kennel Club Grooming Competition. Abby and Ciel won 4th place competing at Crufts 2015 for the first time in the YKC grooming final. They have also qualified to compete in the grooming final at Crufts 2016. To date Abby's other wins include

8 x 1st, 8 x 2nd, 8 x 3rd, 1 x Res, 5 x 5th.

Abby would like to thank all the judges who have recognised her potential and all those who have supported her and is very much looking forward to competing through 2016, with her two best friends by her side, Adalia and Ciel.

TSUSELENA

Percy & Jenson

SUE LEE
www.tsuselena.com

Sh Ch Petsalls Pride Cedar

3 CCs (1 BOB)
4 RCCs

We would like to thank all of the judges who have thought so highly of Cedar throughout his show career, we are thrilled that he has gained his title!

photo Greg Knight

Many thanks must also go to our handlers: Shannon Roberts, Maria Kapasali, Lizzie Greenslade and, finally, James Newton who handled him to his 3rd and crowning CC!

www.petsallspridechesapeakes.co.uk
Paula Graystone: 07966 971519 Roly Hoare: 07834 321143

Madire Tibetan Mastiffs

HERONSVIEW BUNI BEA FOR MADIRE
1st ever Bitch CC and BOB
CRUFTS 2015
2nd CC Darlington
Twice RBIS at TMCGB Open Show.

MADIRE SNOW ANGEL
Best Bitch and Reserve Best In Show
Tibetan Mastiff Club of GB Open Show
Twice Reserve Best Bitch

MADIRE SNOW BLADE
BOB Leeds and Driffield 2015
Twice RBD.

Owned by Pat and Mark Leak
Loved and Shown by
Pat, Mark and Megan Lewis
01623 747827
www.Madire.Com
Follow us on Facebook
'Madire Tibetan Mastiffs'

WOOLLINOZE BUMI BEAR FOR MADIRE
Reserve Best Dog
Tibetan Mastiff Club of GB Open Show
2 Reserve Best Dog

482

JAROT
Lakelands and Jack Russells
LC-E UNRETOUCHED
Owned by Jennifer Hetherington
Handled by Geoff Corish and Michael Coad
01772 612939
White House Farm Kennels, Gill Lane, Langton, Preston, Lancs PR4 4SS

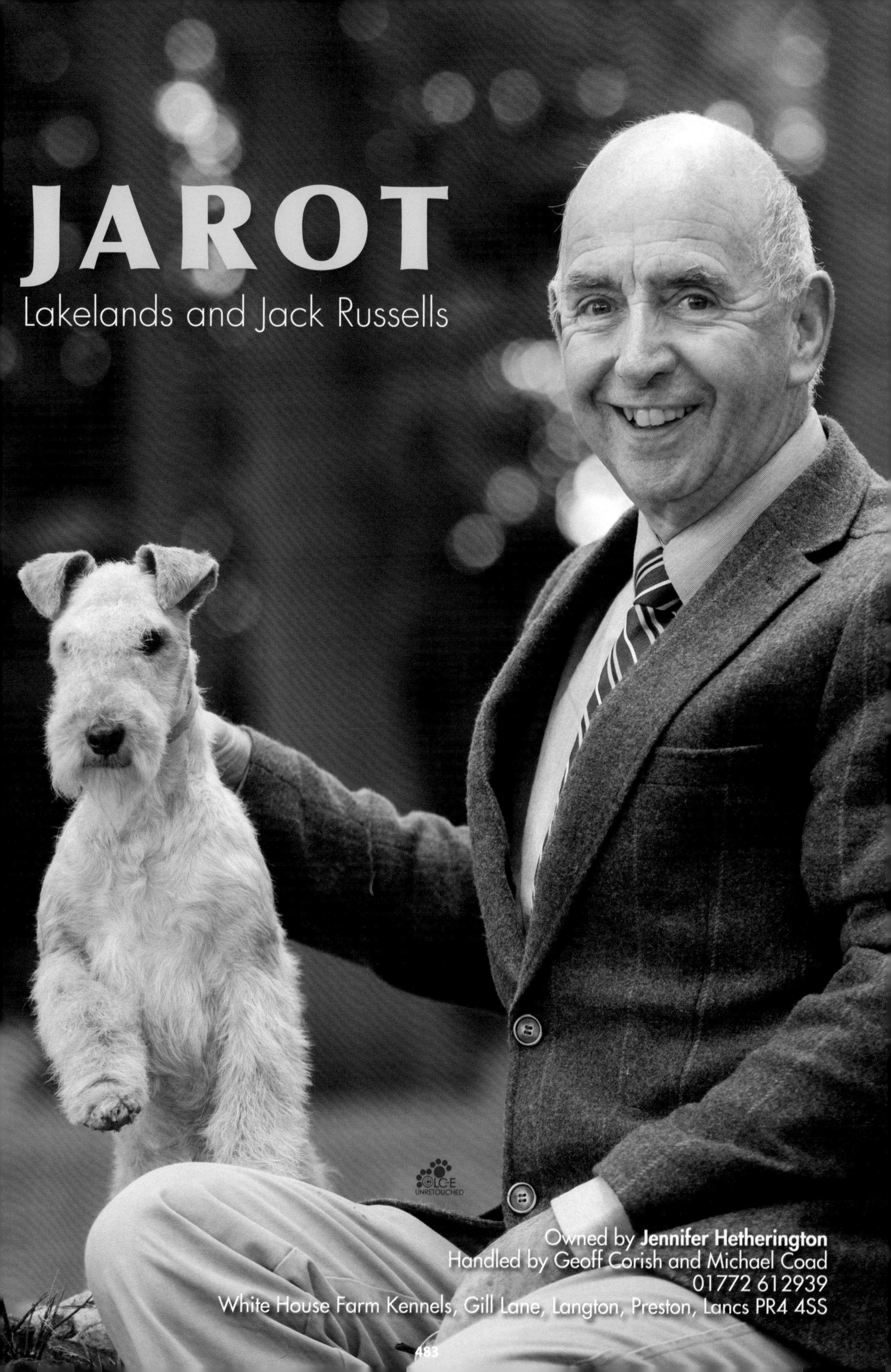

Gayteckels

Adrian, Chris and Russell Marett

LASTAREAN GRACE AND FAVOUR FOR GAYTECKELS P'DH

5 Best of Breeds
7 Best Bitch wins
2 Jersey Challenge Certificates
Runner-up Channel Island Dog of the Year 2012
Best in Show and Reserve Best in Show Winner

Her son GAYTECKELS BAK IN THE ABBOTT has won 5 Puppy Groups

Our Polish import IDEFIX DAY BREAK AT GAYTECKELS has 1 Jersey CC

Also home to...

LASTAREAN KRAL OF ZIDOUT P'DH

3 Best of Breeds
7 Best Dog wins
Small Channel Island Agility Dog of the Year Winner

LIMIER DIDIER AT GAYTECKELS PD'H

Best in Show Winner
Multiple Group Winner

Around the WORLD OF DOGS

PHOTO KIF

Best in show under Andrew Brace at the Turkish Kennel Club show at Silivri was Svetlana Zasimovich's Yorkshire Terrier Life Image Mary Queen.

PHOTO ANDREW BRACE

At an international show in Reykjavik, Iceland, Andrew Brace gave Best in show to Vikingur Hauksson's Papillon puppy Multi Star's Arjen Robben, handled by Erna Omarsdottir.

PHOTO BARBARA GREENIDGE

Geoff Corish judged the last Barbados KC show of 2014 and chose the UK-bred French Bulldog Jafrak Passing Ship, owned by Henry Jordan and handled by Stefan Phillips. Sponsor Pedigree was represented by Lisa Clarke.

PHOTO BARBARA GREENIDGE

At Barbados KC's first show of 2015 Derek Smith chose for best in show Jenni Wilson's Boxer Sundial's Sun God Apollo at Kalbo. Dennis Maynard represented sponsor Vitamin Pet Foods.

At Malta CS' April show, Ernie Paterson's best in show was Ivan Calleja and Johann Schembri's Wire Fox Terrier Mastini di Rihana Goes To Casino.

Jill Peak judged Malta CS' Crufts qualifying show of 2014 and gave best in show to Tony Barker's Irish Terrier Kells Touch Of Fleet St, previously a BIS winner in the UK.

Tom Mather judged best in show at Malta CS' winter show and chose Keely Carabott's Afghan Hound Gold'n Copper Diamonds For Men.

Malta CS' first back-to-back shows were judged by Jeff Horswell and Margaret Wildman. On the first day Jeff gave best in show to Adrian and Ritianne Hili and Dawn Rathmell's Basset Hound Yogi Bear dos Sete Moinhos and reserve to Victor Gatt's Keeshond puppy Samkees Purrsonal Love who was Margaret's BIS the following day.

Three shows took place concurrently in Lima, Peru where the best in show winners were the Dobermann Gary de Akido San, judge Andrew Brace; Bull Terrier Magor McBeatty, judge Michael Canalizo, and White Bull Terrier Evolution Bull's Nando, judge Greg Eva.

Championship Shows 2016

MIDLAND
CANINE

COUNTIES
SOCIETY

GENERAL CHAMPIONSHIP SHOW 2016
A Quality Affordable Show
Bingley Hall, Stafford County Showground ST18 0BD

THURSDAY OCTOBER 27th: TERRIERS & WORKING
FRIDAY OCTOBER 28th: TOYS & UTILITY
SATURDAY OCTOBER 29th: GUNDOGS
SUNDAY OCTOBER 30th: HOUNDS & PASTORAL

POSTAL CLOSING DATE: MONDAY SEPTEMBER 12, 2016
ON-LINE CLOSING DATE: MONDAY SEPTEMBER 19, 2016

Secretary Mr Rodney Price, Pen Bryn Llech, Llanrhaeadr, Denbigh LL16 4PH
Tel/Fax 01745 890368
Web site: www.fossedata.co.uk   Email: pricerodney1@gmail.com

---

LEEDS CHAMPIONSHIP
DOG SHOW LTD

HAREWOOD ESTATE, HAREWOOD
NR LEEDS LS17 9LQ

Friday July 22nd, 2016 – WORKING, PASTORAL & TERRIER
Saturday July 23rd, 2016 – UTILITY & TOY
Sunday July 24th, 2016 – HOUND & GUNDOG

105 BREEDS WITH CCs
MANY NON-CC BREEDS SCHEDULED
MANY BREED OPEN SHOWS SCHEDULED ON THE SAME DAYS

For further information and schedules contact Secretary LIZ STANNARD
SUMMERHILL, SUTTON, MACCLESFIELD SK11 0JD
Tel: 01260 252834   leedssecretary@gmail.com

Best wishes to all exhibitors old and new

Index to Trade Advertisements

Index to breeders' advertisements

Index to breeders' advertisements

Index to breeders' advertisements